The Regulation and Supervision of Banks

T0358399

Over the past two decades, the banking industry has expanded and consolidated at a stunningly unprecedented speed. In this time banks have also moved from focusing purely on commercial banking activities to being heavily involved in market-based and transaction-oriented wholesale and investment banking activities. By carrying out an all-encompassing set of activities, banks have become large, complex, interconnected, and inclined to levels of risk-taking not previously seen. With the onset of the 2008 global financial crisis it became apparent that there was an issue of institutions being too big to fail.

This book analyses the too-big-to-fail problem of banks in the EU. It approaches the topic from an interdisciplinary perspective using behavioural finance as a tool to examine the occurrence of the global financial crisis and the emergence of the structural problem in large banking institutions. The book draws a comparison between the EU, the US and the UK and the relevant rules to assess the effectiveness of various approaches to regulation in a global context. Chen Chen Hu goes on to use behavioural analyses to provide new insights in evaluating the current structural reform rules in the EU Proposal on Bank Structural Regulation and the newly adopted bank recovery and resolution regime in the EU Bank Recovery and Resolution Directive and the Single Resolution Mechanism (SRM) in the Single Resolution Regulation.

Chen Chen Hu is a Legal Consultant at Kromann Reumert, Denmark.

Routledge Research in Finance and Banking Law

Available:

Law and Finance after the Financial Crisis
The Untold Stories of the UK Financial Market
Abdul Karim Aldohni

Microfinance and Financial Inclusion
The Challenge of Regulating Alternative Forms of Finance
Eugenia Macchiavello

Law and Regulation of Mobile Payment Systems
Issues Arising 'Post' Financial Inclusion in Kenya
Joy Malala

Management and Regulation of Pension Scheme
Australia: A Cautionary Tale
Nicholas Morris

The Regulation and Supervision of Banks
The Post Crisis Regulatory Responses of the EU
Chen Chen Hu

Regulation and Supervision of the OTC Derivatives Market
Ligia Catherine Arias-Barrera

For more information about this series, please visit: www.routledge.com/Rout
ledge-Research-in-Finance-and-Banking-Law/book-series/FINANCIALLAW

The Regulation and Supervision of Banks

The Post Crisis Regulatory Responses of the EU

Chen Chen Hu

Routledge
Taylor & Francis Group

LONDON AND NEW YORK

First published 2018
by Routledge

2 Park Square, Milton Park, Abingdon, Oxfordshire OX14 4RN
52 Vanderbilt Avenue, New York, NY 10017

Routledge is an imprint of the Taylor & Francis Group, an informa business

First issued in paperback 2020

British Library Cataloguing in Publication Data
A catalogue record for this book is available from the British Library

Library of Congress Cataloging in Publication Data
A catalog record for this book has been requested

ISBN: 978-1-138-29188-1 (hbk)
ISBN: 978-0-367-59135-9 (pbk)

Typeset in ITC Galliard Std
by Swales & Willis Ltd, Exeter, Devon, UK

Contents

Preface

The subprime mortgage crisis has significantly affected financial markets around the world including the EU. The too big to fail (TBTF) bank structural problem and its corresponding legislative progress have been at the forefront of comprehensive regulatory reform.

In this book I have dedicated my endeavours to comments on the current regulatory changes from the behavioural finance (BF) perspective and made some recommendations for the corresponding EU reform on the TBTF bank structural problem. I wish the arguments could be of certain help in terms of providing some different perspectives for future legislation or reform.

It has been a great pleasure to conduct the research under the supervision of Prof. Jesper Lau Hansen at University of Copenhagen (academic member of European Securities and Markets Authority (ESMA)'s Stakeholder Group), who is very friendly in terms of freely exchanging views yet very strict in terms of academic requirements. His support in all aspects has made this research period especially different and productive for me. I also sincerely appreciate all the help received from Prof. Mads Bryde Andersen at University of Copenhagen (chairman of the Board of Directors of the Danish Financial Regulatory Authority), who periodically offered many priceless comments on my book draft and kindly provided much general guidance on academic research in this area.

I also need to deliver my sincere gratitude to those whose comments have been of valuable help to my research. The comments were gained from formal evaluation, interviews, informal discussions, conferences, etc: Prof. Camilla Hørby Jensen, Prof. Henrik Palmer Olsen, Prof. Ebrahim Afsah, Prof. David Ruder, Prof. Claus Hopt, Prof. Shen Wei, Prof. Stephen B. Presser, Prof. Kenneth Ayotte, Prof. Omri Ben-Shahar, Allan Horwich, John E. Freechack, Dennis R. Wendte, Edward F. Greene, Jacob Gyntelberg, Dr. Lin Lin, Dr. Knut Benjamin Pißler, Dr. Anna Simonova, and Dr. Yi Shin Tang.

This book is a revised version of the doctoral dissertation that I defended at the University of Copenhagen. I hereby genuinely thank my assessment committee, Prof. Emilios Avgouleas at University of Edinburgh, Prof. Daniel Stattin at Uppsala University and Prof. Christian Bergqvist at University of Copenhagen. A special thank you to Prof. Georg Ringe at Copenhagen Business School and University of Oxford.

Chen Chen Hu
Copenhagen
January 2016

Abbreviations

ACBP	Asset Backed Commercial Paper
AIF	Alternative Investment Fund
AIFMD	AIF Mangers Directive
AMH	Adaptive Market Hypothesis
Bafin	Bundesanstalt für Finanzdienstleistungsaufsicht
BCBS	Basel Committee on Banking Supervision
BF	Behavioural finance
BHC	Bank Holding Company
BIS	Bank for International Settlements (BIS)
BOE	Bank of England
BRR	Bank Recovery and Resolution Mechanism
BRRD	Bank Recovery and Resolution Directive
BSR	Bank Structural Regulation (as a proposal from the European Commission)
CBA	Cost benefit analysis
CCI	Core credit institution
CCPs	Central clearing counterparties
CDOs	Collateral debt obligations
CDS	Credit default swap
CLOs	Collateralised loan obligations
CRAs	Credit Rating Agencies
CRD IV	Capital Requirements Directive IV
CRR	Capital Requirements Regulation
CSDs	Central securities depositories
DGS	Deposit Guarantee Scheme
DIP	Debt in possession financing
EBA	European Banking Authority
EBU	European Banking Union
EC	European Commission
ECB	European Central Bank
ECON	Committee on Economic and Monetary Affairs (EP)
EFSF	European Financial Stability Facility
EIOPA	European Insurance and Occupational Pensions Authority
ELTIFs	European Long Term Investment Funds (ELTIFs)

EMH	Efficient market hypothesis
ESCB	European System of Central Banks
ESFS	European System of Financial Supervision
ESM	European Stability Mechanism
ESMA	European Securities and Markets Authority
ESRB	European Systemic Risk Board
EU-SIIs	The EU Systemically Important Institutions as defined in art 3(b) of the BSR
FCA	Financial Conduct Authority (UK; formerly FSA)
FDIC	Federal Deposit Insurance Corporation
FED	Board of Governors of the Federal Reserve System
FINMA	Swiss Financial Market Supervisory Authority
FSA	Financial Supervisory Authority (UK; now FCA)
FSB	Financial Stability Board
FSOC	Financial Stability Oversight Council (US)
GFC	Global financial crisis
GSE	Government-Sponsored Enterprises
G-SIIs	Global Systemically Important Institutions
ICB	Independent Commission on Banking
IGA	Intergovernmental Agreement
IMF	The International Monetary Fund
JST	Joint Supervisory Team
LAC	Loss absorbency capacity
LSE	London Stock Exchange
LTR	Liquidity coverage ratio
MFA	Market Failure Analysis
MFI	Monetary Financial Institution
MiFID	Markets in Financial Instruments Directive II
MiFIR	Markets in Financial Instruments Regulation
MMFs	Money market funds
MoU	Memorandum of Understanding
MPE	Multiple point of entry
MREL	Minimal Requirement for Own Funds and Eligible Liabilities
MTFs	Multilateral trading facilities
NCAs	National Competent Authorities
NRAs	National Resolution Authorities
NSFR	Net stable funding ratio
OCC	Office of the Comptroller of the Currency (US)
OLA	Orderly Liquidation Authority (US)
O-SII	Other Systemically Important Institutions
OTS	Office of Thrift Supervision (US)
PE	Private equity fund
PONV	Point of no viability
PR	Prohibitive rule (BSR)
PRA	Prudential Regulation Authority (Bank of England)

RF	Ring-fence rule (BSR)
RMBS	Residential mortgage backed securities
RRP	Recovery and resolution planning
RWAs	Risk Weighted assets
SBICs	Small Business Investment Companies
SEC	US Securities and Exchange Commission
SIFIs	Systemically Important Financial Institutions
SMEs	Small and medium-sized enterprises
SPE	Single point of entry
SRB	Single Resolution Board
SRF	Single Resolution Fund
SRM	Single Resolution Mechanism
SRR	Single Resolution Regulation (also referred as SRM Regulation)
SSM	Single Supervisory Mechanism
TBTF	Too big to fail
TFEU	Treaty on the Functioning of the European Union
VaR	Value at risk model
VC	Venture capital

Introduction

Over the past two decades, the banking industry has consolidated and expanded at a stunningly unprecedented speed, riding on the wave of the financial de-regulation era.[1] The European Union (EU), as one of the largest economic entities, also witnessed a dramatic expansion of its banking sector, with the total assets of Monetary Financial Institutions (MFIs) reaching EUR43 trillion by 2008, about 350% of the entire EU GDP.[2] The banking sector landscape has significantly changed over the course of worldwide prevailing financial deregulation, i.e. the lax monetary policy and the liberalisation economic doctrine.[3] Against the background of loose macroeconomic policy, the banking industry boom was further fuelled by many microeconomic factors, such as speculative investment strategies and excessive encouragement of innovation in the banking sector. In addition, behavioural factors and bounded rationality of the financial market participants also contributed significantly to the irrational banking exuberance.[4]

1 Issue: the too big to fail bank structural problem in the EU

1.1 Definition

1.1.1 Too big to fail bank structural problem

The too big to fail (TBTF) bank structural problem is the key issue in this book. It refers to the ineffectiveness of supervision and regulation of banks due to the unrestricted co-existence of core banking activities, investment banking activities, and trading activities within institutions with the universal banking

---

1 Jacques De Larosière, *The High-level Group on financial supervision in the EU: report* (European Commission 2009), pp. 7–10.
2 Liikanen Erkki, *High-level Expert Group on reforming the structure of the EU banking sector* (Final Report, Brussels, 2012), p. 12.
3 De Larosière, *The High-level Group on financial supervision in the EU: report*, p. 7.
4 Emilios Avgouleas classified the causes of crisis into two categories. First, the causes relating to more general policies are called macro-causes. Second, those factors that are originated from the financial institutions due to misaligned incentives are called micro-causes.

model (Figure 0.1).[5] It denotes the banking transformation from focusing on commercial banking activities to market-based and transaction-oriented whole-sale and investment banking activities. By carrying out an all-encompassing set of activities, banks have become large, complex, interconnected, and inclined to risk-taking. Such activity expansion rendered pre-crisis bank regulation and supervision ineffective. In addition, the failure of these banks could be extremely disastrous to the overall economy.[6]

In the pre-crisis era, the banking sector exploited the economies of scale and economies of scope in an unprecedented way. And the direct consequence was that the large institutions became too important to fail because the consequences of their failure would be unbearable for society as a whole.[7] For instance,

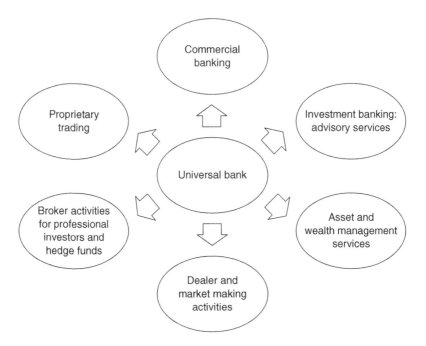

Figure 0.1 Structure of the universal bank

5 European Commission, *Commission staff working document impact assessment accompanying the document Proposal for a Regulation of the European Parliament and of the Council on structural measures improving the resilience of EU Credit Institutions and the Proposal for a Regulation of the European Parliament and of the Council on reporting and transparency of securities financing transactions, SWD/2014/030 final.* (January 29, 2014), pp. 8–9. See also Liikanen Erkki, *High-level Expert Group on reforming the structure of the EU banking sector*, pp. 11–19.
6 European Commission, *Proposal for a Regulation of the European Parliament and of the Council on structural measures improving the resilience of EU credit institutions, COM/2014/043 final* (January 29, 2014), recital (1)–(3).
7 Liikanen Erkki, *High-level Expert Group on reforming the structure of the EU banking sector*, pp. 11–13. See also Financial Stability Board, *Reducing the moral hazard posed by systemically important financial institutions, Basel* (October 2010).

frightened by the potential domino effect and market panic as a result of the bankruptcy of Dexia, a guarantee limit of EUR85 billion was approved by Belgium, France, and Luxembourg to preserve the stability of markets and economic confidence.[8] Thus, for these entities, bankruptcy costs were carelessly neglected over the expansion process. Therefore, the bank structural problem, the co-existence of activities, and the inefficiency of regulation, are seen as the drivers of another concept, the too big to fail problem.

To avoid confusion, the following subsection defines two deeply related but different concepts: the too big to fail problem and the too big to fail institutions.

1.1.2 Two relevant concepts

(a) Too big to fail problem. The TBTF problem is actually seen as a consequence of bank expansion and the co-existence of activities. In other words, the bank structural problem is the trigger for the TBTF problem.[9] According to the Financial Stability Board (FSB), the TBTF problem happens 'when the threatened failure of a SIFI leaves public authorities with no option but to bail it out using public funds to avoid financial instability and economic damage'.[10] The FSB further points out that 'the knowledge that this can happen encourages SIFIs to take excessive risks and represents a large implicit public subsidy of private enterprise'.

However, in some related legislative documents on structural reform in the EU,[11] the definition of the bank structural problem and the TBTF problem are not clearly defined. In the *High-level Expert Group* on reforming the structure of the EU banking sector (Liikanen report), it discusses the need for proposals on structural measures in the EU, but it does not specifically define or differentiate the bank structural problem and the TBTF problem except in its descriptive narrative of pre-crisis EU banking development, which corresponds with the above definitions.[12] In the current proposals in the EU Bank Structural Regulation (BSR) on structural reform (the European Commission adopted the 'proposal for a regulation on structural measures improving the resilience of EU credit

---

8 Dexia, 'Execution of the definitive funding guarantee agreement by the Belgian, French and Luxembourg States'. www.dexia.com/EN/journalist/press_releases/Pages/Execution_definitive_funding_guarantee_agreement_Belgian_French_Luxembourg_States.aspx, accessed November 3, 2014.

9 European Commission, *Commission staff working document impact assessment accompanying the document Proposal for a Regulation of the European Parliament and of the Council on structural measures improving the resilience of EU Credit Institutions and the Proposal for a Regulation of the European Parliament and of the Council on reporting and transparency of securities financing transactions, SWD/2014/030 final.*

10 Financial Stability Board, *Progress and next steps towards ending Too-Big-To-Fail (TBTF)* (2 September 2013), p. 2. See also Simon Johnson, 'Eugene Fama: too big to fail perverts activities and incentives' http://baselinescenario.com/2010/06/02/eugene-fama-too-big-to-fail-perverts-activities-and-incentives/, accessed June 15, 2013.

11 For details of the structural reform see infra Chapter 3, Section 2.

12 Liikanen Erkki, *High-level Expert Group on reforming the structure of the EU banking sector,* pp. 11–19.

institutions' on January 29, 2014), it also only generally refers to the concept of TBTF institutions in the explanatory memorandum and the recital.[13]

But according to the above FSB definition of the TBTF problem, it has a broader scope or denotation than the concept of the bank structural problem, although their connotations might largely coincide. Possible solutions for the TBTF problem would also be more inclusive including effective resolution, intense supervision, strengthening market infrastructures, and structural measures.[14]

(b) Too big to fail institution. To explain the TBTF bank structural problem, a closely related concept is the TBTF institution, also called Systemically Important Financial Institutions (SIFIs). It is normally defined as:[15]

> An institution (including investment firms, funds and insurance companies), the failure of which would mean serious disruption to the function of the financial system, distorting its ability to facilitate orderly payments and settle transactions between institutions and between institutions and consumers within domestic or the international markets.

Due to the size, market importance, and interconnectedness of SIFIs, a failure in one or more of them can cause significant dislocation in the financial system and create adverse economic consequences.[16]

It should be noted that although TBTF institutions or SIFIs are the carriers of the TBTF problem, in this book the entities relevant to the TBTF bank structural problem include mainly SIFIs, but do not exclude other entities that are not on the FSB's SIFI list.[17] The fact is, the bank structural problem can still arise and pose severe disruptive consequences even if an institution is not an SIFI, such as what happened after the fall of the Northern Rock bank in 2007.[18] There are two reasons for the entity scope in this book.

---

13 European Commission, *Proposal for a Regulation of the European Parliament and of the Council on structural measures improving the resilience of EU credit institutions, COM/2014/043 final*, p. 2 and p. 13.

14 Financial Stability Board, *Progress and next steps towards ending Too-Big-To-Fail (TBTF)*, pp. 24–26.

15 Emilios Avgouleas, *Governance of global financial markets: the law, the economics, the politics* (Cambridge University Press 2012), pp. 134–135. See also Andrew Ross Sorkin, *Too Big to Fail: The inside story of how Wall Street and Washington fought to save the financial system – and themselves* (Penguin 2010). See also Simon Johnson, 'Eugene Fama: Too Big to Fail perverts activities and incentives'.

16 Financial Stability Board, *Progress and next steps towards ending Too-Big-To-Fail (TBTF)*, p. 2. See also Financial Stability Board, 'Reducing the moral hazard posed by systemically important financial institutions', p. 2.

17 The FSB periodically updates the list of SIFIs. For example, Financial Stability Board, '2013 update of group of global systemically important banks(G-SIBs)' www.financialstabilityboard. org/wp-content/uploads/r_131111.pdf?page_moved=1, accessed February 25, 2015.

18 For details on the fall of Northern Rock, see infra Chapter 2, Section 4.2.

First, the TBTF bank structural problem happens not only in SIFIs but also in other entities; size does not necessarily function as the decisive role in the problem. Based on statistical research by the International Monetary Fund (IMF) on the relationship between trading activities and financial stability with a sample of 79 SIFIs, it shows two points that are relevant here: (i) the root causes of the instability of these institutions are both the structure and the cyclicality inclination in banking entities; and (ii) the sample from the Asian countries fared well in the 2008 crisis despite the fact that they are also SIFIs.[19]

Second, when it comes to the special resolution as a solution to the bank structural problem, the entity scope of the current EU Bank Recovery and Resolution Directive (BRRD) includes not only SIFIs but also other entities that meet the resolution conditions.[20] The fact is, it is hard to have different resolution policies based on a classification of SIFIs and non-SIFIs. Entities that are not on the list of SIFIs might equally cause a negative spillover effect due to the interconnectedness of the banking sector.[21]

1.2 Development of the problem

1.2.1 Origin and consequences

How has the TBTF bank structural problem come about? The banking sector, which is supposed to provide market intermediation and finance to the real economy, was widely criticised for gradually becoming detached from it.[22] To a certain extent, instead of functioning as a tool to foster and boost real economic growth, many banks have transformed to become entities that are excessively engaged in pursuing business expansion at the expense of the rational development of the real economy. The overall size of the banking sector was more than three times the size of the EU's GDP, which would cast reasonable doubt on the plausibility of the surge of the banking sector in the EU.[23] The rapid development brought

---

19　Julian T.S. Chow, *Making banks safer: can Volcker and Vickers do it?* (International Monetary Fund 2011), pp. 14–16. For detail about the two attributes of the bank structural problem, see infra Chapter 3, Section 5.1.

20　Directive 2014/59/EU of the European Parliament and of the Council of 15 May 2014, establishing a framework for the recovery and resolution of credit institutions and investment firms and amending Council Directive 82/891/EEC, and Directives 2001/24/EC, 2002/47/EC, 2004/25/EC, 2005/56/EC, 2007/36/EC, 2011/35/EU, 2012/30/EU and 2013/36/EU, and Regulations (EU) No 1093/2010 and (EU) No 648/2012, of the European Parliament and of the Council [2014] OJ L 173/190/1 (BRRD).

21　For details of the interconnectedness see Chapter 1, Section 3(b).

22　Steve Denning, 'The Volcker Rule make us safer, but not safe', Forbes, www.forbes.com/sites/ste vedenning/2013/12/13/the-volcker-rule-makes-us-safer-but-not-safe/, accessed November 27, 2014. Defending the relationship between banks and the financial industry with the real economy, Steve Denning argued that 'the financial sector has achieved profitability through practices that have caused increasingly serious financial crises: it needs to be reined in and reconnected to the real economy'.

23　Liikanen Erkki, *High-level Expert Group on reforming the structure of the EU banking sector*, pp. 33–35.

with it unprecedented risks threatening not only the stability of the industry but also the entire economy as a whole due to the interdependence relationship between the overall economy and the banking sector.

The transformation of the banking sector and the run up to the TBTF bank structural problem largely stemmed from the development of the universal banking model, which was dedicated to providing one-stop-shop services to financial customers.[24] In the competition-intensive modern financial markets, the profitability of traditional deposit banking was dwarfed by investment banking activities and other trading activities. In the race for survival, the universal banking model was created and loomed large.[25] The various business activities included deposit banking services, investment banking services, proprietary trading, wealth management services, etc. This business expansion exploited the economies of scale and the economies of scope in an extreme way.[26] As a result, to expand other riskier transaction-oriented business, many banking groups exploited the support and tacit subsidisation by the deposit-taking entities that are normally backed by the deposit insurance mechanism in each country.[27] The problem was that the co-existence of activities and subsidisation in the universal banking model brought about a misalignment of incentives, encouraged excessive risk-taking, and caused the moral hazard problem in the banking industry. When the risks in the banking industry actually materialised, the market failure finally escalated into the eruption of the Global Financial Crisis (GFC).

In addition, the TBTF bank structural problem happened within the context of global financial deregulation policy.[28] It dates back to policies of the last century, such as the UK 'Big-Bang' in 1986 and the gradual dismantlement of the Glass-Steagall Act in the US in the 1990s. Besides, ever since the last decade of the twentieth century, lax monetary policy has been prevalent in western countries, starting from the UK and the US and spreading to other developed economies including the EU. Such a policy was meant to stimulate the development of economic and financial markets. It provided excessive liquidity, signalled a promising market outlook, and led to the phenomenon of prevalent overconfidence and wishful thinking.

General market optimism was transformed into an unprecedented financial innovation and securitisation boom together with real estate bubbles as a result of

---

24 Emilios Avgouleas, *The reform of 'Too-Big-To-Fail' bank: a new regulatory model for the institutional separation of 'casino' from 'utility' banking* (2010), pp. 3–4.

25 Ibid.

26 Omar R. Valdimarsson, 'Too-Big-to-Fail prevention is tested in post crisis Iceland'. Bloomberg, www.bloomberg.com/news/2012–08–03/post-crisis-iceland-is-test-site-for-too-big-to-fail-prevention.html, accessed December 5, 2014. Lucian A. Bebchuk, Alma Cohen, and Holger Spamann, 'Wages of failure: executive compensation at Bear Stearns and Lehman 2000–2008', 27 Yale J on Reg 257.

27 Jerome A. Madden, 'A weapon of mass destruction strikes: credit default swaps bring down AIG and Lehman Brothers', 5 Bus L Brief 15.

28 Lynn Stout, 'Derivatives and the legal origin of the 2008 credit crisis', 1 *Harvard Business Law Review* 1, pp. 31–36.

the self-reinforcement cycle of the markets.[29] Through financial innovation, such as structural debt products and credit derivatives, the risks of the banking credit extension to the real estate markets were supposed to be transferred to other entities. However, the risks were spread to more entities rather than being defused due to the interconnectedness and homogeneity of the financial sector.[30] What was worse, the misleading illusion of risk-transference gave rise to bad incentives for more risk-taking, which fuelled the economic bubble.

In fact, the co-existence of activities acted as a problem driver which, in addition to giving rise to distorted incentives for banks, also added impediments to effective resolution.[31] The impediments to effective resolution would directly lead to the TBTF problem defined earlier.

The impediments mainly happened due to the interconnectedness of banks engaging in various activities. The interconnectedness problem was reflected through two channels: (i) intergroup links, which refer to connections between bank group entities, such as central management of short-term liquidity; and (ii) interbank exposures, which refer to connections between different banks, such as wholesale funding and borrowing.[32]

1.2.2 Significance

The bubbles in the markets finally burst starting with the fall of Bear Stearns in March 2008 and the Lehman Brothers' failure in September 2008.[33] That instantly doomed the highly leveraged and interconnected banking sector and contaminated all involved participants in the financial products food chain and caused a crisis in the banking sector. For the EU, this problem became severe because the banking crisis evolved into a sovereign debt crisis and then into an overall economic crisis.[34]

---

29 Daniel Kahneman, Paul Slovic, and Amos Tversky, *Judgement under uncertainty, cap. 6* (Cambridge University Press, 1982). Facing with complicated decision-making such as predicting the outlook of capital markets, people tend to picture themselves in a bull market if there is an existing positive economic fundamental.

30 Avgouleas, *Governance of global financial markets: the law, the economics, the politics*, pp. 35–51. See infra Chapter 1, Section 3(b).

31 European Commission, *Commission staff working document impact assessment accompanying the document Proposal for a Regulation of the European Parliament and of the Council on structural measures improving the resilience of EU Credit Institutions and the Proposal for a Regulation of the European Parliament and of the Council on reporting and transparency of securities financing transactions, SWD/2014/030 final*, pp. 10–11.

32 Ibid.

33 Rosalind Z. Wiggins and Andrew Metrick, 'The Lehman Brothers bankruptcy B: risk limits and stress tests', Yale Program on Financial Stability Case Study. See also Rosalind Z. Wiggins, Thomas Piontek, and Andrew Metrick, 'The Lehman Brothers bankruptcy A'.

34 Liikanen Erkki, *High-level Expert Group on reforming the structure of the EU banking sector*, pp. 4–11. It explains the development of three phases of the crisis, banking crisis, sovereignty debt crisis and overall economic crisis. See infra Chapter 1, Section 1.

Therefore, in the EU, the structural problem is inextricably intertwined with their current economic recession and outlook for the foreseeable future. Due to the ailing banking industry, the overall economy has suffered a lot hitherto and is still unable to find an efficient way out of the recession and its sluggish path of development. The EU economy is unlikely to recover completely without an effective reform of the banking sector to restore market confidence.

1.3 Two legal questions

The book analyses the two attributes of the TBTF bank structural problem: its structural and cyclical attributes.[35] In other words, risks could be accumulated not only because of the structure of the banks with an all-encompassing set of activities, but also due to the cyclical attribute of banking activities, such as their proclivity for risk-taking.[36] Thus, the cyclical attribute acts as the other variable causing instability in banks. Subsequently, the book answers two research questions.

1.3.1 Structural measures

On January 29, 2014, the EC adopted the EU Proposal on Bank Structural Regulation (BSR) to restrict banks from engaging in risky trading activities.[37]

Question 1: Based on the current proposal, how should EU structural reform be established in an effective and efficient way to deal with the structural attribute of the TBTF bank structural problem ex-ante and prevent bank failure?

1.3.2 Effective resolution

The bank recovery and resolution regime in the EU Bank Recovery and Resolution Directive (BRRD) and the Single Resolution Mechanism Regulation (the SRM Regulation) was newly adopted in 2014.[38]

Question 2: Should the EU resolution regime be strengthened to provide an ex-post solution to bank failure triggered by the cyclical attribute of the TBTF bank structural problem?

---

35 See infra Chapter 1, Section 5.
36 See infra Chapter 3, Section 5.2.
37 European Commission, *Proposal for a Regulation of the European Parliament and of the Council on structural measures improving the resilience of EU credit institutions, COM/2014/043 final.*
38 Directive 2014/59/EU of the European Parliament and of the Council of 15 May 2014, establishing a framework for the recovery and resolution of credit institutions and investment firms and amending Council Directive 82/891/EEC, and Directives 2001/24/EC, 2002/47/EC, 2004/25/EC, 2005/56/EC, 2007/36/EC, 2011/35/EU, 2012/30/EU and 2013/36/EU, and Regulations (EU) No 1093/2010 and (EU) No 648/2012, of the European Parliament and of the Council [2014] OJ L 173/190/1 (BRRD). See also *Regulation (EU) No 806/2014 of the European Parliament and of the Council of 15 July 2014 establishing uniform rules and a uniform procedure for the resolution of credit institutions and certain investment firms in the framework of a Single Resolution Mechanism and a Single Resolution Fund and amending Regulation (EU) No 1093/2010 [2014] OJ L 225/1 (SRM Regulation).*

The book analyses the advantages and flaws of current reforms and tries to come up with practical proposals. It also suggests that a closer cooperation between the two reforms, structural reform (see Chapters 3–5) and resolution reform (see Chapter 6), is necessary to deal with the TBTF bank structural problem.[39]

1.4 Geographic scope

The above research questions are mainly discussed within the EU context. Thus, it does not refer to domestic rules at the Member State level, including Denmark. Generally speaking, according to the Rangvid Report, the causes of the financial crisis in Denmark were similar to those discussed in this book about the EU crisis as a whole in the context of global financial internationalisation.[40] But the book will also look at how relevant EU directives and regulations are transposed and applied at the Member State level.

The book refers to a comparative approach, mostly comparing EU reform with UK and US legislative reforms on the structural problem.[41] But it should be noted that the EU model is the primary objective of the analysis, and the US and the UK models are secondary.

2 Research method

2.1 Behavioural finance

Researchers might have different stances on the reasons for the GFC. However, it is undeniable that the bank structural problem contributed greatly in the run up to the GFC.[42] The analyses herein focus on the discussion of TBTF bank structural problems in the EU.

The first main approach is that of Behavioural Finance (BF).[43] The book conducts a behavioural analysis using two channels: (i) BF theory to analyse the TBTF bank structural problem; and then (ii) applying such analyses to relevant bank structural reform and resolution reform. As some researchers argue, EU regulatory responses towards the GFC evolved from a 'financial stability'-oriented perspective, focusing on prudential regulation and institutional and systemic stability, into a 'consumer protection'-oriented reform, which is also

---

39 For more details, see infra Introduction, Section 3 on the abstracts of Chapters 3–6. See infra Chapter 1, Section 5.

40 Rangvid Committee (Rangvid Udvalget), *The financial crisis in Denmark: causes, consequences, and learning (den finansielle krise i danmark – årsager konsekvenser og læring) (Rangvid-rapporten)* (September 8, 2013), pp. 27–50. Compare the opinions with infra Chapter 2, Section 1 on the causes of the global crisis.

41 See infra Introduction, Section 2.2.

42 United States Senate Permanent Subcommittee on Investigations, *Wall Street and the financial crisis: anatomy of a financial collapse* (Cosimo Reports 2011), pp. 15–17. See also Liikanen Erkki, *High-level Expert Group on reforming the structure of the EU banking sector*, pp. 4–11.

43 Ran Spiegler, *Bounded rationality and industrial organization* (Oxford University Press 2011).

known as 'second generation reform'.[44] Compared with current scholarship on these regulatory reforms, the approach employed herein and the analysing perspectives might be largely different.

2.1.1 Theories and analyses

First, the book refers to relevant theories in BF. Departing from the classic economic theory and its assumption of a reasonable person and Efficient Market Hypothesis (EMH), the fundamental hypothesis or starting point of BF is the bounded rationality of individuals, including investors.[45] It means that individuals possess limited capacity for the process of decision-making. For example, as shown by extensive laboratory research, people tend to be less interested in their welfare in the long term and rather prefer to gain immediate rewards for themselves.[46]

In the area of BF, Daniel Kahneman and Amos Tversky have made great contributions in establishing the theory on how investors make their decisions.[47] In discussing the process of investors' decision-making, they replace the 'utility' function with the 'expected value' function, and the 'probabilities' function with the 'weighting' consideration. In other words, different from the widely accepted opinion that investors make decisions based on the utility a decision could bring and the probability of its occurrence, investors instead consider the expected value, i.e. the gains and losses. And they weigh possible gains against possible losses, but the consideration of losses always outweighs the rational gains. This means that investors make irrational decisions because of a fear of loss. Thus, Daniel Kahneman and Amos Tversky suggest that, to a certain extent, investors' investment decisions could be irrational due to their wrong references and approaches in making a choice.[48]

Building on this, BF advocates that there are certain identified market phenomena called anomalies which are not in accordance with the EMH. According to BF, the EMH cannot explain some puzzles due to various heuristics, such as 'representativeness', 'availability', and 'anchoring'.[49] 'Representativeness' refers to situations where people are asked to judge whether A belongs to B. They tend to decide merely according to the degree to which A resembles B.[50] 'Availability' refers to situations where people judge the frequency or the plausibility of a

44 Niamh Moloney and Jennifer G. Hill, *The regulatory aftermath of the global financial crisis* (Cambridge University Press 2012), pp. 111–115.

45 Herbert A Simon, 'Theories of bounded rationality', 1 *Decision and Organization* 161. See Adam Smith, *Wealth of nations* (University of Chicago Bookstore 2005), pp. 18–20.

46 Alina Maria Neaţu, 'The use of behavioral economics in promoting public policy', 22 *Theoretical and Applied Economics* 255, p. 257.

47 Daniel Kahneman and Amos Tversky, 'Prospect theory: an analysis of decision under risk', *Econometrica: Journal of the Econometric Society*, p. 263.

48 Amos Tversky and Daniel Kahneman, 'Judgment under uncertainty: heuristics and biases', 185 *Science*, p. 1124.

49 Ibid.

50 Ibid. p. 1124.

particular event by 'the ease with which instances or occurrences can be brought to mind'. For instance, a person who has experienced a heart attack would think that the incidence of heart attacks would be higher than the expectation of others who have not experienced one.[51] 'Anchoring' refers to the situation where people are asked to give a numerical prediction based on a particular starting point, but who then demonstrate that different starting points yield different results.[52] For instance, the median estimates of the percentage of African countries in the UN were 25 and 45 for groups that were given 10 and 65 respectively as starting points.

Those are heuristics that can affect decision-making, and what matters here is that these heuristics can easily lead to incorrect decisions. In so doing, BF further suggests that the market-based corrective influence of arbitrage is limited in reaching efficient market equilibrium because of behavioural factors.[53]

In addition, Stefano DellaVigna has identified three classes of deviation from rationality: non-standard preferences, non-standard beliefs, and non-standard decision-making.[54] Non-standard preferences refer to some inclinations of investors that tend to lead to incorrect decisions, such as overvaluing current gratification over future gains. Non-standard beliefs refer to irrational views, such as wishful thinking, on the market situation in a bull market. Non-standard decision-making is related to some irrational patterns of decision-making, such as making investments based on social influences that then cause a 'herding' effect.

More importantly, there is a new paradigm shift in the development of BF, which is Andrew Lo's Adaptive Market Hypothesis (AMH). Compared to the above theories by Daniel Kahneman and Amos Tversky, and Stefano DellaVigna, which are mostly built on the bounded rationality assumption, Andrew Lo's AMH modifies the bounded rationality hypothesis of the BF. It argues for a comparative middle ground hypothesis that people tend to be motivated by the need for survival, but are not completely irrational.[55]

Second, the above BF theories act as an interpretative tool to analyse the development of the TBTF bank structural problem in the GFC. By doing so, it shows that the behavioural factors and the universal banking model worked in tandem in the run up to the bank structural problem and the GFC.[56] This opens up new perspectives in understanding the causes of the GFC and the TBTF bank structural problem in the EU and its resulting reforms.[57]

---

51 Ibid. p. 1127.
52 Ibid. p. 1128.
53 Kahneman and Tversky, 'Prospect theory: an analysis of decision under risk'. See infra Chapter 2, Section 2.1.
54 Stefano DellaVigna, 'Psychology and economics: evidence from the field', 47 *Journal of Economic Literature*, pp. 315–372.
55 Andrew W Lo, 'The adaptive markets hypothesis', 30 *The Journal of Portfolio Management*, p. 15.
56 See also Daniel Kahneman, 'Maps of bounded rationality: psychology for behavioral economics', *American Economic Review*, p. 1449.
57 Financial Conduct Authority, *Financial Conduct Authority (2013), Applying behavioral economics in Financial Conduct Authority, Occasional Paper No. 1. (2013)*.

Through the behavioural analyses, the book suggests two further attributes of the bank structural problem:[58] (i) it confirms the structural attribute of the bank structural problem, as behavioural factors were amplified in trading activities;[59] and (ii) it elaborates the cyclicality attribute of the structural problem, such as the inclination for risk-taking by investors.[60]

In addition, these analyses lay the foundations for subsequent discussion on regulatory reforms: (i) the structural attribute corresponds to structural separation reforms; and (ii) the cyclical attribute corresponds to resolution reforms.[61]

2.1.2 Application

As indicated earlier, BF analyses provide a comprehensive understanding of the connection between BF theories and the TBTF bank structural problem, and indicate that behavioural factors are an accurate interpretative tool in explaining the occurrence of the GFC and the trigger for the TBTF bank structural problem.

More importantly, the behavioural analyses provide new insights for assessing the current structural reform rules in the EU BSR[62] and the newly adopted bank recovery and resolution regime in the EU BRRD and the SRM Regulation.[63] The idea of applying BF to promote legal regulation is supported by many behavioural economists such as George Akerlof and Robert Shiller. They argue that the demonstration of bounded rationality lays the foundation for more government legal intervention.[64] By doing so, it is possible to guide people's behaviours and their decision-making processes, and avoid some anomalies.

First, as regards using the BF analyses to assess the structural measures in the EU BSR, the major task is to evaluate the effectiveness of rules in achieving their perceived purposes. Inspired by the UK Financial Conduct Authority (FCA) and its analyses on using BF to promote effective financial regulation, two approaches among others are extremely important: (i) market failure analysis (MFA) and (ii) cost benefit analysis (CBA).[65] The two tests aim at finding out the effectiveness and efficiency of the EU BSR.[66]

For that to happen, it should be noted that BF has normative weaknesses due to the paradox of reconciliation between the 'descriptive' attribute and the 'normative' attribute of a theory. In this context, a 'descriptive' attribute is used

---

58 For detailed analysis of the cyclical attribute see infra Chapter 3, Section 5.
59 See infra Chapter 1, Section 5.
60 See infra Chapter 2, Section 5.
61 See infra Chapter 2, Section 5.
62 European Commission, *Proposal for a Regulation of the European Parliament and of the Council on structural measures improving the resilience of EU credit institutions, COM/2014/043 final*.
63 See generally BRRD; see also generally SRM Regulation.
64 George A. Akerlof and Robert J. Shiller, *Animal spirits: how human psychology drives the economy, and why it matters for global capitalism* (Princeton, NJ: Princeton University Press 2010), pp. 2–10.
65 Financial Conduct Authority, *Financial Conduct Authority (2013), Applying behavioral economics in Financial Conduct Authority, Occasional Paper No. 1*, p. 54.
66 See infra Chapters 4–5.

to assess whether a theory accurately describes the reality, while a 'normative' attribute is used to assess whether the theory has normative utility to guide legal intervention. Amos Tversky and Daniel Kahneman indicated that the EMH is descriptively inaccurate according to reality, while normatively useful because it enables people to predict a reasonable person's actions, and thus provide a basis for legal regulation. BF, however, may be criticised for its normative weakness because it suggests that human behaviour is unpredictable and hence undermines the legitimacy of the rule of law. Specifically, the basis of the rule of law is that people are reasonable, and legal intervention can guide people to do what is preferred by law because they would suffer legal risks if they did not. So the bounded rationality assumption is breached to a certain extent if people are just irrational.

Be that as it may, there is still a valid basis for BF's normative utility. The AMH could compensate for the weakness to a certain extent. That is because it takes a comparative middle ground hypothesis between a reasonable person and bounded rationality. It advocates that people tend to be either rational or irrational, whatever suits the need for survival.[67]

Second, as regards assessing the bank recovery and resolution regime in the EU BRRD and the SRM Regulation, the BF analyses also played a fundamental role. The BF analyses of the TBTF bank structural problem in combination with the conclusion on the remaining weaknesses in the structural measures based on the MFA analysis and the CBA analysis, actually determine the desirability and necessary strength of the ideal resolution reform. The structural measures could tackle the structural attribute to a certain extent on an ex-ante basis. But they do not address the cyclical attribute and the resolvability problem on an ex-post basis.

2.2 *Comparative approach and others*

The second main approach is the comparative method.[68] In analysing the structural reform and the relevant resolution reform, a comparative approach would also be deployed to draw some regulatory reform lessons and experiences from other major economies. For instance, the US orderly liquidation mechanism established through Title II of the Dodd-Frank Wall Street Reform and Consumer Protection Act (Dodd-Frank Act), is comparable to the BRRD in the EU.[69] The Volcker Rule in the Dodd-Frank Act[70] and the UK Vickers Rule are

---

67 Robert J. Schiller, *Irrational exuberance* (2000), pp. 5–30. See also Robert J. Schiller, *The subprime solution* (Princeton, NJ: Princeton University Press 2008), pp. 115–169. Amos Tversky and Daniel Kahneman, 'Rational choice and the framing of decisions', *Journal of Business*, S251. But they also think it is hard for a theory to accommodate both descriptive and normative needs. See Chapter 4, Section 2.3.3. For specific analysis on normative weakness, see infra Introduction, Section 4.2.

68 Gerhard Danneman, 'Comparative law: study of similarities or differences?' *The Oxford handbook of comparative law* (Oxford, UK: Oxford University Press 2006).

69 See Dodd-Frank Wall Street Reform and Consumer Protection Act (US), Titles I–II. See also generally BRRD.

70 The Dodd-Frank Wall Street Reform and Consumer Protection Act (US), section 619.

also comparable to the High-level Expert Group on reforming the structure of the EU banking sector (the Liikanen report) and the BSR.[71]

In addition to the major research approaches including BF, the economic approach,[72] and the comparative approach, the book adopts the basic dogmatic legal approach, i.e. analysing the legitimacy and effectiveness of relevant regulation and analysing whether a new rule could provide good incentives in the banking sector to curb risk-taking.[73]

3 Structure

Figure 0.2 shows the layout of the book. Chapter 1 analyses the major causes of the TBTF bank structural problem. It aims at pointing out the core features of the TBTF bank structural problem: behemoth size, complexity and interconnectedness, ignoring low probability risk, and the spill over effect.[74] It also provides a metaphor for the 'three gorges'. As a metaphor, the demise of the colossal 'chained battleship' can function as a model for the explanation of the bank structural problem to a certain extent.[75] Therefore, the approaches by which the 'chained battleship' could be avoided might shed light on the analyses of the bank structural problem in the EU. This chapter highlights: (i) the first attribute (among two) of the TBTF bank structural problem, i.e. the structural attribute and the necessity of a structural reform; and (ii) also sets out the tentative implications of the second attribute, i.e. the cyclicality attribute, which is explained further in Chapter 2.[76]

Chapter 2 analyses the cyclicality attribute of the TBTF bank structural problem through a behavioural approach. It tries to identify those seemingly unavoidable irrational factors and heuristics that played a significant role in the run up to the TBTF bank structural problem. Taxonomically speaking, these identified heuristics are classified into two groups according to their origins: ignorance and greed.[77] In financial markets, ignorance and greed compromised the rationality of the investors, the industry, and governments. Therefore, the irrationality in

---

71 Independent Commission on Banking, 'Final report, recommendations'. See also Liikanen Erkki, *High-level Expert Group on reforming the structure of the EU banking sector*, p. 99.

72 See infra Chapter 4, Section 1, the economic approach and CBA are part of the behavioural analyses.

73 Edward H. Levi, *An introduction to legal reasoning* (Chicago, IL: University of Chicago Press 2013).

74 Liikanen Erkki, *High-level Expert Group on reforming the structure of the EU banking sector*, pp. 3–11. European Commission, *Commission staff working document impact assessment accompanying the document Proposal for a Regulation of the European Parliament and of the Council on structural measures improving the resilience of EU Credit Institutions and the Proposal for a Regulation of the European Parliament and of the Council on reporting and transparency of securities financing transactions*, SWD/2014/030 final, pp. 8–10.

75 Luo Guanzhong, 'Romance of Three Kingdoms', *DW Three Kingdoms*, pp. 405–451.

76 Chow, *Making banks safer: can Volcker and Vickers do it?* pp. 14–16.

77 Brett H. McDonnell, 'Of Mises and Min (sky): libertarian and liberal responses to financial crises past and present', 34 *Seattle UL Rev*, p. 1279.

beliefs, preferences, and decision-making processes were widely reflected in the TBTF bank structural problem.[78] The analyses show how behavioural factors and bounded rationality increased risk and volatility in the financial markets and led to the systemic market failure. It suggests that the behavioural factors and the universal banking model worked in combination in the run up to the TBTF bank structural problem. By doing so, it makes a case for not only structural reform but also resolution reform.

Normatively speaking, using behavioural analyses, the chapter meditates on how behavioural factors can influence the assessment of current EU reforms. In other words, how might responsive reforms be structured to offset and contain behavioural factors, and to disrupt or reduce the causal effect between behavioural factors and risks in the banking sector? The relevant analyses and discussions are conducted from Chapter 3 through to Chapter 6.

Chapter 3 starts by explaining the structural reform's dual purposes: financial stability and efficiency (having regard to competition). It then gives an introduction to the BSR reform in the EU and draws a comparison between EU reform and that of the US and the UK.[79] In addition, building on the relevant analysis in Chapters 1 and 2, after the detailed introduction of the structural reform rules in the EU, this chapter also summarises the two attributes of the TBTF bank structural problem: the structural and cyclical attributes. It further explains how the two attributes require the cooperation of two reforms: structural reform (see Chapters 3–5) and resolution reform (see Chapter 6).[80]

Against the background of identifying behavioural factors and irrationality in the GFC and the TBTF bank structural problem, Chapters 4 and 5 conduct an MFA and a CBA. The adoption of the two approaches aims at assessing the effectiveness and efficiency of the current BSR and coming up with practical proposals, enlightened by the experience of applying BF in financial regulation in the UK.[81]

Chapter 4 first advocates that price-based measures could be helpful in dealing with the structural problems of the banking industry, but would not affect the behavioural aspects of it, and hence would be unable to avoid a recurrence of the systemic risk. The price-based measures refer to a broad set of regulations, such as capital rules and liquidity rules.[82] Then, by undertaking an MFA[83] of the BSR, the chapter suggests that different from price-based rules, the ongoing structural separation reform could contain the influence of behavioural factors on the development of the structural problems by severing the subsidisation link between the deposit entity and the trading entity. Therefore, the BSR

---

78 DellaVigna, 'Psychology and economics: evidence from the field'.
79 European Commission, *Proposal for a Regulation of the European Parliament and of the Council on structural measures improving the resilience of EU credit institutions, COM/2014/043 final.*
80 Chow, *Making banks safer: can Volcker and Vickers do it?* pp. 14–16.
81 Financial Conduct Authority, *Financial Conduct Authority (2013), Applying behavioral economics in Financial Conduct Authority, Occasional Paper No. 1,* pp. 53–54.
82 See infra Chapter 3, Section 1.2.
83 Financial Conduct Authority, *Financial Conduct Authority (2013), Applying behavioral economics in Financial Conduct Authority, Occasional Paper No. 1.*

could achieve the first major purpose of reform, i.e. financial stability, albeit there would be practical challenges, such as migration risk and the lack of an international concerted effort.

Chapter 5 continues the analyses of the EU BSR and answers whether it can attain the second reform purpose, financial efficiency (having regard to competition), through another approach, the CBA.[84] It advocates that the BSR could achieve the second major purpose of reform, which is maintaining the efficiency and competition edge for EU banks to a certain extent. But it also suggests some practical challenges and its failure to effectively touch upon resolution elements.

Chapter 6 shifts to the second research question of the TBTF bank structural problem, which is tackling the second attribute, i.e. the cyclical attribute. After introducing and analysing the resolution rules in the newly adopted EU BRRD and the SRM,[85] the chapter shows that compared with the Single Point of Entry (SPE) strategy and the US model, the EU resolution mechanism still suffers from fragmented decision-making powers and decentralized execution. The chapter suggests that the US-style SPE strategy could shed some light on the EU resolution mechanism and offer advice on a more centralised and integrated resolution regime.

The chapter also concludes that the reform to deal with the TBTF bank structural problem could be more effectively achieved by combining the bank

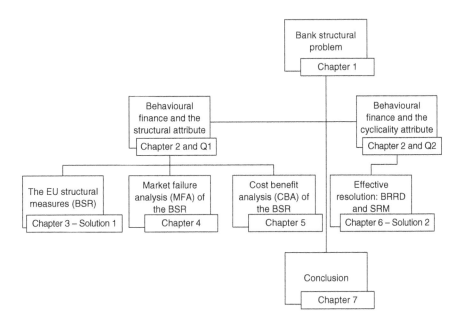

Figure 0.2 Layout of book

---

84 Ibid.
85 See generally BRRD; see also generally SRM Regulation.

recovery and resolution reforms with the structural separation reforms. The latter can contain the misaligned incentives in the industry and deal with the TBTF bank structural problem partly on an ex-ante basis. However, it cannot eradicate the behavioural aspects of the problem. Bank failure or systemic failure might still happen. This demands that ex-post measures be carried out as complementary actions, which could be achieved through the bank recovery and resolution reforms.

4 Possible disagreements and responses

This book starts with the TBTF bank structural problem in the EU, and proceeds with the analysis of the EU structural reforms and the bank resolution reforms. Its focus is the overall picture of the relevant EU reforms. Its approach is not limited to the conventional dogmatic legal research. The reader's attention should be drawn to the following possible disagreements and responses.

4.1 On new legislation progress

Claim 1: The regulation reform in connection with the bank structural separation and resolution regulation has been changing very rapidly in the EU; for instance, a new text emerged from the Council of the European Union on EU bank structural reform on June 19, 2015.[86] This might affect the argument in this book regarding this matter, which is based on the Commission's proposals in January 2014.

Response 1: First, it should be noted that this book is analysing a moving target; the structural reforms' status quo is that the Member States are preparing for legislation in the European Parliament for the coming six months (starting from June 19, 2015).

Accordingly, the book does not adjust the argument for two reasons. The first, general reason is concerned with recent reform updates and even some upcoming legal updates: it is a statement of fact that financial regulation reform in the major economies, including the EU, after the crisis is changing at an unprecedented rate.[87] A book focusing on a particular legal issue can choose to analyse whichever step of the relevant reform it chooses, provided it suits the research purpose. The second, specific reason concerns the Council text: the legislative approach in the Council text is very different from the Commission proposal. The latter mainly adopted an amalgamation between the Volcker style prohibition and the Vickers style ring fence, while the former adopted only the ring fence approach and the narrowly applied non-mandatory ring fence, having regard to prudential

---

86 European Commission, 'Banking structural reform: ECOFIN Council agrees its position' (June 19, 2015) http://ec.europa.eu/finance/bank/structural-reform/index_en.htm#maincontentSec1, accessed June 20, 2015.
87 European Commission, 'Progress of financial reforms', (2015) http://ec.europa.eu/finance/general-policy/policy/map_reform_en.htm, accessed June 1, 2015.

measures.[88] The approach in the latter has many advantages in balancing stability and building efficiency, which is not the case in the new text.[89] Thus, an analysis of the new text would not help the points made in this book.[90]

4.2 On the practicalities of behavioural finance

Claim 2: The BF approach is not sufficiently operational in the convoluted bank structural problem.

Response 2: As indicated earlier, arguing for the irrationality and unpredictability of human behaviour, BF may be criticised for undermining the legitimacy of the rule of law, and not being operational in the TBTF bank structural problem.[91] As a matter of fact, its practicality in regulating the TBTF bank structural problem has both theoretical and realistic grounds.

Its theoretical basis can be more evidently shown by the AMH, representing the new development of BF.[92] Arguing a middle ground between EMH and BF, it suggests that people sometimes act rationally, sometimes irrationally, depending on the strategy that best suits their struggle for survival. Such theoretical modification compensates for the normative inadequacy of BF and strengthens the possibility of applying it to legal regulation.[93]

It should be noted that the book does not advocate tackling or eradicating the irrationality of market participants that played an important role in the development of the TBTF bank structural problem, neither is it possible. But taking behavioural factors into consideration in dealing with the TBTF bank structural problem has a realistic foundation. First, the book suggests simply considering behavioural factors in structural reform. It is possible to use structural separation to provide more incentives for banks to engage in less risky activities, and minimise the interaction between behavioural factors and trading activities and reduce the risks thereof.[94] Second, by suggesting the cyclicality attribute of the structural problem based on behavioural analysis, the book argues that bank failure is unavoidable to a certain extent, even if structural reform were to be implemented.[95] Thus, behavioural analysis is also the basis on which resolution reform is built in this book.

---

88 This reference of EU structural reform is to the latest Council draft available as of June 19, 2015. But the reference of EU bank structural regulation (BSR) in this book is to the European Commission proposal as of January 29, 2014.
89 See infra Chapter 5, Section 6.
90 See also another paper which specifically analyses the new text, Hu Chen Chen, 'The structural reform for EU banks: does it work', Nordic & European Company Law Working Paper 15-05 (2015).
91 See supra Introduction, Section 2.1.
92 Andrew W. Lo, 'Reconciling efficient markets with behavioral finance: the adaptive markets hypothesis', 7 *Journal of Investment Consulting*, p. 21.
93 See infra Chapter 2, Section 4.1. See also infra Chapter 4, Section 1.
94 See infra Chapter 4, Section 3.2.
95 See infra Chapter 6, Section 1.1.

Having said that, critics may then argue that there lacks persuasive precedence of the application of BF in legal regulation. But the fact is that this claim does not show the reality. Although it is still new and unconventional, the practicality of applying BF in financial regulation and other areas of law has been proved to be possible by the UK's FCA in its research.[96] In the UK, a Behavioural Insight Team (BIT) was started as the world's first government institution dedicated to the application of behavioural science in promoting the efficiency of public policies.[97]

4.3 On structural separation

Claim 3: The decoupling approach does not seem to be convincing because universal banking has many advantages.

Response 3: In the book, the case for structural separation is based on two tests: the MFA and the CBA. First, the separation mechanism in the EU BSR can contain the interaction between trading activities and behavioural factors and the risks thereof, and therefore make the banks safer.[98] Second, it tries to maintain the balance between safety and competitiveness by tailoring the scope and strength of separation.[99] Therefore, the separation the book advocates is not absolute separation, disregarding the advantages of universal banking, but one that attempts as far as it is able to preserve the advantages of universal banking.

Critics may then also argue that there are examples where universal banking functions are very successful and therefore advocate absolutely no separation. It is undeniable that there were some countries which performed well in the crisis even though they had also adopted the universal banking model.[100]

But the pure fact that some countries avoided the crisis is not sufficient to support there being absolutely no separation. Take Australia as an example. Its success in largely avoiding the financial crisis was attributable to many factors such as its mining boom, which was dependent on China's miraculous economic growth, its economic stimulus program, and its 'twin-peak' regulatory regime, which turned out to be more effective in containing risk-taking by the banking industry.[101] Unfortunately, there is no known evidence which shows that the impeccability of universal banking was one of them.

---

96 Financial Conduct Authority, *Financial Conduct Authority (2013), Applying behavioral economics in Financial Conduct Authority, Occasional Paper No. 1*, pp. 9–11.
97 Behavioural Insights Team, 'Applying behavioural insights to reduce fraud, error and debt', Cabinet Office, London.
98 See infra Chapter 4, Section 3.2.
99 See infra Chapter 5, Table 5.1.
100 Moloney and Hill, *The regulatory aftermath of the global financial crisis*, p. 210.
101 Ibid, pp. 277–281. See also HM Treasury, 'A new approach to financial regulation: judgement, focus and stability', pp. 3–4. See also infra Chapter 2, Section 2.5.

4.4 On legislative concern

Claim 4: On the analysis of the TBTF bank structural problem and its solutions, readers expect more detailed analysis of the law.

Response 4: This impression may come from two sources: (i) the book adopts the non-conventional BF and economic analysis of relevant rules; and (ii) the analysis is focused on the overall regulatory model in the EU on structural problems and compares it with other jurisdictions where necessary.

On (i), compared with conducting pure dogmatic analysis, an interdisciplinary research analysis might inevitably have much of a reader's attention anchored to it while reading the book.[102]

On (ii), the post crisis regulatory reforms are progressing in leaps and bounds. The reforms have been changing the entire regulatory structure of the financial markets, such as regulatory institutional reform, financial infrastructure reform, traditional banking regulation reform and shadow banking regulation reform.[103] Within such a context of huge change, it is not unusual to focus legal analysis of a new reform mainly on the big picture of a new mechanism, rather than on the detailed analysis of each single piece of legislation.

For example, the European Commission drafted an assessment report on the BSR which basically suggests examining the big picture on the effectiveness, efficiency, and coherence of the new structural separation mechanism.[104] But that situation does not imply that a detailed analysis of each piece of law is not important or ignored in this book.[105] It is of significant importance to conduct analyses of what particular rules mean and how they work in practice. But it is not necessarily of primary importance compared with an evaluation of the big picture of bank structural and resolution mechanisms in the early stages of reform.

---

102 See infra Chapter 2.
103 European Commission, 'Progress of financial reforms'.
104 European Commission, *Commission staff working document impact assessment accompanying the document Proposal for a Regulation of the European Parliament and of the Council on structural measures improving the resilience of EU Credit Institutions and the Proposal for a Regulation of the European Parliament and of the Council on reporting and transparency of securities financing transactions, SWD/2014/030 final*, pp. 38–39.
105 See infra Chapters 4–6.

1 The features of the bank structural problem and its structural attribute

The bank structural problem is at the centre of current world wide regulatory reform. For example, the EC adopted the BSR proposal for structural measures in January 2014. Other major economies are all making similar progress, including the US, the UK and Germany.[1] The TBTF bank structural problem refers to the ineffectiveness in the supervision and regulation of banks with the universal banking model.[2] The co-existence of various activities within the same entity acted as a destabilising factor in the run up to the GFC. The bank structural problem is basically one of the major reasons why the banking sector has become too complex to manage, to supervise, and to fail. Thus, the reform to deal with the TBTF bank structural problem is a significant and indispensable part of the current post-crisis comprehensive financial reform.[3]

1 Bank structural problem in the EU

The structural problem came about within the context of global lax monetary policy, financial liberalisation, and the encouragement of financial innovation both from policy-makers and the financial industry.[4] Financial innovation was at the forefront of the global financial liberalisation; it reflected the inception and key features of the TBTF structural problem.

The structural debt securities represented the forefront of the financial innovation and securitisation. With the rise of real estate prices, mortgages were extended to every potential borrower irrespective of their creditworthiness, credit history, and default risk. The reason was that the innovation of the 'originate-to-distribute model' was designed to transfer the default risk away from the banks.[5] The model made it possible for the banks to sell all the debts to a packager who

---

1 See infra Chapter 3, Section 2.
2 European Commission, *Proposal for a Regulation of the European Parliament and of the Council on structural measures improving the resilience of EU credit institutions, COM/2014/043 final* (January 29, 2014), preamble (1).
3 Ibid, preamble (4).
4 Emilios Avgouleas, *Governance of global financial markets: the law, the economics, the politics* (Cambridge University Press 2012), pp. 89–92.
5 Steven L. Schwarcz, 2009, 'The future of securitization', 41 CL Review, p. 1313.

would act as an originator and repackage them into some structural financial products, such as Residential Mortgage Backed Securities (RMBS), Collateral Debt Obligations (CDOs), through Special Purpose Vehicles (SPV).[6] Then, by selling these structural debt securities to other investors, the risk could be transferred to some institutional investors, such as hedge funds and pension funds. Of course, to increase the creditworthiness of these structural securities, Credit Rating Agencies (CRAs) were also involved to provide marketable ratings. To further diversify the risk, the insurance company designed various credit derivatives, such as Credit Default Swaps (CDS), to ensure the investors of the safety of these products. By these operations, it seemed that the risks had been transferred away from the banks. But due to the interconnectedness of the financial industry, such as interbank wholesale financing, the risks were only spread to more entities, but never addressed.[7] On the contrary, the misleading illusion of risk being transferred away only encouraged all the entities in the above product chain to be less meticulous and more inclined to engage in risk-taking. Riding on the wave of the economies of scope and scale, the banks became larger and larger and reached the scale of systemically important institutions.[8]

On the negative side, the above product chain not only increased the overall leverage of the financial system, but also intensified the risk-taking inclination, the interconnectedness, and homogeneity of the banking sector. It brought about the financial instability of the industry. It was really a debilitating factor to the industry in the long run (Figure 1.1).[9]

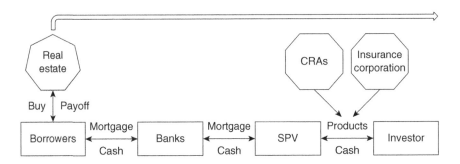

Figure 1.1 Risks and the domino effect

6 *The United States of America v. S&P, 12 U.S.C. § 1833a, 18 U.S.C. § 1341.* The complaint in this case provides a clear elaboration of how the origination of structural debt securities contributed to the run up to the banking sector bubbles.

7 European Commission, *Commission staff working document impact assessment accompanying the document Proposal for a Regulation of the European Parliament and of the Council on structural measures improving the resilience of EU Credit Institutions and the Proposal for a Regulation of the European Parliament and of the Council on reporting and transparency of securities financing transactions, SWD/2014/030 final.* (January 29, 2014) p. 11.

8 Liikanen Erkki, *High-level Expert Group on reforming the structure of the EU banking sector* (Final Report, Brussels, 2012), pp. 12–13.

9 Schwarcz, 'The future of securitization'. Steven L. Schwarcz, 'Understanding the subprime financial crisis', 60 SCL Rev 550.

In the end, the misaligned interests in the above product chain fuelled the economic boom to its extreme, and it went bust starting with the fall of Lehman Brothers and Bear Stearns in 2008. Due to the interconnectedness and homogeneity of banks, the failure of a few entities instantly contaminated all relevant entities in the product chain and the industry as a whole.

As a matter of fact, being one of the most important regions where the banking industry loomed so large, the EU was the first victim due to the contagion effect of the US subprime mortgage crisis.[10] Afterwards, the deteriorating market situation forced the EU to bail out ailing banks, which consequently triggered the downgrade of the sovereign debts and thereafter the sovereign debt crisis. Finally, market confidence further deteriorated into the overall economic crisis.[11]

2 The 'three gorges' metaphor

The analogy of the 'three gorges' battle on the Yangtze River in the three kingdoms dynasty might shed some light on how to tackle bank structural reform in the EU.[12] To a certain extent, the implied 'mechanical theory' and 'let the ship sink wisdom' in the story could be applied to financial regulation.[13]

This was a landmark battle in history because it was a battle of defeating enemy troops using a force that was extremely inferior in number.[14] The rivalry parties in the battle were the powerful and formidable Cao Wei (with a million troops) against a comparably anaemic Sun Wu and Liu Shu alliance (with around a 100,000 troops). The lesson from the battle is about how a weak alliance beat the formidable troops due to the weakness of the 'chained battleships'.

Before the battle, Cao Wei noticed that his soldiers, who had grown up in Northern China and had been trained to fight as land forces, couldn't get used to war on a battleship and easily became nauseated and ill due to the motion of the waves and the unstable battleships fighting in the humid and hot southern area. Cao Wei decided to build colossal battleships, chained together, to accommodate all one million soldiers. The soldiers could run and even ride horses on the huge battleships like they did in the north prairie to overcome the motion of the waves.

The alliance took advantage of the chained and colossal battleships on the Yangtze River by launching a fire attack. A sweeping fire set by the military

---

10 Komisja Europejska, 'Economic crisis in Europe: causes, consequences and responses', 7 *European Economy* 2009. Against the background of the US financial crisis, the EU was instantly affected in 2008–2009. The budget deficits in the EU were more than double in 2009 (to 6% of GDP up from 2.3% of GDP in 2008), and the crisis strongly affected Member States due to the large and open financial sector and strong export-oriented economy.

11 Ibid. See also Rosalind Z. Wiggins, Natalia Tente, and Andrew Metrick, 'Cross-border resolution – Dexia Group', pp. 8–9.

12 Luo Guanzhong, 'Romance of Three Kingdoms', *DW Three Kingdoms*, pp. 405–451.

13 Steven L. Schwarcz, 'Regulating complexity in financial markets'. 87 Wash UL Rev 211. Steven L. Schwarcz argued that the complex financial market is analogous to complex engineering systems, and failures in the financial markets are similar to failures in engineering systems. He suggested applying chaos theory and decoupling methods to analyse complex engineering systems and to shed light on financial regulation.

14 Luo Guanzhong, 'Romance of Three Kingdoms', *DW Three Kingdoms*, pp. 405–451.

alliance from the downriver side was fanned by the strong southeast wind and devastated the million soldiers of Cao Wei on the upriver side of the Yangtze River. Although the probability of a southeast wind was low during the winter on the Yangtze River, geographically speaking,[15] Cao Wei ignored this possibility in its 'chained battleships' plan, with devastating results. When the risk materialised, the fire on one ship and the spill over effect doomed all the ships that accommodated the one million soldiers, because the earlier affected ships could not be sunk as they were all chained together.

To some extent, the demise of the colossal 'chained battleship' can function as a model for the explanation of the TBTF bank structural problem. They are similar in four respects: huge in size; chained battleships are like interconnected banks; ignoring the rare southeast wind is like ignoring the low probability fat-tail risks;[16] and a demise by fire and the banking crisis being caused by the spill over effect.[17]

To avoid the demise of the 'chained battleships', at least two approaches need to be considered. The first is the compartment design.[18] An ideal mechanical approach to the colossal battleship scenario should be that, as a whole, it could exploit the force of scale while also being able to be disaggregated into smaller ships when necessary to attain its original agility. The second approach is that of streamlined procedures to deal with the sinking.[19] After exhausting every rescue opportunity, battleships need to have the capacity to sink earlier failing units to avoid unnecessary further contagion.

3 Key features of the bank structural problem in the EU

The TBTF bank structural problem emerged within the context of the lax macroeconomic policies and the trend for financial innovation. It applied especially to SIFIs, whose failure would seriously disrupt the functioning of the financial system, which is essential for the real economy.[20] The materialisation of the

---

15 When the battle happened in winter, only the northwest wind was prevailing in southeast China because of the specific subtropical climate in East Asia.

16 Avgouleas, *Governance of global financial markets: the law, the economics, the politics*, p. 346. When evaluating the Basel III banks prudential requirement rules, Prof. Avgouleas expressed his concerns about fat-tail risk, 'like Basel II, Basel III risk modelling does not deal effectively with "fat tails". As banks now move to business practices that will not add measurable risk, risk could be pushed to the "tails", because "tail risk" (very low risk of default) is normally ignored. Yet, as explained in Chapter 3, correlations of tail risk, which are notoriously unpredictable and unstable, were at the heart of the GFC'. See also Hal S. Scott, 'Reducing systemic risk through the reform of capital regulation', 13 *Journal of International Economic Law* 763.

17 Europejska, 'Economic crisis in Europe: causes, consequences and responses'. The trading positions and exposures between EU banks with US entities added to the vulnerability of the banking sector when the domino effect happened in the failure of Lehman Brothers.

18 Compartmentalisation is a mechanism used in mechanical design to prevent spill over effect. Steven L. Schwarcz, 'Systemic risk', 97 Geo LJ 193.

19 Basel Committee on Banking Supervision, *Report and recommendations of the Cross-border Bank Resolution Group* (March 2010).

20 Avgouleas, *Governance of global financial markets: the law, the economics, the politics*, pp. 134–135. See also Andrew Ross Sorkin, *Too Big to Fail: the inside story of how Wall Street and Washington fought to save the financial system – and themselves* (Penguin 2010), pp. 10–50.

vulnerability and instability of these institutions triggered a crisis in market confidence in the financial system leading to a chain of failure (systemic failure).[21] But the structural problem also happened in institutions that were not on the list of SIFIs because of the interconnected nature of the industry, which gave rise to the domino spill over effect.[22]

Building on the above analysis, the TBTF bank structural problem showed four essential features: huge scale, interconnectedness and homogeneousness, ignoring the fat tail risk, and the problem of resolvability. The preceding analysis suggests the hypothesis that the aforementioned measures to resolve the 'unchained battleship' could shed light on solving the TBTF bank structural problem in the EU.[23]

By highlighting the key features of the problem, this section provides basic and more specific reference points to analyses in the following chapters on structural and resolution reform in the EU.

(a) **The behemoth size of the banks.** In the run up to the GFC, many large banks had invariably evolved into the universal bank model. The boundary between the traditional commercial banks and the highly risky investment banks had becoming blurred against the background of world-wide financial deregulation policies.[24] Exploiting economies of scope was accompanied by exploiting economies of scale. So these banks became ever-larger entities, or so-called 'mega-banks', amid the financial deregulation policies.[25]

These policies applied to the so-called 'era of great moderation' at the international level.[26] According to Emilios Avgouleas, at least five most important policies need to be specifically referred to among all those paving the way for global financial modernisation: the lax macro-economic and monetary policy, the liberalisation policy in the Washington Consensus, the world trade liberalisation, the financial sector deregulation policy, and the affordable housing policy.[27] He also referred to the subsequent Jackson Hole Consensus which also included a number of economic liberalisation and financial deregulation polices.[28]

Such polices have been commonly adopted and codified in major economies to promote the development of financial markets. In the UK, the milestone

---

21 Robert J. Shiller, *The subprime solution: how today's global financial crisis happened, and what to do about it* (Princeton, NJ: Princeton University Press 2008), p. 69.
22 See infra Chapter 1, Section 3(d).
23 See H. Patrick Glenn, 'Comparative law and legal practice: on removing the borders', 75 Tul L Rev 977.
24 Ian R. Harper, 'The Wallis report: an overview', 30 *Australian Economic Review* 288. The Australian experience of financial deregulation after the Campbell Report directly changed the landscape of the financial markets, such as globalisation, conglomeration, and more efficiency in the banking sector. The same also happened in other major economies, including the EU.
25 Avgouleas, *Governance of global financial markets: the law, the economics, the politics*, pp. 134–135.
26 Ibid, pp. 63–64.
27 The housing policy, which made housing mortgages easily accessible to everybody even those with an unreliable credit history, piled up huge risks in the financial markets, which finally peaked with the collapse of Fannie Mae and Freddie Mac. See Shiller, *The subprime solution: how today's global financial crisis happened, and what to do about it*, pp. 29–39.
28 Avgouleas, *Governance of global financial markets: the law, the economics, the politics*, pp. 63–64. See generally Shiller, *The subprime solution: how today's global financial crisis happened, and what to do about it*.

legislation on its financial deregulation was the 1986 'Big Bang', which abolished the fixed commissions' regime for the London Stock Exchange (LSE) and made the LSE trading and attendant broking service accessible to all financial houses. The direct result of this rule was the trend for acquisitions and activities expansion by traditional commercial banks.[29]

In the US, the financial deregulation and liberalisation legislation dated back to the Banking Act of 1933 (the Glass-Steagall Act) and the subsequent amendment in 1935. It prohibited member banks of the Federal Reserve System from being affiliated with a company that engaged mainly in 'the issue, flotation, underwriting, public sale, or distribution' of securities in section 20. In section 21, it prohibited companies from taking deposits if they were in the business of 'issuing, underwriting, selling, or distributing' securities. It also prohibited member banks from having any officer or director in common with a company 'engaged primarily' in the business of 'purchasing, selling, or negotiating' securities.[30] In addition, the 1956 Bank Holding Company Act stipulated the separation of banking and insurance underwriting business.[31]

However, when it came to financial deregulation, all these rules were eroded gradually, starting with the merger of Citicorp, a banking corporation, with Travelers Group.[32] Further, a form of universal bank and financial conglomerate was legalised by the Gramm-Leach-Billey Financial Services Modernization Act[33] and finally culminated in the acquisition of JPMorgan by Chase Manhattan in 2000 and the new prevailing trend of merger between traditional banks and investment banks.[34]

Compared with the US and the UK, the situation seems a little bit different in the EU. The universal banking model was deeply rooted in the banking industry of continental Europe. It has a much longer history than that in the UK (which only dated back to the 1980s 'Big Bang').[35] The mainly relevant legislation would be the Second Banking Directive of 1989, which allowed the traditional commercial banks to engage in investment market activities through a European pass. It really promoted the universal bank model in the EU, which can be demonstrated by the large number of mergers that took place in Europe from 1990 to 2001.[36]

---

29 Avgouleas, *Governance of global financial markets: the law, the economics, the politics*, p. 63.
30 Banking Act of 1933, 48 Stat. 162, now repealed section 16 and sections 20–21.
31 Bank Holding Company Act of 1956, Pub. L. No. 511, 70 Stat. 133.
32 Matt Murray and Patrick McGeehan, 'Citicorp-Travelers merger shakes up Wall Street rivals', WSJ, http://online.wsj.com/articles/SB891903040436602000, accessed December 5, 2014.
33 Gramm-Leach-Billey Financial Services Modernization Act, Pub. L. No. 106–102, 113 Stat. 1338 (1999).
34 On the full history of financial regulation, and how the legislation has evolved since the Great Depression, see Howell E. Jackson, *Regulation of financial institutions: by Howell E. Jackson and Edward L. Symons, Jr* (Eagan, MN: West Group 1999).
35 Niamh Moloney and Jennifer G. Hill, *The regulatory aftermath of the global financial crisis* (Cambridge University Press 2012), pp. 40–43.
36 Rym Ayadi and Georges Pujals, *Banking consolidation in the EU: overview and prospects* (Centre for European Policy Studies, 2004). As indicated by statistical research, banking consolidation in the EU experienced two successive stages from 1994 to 2000. The first stage, completed in 1998, was mostly small and medium-sized transactions, which accounted for more than 90% of the total. From 1999 to 2000, the second stage was started. Indeed, large-sized transactions accounted for more than 50% of operations.

Yet, in the post-crisis era, when the debate on the need to revamp the banking structure was so intense, the political incentive of separation reform in European countries was still not as strong as that in the UK and the US.[37] De Larosière contended that this model was exactly suitable to the way the European economy was financed and that it should not be made the scapegoat for the post-crisis financial crackdown.[38]

Within the context of these national level policies, in the past two decades of financial modernisation, banks have made great use of the global lax monetary policy and the excessive liquidity in the global financial markets by expanding their activities.[39] They have enhanced credit provision, exploited financial innovation, made speculative investment into risky assets, such as structural debt securities, and depended on excessive maturity transformation and wholesale funding.[40]

The direct result was that colossal banks of behemoth size emerged in the markets. Statistics for 2011 showed that nine banks had total assets of more than EUR1 trillion, with Deutsche Bank having more than EUR2 trillion. The largest bank had total assets equal to 17% of EU GDP. The total assets of financial institutions had reached EUR43 trillion by 2008 in European countries, which was 3.5 times the GDP of the total of all EU countries.[41]

According to the 2011 statistics, in relation to domestic GDP, eight banks had assets greater than the size of their domestic GDP, with Nordea (197%) and Danske Bank (194%) topped the rankings.[42] The ratio of overall assets of financial institutions to GDP varied in Member States. Moreover, in Iceland the overall assets of monetary financial institutions were approximately 12 times the total GDP of Iceland.[43] As one of the largest banks in Iceland, Kaupthing's balance sheet ballooned to USD44 billion and dwarfed the GDP of USD13.5 billion in this country in 2011.[44] What is ironic is that the Moody's rating for the bank was A1, which is a very high level. And like the other two largest banks in Iceland, it also passed the FSA's stress test in 2008 just months before the financial crisis.[45] Thanks to the high interest rate policy in response to high inflation in Iceland, there had been a huge trend towards internationalisation by all Icelandic banks.

37 Moloney and Hill, *The regulatory aftermath of the global financial crisis*, p. 40.
38 Jacques de Larosière, 'Don't punish the banks that performed best', FT, www.ft.com/intl/cms/s/0/1b085c0e-45e1-11e0-acd8-00144feab49a.html#axzz3FTVG2zIg, accessed December 5, 2014.
39 Rok Spruk, 'Iceland's financial and economic crisis: causes, consequences and implications', European Enterprise Institute Policy Paper.
40 Jacques De Larosière, *The High-level Group on financial supervision in the EU: report* (European Commission, 2009), pp. 7–8. For more detailed analysis, see also infra Chapter 6, Section 2.1.1 on how maturity transformation caused the risk of bankruptcy.
41 Liikanen Erkki, *High-level Expert Group on reforming the structure of the EU banking sector*, pp. 38–41.
42 Ibid, p. 41.
43 Tryggvi Thor Herbertsson, 'The Icelandic banking collapse: a story of broken promises'. Available at SSRN 1339170.
44 Ibid.
45 Omar R. Valdimarsson, 'Too-Big-to-Fail prevention is tested in post crisis Iceland', Bloomberg, www.bloomberg.com/news/2012–08–03/post-crisis-iceland-is-test-site-for-too-big-to-fail-prevention.html, accessed December 5, 2014.

The psychological anchoring effect might suggest that the assets to GDP ratio should probably have been the highest in the US, because it was the collapse of Bear Stearns and Lehman Brothers that pulled the trigger on the financial markets.[46] However, the actual statistics showed that the ratio of assets to GDP in the US was just 80%, far less than that of the European countries as a whole.[47]

Thus, the above analysis indicates that the universal banking model and its development were accompanied by the emergence of many colossal financial conglomerates in the EU. The behemoth banks and industry were intertwined creating more possible risks and volatility. It should be noted that the risk and uncertainties are ubiquitous, and they are shown in terms of either a linear or chaos distribution.[48] Once risks in these banks materialised, their sheer colossal size would make their failures devastating to the real economy.

(b) The homogeneity and interconnectedness. With the universal banking model developing and banks becoming larger and larger, interconnectedness was another very prominent characteristic of the pre-crisis banking industry in the EU.[49] The interconnectedness was evident from two aspects: the intragroup link and the intergroup link.[50]

The intragroup link basically facilitates the subsidisation from the deposit entities to the trading entities in the same group. Although the situation varied in different countries, the group links normally included: cross-shareholdings, trading operations, central management of short-term liquidity within the group, and guarantees and commitments at the group entity level.[51]

The interbank link was another source of the banking sector interconnectedness.[52] For the past decades, banking expansion around the world has witnessed a transformation in the funding mix. The motivation of business expansion together with spiking bank assets has outgrown the traditional retail funding capacity. It is no longer sufficient to meet the financing needs of this ever-competitive industry. So, expanding banks relied more and more on wholesale funding sources rather than traditional funding sources.[53] However, the situation varied between different countries. Banks in Central and Eastern Europe had a high proportion of net

---

46   Daniel Kahneman, Paul Slovic, and Amos Tversky, *Judgement under uncertainty, cap. 6* (Cambridge University Press, 1982).

47   Be mindful that there are differences between GAAP rules in the US and IFRS rules in the EU.

48   Stephen A. Ross, Randolph Westerfield, and Bradford D. Jordan, *Fundamentals of corporate finance* (Tata McGraw-Hill Education, 2008), p. 321.

49   Emilios Avgouleas, *The reform of 'Too-Big-To-Fail' bank: a new regulatory model for the institutional separation of 'casino' from 'utility' banking* (2010), pp. 2–3.

50   European Commission, *Commission staff working document impact assessment accompanying the document Proposal for a Regulation of the European Parliament and of the Council on structural measures improving the resilience of EU Credit Institutions and the Proposal for a Regulation of the European Parliament and of the Council on reporting and transparency of securities financing transactions, SWD/2014/030 final*, pp. 10–11.

51   Ibid.

52   Ibid.

53   Liikanen Erkki, *High-level Expert Group on reforming the structure of the EU banking sector*, pp. 14–15, 27, 47.

interest income relative to total assets compared with banks in countries such as Sweden, the UK, Finland, Ireland, and Luxembourg. Banks with a higher degree of interconnectedness tended to benefit from higher implicit guarantees.[54]

The fact that the entire banking sector is closely interconnected makes it a debilitating factor of systemic risk. It was the interconnectedness factor that made the domino and spill over effect of banking failures become possible in the first place.[55]

The universal banking model and the evolution of financial conglomerates were created as tools to better exploit the economies of scale and scope, such as more accessible funds, risk diversification, and diversity of activities that lead to income stability and bank stability.[56] In reality, it achieved the first purpose before the GFC, although not in a healthy way. With regard to diversification, it not only failed but backfired such that the problem of homogenisation emerged in the banking sector.[57]

In fact, the risks within a universal bank or financial conglomerate were not actually diversified. Instead, industry homogenisation, such as homogenous funding resources, similar broad sets of activities, similar securitisation activities, similar exposures to derivative markets, and similar risk concentration led to the banks being less resilient when the negative economic situations arose.[58] That was why the explosion of the subprime crisis on Wall Street instantly plagued the world.

Specifically speaking, there were two significant sources of homogenisation in the universal banking model. First, the prevailing funding sources (balance sheet) and a similar business portfolio were key factors in triggering homogenisation.[59] Banks relied more on retail deposits as sources of major funding, traditionally speaking, but the large banks relied more on the short-term wholesale repo markets and the interbank markets to speed up bank expansion in the pre-crisis era.[60] In addition, it turned out that these banks relied too much on debt maturity transformation, which resulted in the accumulation of exponential risks.[61]

---

54 Independent Commission on Banking, 'Final report, recommendations', p. 286.
55 Liikanen Erkki, *High-level Expert Group on reforming the structure of the EU banking sector*, pp. 14–15.
56 James R. Barth, R. Dan Brumbaugh and James A. Wilcox, 'Policy watch: the repeal of Glass-Steagall and the advent of broad banking', *The Journal of Economic Perspectives*, p. 191.
57 Schwarcz, 'Regulating complexity in financial markets'. Avgouleas, *The reform of 'Too-Big-To-Fail' bank: a new regulatory model for the institutional separation of 'casino' from 'utility' banking*, pp. 22–24.
58 Liikanen Erkki, *High-level Expert Group on reforming the structure of the EU banking sector*. The report indicates that 'Retail deposits grew roughly in line with EU GDP and did not allow bank balance sheet growth to outpace GDP growth. EU banks funded their rapid growth with funding in the interbank markets (unsecured) and wholesale repo markets (secured) instead'.
59 Avgouleas, *The reform of 'Too-Big-To-Fail' bank: a new regulatory model for the institutional separation of 'casino' from 'utility' banking*, pp. 22–23.
60 Banks had a very high leverage ratio, which, on the one hand, facilitated bank expansion, and, on the other, accumulated very high risks and caused instability.
61 Markus K. Brunnermeier and Lasse Heje Pedersen, 'Market liquidity and funding liquidity', 22 *Review of Financial Studies* 2201. With regard to the use of maturity transformation, its assumption is that there would be constant short-term debt to fund long-term assets. The problem is that whenever market risks actually happen, the crisis in confidence dooms this transformation and brings instability to the banks.

Relying on a very leveraged capital structure, many of these large banks similarly had risk exposures to structural debt securities and credit derivative products.[62]

Second, were the short-termist-oriented compensation schemes and thereunder short-termist trading activities. The executive compensation schemes were criticised for focusing too much on short-term performance, thus creating perverse incentives.[63] Focusing on short-term benefits made executives tend to commit to riskier investment to generate the highest returns, even though these might possibly lead to catastrophic long-term consequences.[64] It encouraged investment short-termism and ignored the real value of investing in the banking sector.[65] The issue of how to regulate bankers' compensation is still a very contentious source of debate.[66] When it comes to structural debt securities, over-reliance on CRAs was also an important variable that led to homogenisation. The CRAs, in consideration of boosting market share and advancing competition edge, would always provide customer-friendly ratings, which accelerated the risk accumulating in the financial markets.[67]

Thus, all the financial institutions tended to be more or less interconnected. Links and interconnections included interbank lending and intrabank links.[68] Furthermore, banks' balance sheet and business activities were homogenous and further increased instability. The homogeneity and interconnectedness were also defining characteristics of the TBTF bank structural problem.

(c) **The low probability events.** The ignoring of low probability events can also be seen as an important factor that led to the run up to the GFC and the crisis in the EU.[69] Two significant aspects among others demonstrate how low probability events in financial markets were ignored.

First, in the abovementioned financial securitisation chain, the overconfidence towards the housing and financial markets became prevalent through the self-reinforcement effect and the so-called 'feedback loop'.[70] Within the context of the world's lax interest rate policy and excessive liquidity, investors tended to

---

62 Europejska, 'Economic crisis in Europe: causes, consequences and responses'.
63 Lucian A. Bebchuk, Alma Cohen, and Holger Spamann, 'Wages of failure: executive compensation at Bear Stearns and Lehman 2000–2008', 27 Yale J on Reg 257.
64 Ibid.
65 Guido Ferrarini, Niamh Moloney, and Maria-Cristina Ungureanu, 'Executive remuneration in crisis: a critical assessment of reforms in Europe', 10 *Journal of Corporate Law Studies* 73.
66 Ibid.
67 *The United States of America v. S&P, 12 U.S.C. § 1833a, 18 U.S.C. § 1341.* See the complaint pp. 14–20.
68 Adair Turner, *The Turner Review: a regulatory response to the global banking crisis,* vol. 7 (Financial Services Authority, 2009).
69 See ibid. Many risk evaluation models have been designed to assess risks in the markets; however, it has been accurately indicated by many scholars the view that past distribution patterns carry robust inferences for the probability of future patterns is theoretically inaccurate.
70 In feedback theory, initial price increases in the precipitating factors lead to more price increases as the original price increases feed back to even higher prices in the form of higher demand. The second round of price increases feeds back to the third, and so forth. See Robert J. Schiller, *Irrational exuberance* (Princeton, NJ: Princeton University Press), pp. 60–61.

invest and were easily befuddled by market exuberance. They totally believed that the housing markets would continue to strengthen. Therefore, households tended to borrow more to invest in real estate markets, banks tended to lend more relying on maturity transformation and repo markets, SPVs were largely institutionalised to securitise banks' assets, and institutional investors were willing to invest due to highly inflated ratings by CRAs and credit derivatives provided by insurers.[71] Every participant in the markets was so confident about the outlook for continual increases.

It was like a Ponzi scheme. The asset managers provided an offer of high returns to lure investors, and investors and potential risk-takers were emboldened by significant profits and invested excessive money into the managers' asset baskets.[72] In a Ponzi scheme, unlike in normal assets management, the assets under management are seldom actually invested into profitable projects. Instead, the first investor is paid off by the proceeds of sales to the second round of investors, and the second round of investors are paid off by the proceeds of sales to the third round of investors, and so forth.[73]

As regards the pre-crisis financial securitisation products in the EU and the US, it was, to a certain extent, the story of a Ponzi scheme all over again when it came to investment irrationality and the inevitability of bubbles bursting.[74] When there was the evident upturn in the housing market, investors were lured and befuddled by the illusion that the markets would keep climbing forever and infinite profits were there for the making. That wishful thinking was especially strengthened amid the prevailing optimistic propaganda given out by the mass media.[75] The banks, to exploit profits against the background of lax monetary policy, extended their housing debts even more indiscriminately to those subprime debtors. As prices kept going higher, creditors could use the first real estate as a mortgage to buy a second real estate, and so forth. That magnified their profits through leverage, provided that the markets kept rising.[76] Banks, through excessive use of short-term funding (liabilities) to finance long-term maturities assets, could continue expanding the debt exposures to those frenzied households.[77] Their perverse incentives originated from a mechanism called the 'originate-to-distribute

---

71 Emilios Avgouleas, 'Financial regulation, behavioural finance, and the global credit crisis: in search of a new regulatory model' (September 3, 2008), pp. 20–22.

72 Schiller, *Irrational exuberance*, p. 64.

73 Ibid, pp. 62–68.

74 See Avgouleas, *Governance of global financial markets: the law, the economics, the politics*, p. 47.

75 For instance, before the crisis, the former Icelandic Prime Minister David Oddsson indicated his pride and confidence in their economic boom in addressing the reasons for their success: 'Privatization, strong fiscal management and responsible leadership on the part of labour unions and employers have played a major part in the successful restructuring of the Icelandic economy. But many other factors have been important as well. The Central Bank was granted full independence and the Icelandic currency was floated in the market. Such a framework makes the economy more disciplined and solid'. Spruk, 'Iceland's financial and economic crisis: causes, consequences and implications', p. 11, https://ssrn.com/abstract=1574296, accessed January 10, 2018.

76 Patric Hendershott, Robert Hendershott, and James Shilling, 'The mortgage finance bubble: causes and corrections', 19 *Journal of Housing Research* 1.

77 Avgouleas, *Governance of global financial markets: the law, the economics, the politics*, pp. 129–130.

model', which permitted them to sell all the debts to a packager who would repackage them into some financial tools, such as RMBS and CDOs, through an SPV and resell them to other institutional investors.[78] The ironic part of the product chain designed to transfer and defuse risks was that it could not do the job very well, but only ended up spreading the risk to more entities in the financial markets. Therefore, the profits would keep accumulating for every participant until house prices decreased to levels less than the mortgage debts that had to be paid back. Thus, when the bubble burst in 2008, the defaulting of householders instantly contaminated the entities and participants in the chain.[79]

It is fair to argue that this scenario is different from a Ponzi scheme, because a Ponzi scheme implies that the asset managers commit fraudulent behaviour intentionally, whereas in the GFC, there is not much evidence of fraudulent behaviour.[80] Putting this aside, what happened in the GFC could be deemed to at least be a 'naturally occurring Ponzi process'. This denotes a phenomenon where a speculative feedback loop does play an important role in relation to investors' decision-making and strengthens irrational investment behaviours, especially in the complicated investment dynamics, where there is not much information upon which investors can rely, despite the lack of intentional contrivance by fraudulent managers.[81] Specifically, with house prices continually rising, the illusive impression of prosperity and profits made by others or made by one's own previous investment would provide positive feedback to reinforce the rationality of the investment. Thus the speculative loop reinforced investors' belief to invest for the second round, and so forth.[82]

Irrespective of being deemed as a typical 'Ponzi scheme' or the 'naturally occurring Ponzi scheme', the fact is the investors would not bother to think about the seemingly unlikely yet very possible bubble burst. The analysis of the current crisis denotes that investors ignored the very low probability event of house prices possible plummeting in value.[83] Theoretically, although the prices could keep going higher if people still believed in the housing market and invested in it, once the low probability event eventually happened, the destruction was tremendous.

Second, another direct manifestation of ignoring of low probability events was the prevailing model that the banking industry was using to reap profits in the

---

78 *The United States of America v. S&P*, 12 U.S.C. § 1833a, 18 U.S.C. § 1341.

79 De Larosière, *The High-level Group on financial supervision in the EU: report*, pp. 11–12.

80 So far, only a few bankers in the crisis have been successfully prosecuted. The reasons why are complex, as it has been pointed out by many scholars that, on the one hand, it is difficult to prove any wrongdoing in the financial markets, especially any intent to defraud; on the other, the risk-taking culture in business makes the courts and parliament very reluctant to second guess business decisions and prosecute bankers. Blog by J.R., 'Why have so few bankers gone to jail?' *Economist*, www.economist.com/blogs/economist-explains/2013/05/economist-explains-why-few-bankers-gone-to-jail, accessed December 5, 2014.

81 Schiller, *Irrational exuberance*, pp. 65–68.

82 Ibid, p. 47.

83 Wei-Xing Zhou and Didier Sornette, 'Is there a real-estate bubble in the US?' 361 *Physica A: Statistical Mechanics and its Applications*, 297.

pre-crisis era: the notorious Value at Risk (VaR) model.[84] Practitioners created the model in the 1980s to assess firm risk. It was meant to provide a snapshot of how much money a firm could lose in a single day.[85] The model used historical data to report information of three kinds: (i) the specific dollar amount to be lost; (ii) within what time period; and (iii) with what anticipated level of confidence.[86] The model is the basis for the Basel capital requirements, so the accuracy of it in reflecting real risks in banks' assets is extremely important.[87]

Global trading by large banks contained numerous positions with thousands of market risk factors, such as interest rate risk, exchange rate risk, and equity price risk. Based on the countless factors and risks, it is almost impossible for any model to accurately measure the distribution of all risk factors. So, banks could only rely on approximation and rough calculations of various parameters to provide their portfolio with a risk structure.[88] Over this process, they ignored many seemingly unlikely risks.

The low probability risks tend to be hard to calculate statistically; therefore, based on the above situation, it would normally be treated as zero in reality. This approach was also adopted in the VaR.[89] Low probability events being ignored in modelling created the illusion that it should also be ignored in reality. But the GFC presented a far-fetching admonishment to the markets with regard to the destructibility of low probability events.

The operation of VaR depends on two assumptions: (i) the past asset price volatility shows continuity in the future; and (ii) the variations are distributed around a mean (following a bell curve).[90] But the truth is that the assumptions are not accurate, especially in times of crisis. The distribution curve of the volatility of assets has fat tails,[91] which means that the possibility of extreme events in asset price volatility is significantly higher than in a normal distribution.[92] When events happen more frequently than anticipated by the model, the model itself becomes useless.[93]

---

84 Christine Harper, 'Death of VaR evoked as risk-taking Vim meets Taleb's black swan', Bloomberg, www.bloomberg.com/apps/news?pid=newsarchive&sid=axo1oswvqx4s,> accessed December 5, 2014.

85 Peter Conti-Brown, 'Proposed fat-tail risk metric: disclosures, derivatives, and the measurement of financial risk, A', 87 Wash UL Rev 1461–1462.

86 Ibid, p. 1463.

87 Avgouleas, *Governance of global financial markets: the law, the economics, the politics*, pp. 243–244.

88 Jeremy Berkowitz and James O'Brien, 'How accurate are value-at-risk models at commercial banks?' *Journal of Finance* 1093, pp. 1108–1110.

89 Iman Anabtawi and Steven L. Schwarcz, 'Regulating systemic risk: towards an analytical framework', 86 Notre Dame L Rev 1349, pp. 1379–1380.

90 Tim Morrison, *The risks of financial modeling: VaR and the economic meltdown* (Scribd, 2009).

91 *Financial Times*, 'Definition of tail risk', http://lexicon.ft.com/Term?term=tail-risk, accessed March 14, 2014.

92 Jon Danielsson and Casper G. De Vries, 'Value-at-risk and extreme returns', *Annales d'Economie et de Statistique* 239, p. 243.

93 Conti-Brown, 'Proposed fat-tail risk metric: disclosures, derivatives, and the measurement of financial risk, A', p. 1462.

As the mass media reported, 'Value at risk, the measure banks use to calculate the maximum their trades can lose each day, failed to detect the scope of the US subprime mortgage market's collapse'.[94] Theoretically, a mathematical model can bring desirable predictions to the investors who mostly prefer certainty and tend to be risk averse. But the precondition is that the model is accurate and practical. An inaccurately constructed model could distort market risks and uncertainty and mislead investors who rely on it to make investment decisions.[95] The VaR model turned out to rely on assumptions and incomprehensive historical data, which were definitely not accurate. In fact, it assumed that the housing prices would not depreciate in value and would keep increasing.[96] Addressing the error of this model, Alan Greenspan said when he testified before the Congress that:[97]

> A Nobel Prize was awarded for the discovery of the pricing model that underpins much of the advance in derivatives markets. This modern risk management paradigm held sway for decades. The whole intellectual edifice, however, collapsed in the summer of last year because the data inputted into the risk management models generally covered only the past two decades, a period of euphoria. Had instead the models been fitted more appropriately to historic periods of stress, capital requirements would have been much higher, and the financial world would be in far better shape today, in my judgment.

In addition, there is also evidence to show that banks tended to have conservative calculations of VaR. The reason was that banks that failed certain VaR tests would be subject to higher capital requirements. That provided banks with incentives to be conservative in their risk forecasts.[98] The ICB report also indicates that among the UK's largest banks, the ratio of risk-weighted assets to un-weighted assets fell as financial leverage increased from the year 2000 to the year 2008.[99]

Therefore, banks over exploited the mistaken valuation model being used in the securitisation products.[100] The assumption of continuously increasing house prices simply ignored the low probability of negative market circumstances. Theoretically, investment strategies based on VaR can succeed in many of the cases, but fail with a very low probability.[101] In general, the industry can reap profits using this risk evaluation strategy, but when failure happens, it can be disastrous.

94 Harper, 'Death of VaR evoked as risk-taking Vim meets Taleb's black swan', Bloomberg.
95 Schwarcz, 'Regulating complexity in financial markets'.
96 Avgouleas, *Governance of global financial markets: the law, the economics, the politics*, p. 244
97 Alan Greenspan, 'Greenspan testimony on sources of financial crisis', WSJ, http://blogs.wsj.com/economics/2008/10/23/greenspan-testimony-on-sources-of-financial-crisis/, accessed December 5, 2014.
98 Berkowitz and O'Brien, 'How accurate are value-at-risk models at commercial banks?' pp. 1109–1110.
99 Independent Commission on Banking, 'Final report, recommendations', pp. 98–99.
100 Edward Vincent Murphy, 'Alternative mortgages: risks to consumers and lenders in the current housing cycle', CRS Report RL33775 at 5-6.
101 Burton Gordon Malkiel, *A random walk down Wall Street: including a life-cycle guide to personal investing* (New York: WW Norton & Company 1999), pp. 198–202. The investment theory evolved from the 'castle in the air' theory to the 'solid fundamental' theory. It turned out that neither of them could be used to beat the markets. Then, came Modern Portfolio Theory. However, it turned out that diversification could only function to a certain extent. There are some systemic risks which cannot be diversified. These risks rarely happen, but their results are devastating.

Either from the perspective of naturally occurring Ponzi schemes, or from the perspective of a mathematical model, there is valid evidence to show that the pre-crisis banking industry ignored low probability events.

(d) The domino disruption. As a matter of fact, it seems that a tremendous domino effect of failure is inevitable to a certain extent as a result of the afore-mentioned three attributes of the banking sector in the EU: the colossal size, the homogenisation and interconnectedness, and ignoring low possibility events. The huge scale and scope and homogenisation were the ideal factors by which risks could be accumulated, and the event of low probability disruptive events was the trigger for failure.[102]

The domino effect of failure in the GFC referred to the mechanism where shocks were transmitted both directly and indirectly within the network of the banking industry and led to overall failure.[103] Banks became overly leveraged and excessively exposed to securitisation products whilst expanding their activities. As investors, they bought securities on credit from brokers and dealers, using the securities as collateral. The broker-dealer normally required a minimal level of collateral. When the ignored risk materialised, the securities' prices fell below the minimum collateral required. The broker-dealer issued a marginal call to increase the collateral, which meant firms had to conduct a fire sale, thereby depressing prices, asking for more collateral, leading to more fire sales, and so forth.[104] That was how the sudden volatility in the prices of assets doomed the Wall Street investment banks Bear Stearns and Lehman Brothers and ignited the debate on bailout or bankruptcy.[105]

The failure of one entity contaminated the entire sector in the EU through two means (both directly and indirectly): (i) many EU banks held large structural debt securities positions in their trading book; and (ii) there was an impasse between interbank markets and a loss of confidence between different institutions, which put more pressure on liquidity.[106]

Therefore, the domino effect doomed the whole industry. The EU pressed on with Member States' bailouts, which triggered the sovereign debt crisis. Indebted governments were further thwarted by the entire economic situation in the region and this led to the overall crisis.[107]

With regard to the domino disruptive effect that happened in the EU after the crisis, a good example would be the Deutsche Industriebank IKB, which built a large portfolio of Asset Backed Commercial Paper (ACBP) to invest in RMBS and CDOs. This strategy worked well until Bear Stearns revealed huge losses in its two sub-prime hedge funds on July 16, 2007. Days after that, the ACBP

---

102 Avgouleas, *The reform of 'Too-Big-To-Fail' bank: a new regulatory model for the institutional separation of 'casino' from 'utility' banking*, pp. 2–3.
103 Anabtawi and Schwarcz, 'Regulating systemic risk: towards an analytical framework', p. 1372.
104 Ibid, pp. 1373–1374.
105 Rosalind Z. Wiggins, Thomas Piontek and Andrew Metrick, 'The Lehman Brothers bankruptcy A'.
106 Liikanen Erkki, *High-level Expert Group on reforming the structure of the EU banking sector*, p. 5. See also Independent Commission on Banking, 'Final report, recommendations', pp. 278–279.
107 Liikanen Erkki, *High-level Expert Group on reforming the structure of the EU banking sector*, pp. 6–8.

market was closed and IKB was unable to roll over its funds' short-term debts. It finally ended up receiving a rescue package from KFW, its owner, arranged by the German central bank.[108]

Statistical data shows that, among the three eurozone countries that were rescued, Greece, Ireland, and Portugal, only one would emerge from its bailout plan as scheduled. In Ireland, two years after it was rescued with a bailout of USD97 billion, government debts were still at 125% of GDP, which means it needed a further bailout. Greece, with a rescue package of EUR240 billion, still had debts as high as 175% of its GDP three years after their bailout.[109] Even now, the 'extend the debt or let it default' dilemma in Greece has been tasking policy-makers in the EU.[110] These data demonstrate that the crisis originating from the disruptions in the financial markets was huge and caused great suffering.

Thus, the TBTF bank structural problem shows the four attributes: colossal scale, homogeneity and interconnectedness, ignoring of low probability events, and the domino failure effect. All these aspects need to be tackled as part of the post-crisis regulation reforms.[111]

4 Bank structural problem in the EU and possible solutions

The aforementioned analyses show the key features of the TBTF bank structural problem. This leads onto the next question: what would be some practical solutions to solve the TBTF bank structural problem? From the perspective of current regulatory reform in the EU, the following are the main issues that might need to be highlighted and strengthened.[112]

(a) **Solution 0: the traditional price-based approach.** This solution covers mainly, but is not limited to, an enhanced regulatory framework, active supervision, enhanced transparency and disclosure, and strengthening market infrastructures.[113] In terms of banking regulation, such price-based regulations as

108 Carrick Mollenkamp and Edward Taylor, 'How subprime mess ensnared German Bank; IKB gets a bailout', WSJ, http://online.wsj.com/articles/SB118670471880693703, accessed December 5, 2014.

109 *Economist*, 'Europe's bail-out programmes: what Angela isn't saying – Euro-zone rescues have left sovereign debt too high to be sustainable', www.economist.com/news/finance-and-econo mics/21583257-euro-zone-rescues-have-left-sovereign-debt-too-high-be-sustainable-what-angela, accessed December 5, 2014.

110 *Economist*, 'Greece's debt negotiations: extension granted, www.economist.com/news/ europe/21653710-despite-delayed-payment-imf-deal-between-greece-and-its-creditors-remains-sight-extension, accessed June 5, 2015.

111 Anabtawi and Schwarcz, 'Regulating systemic risk: towards an analytical framework'.

112 European Commission, 'Progress of financial reforms', (2015) http://ec.europa.eu/finance/ general-policy/policy/map_reform_en.htm, accessed June 1, 2015.

113 Julian T.S. Chow, *Making banks safer: can Volcker and Vickers do it?* (Washington, DC: International Monetary Fund, 2011), pp. 5–6. These measures and rules are also called price-based regulation. This report discusses the problem of too important to fail (TITF). It also discusses the two fundamental approaches to deal with this problem: the price-based approach, including mainly the capital requirement regime, and the structure-based approach.

the capital rules and liquidity rules were deemed to be helpful standards for controlling bank risk. But it transpires that the Basel II regime was flawed in lacking a specific level of liquidity, failing to restrain bank leverage, and the risk-weighting model being inaccurate.[114]

The on-going price-based reform raised some questions: is the current reform in the Basel III regime sufficient to control risks in the TBTF bank structural problem?[115] To which extent would other measures be helpful to contain the bank structural problem, such as stronger overview of the CRAs, stronger supervision of TBTF institutions, realignment of different incentives, and improved corporate governance? Would the approach be effective to deal with the problem in terms of the relevant behavioural factors in the GFC?

The book does not elaborate this approach in much detail. However, the traditional price-based regulation and its insufficiency in dealing with the structural problem provide a backdrop against which the assessments of the current structural and resolution reform in the EU can be conducted.[116] The fact is that the price-based approach does not exactly target the structural problem and its features. The Basel Committee on Banking Supervision (BCBS) has adopted more robust rules, such as capital requirements with higher loss absorbency, higher liquidity standards for short-term and long-term funds, capital conservation buffer requirements, etc. They are of help to a certain extent, but the complexity of banks' activities and organisation, as suggested by an International Monetary Fund (IMF) report, would continuously cast doubt on the rules' ability to address fat-tail risks and systemic risk.[117]

(b) Solution 1: the decoupling method and tackling complexity. Steven Schwarcz pointed out that the problem faced by the banking sector resembles that for engineers.[118] Therefore, the solutions that engineers use may contribute to a meditation on the structural problem. This leads onto the engineering method of decoupling. A decoupling system with the characteristics of modularity could reduce the possibility that the failure of one part of a complex system could cause the failure of other parts of the system.[119] The mechanism prevents the spill over effect on failure.

Similarly, the efficiency of a structural regulatory reform could possibly rely on a banking structure that arms banks with a buffer against any possible attack

---

114 Avgouleas, *Governance of global financial markets: the law, the economics, the politics*, pp. 344–347. See also Jon Danielsson et al., *An academic response to Basel II* (London: LSE Financial Markets Group, 2001).

115 See generally, Basel Committee on Banking Supervision, *Basel III: International framework for liquidity risk measurement, standards and monitoring* (December 2010).

116 See infra Chapter 4, Section 1.4.

117 José Viñals et al., *Creating a safer financial system: will the Volcker, Vickers, and Liikanen Structural measures help?* (Washington, DC: International Monetary Fund, 2013), p. 7.

118 Schwarcz, 'Regulating complexity in financial markets'.

119 Ibid. As indicated by Steven Schwarcz's analyses, in the decoupling mechanism, 'Modularity allows complexity to become manageable by partially closing off some parts of the system and allowing these encapsulated components to interconnect only in certain ways'.

arising from a financial crisis. A new regulation towards the banking industry would probably be an effective one if it were to provide two strands: (i) the core banking business (relationship-oriented)[120] could be insulated from a possible crisis emanating from risky activities (transaction-oriented activities); and (ii) healthy entities could provide assistance to ailing entities, such as infusing liquidity when necessary.[121]

This approach would raise another significant question to be addressed: how should the segregation approach be structured in an effective way? Some advocate a wholesale return to the Glass-Steagall Act regulation style, while others argue that it is impossible because that could make the capital markets inaccessible to commercial banks and cause unbearable economic costs.[122] The Dodd-Frank Act, which made a compromise to curb the most speculative investment banking through the Volcker Rule, was criticised for not eradicating the TBTF bank structural problem completely. It seems to be unable to deal with the problems of complexity and connectedness.[123] Within the EU, researchers are now focusing on evaluating the effectiveness of the Vickers Rule, the Liikanen Report, and the BSR, arguing for different restrictions on scope and strength of activities.[124] Some argue that a more moderate and acceptable way would be preferred in terms of the subtle relationship between EU Member States, dubbed 'a system of battle'.[125]

In summary, the issue that needs to be addressed under this approach is how should segregation be structured based on the current BSR so as to be effective in dealing with the TBTF bank structural problem in the trade-off between innovation and stability?

(c) Solution 2: the EU bank recovery and resolution mechanism as a complementary approach. Despite the above approaches, a bank failure could still be inevitable in certain circumstances, especially in terms of behavioural finance.[126] So, a resolution reform seems to be an indispensable part in solving the problem. It is said that the reason why the EU banking crisis escalated into a sovereign debt

---

120 European Commission, *Commission staff working document impact assessment accompanying the document Proposal for a Regulation of the European Parliament and of the Council on structural measures improving the resilience of EU Credit Institutions and the Proposal for a Regulation of the European Parliament and of the Council on reporting and transparency of securities financing transactions, SWD/2014/030 final*, pp. 12–13.

121 Avgouleas, *The reform of 'Too-Big-To-Fail' bank: a new regulatory model for the institutional separation of 'casino' from 'utility' banking*, pp. 6–9.

122 Ibid.

123 The Dodd-Frank Wall Street Reform and Consumer Protection Act (U.S), section 619.

124 See generally Independent Commission on Banking, 'Final report, recommendations'.

125 Moloney and Hill, *The regulatory aftermath of the global financial crisis*, pp. 55–83. The authors explain how conflicting opinions between the Commission and the Parliament and between different Member States have exerted influence on the regulatory progress.

126 Daniel Kahneman and Amos Tversky, 'Prospect theory: an analysis of decision under risk', *Econometrica: Journal of the Econometric Society* 263.

crisis and an overall economic crisis was in part due to the absence of a recovery and resolution procedure.[127]

Therefore, the EC put forward proposals for a series of measures: preparatory and preventative measures, early intervention, and resolution powers and tools.[128] The proposals in the EU seem to be innovative in some respects. For instance, both recovery planning and resolution planning could be done at the entity and group level. The resolution tools include the bail-in mechanism, which converts the debts of troubled institutions into equity.[129] However, there still remain some difficult problems that need to be addressed in the reforms, such as the harmonisation of bank insolvency and resolution laws, and the establishment of resolution funds in terms of cross-border groups.[130]

In December 2012, great progress was made when eurozone finance ministers agreed a plan to cede power to a common bank supervisor. The European Banking Union (EBU) includes a Single Supervisory Mechanism (SSM), a Deposit Guarantee Scheme (DGS), and the Bank Recovery and Resolution Directive (BRRD).[131]

On May 15, 2014, the EU adopted the BRRD.[132] Further, the Parliament and the Council approved the SRM regulations in July 2014.[133] Although progress has been made, there are still many criticisms of the effectiveness of the mechanisms of the EBU, such as the flaws with regard to non-effective governance, the relationship with non-euro States, the National Competent Authority (NCA), and EU conflicts.

Overall, the questions that need to be answered are: would the resolution rules in the BRRD and SRM be effective to supplement the structural reform and how could the current resolution rules be strengthened in reality?

---

127 Kenneth Ayotte and David A. Skeel Jr, 'Bankruptcy or bailouts', 35 J Corp L 469.
128 European Commission, *An EU framework for crisis management in the financial sector* (October 20, 2010), pp. 4–5.
129 Jim Brunsden and Rebecca Christie, 'German push to accelerate bank bail-ins joined by Dutch', www.bloomberg.com/news/2013–02–04/german-push-to-accelerate-bank-bail-ins-joined-by-dutch-finns.html, accessed December 5, 2014. It was pointed out that the major powers in the EU were advocating the Danish style bail-in legislation to solve the state bailout dilemma.
130 Avgouleas, *Governance of global financial markets: the law, the economics, the politics*, p. 425.
131 European Commission, *Communication from the Commission to the European Parliament and the Council: a roadmap towards a banking union, COM(2012) 510 final* (September 12, 2012).
132 Directive 2014/59/EU of the European Parliament and of the Council of 15 May 2014, establishing a framework for the recovery and resolution of credit institutions and investment firms and amending Council Directive 82/891/EEC, and Directives 2001/24/EC, 2002/47/EC, 2004/25/EC, 2005/56/EC, 2007/36/EC, 2011/35/EU, 2012/30/EU and 2013/36/EU, and Regulations (EU) No 1093/2010 and (EU) No 648/2012, of the European Parliament and of the Council [2014] OJ L 173/190/1 (BRRD).
133 See *Regulation (EU) No 806/2014 of the European Parliament and of the Council of 15 July 2014 establishing uniform rules and a uniform procedure for the resolution of credit institutions and certain investment firms in the framework of a Single Resolution Mechanism and a Single Resolution Fund and amending Regulation (EU) No 1093/2010 [2014] OJ L 225/1 (SRM Regulation).*

5 Conclusion: two attributes and possible reforms

In sum, the above analyses demonstrate the co-existence of various activities and features of the TBTF bank structural problem. The problem is denoted by the difficulties of risk control, and supervision and regulation along with the huge scale and comprehensive scope of bank activities, as reflected by the four features. This also represents the first attribute of the TBTF bank structural problem: the structural attribute (transaction-based activities bring about financial stability).[134]

However, it turns out that the bank structural problem has two attributes: (i) the structural attribute as indicated earlier; and (ii) the cyclicality attribute. It is not only a problem with the structure of the banks but also one that is inextricably linked with the inclination towards cyclicality in the banking industry.[135] According to an IMF paper, in the TBTF bank structural problem, trading activities are not the sole source of instability; risks also come from the endogenous cyclicality of banking activities, such as the inclination for risk-taking. In other words, even by committing to some seemingly beneficial activities, such as hedging and market-making activities, it is still likely that risks can be accumulated due to the cyclical nature of banking activities.[136]

The cyclicality attribute is normally intertwined with and further aggravated by behavioural factors.[137] Bounded rationality and various heuristics tend to tilt the scale of decision-making in favour of risk-taking rather than safety in the banking sector.

In the pre-crisis era, the cyclicality attribute of the banking industry acted as an endogenous source of risk. Cyclicality is the second attribute of the TBTF bank structural problem, and it interacts with the structural attribute. Finding a way to deal with the TBTF bank structural problem is of critical importance to the revival of the EU banking sector and its economy. For that to happen, both the structural attribute and the cyclical attribute need to be addressed.

First, the EU structural measures can be linked to the structural attribute, because it is possible that the measures could bring about a change in the structure of the banks. Specifically, the questions that need to be answered are: is institutional separation reform desirous in terms of BF? Are the BSR[138] and the Liikanen Report sufficient to enhance the financial stability of the industry when

---

134 Chow, *Making banks safer: can Volcker and Vickers do it?* pp. 14–16. See infra Chapter 3, Section 5.

135 Conti-Brown, 'Proposed fat-tail risk metric: disclosures, derivatives, and the measurement of financial risk, A'. No matter which kind of risk model is applied, there are always some unpredictable factors, such as fat-tail risks and the cyclical inclination, that bring instability to banks. See infra Chapter 2, Section 4. For detailed analysis of the cyclical attribute, see infra Chapter 3, Section 5.

136 Chow, *Making banks safer: can Volcker and Vickers do it?* pp. 14–16.

137 Financial Conduct Authority, *Financial Conduct Authority (2013), Applying Behavioral Economics in Financial Conduct Authority, Occasional Paper No. 1.* (2013).

138 See European Commission, *Proposal for a Regulation of the European Parliament and of the Council on structural measures improving the resilience of EU credit institutions, COM/2014/043 final.*

comparing the EU rules with those in other economies, such as the UK[139] and the US?[140] Would the BSR and Liikanen rules be economically efficient in dealing with the structural problem and preserving economic competitiveness?[141]

Second, an effective resolution reform could be linked to the cyclical attribute. It is possible that effective resolution measures can be complementary to the structural measures and act as an ex-post exit mechanism to minimise moral hazard, cyclicality, and behavioural factors in the banking sector. The separation reform could be constructed to provide an ex-ante regulatory mechanism to prevent the recurrence of crises originating from the structural problem. The resolution mechanism could be constructed to provide an ex-post measure to deal with unavoidable failure. In specific, the question that needs to be answered is: would the current resolution reform under the BRRD and the SRM be effective in cooperation with structural separation and delink the causal relationship between behavioural factors and banking instability and volatility?[142]

In sum, this chapter elaborates the TBTF bank structural problem, its first attribute, and possible corresponding reform. It also briefly refers to the second attribute and its possibly corresponding reform. Before the imploration and assessing of separation reform (BSR) in Chapters 3–5 and the resolution reform (BRRD and SRM) in Chapter 6, Chapter 2 focuses on the behavioural analysis of the TBTF bank structural problem. It provides: (i) behavioural evidence to prove that irrationality and the universal banking structure work in combination as a destabilising force and thereby make a case for separation; and (ii) BF evidence to prove the cyclicality attribute and unavoidability of failure and resolution in extreme circumstances.[143]

139 Independent Commission on Banking, 'Final report, recommendations'.

140 Bank Holding Company Act of 1956, Pub. L. No. 511, 70 Stat. 133, section 13(a)(2).

141 Édouard Fernandez-Bollo, 'Structural reform and supervision of the banking sector in France', 2013 *OECD Journal: Financial Market Trends* 1.

142 Directive 2014/59/EU of the European Parliament and of the Council of 15 May 2014, establishing a framework for the recovery and resolution of credit institutions and investment firms and amending Council Directive 82/891/EEC, and Directives 2001/24/EC, 2002/47/EC, 2004/25/EC, 2005/56/EC, 2007/36/EC, 2011/35/EU, 2012/30/EU and 2013/36/EU, and Regulations (EU) No 1093/2010 and (EU) No 648/2012, of the European Parliament and of the Council [2014] OJ L 173/190/1 (BRRD).

143 Kahneman and Tversky, 'Prospect theory: an analysis of decision under risk'.

2 The behavioural factors related to the bank structural problem

This chapter analyses the manifestations of identified behavioural factors in the TBTF bank structural problem. These analyses act as the foundation for further discussion of the regulation revamp on separation and resolution to deal with the TBTF bank structure problem. Specifically, by analysing how behavioural factors loomed large and were magnified through the trading-oriented activities within the universal banking model, the behavioural analysis provides fundamental theoretical support for the necessity and extent of a structural separation reform. In addition, by explaining the provident cyclical attribute in universal banking, it also provides a fundamental basis for the need for a resolution reform as a complementary measure against the background of the structural separation reform.

1 Introduction to behavioural finance

To analyse the behavioural aspect of the TBTF bank structural problem, it needs to start with behavioural theory and its origin.[1] Theorised by Adam Smith, classic economy theory advocates the value of a free market, the invisible hand and non-intervention from governments, and the wisdom of nature.[2] Specifically, a free market means that each individual is presumed to be rationally pursuing the maximisation of personal economic interest. By doing that, society as a whole could exhaust all mutually beneficial opportunities. The direct result is that all social resources are appropriately allocated, and job markets reach the ideal status of full employment. Consequently, this process leads to the maximisation of social welfare and social benefit.[3] As Adam Smith points out:[4]

1 Daniel Kahneman and Amos Tversky, 'Prospect theory: an analysis of decision under risk', *Econometrica: Journal of the Econometric Society* 263.
2 See generally Adam Smith, *Wealth of nations* (Chicago, IL: University of Chicago Bookstore 2005), pp. 18–20. Maurice Dobb and Maurice Herbert Dobb, *Theories of value and distribution since Adam Smith: ideology and economic theory* (Cambridge University Press 1975), pp. 39–43.
3 Smith, *Wealth of nations*, pp. 18–20.
4 Ibid, pp. 362–363. See also Jacob Viner, 'Adam Smith and laissez faire', *The Journal of Political Economy* 198.

Every individual is continually exerting himself to find out the most advantageous employment for whatever capital he can command. It is his own advantage, indeed, and not that of the society, which he has in view. But the study of his own advantage naturally, or rather necessarily, leads him to prefer that employment which is most advantageous to the society.

Arguably, this free market theory based on the economic person hypothesis is right, at least based on the fact that it has been a prevailing theory for many centuries guiding the establishment and development of capitalism. The theory witnessed the history of New York City transforming from a ship harbour to a world hub of finance and trade,[5] the century debate between Hayek and Keynes and the world trend towards liberalisation reform,[6] and the economic liberalisation policies leading to the rise of the City of London after the 1980s.[7] It should be noted that the free market theory is a paradigm that not only thrives in these traditional capitalism countries, but also has been exerting more and more influence on the emerging world, such as China and India.[8]

However, the development of economic theories showed that people are not entirely convinced the above argument is unassailable. A fundamental reason is that the principle of a free market based on the economic person hypothesis and the embodiment thereof, the world's overall capitalism upturn, cannot represent a complete picture of world economic history. It indicates only the overall trend of the industrialisation process and the development of capitalism, but ignores periodic economic volatility.[9] If we depict world economic development in a graph, its path is not an upward trend all the way; rather, it shows a zigzag and volatile continuity, according to Robert Schiller's viewpoint.[10]

Therefore, what was argued by Adam Smith is partly right. The upward trend of the world economy that is mainly based on the free market principle can be proved by a statistical approach. However, it is not absolutely right in terms of the constant volatility of economy development that is overlooked in favour of

---

5 John Steele Gordon, *The Great Game: the emergence of Wall Street as a world power* (New York: Texere 2000), pp. 10–20.

6 See Gilles Dostaler, 'The debate between Hayek and Keynes', 6 *Perspectives on the History of Economic Thought 77*. See also generally Joel Seligman, *The transformation of Wall Street: a history of the Securities and Exchange Commission and modern corporate finance* (Boston, MA: Houghton Mifflin 1982).

7 Emilios Avgouleas, *Governance of global financial markets: the law, the economics, the politics* (Cambridge University Press 2012), p. 68.

8 See generally Ronald Coase and Ning Wang, *How China became capitalist* (New York: Palgrave Macmillan 2012). Over the past three decades, China has embraced capitalism in many aspects of society including mostly its economy and culture. For instance, the economic theory of Adam Smith was widely accepted. *The theory of moral sentiments* (Harmondsworth, UK: Penguin 2010 [1759]) has more than a dozen Chinese editions; the book won the affection of former premier Wen Jia Bao. The theory of Adam Smith corresponds with the Chinese economic development in a harmonious way.

9 Brett H McDonnell, 'Of Mises and Min (sky): libertarian and liberal responses to financial crises past and present', 34 Seattle UL Rev 1279.

10 Robert J Schiller, *Irrational exuberance* (2000), pp. 8–9.

the overall upward trend.[11] The economic history analysed by Robert Schiller indicates that the periodic drastic upturns and downturns did exist. That means that the free market economy based on the economic person hypothesis does not necessarily lead to efficiency. Many scholars attribute the volatility to the exertion of influence on the economy by specific factors, such as information asymmetry and externality.[12]

Another reason could be irrational factors, also called the irrationality or bounded rationality of human beings.[13] It denotes that the standard predictable and rational economic decisions of mankind could be distorted or even occasionally replaced by some unexpected deviation and irrationality, and hence lead to abnormal performance of the overall economy, namely, the volatility of markets.[14]

The problem of the classic economic theory is that it is premised only on the assumption of the functioning of an economy driven by economic motive and people's rational responses.[15] If we draw a square with four boxes, representing economic motives and non-economic motives, people's rational responses and irrational responses, the classic economic model is based on only the upper left-hand box, which means the economy functions according to the premise of people driven only by economic motive and rational responses to market changes. It intentionally or inadvertently excludes: (i) the upper-right box, which denotes that the economy functions based on the premise of non-economic motives and rational responses; (ii) the lower-left box, which means the economy functions based on the hypothesis of economic motives and irrational responses; and (iii) the lower-right box, which means the economy functions based on the assumption of non-economic motives and irrational responses.[16] Behavioural economists believe that if we want to explore the real truth of how to predict the overall evolution of the economy and how to improve it when it encounters a problem, the answers lie in these three untouched boxes (Table 2.1).[17]

The behavioural finance theory focuses on the overlooked three boxes. Every time an economic bubble bursts, there would be a heated debate with regard to how to revamp market regulation to both boost economic development while preserving stability. After the GFC swept across the world, the research attention was fixated again intensively on the Hayek and Keynes debate.[18] Austrians and

---

11   Gordon, *The Great Game: the emergence of Wall Street as a world power*, pp. 10–20.
12   Steven Shavell, *Foundations of economic analysis of law* (Cambridge, MA: Harvard University Press 2009), pp. 10–30.
13   Ran Spiegler, *Bounded rationality and industrial organization* (Oxford, UK: Oxford University Press 2011).
14   George A. Akerlof and Robert J. Shiller, *Animal spirits: how human psychology drives the economy, and why it matters for global capitalism* (Princeton, NJ: Princeton University Press 2010), pp. 1–3.
15   Ibid, pp. 167–176.
16   Ibid, pp. 170–176.
17   Andrei Shleifer, *Inefficient markets: an introduction to behavioral finance* (Oxford, UK: Oxford University Press 2000), pp. 10–20.
18   McDonnell, 'Of Mises and Min (sky): libertarian and liberal responses to financial crises past and present'.

Table 2.1 Classic economic theory vs.behavioural finance theory

R \ M	Economic motives	Non-economic motives
Rational responses	Adam Smith Theory	Behavioural Theory
Irrational responses	Behavioural Theory	Behavioural Theory

followers advocated a strongly anti-intervention approach, while the Keynesians and supporters strongly contended an active government intervention. After the GFC, the debate on intervention by the two parties was intensified again.

Brett H. McDonnell, in analysing the libertarian and liberal responses to financial crises categorised various approaches of government intervention into mainly four types according to two variables:[19] (i) the subject that we distrust: either the market or the government; and (ii) the sources of distrust of governments and markets: either ignorance or greed. These two distinctions will be used in the taxonomy of behavioural factors in the following analysis.

The identification of behavioural factors stems from the concept of 'bounded rationality'. In theory it means that the rationality of human beings in decision-making is limited due to finite information sources, finite cognitive ability, and the limited time they have in making a particular choice.[20] What needs to be focused on here as a prelude to the discussion on the TBTF bank structural problem is how bounded rationality and human irrationality occur, and why human beings as choice-makers should be distrusted.

The above classification based on the sources of distrust and the subjects whom we distrust can also be used to categorise all those behavioural factors in our analysis of the causes of the TBTF bank structural problem: (i) the subjects whom we distrust in this problem include: investors, industry, and regulators; and (ii) the sources of distrust in this problem include: greed and ignorance. But, after the combination of the two variables, the ignorance of investors and governments and the greed of industry will be the main ones discussed in detail (Table 2.2). This is because they are more commonly referred to in the current scholarship, and they are more providently reflected in the GFC and the TBTF bank structural problem, among others. Each of them is worth writing a monograph about from an economic perspective.[21] But in this book, we focus on their links with future financial regulation.

19 Ibid, pp. 1282–1283.
20 Herbert A. Simon, 'Models of man: social and rational'. See also Shleifer, *Inefficient markets: an introduction to behavioral finance*, pp. 15–30.
21 J.R., 'Why have so few bankers gone to jail?' *Economist*, www.economist.com/blogs/economist-explains/2013/05/economist-explains-why-few-bankers-gone-to-jail, accessed December 5, 2014; the ignorance of the industry is relevant to the accountability mechanism and the incriminating of bankers, on which little progress has been made in legislative reform so far in the major economies.

Table 2.2 The classification of behavioural factors

	Ignorance	*Greed*
Investor	√	?
Industry	?	√
Government	√	?

To discuss how behavioural factors played a significant role in the develop-ment of the GFC and the bank structural problem, it is necessary to first identify what are the generally accepted causes of the GFC and the TBTF bank structural problem, and then analyse their behavioural aspects. Emilios Avgouleas's discus-sion of the causes of the GFC is in two parts. The first part is the macro causes of the crisis:[22]

(1) Relaxed monetary policies and trade imbalances that fuelled massive asset bubbles and irrational exuberance;
(2) Flawed government policies: promoting universal housing (e.g. the US), pursuing mono-dimensional development, and placing excessive reliance on one or two industries (e.g. Iceland and its banking sector);
(3) Regulatory failure (e.g. the incapacity to deal with cross-border financial crises);
(4) Overexploitation of financial innovation.

In the second part, Emilios Avgouleas also emphasises several micro reasons for the GFC:[23] (i) traders and bankers' short-termist-oriented compensation struc-tures; (ii) the originate-to-distribute model and its impact on credit extension and loan underwriting standards;[24] and (iii) the flaws in credit ratings and the overdependence on them.

2 Behavioural factors: ignorance and the bank structural problem

This section will start to analyse the behavioural bias caused by ignorance identi-fied in behavioural economics and how this bias played a significant role in the development of the TBTF structural problem.

2.1 Human tendency to err and the bank structural problem

Adam Smith's free market based on economic individual hypothesis suggests a free market system and non-intervention lead to the state of full employment

---

22 Avgouleas, *Governance of global financial markets: the law, the economics, the politics*, pp. 89–90.
23 Ibid, p. 90.
24 See supra Chapter 1, Section 1.

and the maximisation of social welfare.[25] On the contrary, John Maynard Keynes explained Adam Smith's premise in a different way by exploring the individual's departure from rationality and hence the economy departure from full employment from the perspective of animal spirits. He pointed out that when people are making investment decisions, 'the basic of knowledge for estimating the yield ten years hence of a railway, a copper mine, a textile factory, the goodwill of patent medicine, amounts to little and sometimes to nothing'.[26] He further concluded that 'a large proportion of our positive activities depend on spontaneous optimism rather than a mathematical expectation'.[27] Therefore, what is indicated is that Adam Smith's premise is not completely right, and that human beings tend to be irrational and make mistakes, especially during a complicated decision-making process.[28]

That analysis leads to the questions: why do people make mistakes and how do people evaluate uncertain events and possibilities? Based on subjective experience, a person may rely on his or her intuition, hunch, guess, instinct, etc. In reality, people's decision-making shows some cognitive patterns which might be erroneous. Amos Tversky and Daniel Kahneman argued that people depend on the heuristics of 'representativeness' when they are asked to categorise A or B; the heuristics of 'availability' when they are asked the frequency or the plausibility of a particular development; and the heuristics of 'anchoring' when they are asked to give a numerical prediction.[29] These are all heuristics that can affect decision-making, and what matters here is that these heuristics can easily lead to wrong decisions.

The fact that people tend to err can also be seen from the cognitive process. Scientists categorised three systems of cognition: the perception system, the intuition system, and the reasoning system.[30] Perception means a kind of automatic, effortless cognition towards the current stimulus, such as the perception of temperature when people touch boiling water. Intuition is also an effortless way of thinking, but in the form of conceptualisation, e.g. it will take ten hours to fly from Beijing to Copenhagen. Reasoning is a sophisticated way of logical and effortful thinking, such as to what extent should the regulator loosen the control

25 Smith, *Wealth of nations*, pp. 362–364.
26 Akerlof and Shiller, *Animal spirits: how human psychology drives the economy, and why it matters for global capitalism*, p. 3.
27 John Maynard Keynes, *General theory of employment, interest and money* (Rickmansworth, UK: Atlantic Publishers 2006), p. 103. See also Akerlof and Shiller, *Animal spirits: how human psychology drives the economy, and why it matters for global capitalism*, pp. 1–7. It refers to animal spirits, i.e. some human psychology affecting their behaviours, such as over-confidence, fairness, and corruption.
28 Keynes, *General theory of employment, interest and money*, p. 104.
29 Amos Tversky and Daniel Kahneman, 'Judgment under uncertainty: heuristics and biases', 185 *Science* 1124.
30 Daniel Kahneman, 'Maps of bounded rationality: psychology for behavioral economics', *American Economic Review* 1449. Amos Tversky and Daniel Kahneman mapped a figure to analyze and compare the differences between the perception system, the intuition system, and the reasoning system.

of Chinese banks' interest rates, and are the lending floor and deposit ceiling desirable?[31] As analysed by Amos Tversky and Daniel Kahneman, the indicator of whether a task will be assigned to the intuition system or the reasoning system mostly depends on how much effort is consumed in the task. The intuition system takes a position between the automatic perception and the conceptually deliberate reasoning process. It assembles the perception system from the perspective of the attribute of process (a fast and automatic process, compared with the slow and rule-governed process for the reasoning system) and the reasoning system from the perspective of the attribute of content.[32]

Building on the three systems of cognition, Amos Tversky and Daniel Kahneman further explored how intuition is activated and how people make mistakes. This is through the concept of accessibility: 'the ease with which mental contents come to mind'.[33] For instance, people can easily calculate in their mind that 500 metres is approximately the distance from the Church of Our Lady to the Round Tower in Copenhagen city centre. However, when you ask people to say how far 3,000 metres is, again starting from the Church of Our Lady without using any technical tools, most people cannot answer the question as the information needed is not easily accessible. There are many decisions which do not require much effort, logic, or serial thinking. This can be called natural assessment, which is based on intuition. Amos Tversky and Daniel Kahneman concluded that accessibility is not a dichotomy; rather, it is a continuum. Some decisions consume more efforts than others, and it is human tendency to simply ignore uncertainties while relying on intuition due to the accessibility mechanism to confront complex and obscure tasks.[34]

In the dynamics of the economic world, participants also tend to have many intuitive concepts in their minds, such as being overconfident towards the market situation in an economic boom. This can be vividly demonstrated by world financial history, with periodically occurring boom and bust cycles being repeated as a result of people's short memory and illusion.[35] A salient characteristic of economic bubbles is that there are always general similarities despite the different contexts: public frenzy, overconfidence in the market, and regret and repentance after the crisis.

In the development of the TBTF bank structural problem, the inclination of market participants to make mistakes also played a considerable role. The

---

31 L.W. Tom Orlik, 'China loosens a key control over banks: move signals Beijing's commitment to undertake financial overhauls', *Wall Street Journal*, http://online.wsj.com/article/SB10001424 127887324448104578615430573714510.html, accessed December 8, 2014.

32 Kahneman, 'Maps of bounded rationality: psychology for behavioral economics'.

33 Tversky and Kahneman, 'Judgment under uncertainty: heuristics and biases'.

34 Kahneman, 'Maps of bounded rationality: psychology for behavioral economics'.

35 Richard Scott Carnell, Jonathan R. Macey and Geoffrey P. Miller, *The law of banking and financial institutions* (Netherlands: Wolters Kluwer Law & Business 2009), pp. 16–27. The banking industry and consumers certainly knew of the risks and volatility of financial markets in previous crises. However, when the anguish of previous crises gradually disappeared in people's consciousness, they tended to gamble again, and the industry would lobby for lax regulation. So, the psychology of investors is also an important reason why periodic crises happened.

governments in the major economies were announcing the coming of a new financial modernisation era and dismantled as many restrictions as they could to improve financial efficiency.[36] The mass media were preaching the coming of a big economic boom. The financial industry was comprehensively accelerating the pace of business expansion driven by loose macro-economic policies and the urge for more profits within the competitive market environment.[37] In addition, the market boom was further strengthened by investors' frenzy to invest. In the structural debt securities product chain, none of the participants took the flaws of mathematical modelling seriously.[38]

In the Icesave dispute,[39] it is impossible to understand, except through behavioural analysis, why investors trusted the financial institutions and conglomerates in Iceland and kept investing in them. They held assets including many structured debt securities that were worth more than ten times the GDP of the whole country.[40] The EFTA court made the judgment in favour of Iceland mainly according to a narrow interpretation of the Deposit Guarantee System. It shows that the necessity of preserving overall social and economic stability justified the discrimination of the Icelandic depositor guarantee scheme against foreign depositors.[41] It provides a bitter example of the inclination for humans to make mistakes, leading to systemic bank failure.

So many investment decisions were made without investors being fully aware of the economic rationality.[42] In terms of the investment in real estate markets via mortgages, due to the complexity of the markets millions of households made huge returns while nobody actually understood or was familiar with what was really going on in the markets that triggered the huge profits. In the securitisation products, the answers to many question were uncertain, such as how are RMBS and CDOs structured? How does maturity transformation operate in banks? Can the CDO evaluator identify the potential risks in the products? Yet, most of the market participants were crazy about investing in it under the herding effect, despite the risks.[43]

---

36 See supra Chapter 1, Section 3(a).

37 Rok Spruk, 'Iceland's financial and economic crisis: causes, consequences and implications', *European Enterprise Institute Policy Paper*, pp. 7–10.

38 Tim Morrison, *The risks of financial modeling: VaR and the economic meltdown, 2009*. The flaws of the VaR model were noticed by some experts, but they were almost ignored in the trend for huge financial expansion. See supra Chapter 1, Section 3(c).

39 *Case E-16/11 [2013] EFTA Surveillance Authority v Iceland, not yet reported.*

40 Eyvindur G Gunnarsson, 'The Icelandic regulatory responses to the financial crisis', 12 *European Business Organization Law Review* 1.

41 Arwin G. Zeissler, Thomas Piontek and Andrew Metrick, 'Ireland and Iceland in crisis C: Iceland's Landsbanki Icesave', *Yale Program on Financial Stability Case Study*.

42 Warren Buffett deemed derivatives to be 'financial weapons of mass destruction'. Its obscurity makes it easier for investors to make incorrect investment decisions.

43 Mark Riddix, 'Down the rabbit hole: deciphering CDOs', Forbes, www.forbes.com/2010/05/17/what-are-collateralized-debt-obligations-personal-finance-cdos.html, accessed December 8, 2014. The author indicates, 'CDOs are collateralized debt obligations. If you don't know what that is, you're not alone; no one on Wall Street seems to know what they are either'.

2.2 Consumer preferences in the bank structural problem

After analysing how and why people always tend to make mistakes from the perspective of economic analysis and cognitive analysis, the next three sections dig further into the taxonomy of those identified biases and anomalies and explain their influence on the development of the bank structural problem. Stefano DellaVigna has identified three classes of departure from rationality: (i) non-standard preferences, (ii) non-standard beliefs, and (iii) non-standard decision-making.[44]

The first class is non-standard preferences including time preference, risk preference, and regret and other emotions.[45] Time preference is related to the concept of present bias, which is how people overvalue current gratification over the future. There are many examples of present bias, such as overuse of credit cards with near zero teaser rates due to people underestimating the potential for future consumption, and the phenomenon of low rates of savings in the US due to people's illusion that future savings' potential is bigger than at present. Present bias normally leads to a problem of self-control and procrastination.[46]

Risk preference normally refers to reference dependence and loss aversion, which means people tend to avoid loss when making investment decisions. According to prospect theory by Amos Tversky and Daniel Kahneman, during the investment decision-making process, value functions are concave for gains and convex for losses, and the losses are steeper than the gains. This means that the consideration of losses always outweighs the consideration of rational gains in the decision-making process for an investment.[47]

Regret and other emotions are related to the phenomenon that people tend to make decisions based on certain emotions, especially, the fear of regret. Thus, people tend to buy some expensive, inappropriate insurance plans for fear of future unlikely losses.[48] Decisions are made due to a fear of regret rather than for an underlying reasonable value.

The investor's time, risk, and other preferences were manifested in many aspects of the TBTF bank structural problem. A very noticeable aspect was the overdependence on Credit Ratings Agencies (CRAs).[49] In the whimsical world of investment with complex financial products, both sophisticated and unsophisticated investors tend to rely on something definite and certain, despite the likely impossibility it will meet their preferences for risk aversion and regret avoidance.

---

44 Stefano DellaVigna, *Psychology and economics: evidence from the field* (2007). See also Kahneman, 'Maps of bounded rationality: psychology for behavioral economics'. Tversky and Kahneman, 'Judgment under uncertainty: heuristics and biases'.

45 DellaVigna, *Psychology and economics: evidence from the field*.

46 Dan Ariely and Simon Jones, *Predictably irrational* (New York: HarperCollins 2008), pp. 109–126.

47 Kahneman and Tversky, 'Prospect theory: an analysis of decision under risk'. There was a figure drawn by Amos Tversky and Daniel Kahneman to explain the value function. See also supra Introduction, Section 2.1.

48 DellaVigna, *Psychology and economics: evidence from the field*.

49 *The United States of America v. S&P, 12 U.S.C. § 1833a, 18 U.S.C. § 1341*, see the complaint, pp. 38–59.

Therefore, nothing was better than the CRA ratings in terms of providing simple and succinct investment guidance. The result was that the three big CRAs thrived unprecedentedly and were depended on to a great extent by investors in the securitisation products.

The reckless CRAs were widely criticised as a significant cause of the housing bubble and subprime mortgage expansion.[50] The CRAs are good examples of an oligopoly because there are only three major agencies: Standard & Poors, Fitch, and Moody, who dominated the markets. Current scholarship suggests that the root problems of the credit rating service and the critical causes of the financial crisis were ratings inflation and conflicts of interest.[51] In other words, CRAs tended to provide customer friendly ratings due to a conflict of interest.

Yet, investors and even the regulators were still extremely dependent on the ratings, and nobody really thought about the real risks hidden behind the structural debt products. In the US, there were even some statutes and regulations provided by Nationally Recognized Statistical Rating Organizations (NRSRO) that made the 'investment grade' the threshold for investment by specific investors.[52] In accordance with the rule, the credit union was only allowed to invest in those financial products with a grade no lower than AA–.[53]

Due to an irrational overdependence, investors were susceptible to the CRAs, who constantly represented to the markets that their ratings were impartial and independent while rarely warning investors of the flaws of their ratings.[54] The three credit rating giants were definitely aware of the fact that their rating grades were of material importance to investors, especially as existing rules deliberately deployed its 'investment grade' as a shelter for market volatility risk and possible default losses. S&P, for example, continuously represented to the public that their ratings grades were 'high quality, independent, objective, and rigorous[ly] analytical'. Actually, it turned out that many of its ratings were materially flawed.[55]

The point to be made here is that people were irrationally dependent on the CRAs' ratings despite their lack of objectivity, and that the CRAs' awareness of investors' overdependence made the investors even more susceptible. The root causes of the susceptibility of investors were largely their risk aversion and regret aversion preferences. Such behavioural bias and the influence on investors were magnified in the trading-related activities engaged in by universal banks.

---

50 Avgouleas, *Governance of global financial markets: the law, the economics, the politics*, pp. 130–131.

51 Ibid, pp. 130–133.

52 *The United States of America v. S&P, 12 U.S.C. § 1833a, 18 U.S.C. § 1341*, see the complaint, p. 11.

53 See 12 C.F.R. § 704.6(f). *'At the time of purchase, investments with long-term ratings must be rated no lower than AA- (or equivalent) by every NRSRO that provides a publicly available long-term rating on that investment, and investments with short-term ratings must be rated no lower than A-1 (or equivalent) by every NRSRO that provides a publicly available short-term rating on that investment'.*

54 Avgouleas, *Governance of global financial markets: the law, the economics, the politics*, p. 124. The CRAs warned the investors of the functioning of their ratings. However, they never did this in a very comprehensive or prominent way, at least not enough for non-sophisticated investors to be aware of the potential risks behind these structural debts products.

55 *The United States of America v. S&P, 12 U.S.C. § 1833a, 18 U.S.C. § 1341*.

2.3 Consumer beliefs in the bank structural problem

The second class of irrationality according to Stefano DellaVigna is non-standard beliefs consisting of systemic overconfidence (such as wishful thinking investment),[56] overextrapolation (such as people's tendency for 'gambler's fallacy'),[57] and projection bias (such as buying so-called 'blue chip stocks' solely as a result of current statistics).[58]

Overconfidence is normally defined as the psychological state of being over-confident about one's own decision-making and overestimating the possibility of positive events.[59] For instance, in the 1630 Dutch Tulip mania, the tulip was highly esteemed as a representation of fashion and nobility. Investors were in a frenzy about the rocketing high price of tulip bulbs, the peak of which was when a single tulip bulb could be sold for more than ten times the total annual income of a craftsman. In 1935, there was a tulip bulb called 'Childer', which was worth 1615 florins.[60] By comparison, you could have bought 4 bulls or a tow truck for only 480 florins.[61] The psychological state and mental frenzy of investors at that time is a good example of overconfidence.

Overextrapolation is also called overinference, which refers to the tendency of people making decisions on the basis of only limited observations and over-estimating the representativeness of the available data.[62] Some experimental research about gambling shows that in the simple 'pick-three-numbers game' where the fewer the number of people who choose a number, the higher the expected pay-out,[63] people tend to exclude the numbers that recently won one or two weeks ago. They think that the same number won't happen twice within two consecutive weeks based on their extrapolation bias. The reason why people make irrational decisions in the game is that they make an overinference based on unrepresentative data.

Projection bias is used to define the tendency of investors expecting their current status to continue into the future, which is to say, they hypothesise there is a logical continuity of their current status into the future.[64] For instance, research shows that most employees invest their money in their employers' companies by relying only on the past performance of the stock. Specifically, a higher percentage of money is invested in an employer's company if its past stock performance

---

56   Tversky and Kahneman, 'Judgment under uncertainty: heuristics and biases'.
57   Schiller, *Irrational exuberance*, pp. 62–64.
58   Ibid, pp. 3–6.
59   Ibid, p. 45.
60   John Steele Gordon, *The Great Game: the emergence of Wall Street as a world power* (Beijing: China Citic Press Corp 2005), pp. 7–10.
61   Gordon, *The Great Game: the emergence of Wall Street as a world power.* See also Schiller, *Irrational exuberance*, pp. 71–72.
62   DellaVigna, *Psychology and economics: evidence from the field.*
63   Ibid, p. 27.
64   George Loewenstein, Ted O'Donoghue and Matthew Rabin, 'Projection bias in predicting future utility', *The Quarterly Journal of Economics* 1209.

is better.[65] Projection bias is also manifested in modern investment theories, especially the 'castle in the air theory' and the 'technical analysis'.[66] The principle of the 'technical analysis' suggests that a chart of a company's past prices and volumes of trading shows all the necessary information you need for investment decision-making. It seems plausible to some extent because the herding instinct of the masses may make the trend continue. Therefore, it sounds very rational and attractive to non-sophisticated investors who suffer greatly from the disadvantage of information asymmetry and knowledge asymmetry. However, it is not as rational as it seems. The reason is that chart-dependent investors buy when trends have been established and sell when trends have been broken, while the reality is that on most occasions, the trends can just abruptly change and leave insufficient time for even the swiftest chartist to adapt their strategy.[67]

In the run up to the bank structural problem in the pre-crisis era, investors and participants in the securitisation products either could not properly manage the risks of their investments due to a lack of information and quantitative skills to analyse their complexity, or lacked the due incentive to conduct comprehensive research, believing in the transference of risk through the originate-to-distribute model.[68] Therefore, they chose to assess the risks behind the financial innovation by 'accessibility', 'the ease with which mental contents come to mind'.[69]

That is to say, they tended to rely on some basic anomalies, such as overconfidence, overextrapolation, and projection bias.[70] A large part of the securitisation products investors tended to make their investment decision without conducting thorough research regarding the quality of the underlying assets. But they were still so decisive and resolute in their speculative investment decisions. The reasonable explanation is that they were very confident of the outlook of the financial products, due to their confidence euphoria and projection bias based on previous irrational exuberance. They speculatively believed that through the pre-crisis financial product chain, their investment would be vastly profitable if the current rising housing prices were to continue.[71]

The TBTF bank structural problem can be likened to be a 'natural occurring Ponzi scheme'.[72] Non-standard preferences played a significant role in the scheme. The mortgage extension for investment in the housing market promised

65 DellaVigna, *Psychology and economics: evidence from the field*, p. 28.
66 Burton Gordon Malkiel, *A random walk down Wall Street: including a life-cycle guide to personal investing* (New York: WW Norton & Company 1999), pp. 99–110.
67 Ibid.
68 See supra Introduction, Section 1.1.
69 Tversky and Kahneman, 'Judgment under uncertainty: heuristics and biases'.
70 Avgouleas, *Governance of global financial markets: the law, the economics, the politics*, pp. 61–62. Investors had no idea how the envisioned diversification through CDSs and envisioned transference of risks through the financial product chain ended up leading to homogeneity and causing instability.
71 Robert J. Shiller, *The subprime solution: how today's global financial crisis happened, and what to do about it* (Princeton, NJ: Princeton University Press 2008), pp. 10–30.
72 Niall Ferguson, *The ascent of money: a financial history of the world* (Harmondsworth, UK: Penguin 2008), pp. 55–67. See supra Chapter 1, Section 3(c).

high revenues and profits for both banks and households. That attracted the first round of customers. Banks transferred the mortgage assets through the originate-to-distribute model, so that they could keep providing loans to customers in the second round, and so forth.[73] SPVs would also be willing to securitise more loans, and investors were also very willing to keep trading the securitisation products.[74] Therefore, a wave of euphoria swept the markets and kept fuelling the bubbles. However, such was the euphoria of continually earning money that all participants assumed that the price of real estate would always increase.

Therefore, the heuristics of overconfidence and projection bias contributed non-negligibly to the prosperity of trading-oriented activities and the 'natural Ponzi scheme' of the real estate bubble and the securitisation product bubbles.

2.4 Consumer decision-making in the bank structural problem

The third class of irrationality is the non-standard decision-making process including: narrow bracketing (such as the neglect of portfolio consideration),[75] the salient framing effect (such as the inclination of choosing the most prominently framed option among others), relying on heuristics (such as anchoring to a particular number when doing a numerical prediction),[76] and social influence (such as the investment feedback loop phenomenon).[77]

Narrow bracketing is conceptualised as people making decisions on an isolated basis rather than trying to think through everything systemically. Amos Tversky and Daniel Kahneman conducted an experiment in which people were offered a two-stage choice where they had a 0.75 possibility of failing in the first stage and 0.25 chance of reaching the second stage. In the second stage, they were offered a choice between A (4,000, .80) and B (3,000, 1). In the experiment 78% chose choice B. But, according to mathematics, the final utility of choice B is: $0.25 \times 3000 = 750$, while choice A is: $0.25 \times 0.8 \times 4000 = 800$. The reason why people made the wrong decision was that they didn't consider the first step and second step together in their calculation but on an isolated basis.[78]

Salient framing concerns how the decision-making process can be influenced by inconsequential variances due to the fact that limited attention tends to be fixated on the salient aspects of a situation.[79] Amos Tversky and Daniel Kahneman categorised three kinds of framing which can influence decision-making: framing of act, framing of contingency, and framing of outcome.[80] Among them, framing of outcome is most frequently reflected in investors' behaviours associated with market inefficiency and information asymmetry. A telling example is the

73 Avgouleas, *Governance of global financial markets: the law, the economics, the politics*, pp. 40–41
74 See supra Chapter 1, Section 1.
75 Malkiel, *A random walk down Wall Street: including a life-cycle guide to personal investing*, p. 179.
76 Tversky and Kahneman, 'Judgment under uncertainty: heuristics and biases'.
77 DellaVigna, *Psychology and economics: evidence from the field*, pp. 29–30.
78 Kahneman and Tversky, 'Prospect theory: an analysis of decision under risk'.
79 DellaVigna, *Psychology and economics: evidence from the field*.
80 Amos Tversky and Daniel Kahneman, 'The framing of decisions and the psychology of choice', 211 *Science* 453.

'gambler's fallacy'. If an investor loses 140 dollars in an investment, and he or she has the final chance to invest another 10 dollars to win back the 140 dollars, there can be two different framings of the same result. A is based on the status quo as a reference point (140, –10), and B is based on an adapted reference point (0, –150).[81] As the data indicate, the latter seems riskier; however, people in a frenzied state always forget to adapt their reference point and tend to choose the risky business.[82] Framing of contingency can also be explained by the former example, the two-stage experiment. The reason why most people choose B is because of the so-called pseudo certainty, where they forget to calculate the previous contingency in their math calculation.[83] Framing of act is always associated with a compound decision consisting of many different but interrelated decision units; the complexity of them and their befuddling relationships can always lead people to make the wrong choice.[84]

Heuristics refers to many anomalies that can lead to erroneous decisions.[85] Among those identified, there are a few which can exert a huge influence on investors: the heuristics of representativeness when people are asked to categorise A to B; the heuristics of availability when they are asked about the plausibility of a particular development or event; and the heuristics of anchoring when they are asked a numerical prediction.[86]

Persuasion denotes the tendency of investors to be susceptible to social influence.[87] People tend to trust others and reinforce their beliefs through social influence and the feedbacks they receive. The feedback theory of economic bubbles, or the 'feedback loop', indicates that the initial price increase can lead to further price increases as the initial price increase feeds back into the second round of price increases as a result of increasing consumer demand; then the second round of increase feeds back to the third round, and so forth.[88] This can also be explained in a negative way: the initial downturn in the price can lead to further price decreases because the initial decrease feeds back to the second round of decrease through the decrease of demands, and the second round then further aggravates the price. Therefore, the feedback loop increases the accumulation of risk in a boom and aggravates the situation of loss in a period of bust.

In the TBTF bank structural problem, the complexity in the banking sector was one of the most important factors that led to the GFC, reflecting the link between the behavioural decision-making process and the accumulation of risks.[89]

---

81 Ibid.
82 Kahneman and Tversky, 'Prospect theory: an analysis of decision under risk'.
83 DellaVigna, *Psychology and economics: evidence from the field*, p. 27.
84 Tversky and Kahneman, 'The framing of decisions and the psychology of choice'.
85 Emilios Avgouleas, 'Financial regulation, behavioural finance, and the global credit crisis: in search of a new regulatory model', *Behavioural finance, and the global credit crisis: in search of a new regulatory model* (September 3, 2008), pp. 12–15.
86 Tversky and Kahneman, 'Judgment under uncertainty: heuristics and biases'. See supra Chapter 2, Section 2.1.
87 Schiller, *Irrational exuberance*, p. 44.
88 Ibid, pp. 60–64. See supra Chapter 1, Section 3(c).
89 Steven L. Schwarcz, 'Regulating complexity in financial markets' 87 Wash UL Rev 211.

Although complexity is not necessarily produced to befuddle investors, its emergence could impair market transparency and information efficiency in many ways.[90] For instance, the complexities of structural debt securities and the originate-to-distribute model could lead to a higher possibility of default in the long run. As indicated by the analysis on risk modelling, due to the impossibility of assessing different risks for innumerable kinds of assets underlying the structural debt securities, the risk model simply evaluated approximate risks by intentionally omitting many significant but immeasurable risks.[91] Therefore, the complexities of securities could impair disclosure, obfuscate consequences, and increase financial product uncertainties for investors.

First, the limited disclosure and complicated structural debt securities are a good example of how complexity framing could impede rational investment decision-making. Complexity exacerbated the reliance on other heuristics and social persuasion because experiments show that people are prone to conduct decision-making processes irrationally when faced with complicated decisions as they are affected by the 'accessibility' effect.[92]

As a matter of fact, it is even fair to say that in the securitisation of structural debt securities, the framing effect was orchestrated and exploited by the banks and CRAs to a certain extent to significantly affect the decision-making processes of investors.[93] Apparently, according to industry practice, the charge for rating services by CRAs of the originators would ultimately be transferred to the investors in the securitisation products, who care only about profitability.[94] The rating of structured debt securities for the CRAs was a very significantly profitable business. Thus, a misaligned incentive was created: the CRAs provided satisfactory ratings to attract investors, and the CRAs and the banks would then benefit.[95]

Within the context of the misaligned incentive of banks and CRAs and the resulting complexities, the eagerness of investors to 'beat the market' made them more susceptible to the banking sector and the CRAs.[96] The investors include direct investors in securitisation products and other indirectly related households who kept investing in the real estate markets.[97] Many scholars argue that

---

90 Ibid.
91 Morrison, *The risks of financial modeling: VaR and the economic meltdown, 2009.* See supra Chapter 1, Section 3(c).
92 When the decision-making is too complicated, people tend to simply ignore complexity and make decisions based on some rules of thumb. See Kahneman, 'Maps of bounded rationality: psychology for behavioral economics'. See supra Chapter 2, Section 2.1.
93 *The United States of America v. S&P, 12 U.S.C. § 1833a, 18 U.S.C. § 1341,* see the complaint, pp. 19–21.
94 S&P normally charges a maximum USD150,000 per non-prime RMBS to be rated, a maximum USD500,000 per CDO to be rated, and USD750,000 per synthetic CDO product to be rated.
95 *The United States of America v. S&P, 12 U.S.C. § 1833a, 18 U.S.C. § 1341,* see the complaint, p. 39.
96 Malkiel, *A random walk down Wall Street: including a life-cycle guide to personal investing,* pp. 1–10.
97 Mark Riddix, 'Down the rabbit hole: deciphering CDOs', Forbes. Warren Buffett said that structural debt products are mass destruction weapons; he could not understand the complexity of them.

investors' eagerness to engage in risk-taking for higher profits was the driver for continuous financial innovation, such as the subprime mortgage.[98]

Specifically speaking, complexity was manifested in many aspects of the structural debt securities: the complicated securitisation process, various types of underlying assets, various kinds of structured debt products, and different risk evaluation models (such as 'LEVELS' for RMBS products and the 'CDO evaluator').[99] Each was beyond the wildest imagination of investors, and this undoubtedly led to problems with full disclosure and impaired the products' transparency. Thus, many important details about products, such as the possibility of higher-than-expected defaults and the high contagion effect were not known by investors. According to the concept of 'accessibility', the eagerness to make profits left the investors with no alternative but to find an arbitrary but simple way to face the complexities.

Eventually, in order to deal with complexity, investors seek certainty, that is a 100% instant profit of USD100 is apparently more attractive to investors than 50% of a USD500 future interest.[100] The rating service catered to this need perfectly. With regard to the desirability for certainty in investment in structural debt securities, the grading scales provided by CRAs were nothing but a simple embodiment of the impossibly convoluted securitisation products.[101] In S&P, the grading levels are from AAA, AA, A, BBB, BB, B, CCC, CC, SD (Selective Default), down to D (Default).[102] Obviously, the most prominent characteristics of the grades were clearness and simplicity, which made the originally unpredictable and convoluted financial products become very clear and certain to investors. Therefore, the simplicity framing of the rating grades catered to the need for certainty and risk aversion for investors. It directed investors to make easy decisions based on their succinct yet probably not accurate ratings.

That complexity framing of securitisation products clouded any reasonable judgement by investors, and that made them very vulnerable in negative market situations.[103] In the EU, Deutsche Industriebank IKB, which was originally a traditional bank serving small- and medium-sized firms, was one of the first European banks to be hit by the crisis due to its securitisation products' exposures. Amid the tidal wave of investment in structural debt securities, it built a large portfolio of ABCP funds to invest in high rated RMBS, collateralised loan obligations (CLOs), and commercial real estate. IKB's ABCP structured vehicles were refinanced in the short term in the commercial paper markets. When Bear Stearns revealed losses on July 16, 2007, IKB's finance strategy was under

---

99 *The United States of America v. S&P, 12 U.S.C. § 1833a, 18 U.S.C. § 1341*, see complaint, pp. 8–20. CDOs were categorized into three types according to different combinations of assets: cash CDOs, synthetic CDOs, and hybrid CDOs, each requiring a different risk evaluation model.
100 Kahneman and Tversky, 'Prospect theory: an analysis of decision under risk'.
101 *The United States of America v. S&P, 12 U.S.C. § 1833a, 18 U.S.C. § 1341*.
102 Ibid. See the pleading, p. 10.
103 Schwarcz, 'Regulating complexity in financial markets'. See Chapter 1, Section 3(d).

extreme stress. Soon IKB depleted its liquidity to roll over its short-term debts. The high ratings were not of much help in a negative financial situation.[104]

Second, the marketing of structural debt securities also portrayed the feedback loop in the pre-crisis era and the run up to the TBTF bank structural problem. The reason why incredible trust was had in the CRAs, despite their dubious rating model and suspicious conflicts of interest, is that people tend to make decisions affected by social influences when faced with complexity.[105] The CRA ratings were also a kind of feedback among others.[106]

In the first place, macro- and micro-economic tools led to the price increase in the housing markets and attracted many investors.[107] That created a general economic optimism due to the social influence effect from the banking sector, the CRAs, other investors, the mass media, etc. Thus, the higher price of the first round fed the investment with more demands in the second round, and so forth. Finally, nobody cared about discovering the real values, only following the precedence of others despite the lack of plausibility.

Therefore, the identified irrationality over investors' decision-making processes was also evidently reflected by the complexity of trading-related activities in universal banks.

2.5 Regulators and policies in the bank structural problem

Regulators are the guardians of the financial markets' safety and soundness. Ignorant or reckless decision-making about economic or monetary policies can affect the functioning of the financial markets. With regard to the TBTF bank structural problem, it is widely accepted that the regulatory policies were flawed in many respects, which gave rise to the irrational expansion in bank activities.[108]

First, the pre-crisis era was characterised by lax monetary policies and the expansion of global financial markets. It was esteemed as the 'era of great modernisation'.[109] Most of the related deregulation policies were established in the 'Jackson Hole Consensus', which asserted the importance of monetary policies,[110] central bank independence, and the efficient market paradigm. The regulators believed that price stability was necessary for economic growth and financial stability, and that price stability and financial stability are not in conflict. Rather, they are complementary to each other.[111] In fact, the success of price stabilising is always accompanied by asset inflation. That was also what happened in the pre-crisis era. Most of the central banks around the world, the US Federal Reserve Bank (FED),

---

104 Liikanen Erkki, *High-level Expert Group on reforming the structure of the EU banking sector* (Final Report, Brussels, 2012), p. 5.
105 Tversky and Kahneman, 'Judgment under uncertainty: heuristics and biases'.
106 Schiller, *Irrational exuberance*, pp. 44–60.
107 Ibid.
108 Avgouleas, *Governance of global financial markets: the law, the economics, the politics*, pp. 91–93.
109 Ibid, pp. 64–67.
110 Matthias Paustian Charles Bean, Adrian Penalver, and Tim Taylor, '"Monetary policy at the fall", Paper in the Federal Reserve Bank of Kansas City Annual Conference, Jackson Hole', www.kansascityfed.org/publicat/sympos/2010/2010-08-23-bean.pdf, accessed December 8, 2014.
111 Avgouleas, *Governance of global financial markets: the law, the economics, the politics*, p. 66.

the European Central Bank (ECB), and the Bank of England (BOE), decided to maintain price stability, even at the risk of asset bubbles. The direct result of the policy orientation was that the regulators in most of the countries failed to prevent the asset bubbles from forming and looming ever larger.[112] The bankers further exploited and exacerbated the situation through profitable yet reckless expansion of the provision of credit and various financial innovations.

However, recognising the seriousness of the asset bubbles was not directly transformed into effective policy interventions, such as tightening monetary policy. The reason was obvious: raising interest rates and appeasing the asset bubbles must be undertaken at the expense of economic growth, which, unfortunately, was not what all the regulators were willing to embrace.[113]

Second, the deregulation of financial markets was too aggressive. The EMH considers price to be the correct mechanism to accurately signal the degree of soundness of the financial markets. It believes that financial markets could address failure through the price discovery mechanism and arbitrage behaviours.[114] Believing in this assumption, the trend for deregulation prevailed in world financial markets. For instance, in 1986 there was the 'Big Bang' financial deregulation in the UK, followed by the Gramm-Leach-Billey Financial Services Modernization Act in the US, and the Second Banking Directive in the EU in 1989, which allowed traditional commercial banks to engage in investment banking activities in the EU.

The regulators showed bounded rationality in financial regulation policies that fostered the irrational expansion of banks into trading-oriented activities.[115] They failed to see in advance how banks would take advantage and exploit these lax macro-economic circumstances by resorting to massive financial innovations, leveraging their balance sheets, and riding the wave of excessive liquidity, gradually evolving into TBTF banks.[116]

In terms of positive regulatory policies, Australia was largely deemed a safe haven that evaded the GFC.[117] This was largely because it had tightened its regulations after the Wallis report in 1997, observing the huge risks underlying its financial liberalisation process. It controlled its regulatory structure by balancing prudential and business conduct regulation through the 'twin-peak' regulation model, which was also adopted by the UK after the crisis.[118]

---

112   J. B. Taylor, 'Housing and monetary policy (No. w13682)'. National Bureau of Economic Research. www.nber.org/papers/w13682, accessed December 8, 2014.

113   Avgouleas, *Governance of global financial markets: the law, the economics, the politics*, pp. 92–96.

114   Andrew W. Lo, 'Reconciling efficient markets with behavioral finance: the adaptive markets hypothesis', 7 *Journal of Investment Consulting* 21.

115   Kahneman, 'Maps of bounded rationality: psychology for behavioral economics'.

116   Morrison, *The risks of financial modeling: VaR and the economic meltdown, 2009*. The risks of financial innovation and risks underlying the securitisation products should have been better understood. But the regulators obviously failed to see them.

117   Eilís Ferran, *The regulatory aftermath of the global financial crisis* (Cambridge, UK: Cambridge University Press 2012), pp. 209–211.

118   Ibid, pp. 216–219. See also Ian R. Harper, 'The Wallis report: an overview', 30 *Australian Economic Review* 288. See also HM Treasury, 'A new approach to financial regulation: judgement', *Focus and Stability*.

Thus, macro-economic and regulatory policies irrationally failed to discover the risks underlying the universal banking model, which they should have uncovered through reasonable due diligence.

2.6 Case study of Iceland, Lehman Brothers, and Washington Mutual bank

The Iceland case is a good example to show how an erroneous interest rate policy can lead to the accumulation of gargantuan risks. When assessing what happened in Iceland, many current researchers attribute its failure and the Icesave debacle to the liberalisation process, financial deregulation, the privatisation policy, the Oddsson reform, the trading exposure to securitisation products, etc.[119]

However, Spruk Rok argued 'according to many empirical and statistical analyses that the main reason triggered the crisis was the failure of the central bank and the historical deviation of the monetary policy'.[120] Specifically, Iceland had been haunted by the inflationary problem ever since 1980s.[121] That laid down the context of Icelandic government's intervention targeting inflation through persistent high interest rate policy. This policy was distinct to the world trend of lax monetary policy. It brought about the tidal wave of foreign currency inflow and domestic financial institutions overseas expansion simply by taking advantage of the interest rate differences.

The direct result was a rapid appreciation in the domestic currency.[122] Therefore, foreign currency inflow, domestic currency appreciation, and financial institution expansions triggered by the high interest rate policy fuelled the overheated economy and conversely added to the inflationary pressure rather than appeasing it. Therefore, the central bank raised the interest rate to ease inflation, but this backfired as too much foreign money was attracted in by the high interest rate, thereby adding to inflation.

> In addition, market internationalization like that in Iceland usually requires foreign currency reserves to diversify market risks in case of any market volatility. However, that was completely ignored by the Iceland government and its central bank. Therefore, once the crisis started in the US as Bear Stearns and Lehman Brothers collapsed, it instantly plagued the world including Iceland where risks have enormously piled up.[123]

---

119 See Gunnarsson, 'The Icelandic regulatory responses to the financial crisis'. On the risk accumulation and the policy transformation in the pre-crisis era, see Kaarlo Jännäri, 'Report on banking regulation and supervision in Iceland: past, present and future', 30, report commissioned by the Icelandic government as part of its Stand-By Arrangement with the International Monetary Fund.

120 Spruk, 'Iceland's financial and economic crisis: causes, consequences and implications'.

121 It was shown that before the Oddsson reform, Iceland had the highest inflation rate in the OECD countries at 16.51% from 1980–2009. This created the need to tame the extreme inflation by introducing high interest rates.

122 Jännäri, 'Report on banking regulation and supervision in Iceland: past, present and future'.

123 Spruk, 'Iceland's financial and economic crisis: causes, consequences and implications'.

Therefore, it is plausible to say, if trading exposures to securitisation products were the trigger for the Icelandic crisis, it was the wrongful monetary policy that doomed Iceland from the beginning.[124]

The Lehman Brothers case proves the flaws in the excessive deregulation policy and the ignoring of regulatory mechanisms. For example, there was no recovery and resolution scheme at all for the TBTF banks.[125] This was evident from the difficulties in the liquidation proceedings of Lehman Brothers: the disorder in the process; the unsettling of creditors, shareholders and stakeholders; and the subsequent colossal market volatility.[126] Such problems adversely impeded an orderly liquidation and triggered an unnecessary massive evaporation in the value of the assets in the liquidated entities.

A Federal Deposit Insurance Corporation (FDIC) article showed that the filing for liquidation according to the Bankruptcy Act had several adverse effects. It brought about the spill over effect within the group, uncertainties for its creditors,[127] and devastation to derivatives and swap markets, as a result of Lehman Brothers Holding Inc. acting as the final guarantor of the exposures of its subsidiaries and affiliates in the commodity markets.[128] If an appropriately swift resolution process had been established, it could have preserved a large proportion of the group's asset values that had evaporated because of the liquidation disorder. It could also have avoided the unnecessary market volatility and been better able to meet the claims of all the stakeholders.[129] Some of necessary measures are reflected in the Dodd-Frank Act, such as the 'living will',[130] the liquidity provision from the Treasury, and resolution tools.[131]

If these rules had been adopted and implemented earlier, things would have been totally different in terms of minimising the risk of spill over within the financial markets.[132] Therefore, the regulators of financial markets were, to some extent, not fully rational in their decision-making because of bounded rationality.

---

124 Ibid.
125 Rosalind Z. Wiggins, Thomas Piontek and Andrew Metrick, 'The Lehman Brothers bankruptcy A'.
126 Federal Deposit Insurance Corporation, 'The orderly liquidation of Lehman Brothers Holdings Inc. under the Dodd-Frank Act', www.fdic.gov/bank/analytical/quarterly/2011_vol5_2/lehman.pdf, accessed November 15, 2014.
127 Such as Reserve Primary Fund, who had a claim of USD785 million against Lehman Brothers Holding Inc. The liquidation created uncertainties for its own financial situation.
128 Federal Deposit Insurance Corporation, 'The orderly liquidation of Lehman Brothers Holdings Inc. under the Dodd-Frank Act'. See also David A. Skeel, 'Single point of entry and the bankruptcy alternative', *Across the Great Divide: New Perspectives on the Financial Crisis* 14, pp. 3–6.
129 Federal Deposit Insurance Corporation, 'The orderly liquidation of Lehman Brothers Holdings Inc. under the Dodd-Frank Act'.
130 Dodd–Frank Wall Street Reform and Consumer Protection Act (US), section 204 of Title I, section 165(d).
131 Ibid, Title I section 204. See also the Orderly Resolution of Covered Financial Companies – Special Powers under Title II.
132 Rosalind Z. Wiggins and Andrew Metrick, *The Lehman Brothers bankruptcy H: the global contagion* (2015).

The Washington Mutual Bank (WaMu) case shows how regulators failed to ensure the bank's risk compliance because of their bounded rationality.[133] At the time of its failure, WaMu was the largest US thrift bank with USD300 billion in assets and USD180 billion in deposits. Starting from the time of the financial modernisation process after the deregulation legislation at the beginning of the twenty-first century, it gradually embarked on a journey of pursuing higher profits by extending risky loans despite the high default risk.[134]

Starting in 2006, even before the onset of the GFC, many of its high-risk loans were incurring high rates of delinquency. At the time, its mortgage-backed securities were also experiencing downgrades and losses. With its portfolio suffering more losses due to poor-quality loans and securities, its share price plummeted and that caused a liquidity draught and a run on the bank. Finally, WaMu was seized by its regulators and placed in receivership with the FDIC and then sold to JPMorgan.[135]

The case demonstrates the bank's failure as a result of excessive risk-taking and exposure to securitisation products. But more importantly, it reflects the failure of the Office of Thrift Supervision (OTS) in restraining unsafe lending practices.[136] Due to the trend of deregulation, the OTS believed in minimal regulatory intervention, and it was very hesitant to actually intervene in the hypothetically effective risk management conducted by the bank. Therefore, the OTS displayed a very high degree of deference to the apparent good management and sound practices of the industry.[137]

According to some researchers, although the OTS had officially identified over 500 serious deficiencies in five years (2004–2008), it never took any enforcement action against WaMu to correct its unsafe practices.[138] In addition, it never lowered the ratings of the firm in business safety and soundness either. Even though there were some occasional enforcement actions, they also did not bring about any effective changes to the firm's practice. As the FDIC Inspector General John Rymer said:

> The examiners, from what I have seen here, were pointing out the problems, underwriting problems, riskier products, concentrations, distributions, and markets that may display more risk – they were all significant problems and they were identified. At the end of the day, though, I don't think forceful enough action was taken.[139]

Furthermore, the OTS was involved in a serious turf war against the FDIC, another regulator of WaMu.[140] Through the supervision process, the OTS had

---

133 Simon, 'Models of man: social and rational'.
134 United States Senate Permanent Subcommittee on Investigations, *Wall Street and the financial crisis: anatomy of a financial collapse* (Cosimo Reports 2011), pp. 48–56.
135 Ibid, pp. 109–120.
136 Ibid, pp. 165–167.
137 Ibid.
138 Ibid, pp. 195–196.
139 Ibid, p. 195.
140 Ibid, pp. 196–200.

become increasingly protective of the industry, while the FDIC was becoming increasingly aggressive in supervision, witnessing the identified risks in the firms. Therefore, the OTS frequently expressed its discontent towards the FDIC. It intentionally resisted the FDIC's advice, denying office space and information access to FDIC examiners, and restricting the FDIC's examinations.[141]

Therefore, the three cases indicate the bounded rationality of the regulators in the run up to the TBTF bank structural problem from different aspects: making macro- and micro-economic policies, the failure of banking regulation, and the failure in ensuring compliance by the banks.

3 Behavioural factors: greed and the bank structural problem

This section analyses the bias caused by greed that contributed to the irrationality of market participants, mainly the industry, in the development of the TBTF bank structural problem. Within the context of BF, so-called 'animal spirits' played an important role in the economic wax and wane in history.[142] The classic economic assumption of the economic person is incomplete to a certain extent.[143] In the earlier poetic burgeoning period of capitalism, it might be fair to conclude that consumer protection was not the 'Achilles Heel' of capitalism. The reason is that the basic assumption of the economic person means that consumers are sufficiently rational such that they are always fully informed and well educated to know all relevant material facts in accordance with which decisions are to be made.[144]

Things have changed; the consumer protection problem has become more and more acute. Modern financial markets have grown to be so convoluted with ubiquitous uncertainty and obscurity. The markets and relevant products are so incomprehensible even for sophisticated investors and institutional investors.[145] In the pre-crisis financial boom, some of the most conspicuous characteristics of the markets were their ever-increasing complexity, interconnectedness, and homogeneousness. Complexity can impede sufficient disclosure and befuddle financial consumers.[146] Homogeneity and interconnectedness, however, could increase the possibility of contagion, aggravate an adverse situation, and lead to a domino effect should any negative situations arise.[147] Thus, investors were becoming so susceptible to the increasingly complicated financial markets that they could easily be exploited or manipulated. Contrary to the argument in classic economy theory, consumer protection is the 'Achilles Heel' of capitalism to a certain extent.

---

141 Ibid.
142 Akerlof and Shiller, *Animal spirits: how human psychology drives the economy, and why it matters for global capitalism*, pp. 11–56. See infra Chapter 4, Section 2.1.
143 Smith, *Wealth of nations*, pp. 362–363.
144 See supra Chapter 2, Section 1.
145 Schwarcz, 'Regulating complexity in financial markets'.
146 Steven L. Schwarcz, 'Disclosure's failure in the subprime mortgage crisis', Utah L Rev 1109.
147 Schwarcz, 'Regulating complexity in financial markets'.

For instance, the Save and Loan Association (S&Ls) recession in the 1990s happened in the days when the US government was trying to energise the gloomy economy. With government support, the S&Ls kept borrowing money from banks and engaging in risky credit extension. With the growth in the economy, inflation increased and put severe pressure on the S&Ls, as the cost of borrowing money became greater than the receipts from the mortgages they had issued. On the brink of collapse, the government allowed the S&Ls to invest in Milken junk bonds to refinance their debts for fear of more bankruptcies. These junk bonds further aggravated the risk underlying the S&Ls and finally doomed many to bankruptcy.[148] During the period of the boom and bust of the S&Ls, the investors definitely had no idea of the fraudulent behaviour that connected S&L assets with Milken junk bonds.

3.1 Firms' greed in the bank structural problem

It is widely accepted that the existence of misaligned incentives played a significant role in the development of the TBTF bank structural problem.[149] The proverbial culture of 'ripping off the client' helps us to figure out how the banking sector operated in the pre-crisis era.[150] When Greg Smith left Goldman Sachs, his criticism was that this largest and most important investment bank had veered far away from the place he had joined from college, and that the interests of the clients had been marginalised continuously. As a Goldman Sachs executive director and head of the firm's US equity derivatives business in Europe, the Middle East and Africa, he revealed many details about the exploitation of clients in this firm when he resigned.[151]

Various existing biases were identified earlier about the decision-making processes which make consumers susceptible to external risks in the banking sector.[152] It is plausible to argue that being familiar with all those biases, firms could devise specific product structures to make it more transparent or to use special marketing tactics so that they can minimise the influence that bias can have on investors' decision-making. At the very least, firms could avoid intentionally taking advantage of consumers' biased decision-making tendencies.

---

148 Akerlof and Shiller, *Animal spirits: how human psychology drives the economy, and why it matters for global capitalism*, pp. 30–33.
149 European Commission, *Commission staff working document impact assessment accompanying the document Proposal for a Regulation of the European Parliament and of the Council on structural measures improving the resilience of EU Credit Institutions and the Proposal for a Regulation of the European Parliament and of the Council on reporting and transparency of securities financing transactions, SWD/2014/030 final.* (January 29, 2014), pp. 12–13.
150 Greg Smith, *Why I left Goldman Sachs: a Wall Street story* (Oxford, UK: Hachette 2012), pp. 5–10.
151 Greg Smith, 'Why I am leaving Goldman Sachs', *New York Times*, www.nytimes.com/2012/03/14/opinion/why-i-am-leaving-goldman-sachs.html?_r=0, accessed December 12, 2013.
152 Amos Tversky and Daniel Kahneman, 'Rational choice and the framing of decisions', *Journal of Business* S251, see supra Chapter 2, Section 2.2.

However, animal spirits indicate that the firms would sometimes exploit these consumers' anomalies to maximise their own interests.[153] Even worse, knowing the behavioural attributes of investors' decisions and some 'predictable irrationality', firms could adjust their products, pricing, and promotion strategies to elicit wrong decisions by consumers.[154] Predictably irrational means that people are not only irrational but also predictably so. This means they can be easily tricked by others who are aware of this. An experiment conducted by Dan Ariely provided an *Economist* subscription offer to 100 students in MIT's Sloan School of Management. Among the three options: internet-only subscription for USD59, print-only subscription for USD125, and print-and-internet subscription for USD125, 16 chose the first, none chose the second, while 84 chose the third option. It seems that the second option is pointless compared with the third; however, Dan Ariely argued that the second option only acted as a decoy to elicit more students to choose the more expensive one rather than choose the more economic internet-only subscription. This experiment indicates that others who are aware of it could easily use the predictable irrationality of people.

Generally speaking, in the banking sector, being familiar with how investors make their decisions under the influence of anticipated preferences, beliefs, and decision-making anomalies, banks could easily take advantage of that knowledge.

For instance, knowing the social persuasion and 'feedback loop' propensity of investors, banks could always find a way to manipulate the feedback and persuasion channel. They do this through many strategies: investing more money in public media advertising, bragging about the fantastic economic outlook, exaggerating the advantage of the products, or enticing potential investors by providing some fresh examples of how people have attained double-digit investment returns. Before the crisis, Robert Schiller inferred that he had been repeatedly requested by some newspapers to provide a statement in support of some extremely radical view with regard to market outlook, and it was suggested he recommend some other scholars when he refused to do it.[155] Through reporting a radically optimistic economic outlook, the public's attention would be fixated on the marvellous economic outlook and the seemingly attractive investment opportunities. That is the reason why Schiller called the mass media a 'precipitating factor of the bubble'.[156]

Another example is that a firm could exploit the framing and limited attention propensity of investors. As indicated in the complaint of the S&P case, by providing more elusive presentations about the same information on their products, the banks and CRAs could influence consumers' decision-making. In other words, knowing the salience framing and the 'accessibility' mechanism of consumers,[157] firms tended

---

153 United States Senate Permanent Subcommittee on Investigations, *Wall Street and the financial crisis: anatomy of a financial collapse*, pp. 318–325.
154 Ariely and Jones, *Predictably irrational*, pp. 4–10.
155 Schiller, *Irrational exuberance*, pp. 71–95.
156 Ibid, pp. 17–44.
157 *The United States of America v. S&P, 12 U.S.C. § 1833a, 18 U.S.C. § 1341.*

to represent the same product information with some inconsequential framing to exactly take advantage of those consumers' irrationality. By doing so, they made investors choose in favour of firms without any awareness of the probable detriment to themselves.[158] The common approaches were changing the price structures, making it so complicated that it was beyond the comprehension of common consumers, or intentionally tailoring their products so that they were appealing to customers while actually not necessarily serving the best interests of the customers in the long run.[159]

In addition, behavioural factors would also facilitate a firm to gain market power or strengthen their market position. Because of the present bias, people tend to try to make decisions to preserve the status quo to a certain extent. As reported by some mass media, there is a higher possibility of people changing their wives or husbands rather than changing their bank accounts in modern times.[160] Therefore, it could be very easy for firms to gain and abuse their market power.[161] What is more, it should be noted that this situation could be further aggravated by the long-seated market inefficiency problems, such as information asymmetry, knowledge asymmetry, and market externalities.[162]

Among these currently widely accepted reasons for the bank structural problem, many correspond to greed-based irrationality: the executive compensation scheme and the corporate governance failure, the originate-to-distribute model, and the flawed CRA.[163] Due to a hunger for profits amid fierce competition, the executive compensation scheme developed into a kind of industry short-termism, which contradicts the principle of investment for the long run.[164] Industry greed was a driving force for the development of the originate-to-distribute model, which led to reckless credit extension and encouraged the expansion of securitisation disregarding potential risks, because the originator's revenues were tied to the volumes of transactions rather than the quality

---

158 Tversky and Kahneman, 'Rational choice and the framing of decisions'. See also Peter Hammond, 'Consequential behavior in decision trees and expected utility', *Institute for Mathematical Studies in the Social Sciences Working Paper*. It specifically introduces how people respond to immaterial changes with different decisions. It suggests that people should focus on material changes of factors.

159 Financial Conduct Authority, *Financial Conduct Authority (2013), Applying behavioral economics in Financial Conduct Authority, Occasional Paper No.1.* (2013).

160 Ibid, p. 9.

161 Financial Services Authority, 'A guide to market failure analysis and high level cost benefit analysis', www.fsa.gov.uk/pubs/other/mfa_guide.pdf, accessed December 8, 2014.

162 Steffen Huck and Jidong Zhou, 'Consumer behavioural biases in competition: a survey'. See also Spiegler, *Bounded rationality and industrial organization*.

163 See supra Chapter 2, Section 1.

164 Jeremy J. Siegel, *Stocks for the long run: the definitive guide to financial market returns and long-term investment strategies* (New York: McGraw-Hill 1998), pp. 21–22. Jeremy J. Siegel argued that over the past 200 years, the annual return of diversified portfolios was nearly 7%. The reason for this stock market consistency could be the fundamental forces producing economic growth led the stock market to pick up its value in spite of various economic or political turmoil. Siegel proposed a long-term investment strategy based on the fact that nobody can beat the market in the short term.

of their assets.[165] As regards the CRA, conflicts of interest compromised their rating independence and objectivity.[166]

Therefore, driven by greed in the industry, banks had the incentive to take advantage of investors' anomalies, and that played a significant role in the development of the TBTF bank structural problem.

3.2 Case study of S&P

The case study of S&P indicates how intentionally inflated credit ratings driven by the greed of the CRAs contributed to the development of the GFC and the TBTF bank structural problem.[167] S&P was actually sued by the US government for mail fraud, wire fraud, and financial institution fraud. The *United States v. S&P* reflects the problem that financial service providers could exploit heuristics of consumers and mislead their decision-making.[168]

(a) **CRAs and issuer's friendliness compromises rating objectivity.** Indicated by the US subcommittee's investigation, one of the key factors attributed to the inflation of ratings was the inherent conflict of interest arising from the system used to pay for CRAs' services.[169] As shown in the complaint of the case, S&P as one of the largest CRAs, represented on all relevant occasions before the crisis that its Structured Finance segment was considered by them to be a profit centre, and that Global CDO and Global ABS were growing areas of revenues. Therefore, the ratings agency treated issuers as customers and sources of profits.[170] For the sake of preserving the profit source, the aim of S&P was to preserve a 'business friendly' relationship with those issuers. That was evidenced by the fact that any time issuers withdrew their application for rating, S&P deemed it to be a 'lost deal'.[171] This implies that they simply treated the ratings as a profitable business, rather than purely a fair and impartial risk assessment service.[172]

Over the process of the development and modification of securitisation product evaluators, it was also found that due to conflicts of interest, S&P tended to

---

165 Avgouleas, *Governance of global financial markets: the law, the economics, the politics*, pp. 129–130.
166 Ibid, p. 130.
167 United States Senate Permanent Subcommittee on Investigations, *Wall Street and the financial crisis: anatomy of a financial collapse*, p. 5.
168 *The United States of America v. S&P, 12 U.S.C. § 1833a, 18 U.S.C. § 1341*, see the complaint.
169 United States Senate Permanent Subcommittee on Investigations, *Wall Street and the financial crisis: anatomy of a financial collapse*, pp. 7, 267.
170 *The United States of America v. S&P, 12 U.S.C. § 1833a, 18 U.S.C. § 1341*, see the complaint, p. 14. S&P really focused attention on boosting market share and strengthening their market competition. Providing ratings for structural debt securities was deemed to be one of the most important segments of their profits.
171 Ibid.
172 S&P's many interior documents, such as 'Code of Practices and Procedures' and 'Code of Conduct' constantly revealed that their ratings were objective and independent. See ibid, see the complaint, pp. 28–30.

let diligent risk evaluation give way to profit-making irrespective of the market deterioration before the crisis.[173] Long before the occurrence of crisis, quantitative analysis conducted by S&P indicated that the markets were changing and so did the risk potentials of those rated products. It was also known through research that the default assumption, which acted as the basic premise of the CDO Evaluator and the specific rating result it provided, was inaccurate and not consistent with the newly updated data. To adapt to the changing risks, a new CDO evaluator named E3 (CDO evaluator Version 3.0) was devised based on the former edition after dealing with some flaws. But, it was not implemented instantly because of the negative feedbacks it received from issuers. S&P conducted a poll among those issuers before implementation. Bear Stearns, among others, provided negative feedbacks and indicated that the updated high standard of ratings would harm those lowly rated asset pools (of which S&P had a huge market share) while contributing nothing to the highly rated asset pools (which S&P were trying to expand into).[174]

Therefore, it is not unfair to say that S&P had always been trying to maintain a benign client relationship with all those issuers who brought it profitable business. So, the two parties' interests were aligned in exploiting consumers' heuristic preference for certainty.[175] This can be reflected from its stance towards the need to update the CDO evaluator. It chose to preserve its currently high market share in non-investment grade deals and improve its currently low market share in investment grade synthetic CDO business by providing a client-favourable rating model.[176]

CRAs are supposed to be impartial and independent in terms of their rating service. However, if S&P esteemed revenue enhancing and profit maximisation as its main purposes, it cast enough doubt on its objectivity based on its conflicts of interest and the animal spirit theory.[177]

(b) They delayed and compromised the update of the RMBS and CDO evaluator model. For the sake of business need, S&P even delayed the update process of its risk evaluation model.[178] As a credit ratings agency, S&P was aware of the importance of the objectivity and independence of risk evaluation and its final rating grade. However, when it came to it in practice, principles gave way to

173   Ibid, see the complaint, pp. 48–55.
174   Ibid, see the complaint, pp. 49–50.
175   Tversky and Kahneman, 'Judgment under uncertainty: heuristics and biases'. See also DellaVigna, *Psychology and economics: evidence from the field.*
176   *The United States of America v. S&P, 12 U.S.C. § 1833a, 18 U.S.C. § 1341.* See the complaint, pp. 53–54. This business expansion plan could be seen from its many representations to the public and some correspondence of its employees.
177   Akerlof and Shiller, *Animal spirits: how human psychology drives the economy, and why it matters for global capitalism*, pp. 5–10.
178   United States Senate Permanent Subcommittee on Investigations, *Wall Street and the financial crisis: anatomy of a financial collapse. The United States of America v. S&P, 12 U.S.C. § 1833a, 18 U.S.C. § 1341,* see the complaint, p. 297.

pragmatism. According to its 2006 Strategic Plan, within the context of updating the evaluation model and the database, it believed:[179]

> Continuing to encourage and increase the need for rating overall is important as it ensures transactions will continue to be rated, however, having criteria and analytical tools that enable us to rate transactions and meet the needs of players in the market will ensure that S&P will continue to be the one agency rating [with] the largest share of transactions.

Although S&P regularly represented its trustfulness to the public, it did not practise what it preached.[180] In or around 2003, S&P assured investors that it had adapted its LEVELS model to the changing hidden risks of collateralised assets. However, this did not actually happen until around mid-2004 when S&P incorporated new data into the LEVEL model and launched the LEVELS 6.0 plan. This required a higher coverage of losses in order to receive an investment grade. After contentious debate within the company, LEVELS 6.0 plan was not successfully implemented as planned due to considerations of market share and profit levels. During 2005–2006, a modified version of the LEVELS 6.0 plan was issued, and it was not until 2007 that S&P finally published the LEVELS 6.0 plan. It was labelled LEVELS 6.0, but it was actually an adjusted version of the former LEVELS 6.0 plan made more favourable to issuers for the sake of boosting its market share.[181]

(c) Abuse of power, conflicts of interest, and knowingly disregarding changing circumstances added to risks. Prior to the growth in structural debt securities and the increasing dependence on ratings, the CRAs also had a good reputation for their independent and objective judgement. But that culture shifted starting in about 2000. After 2000, the previous academically oriented and conservative CRAs became more and more market oriented[182] due largely to the 'issuer-pays' model.

As indicated in the complaint, starting in or around 2006, the analysts in S&P noticed through statistical research that the markets were deteriorating and there was a rising ratio of delinquencies in the mortgages that were the underlying assets for the RMBS products. It predicted a high probability of the default risk bursting. Some working notes by employees in S&P revealed that 'the market is a wildly spinning top which is going to end badly'.[183] The official

---

179 *The United States of America v. S&P, 12 U.S.C. § 1833a, 18 U.S.C. § 1341*, see the complaint, pp. 52–56.
180 Ibid.
181 Ibid, see the pleading, pp. 48–49. It revealed much correspondence with regard to how the firm changed the evaluation model to finally get a favourable version for the client.
182 United States Senate Permanent Subcommittee on Investigations, *Wall Street and the financial crisis: anatomy of a financial collapse*, pp. 272–273.
183 *The United States of America v. S&P, 12 U.S.C. § 1833a, 18 U.S.C. § 1341*, see complaint, p. 62.

RMBS surveillance, which was responsible for the RMBS market volatility, also revealed that there was a bubble in the mortgage markets and that the bubble was deflating. This was further confirmed in an RMBS surveillance committee meeting that stated that these RMBS tranches were experiencing 'higher than expected delinquency and loss performance'.[184]

According to the model used to produce the CDOs,[185] if the RMBS products undergo a risk expansion and delinquency danger, it axiomatically means that those CDOs products would also undergo a higher default risk. This is because among the three kinds of CDOs, both Cash CDOs and Hybrid CDOs are collateralised fully or partly by RMBS products. Thus, a rational way of risk assessment is to downgrade accordingly those CDO products using RMBS assets as underlying assets. However, the standard practice at S&P when rating CDOs was simply to accept the underlying assets at face value.[186]

Therefore, based on the given conflict of interest in the 'issuer-pays' model, it was not in the interests of the CRAs to provide accurate ratings for the risky structural debt securities. The desire for profit and greed within the industry made them easily take advantage of investors' predictable irrationality.

Other than CRAs' conflicts of interest, there was even evidence to suggest that investment banks and hedge funds conspired to exploit the irrational investors after the negative situation started to emerge. For instance, Goldman marketed Abacus securities to clients knowing that the underlying assets for this CDO were intentionally poorly chosen by Paulson & Co. Inc. It even knew that as a result of these poorly chosen assets, Paulson & Co. Inc. would actually bet against the CDO. Finally, it transpired that Paulson & Co. Inc. profited hugely from the scheme, while ignorant investors such as IKB suffered enormous losses.[187]

Therefore, the S&P case shows that inflated credit ratings driven by the greed of the CRAs exploited the predicable irrationality of investors and contributed to the development of the GFC and the TBTF bank structural problem.

4 Adaptive market hypothesis and the bank structural problem

Having undertaken much analysis on irrationality in the preceding sections, it should be noted that the purpose of behavioural analysis is to apply it to improving legal regulation in the banking sector, which we look at in Chapters 3 to 6. For that to happen, a theoretical argument on the normative attribute of behavioural finance theory needs to be addressed.[188]

---

184 Ibid, see the complaint, pp. 62–66.
185 All the CDOs structural debt securities are structured on the basis of many underlying assets, which include RMBS, credit derivatives, or a hybrid of RMBS assets and credit derivatives. See also Avgouleas, *Governance of global financial markets: the law, the economics, the politics*, pp. 40–49.
186 *The United States of America v. S&P, 12 U.S.C. § 1833a, 18 U.S.C. § 1341*, see the complaint, p. 97.
187 *Securities and Exchange Commission v. Goldman, Sachs & Co. and Fabrice Tourre.*
188 Tversky and Kahneman, 'Rational choice and the framing of decisions', pp. 251–253.

4.1 Adaptive Market Hypothesis and firms' greed in the bank structural problem

As regards applying behavioural theory normatively to law, there is always a criticism: compared with the reasonable person assumption under classic economy theory, behavioural finance might be more 'descriptively' accurate in terms of arguing the irrational aspects of humans, but it can do no better than the reasonable and economic person assumption in guiding legal regulation 'normatively', because it implies the existence of uncertainties but is unable to capture or predict them. The rule of law could be more effectively established based on the predictability of human behaviours, not the contrary.[189]

To a certain extent, the emergence of the Adaptive Market Hypothesis (AMH) makes up for the drawbacks of the previous BF theory by compensating for its normatively inadequate attribute. Andrew Lo theorises the AMH. He advocates that:

> Market actors ultimately struggle not for optional returns (as the EMH holds) – optimization is costly – but for survival, like all living species in an evolutionary framework, they behave sometimes rationally, sometimes irrationally, depending on the strategy that suits best their struggle for survival.[190]

The AMH disagrees with the EMH hypothesis of rationality; it also modifies the BF bounded rationality hypothesis. It argues a comparative middle ground hypothesis that people act motivated by the need for survival; they are neither completely rational nor complete irrational.[191]

He argues that valid evidence for the evolution of the human brain suggests that the reason for evolution is to maximise the survival potential of human beings, first serving basic survival needs and then facilitating the natural selection process.[192] The new approach implies that people's behaviour is not necessarily driven by intrinsic and exogenous motivations, but by natural selection processes and maximising the possibility of preserving their genetic material.

Different from Daniel Kahneman and Amos Tversky's irrationality hypothesis, AMH provides limited certainty behind the irrationality assumption in BF. This adds to the predictability of the theory and makes up for the normative paradox to a certain extent. From this perspective, the financial institutions were not completely irrational; their irrationality was driven by their need for survival. They

---

189 Ibid. See supra Introduction, Section 4.2. See also infra Chapter 4, Section 2.3.3.
190 Avgouleas, *Governance of global financial markets: the law, the economics, the politics*, pp. 62–64. See also Lo, 'Reconciling efficient markets with behavioral finance: the adaptive markets hypothesis'.
191 Tversky and Kahneman, 'Rational choice and the framing of decisions'.
192 According to Lo, there is a time sequence in the evolution of three main important parts of the brain. First, the brainstem which controls the basic body movements; then the limbic system which controls human emotion and instinct; and finally, cerebral cortex which allows us to think logically.

were acting irrationally under the pressure of survival so that they emphasised the short-term interest-oriented investment strategy and the transaction-volume-based compensation scheme, regardless of the hidden risks.[193]

This argument is reflected to some extent by the irrational exuberance of the financial markets and the banking industry before the crisis in Europe.[194] For instance, in Iceland, the emergence of the bank expansion overseas was because of the survival needs of the banks amid the interest rate policy introduced to fight against high inflation in the country in the last decades of the twentieth century. To develop under fierce competition, domestic banks needed to expand overseas to take advantage of the interest rate difference. This could be seen in the disproportional overseas business in the three biggest banks in Iceland.[195] Furthermore, the acceleration of the overseas strategy was also intertwined with the change in the debt structure: the overdependence on short-term wholesale markets rather than traditional deposit markets.[196] The Icelandic bank international expansion to the UK, Luxembourg, and other Nordic countries was accompanied by high indebtedness. Banks did not realise or intentionally neglected the fact that such an aggressive race for survival could backfire on them.

Thus, AMH could be a plausible theory to analyse the expansion in the pre-crisis banking industry. It could be advocated that those expansionary behaviours were driven by the survival need of firms within a competitive industry, so that they tended to disregard the catastrophic impact of their behaviour.[197] By taking the middle ground between classic economy theory and BF, AMH, as a new school of BF, adds limited certainty to people's irrationality and offers a more solid basis for normative legal intervention.

4.2 Case study of Northern Rock

The Northern Rock case could illustrate how the greed of the industry promoted a business expansion driven by the need for survival. When it comes to reflecting on the Northern Rock collapse, one could easily characterise it as a typical case of a 'bank run', which technically means that the customers or the depositors of the bank line up in front of the bank to withdraw money due to fears over the safety of their deposits and market volatility.[198] The distinctive part of this case was that the damage to the bank had already been done before

---

193 See Lo, 'Reconciling efficient markets with behavioral finance: the adaptive markets hypothesis', see also Andrew W Lo, 'The adaptive markets hypothesis', 30 *The Journal of Portfolio Management* 15.
194 Liikanen Erkki, *High-level Expert Group on reforming the structure of the EU banking sector*, pp. 11–19.
195 Spruk, 'Iceland's financial and economic crisis: causes, consequences and implications'.
196 Liikanen Erkki, *High-level Expert Group on reforming the structure of the EU banking sector*, pp. 14–15.
197 Ibid, pp. 38–39.
198 Gunnarsson, 'The Icelandic regulatory responses to the financial crisis'. See also Jännäri, 'Report on banking regulation and supervision in Iceland: past, present and future'.

the retail depositors withdrew their money. This enables us to think of this bank liquidity crisis in a different way.

Northern Rock was originally a 'building society' because it was mutually owned, and it can be dated back to the nineteenth-century cooperative movement. So, Northern Rock was originally a traditional local bank serving local clients. But, after the 'Big Bang', many traditional banks took advantage of the changes to expand their businesses amid ever intensifying competition. Northern Rock's assets grew from £17.4 billion to £113.5 billion, with an annual growth of 23.2%.[199] As the fifth biggest mortgage bank, its ever-increasing mortgage business and services pressed on with a change to the traditional retail deposits-based funds. Thus, non-retail funds loomed large and were employed to serve the business's expansion. Statistics showed that the retail to total assets ratio fell from 60% in 1998 to 23% in June 2007.

Among the various sources of funding, the most popularly used by Northern Rock were securitised notes, interbank deposits, and covered bonds.[200] Securitised notes were similar in nature to the securitisation process, though the way in which they operated was different from that in the US or other EU countries.

Acting as the originator, Northern Rock initially transferred part of the mortgage assets into a trust company, which entered into a contract with special purpose entities.[201] Then, the special purpose entities signed a contract with another note-issuing company who acted as the note-issuer. A prominent difference with the Northern Rock securitised note was that it normally had a long maturity period, which was in contrast to the short-term maturity liabilities (needing to be rolled over several times a year) in the US and other EU countries. In that sense, it seemed that this kind of securitised note was even a little safer than that in other countries.[202]

However, the irrationality here was the overdependence on different kinds of non-retail funds while marginalising the importance of the retail deposits. According to Northern Rock's 2007 annual report, one of the most prominent differences about the funds was that retail deposits in the form of postal accounts, offshore accounts, Internet accounts, or branch accounts dropped significantly from £24.4 billion to £10.5 billion.[203]

In addition, leverage finance was overutilised. It is common for monetary financial institutions to make use of leveraging. But a balance should be maintained between profit maximisation through excessive risky leveraged finance, and safety and soundness. In principle, the way to determine the leverage ratio should

---

199 Hyun Song Shin, 'Reflections on Northern Rock: the bank run that heralded the global financial crisis', *The Journal of Economic Perspectives* 101, pp. 101–103.

200 Ibid, pp. 103–104. 'Covered bonds are long-term liabilities written against segregated mortgages assets', so they are illiquid in nature.

201 Avgouleas, *Governance of global financial markets: the law, the economics, the politics*, pp. 40–44.

202 Ibid, pp. 40–47.

203 Hyun Song Shin, 'Reflections on modern bank runs: a case study of Northern Rock' 23 *Journal of Economic Perspectives* 101.

be in line with the market environment. Specifically, it is normally determined by the maximum leverage possible in repurchase agreements according to the 'haircut'.[204] The haircut fluctuates a lot in accordance with funding conditions, and the fluctuations largely determine the leveraging of banks.

The characteristic of the leverage (assets to equity ratio) is that it always fluctuates according to the slightest volatility in the haircut because of the interaction of the borrowing multipliers.[205] In terms of the risk of using leveraging, any identification of more risk could cause a significant pullback in leveraging, which would put a lot of pressure on a highly leveraged bank. Thus, a reasonable bank would need to maintain a balanced and flexible balance sheet to deal with such unexpected situations.

Building on this and assuming a static environment where the haircut is constant, what would make the fluctuation more severe and the leverage more vulnerable would be the broad categorisation of the denominator. This means that although the nominal leverage is constant according to the constant haircut, the asset exposures could be larger if one applies an oddly broad categorisation of equity. This was what Northern Rock did.[206] It deliberately included not only common equity, but also preferred shares and subordinated debt, which were not supposed to be categorised as equity because they are not within the firm's direct control, and hence should not be in the total equity denominator. The direct result was that the leverage ratio was even more vulnerable as a result of this manipulation.

Under the competitive financial markets and the context of the 'Big-Bang' policy, banks tended to expand their business and enhance their market shares to survive, and that makes sense according to the AMH theory.[207] However, under the motive of survival, leveraged banks also made themselves more susceptible to market fluctuations.[208] Northern Rock's failure was a leverage-based failure isolated from other companies.[209] This is how it happened: the bank's funding relied largely on wholesale funding from another monetary financial institution (MFI) (B), which occasionally also had exposures to another MFI (C). When B suffered losses through its exposure to C, then B has to wind down its current assets and

204 The repurchase agreement is to sell a security at a price lower than the current market price, then buy it back in the future at a designated price set in advance; the difference between the price at which it is sold, and the current market price is called a haircut. For instance, if the haircut is 2%, then the borrower can get USD98 for each USD100, and then use the USD98 as a guarantee to borrow more, and so forth. See also Financial Stability Board, 'Strengthening oversight and regulation of shadow banking: an overview of policy recommendation' (August 29, 2013).

205 According to the leverage algorithm, if the haircut is 2%, the leverage is 50, which means that if one wants to borrow USD100 one must come up with a guarantee of USD2. If market conditions turn bad and the haircut changes to 4%, then the maximum leverage is 25. For a bank with an original leverage of 50, the losses would be catastrophic. It is obvious that fluctuations in the leverage could be massive, even from a slight change in the haircut rate.

206 Shin, 'Reflections on Northern Rock: the bank run that heralded the global financial crisis', pp. 113–115.

207 Lo, 'Reconciling efficient markets with behavioral finance: the adaptive markets hypothesis'.

208 Lo, 'The adaptive markets hypothesis'.

209 Shin, 'Reflections on modern bank runs: a case study of Northern Rock'.

debts, which meant reducing its lending to Northern Rock and thereby drying out its funds. The transformation of short-term liability and long-term asset (such as loans) is always a paradox: it is desired by all MFIs but also brings extra risks.[210]

5 Conclusion: behavioural finance, two attributes, and possible solutions

In sum, this chapter has looked at the behavioural analyses of the TBTF bank structural problem. It has shown that behavioural factors played a significant role in the development of the bank structural problem from many aspects: (i) the preferences, beliefs, and decision-making processes of investors; (ii) the ignorance of government policies; (iii) the greed of the banking sector and other participants including CRAs; and (iv) banks' level of risk-taking driven by the need for survival.

We explained the two attributes of the structural problem.[211] First, it further confirmed the structural attribute of the TBTF structural problem, which was discussed in detail in Chapter 1.[212] The analysis showed that in the development of the problem, behavioural factors loomed large in the trading-oriented entities and activities, rather than in traditional banking activities. Second, it elaborated and highlighted the risk-taking and cyclicality attribute of the structural problem, which was briefly referred to in Chapter 1.[213] It can be seen in aspects, such as the risk-taking inclination of investors, the naturally Ponzi scheme, the greed of the banking sector and CRAs, the need for survival of the banks, etc.[214]

These analyses also act as the foundation for further discussion on the revamp of regulations on separation and resolution to deal with the TBTF bank structure problem. The behavioural analyses provide a fundamental theoretical support for the necessity for and extent of a structural separation reform. By explaining the provident cyclical attribute in the universal banking model, it also provides a fundamental basis for the necessity and extent of resolution reform as a complementary measure against the backdrop of structural separation reform.[215]

---

210 Shin, H. S. (2009). 'Reflections on Northern Rock: the bank run that heralded the global financial crisis', *The Journal of Economic Perspectives* 101–120.
211 For detailed analysis of the cyclical attribute see infra Chapter 3, Section 5.
212 See supra Chapter 1, Section 5.
213 See supra Chapter 1, Section 5.
214 See supra Chapter 2, Section 4.
215 See infra Chapter 5, Section 6.3.

3 The decoupling approach
Bank structural reform in the EU

After analysing the non-negligible influence that behavioural factors had on the development of the TBTF bank structural problem, Chapter 3 concentrates on explaining the current Bank Structural Reform (BSR) proposal that has been made by the EC, with a reference to the similar yet different regulation reforms in the US (the Volcker Rule) and the UK (the ring-fence rule). Chapter 4 conducts a Market Failure Analysis (MFA) of the BSR. It tries to argue that the structural separation rule, unlike other price-based reforms that have no regard to behavioural factors, can directly contain the behavioural anomalies that contributed to the development of the TBTF bank structural problem. Then, Chapter 5 carries out a Cost Benefit Analysis (CBA) of the BSR, which aims to analyse the economic efficiency of the reform from a comparative perspective.

The rationale for the structural reform can be explained by the decoupling approach used by engineers referred to as the 'chained battleship' metaphor.[1] Chapter 1 concludes that the engineering problem and the TBTF bank structural problem have some similarities: the huge size, their interconnectedness and complexity, ignorance of low probability events, and the domino effect in a collapse.[2] Thus, the solution to the TBTF bank structural problem may be similar to the solutions offered by engineers.

The decoupling method used by engineers refers to the design of different and independent compartments to prevent the failure of one part of an entity from automatically giving rise to the failure of the remaining parts. Similarly, a new regulation towards banks would probably be effective if it were to separate relationship-oriented activities (mostly traditional banking activities) from the risky transaction-oriented activities and even provide a channel whereby healthy entities can offer the ailing entities assistance when necessary.[3]

Steven Schwarcz also advocates such a proposition. He points out that decoupling mechanisms with the characteristics of modularity would reduce

---

1 See supra Chapter 1, Section 2.
2 See Financial Stability Oversight Council, *Study of the effects of size and complexity of financial institutions on capital market efficiency and economic growth* (January 2011). See also Steven L. Schwarcz, 'Protecting financial markets: lessons from the subprime mortgage meltdown', 93 Minn L Rev 373.
3 Emilios Avgouleas, *The reform of 'Too-Big-To-Fail' bank: a new regulatory model for the institutional separation of 'casino' from 'utility' banking* (2010), pp. 6–9. See supra Chapter 1, Section 4(b).

the possibility that the failure of one part of a complex system could cause the failure of other parts.[4] When a component of a system fails, modularity allows repairs to be undertaken before the entire system is contaminated and destroyed.[5] The structural reform and compartment solution is also consistent with the 'chaos theory', which advocates that failure tends to happen in a complex system, but a good system is the one which minimises the consequences of a potential failure.[6]

The argument sounds very rational, but there are controversies with regard to how the decoupling approach should be structured.[7] In terms of a wholesale return to the Glass-Steagall Act regulations, many argue that it is overly costly. On the compromise made by the Dodd-Frank Act to curb speculative investment banking and other risky activities through the Volcker Rule, there are also many critiques suggesting that it does not eradicate the structural problem completely.

Within the EU, research originally focused on the Vickers Rule and the Liikanen Report arguing for ring-fencing through two different approaches. The ring-fence approach gained a certain momentum because many believed that a moderate rule rather than an absolute separation rule would be more economically appropriate. That makes sense in terms of the fact that the EU is dubbed 'a system of battle' and it is not easy to implement a radical reform that requires resolute political choice.[8]

However, the EC proposal (the BSR) adopted a mixed approach between the Volcker prohibition rule and the Vickers ring-fence rule. In the trade-off between financial competitiveness and stability, how to structure the separation rule to effectively deal with the TBTF structural problem warrants closer examination.

1 The regulatory context of the EU bank structural reform

The IMF report (2013) introduced two fundamental approaches to deal with the structural problem: the price-based approach and the structural approach.[9]

1.1 The price-based approach

The price-based approach mainly referred to the capital requirement, the leverage requirement, and additional capital buffer requirement. The structural-based

---

4 Steven L. Schwarcz, 'Regulating complexity in financial markets', 87 Wash UL Rev 211.
5 Henry E. Smith, 'Modularity in contracts: boilerplate and information flow', Michigan Law Review 1175.
6 Lawrence A. Cunningham, 'From random walks to chaotic crashes: the linear genealogy of the efficient capital market hypothesis', 62 Geo Wash L Rev 546.
7 Julian T.S. Chow, *Making banks safer: can Volcker and Vickers do it?* (New York: International Monetary Fund 2011)
8 Niamh Moloney and Jennifer G. Hill, *The regulatory aftermath of the global financial crisis* (Cambridge, UK: Cambridge University Press 2012), pp. 55–83. Eilis Ferran explains how conflicting opinions between the Commission and the Parliament and between different Member States influence the regulatory progress. Eilis Ferran and Valia S.G. Babis, 'The European single supervisory mechanism', University of Cambridge Faculty of Law Research Paper.
9 See supra Chapter 1, Section 4.

approach is to limit the scope and size of banks so that the hidden risks can be restricted to an appropriate scale.[10] Based on the evolution of post-crisis regulatory reform, it transpires that the former and on-going relevant price-based regulation reforms cannot deal with the structural problem directly and effectively by itself. The reason is that they only enhance the resilience of the banking sector insofar as they promote the loss-absorbency capacity. But, they could not contain the fundamental reason for loss, such as interconnectedness and the complexity and resolvability problem, let alone the underlying behavioural factors.[11] So far, the regulatory authorities in the EU have adopted several price-based measures, most of which are explained below.

1.2 The price-based measures

The first price-based rule that is worth mentioning is the capital requirements in Capital Requirements Directive IV (CRD IV) and Capital Requirements Regulation (CRR).[12] Similar to the Basel III capital requirements, they address the capital inadequacy problem in the banking industry directly by requiring a higher tier 1 capital ratio, additional tier 1 capital ratio, and total assets capital ratio and leverage ratio.[13] These standards can make banks safer and more resilient in any situation of financial deterioration or market instability because of the higher capacity to absorb losses. However, it does not address the systemic risk in financial market transactions. Specifically, the risk-weighted assets model, upon which capital requirements depend, cannot capture or reflect all of the underlying risks in financial markets, especially fat-tail risk and systemic risk.[14] This means that the capital requirements could not provide sufficient capacity to absorb bank losses because of the limits to economic models, even though they would be strictly implemented. Statistics indicate that the ratio of Risk-Weighted Assets (RWAs) to non-RWAs was decreasing in the run up to the GFC.[15] Unfortunately, it was exactly those risks that were not captured that triggered the TBTF bank structural problem, and that the legislators have now been trying to resolve.

Second, a reform of corporate governance is also being carried out. Although there are many corporate governance requirements advocated by the CRD IV,

---

10 José Viñals and others, *Creating a safer financial system: will the Volcker, Vickers, and Liikanen Structural measures help?* (New York: International Monetary Fund 2013), pp. 5–6.

11 Liikanen Erkki, *High-level Expert Group on reforming the structure of the EU banking sector* (Final Report, Brussels, 2012), pp. 88–90.

12 See Directive 2013/36/EU of the European Parliament and of the Council of 26 June 2013 on access to the activity of credit institutions and the prudential supervision of credit institutions and investment firms, amending Directive 2002/87/EC and repealing Directives 2006/48/EC and 2006/49/EC [2013] OJ L 176/338(CRD IV). See also Regulation (EU) No 575/2013 of the European Parliament and of the Council of 26 June 2013 on prudential requirements for credit institutions and investment firms and amending Regulation (EU) No 648/2012 [2013] OJ L 176/1(CRR). They stipulate general rules with regard to capital requirement, risk exposure, etc.

13 Basel Committee on Banking Supervision, 'Basel III: a global regulatory framework for more resilient banks and banking systems', Basel Committee on Banking Supervision, Basel, pp. 68–69.

14 See supra Chapter 1, Section 3(c).

15 Independent Commission on Banking, 'Final Report, recommendations', pp. 98–99.

they can only be useful on the condition that an authoritative management mechanism and board of directors, and a stringent accountability system can be established.[16] Otherwise, the effectiveness of the entire corporate governance mechanism would still be unpredictable.

Third, the supervision system has also been strengthened. In December 2012, great progress was made; eurozone finance ministers agreed a plan to cede power to a common bank supervisor based on an EC proposal on EBU in September 2012.[17] The EBU includes an SSM (Single Supervisory Mechanism). The EU adopted the SSM Regulation in 2013.[18] Some argue that the SSM is flawed in its ambiguity of governance, its relationships with non-euro States and NCAs.[19] Therefore, the problem of a lack of coordination persists whilst the Member States are still the main power to exert the mandate of supervision. The direct result will be a lack of consistency in implementation.

Fourth, there are also higher requirements of transparency, disclosure, and consumer protection.[20] The fact is that increasing evidence shows enhanced transparency and disclosure would not be as effective as expected in making investors better informed due to their incentives for risk-taking and the problem of consumers' limited cognitive competency.[21] In the EU, consumer protection might be strengthened by disclosure requirements in the Markets in Financial Instruments Directive II (MiFID II) and MiFIR, but disclosure is not sufficient to deal with consumer protection by itself.

Overall, the price-based measures are unable to efficiently deal with systemic risk. They do not tackle certain core problems, such as interconnectedness and the resolvability problem, nor the underlying behavioural factors. The two aspects of the structural problem, the co-existence of activities and the systemic risk and

16 See CRD IV, art 88 and art 95.
17 European Commission, *Communication from the Commission to the European Parliament and the Council: a roadmap towards a banking union, COM(2012) 510 final* (September 12, 2012), pp. 2–3.
18 Regulation (EU) No 1024/2013 of 15 October 2013 conferring specific tasks on the European Central Bank concerning policies relating to the prudential supervision of credit institutions [2013] OJ L 287/63 (SSM Regulation).
19 Eddy Wymeersch, 'The European Banking Union, a first analysis'. Zhai Xiaowei, 'The EU's crisis management and financial law reform: analysis of a Consolidated EU banking regulatory mechanism', 3 *Journal of Yunnan University Law Edition* 153.
20 Directive 2014/65/EU of the European Parliament and of the Council of 15 May 2014 on markets in financial instruments and amending Directive 2002/92/EC and Directive 2011/61/EU[2014] OJ L173/349(MiFID II). Regulation (EU) No 600/2014 of the European Parliament and of the Council of 15 May 2014 on markets in financial instruments and amending Regulation (EU) No 648/2012[2014] OJ L173/84(MiFIR). See generally MiFID II and MiFIR.
21 Omri Ben-Shahar and Carl E. Schneider, 'The futility of cost-benefit analysis in financial disclosure regulation', 43 *The Journal of Legal Studies* S253. See also Omri Ben-Shahar and Carl E. Schneider, 'The failure of mandated disclosure', *University of Pennsylvania Law Review* 647. There are two basic reasons for the ineffectiveness of the enhanced transparency and disclosure rule. The first one is the motivation and the competency of the investors. Disclosure is always about complicated and convoluted issues. Piling up of information would somehow make it impossible for the investors to handle the burden of understanding and analysing the information they are exposed to. In that circumstance, according to behavioural theory, the human cognitive mechanism tends to

resolvability problem, are intertwined. They need to be dealt with in tandem by additional reforms other than price-based measures.

2 Bank structural reform in the EU and other jurisdictions

As referred to in Chapter 1, the TBTF bank structural problem has four main features that bring about immense perils to the entire financial sector and the overall economy: (i) behemoth size, (ii) complexity and interconnectedness, (iii) ignoring low probability events (systemic risk) in trading-oriented services, and (iv) the domino effect of collapses (the spill over effect).[22]

2.1 The EU bank structural problem

The connotation of the TBTF bank structural problem is very broad. As indicated in an EC consultation paper, large EU banking groups are faced with many problems: 'balance sheet expansion, higher leverage, lack of market discipline, lack of bank resolvability, excessive risk-taking, trading and market based activities, implicit bail-out expectation, competitive distortion, and conflict of interest'.[23] These issues should not be discussed on a stand-alone basis. They are all intertwined, and all of these issues converge on the bank structural problem to a certain extent.

But the core and denotation of the TBTF bank structural problem is still the 'unrestricted co-existence of core banking functions and trading activities within large banks', distorted incentives for banks, and difficulties in supervision and resolution.[24] It represents the transformation from customer-oriented services to trade-oriented services. Given that the systemic risk and the resolvability problem could not be addressed by price-based measures,[25] structural separation reform is probably the most promising instrument in the future to deal with the current unresolved structural problem in the EU.

---

simplify information they are exposed to and meaning they rely on some heuristics, such as wishful thinking. The direct result is that being provided with probably all the necessary information, the investors would still fail to grasp the potential risks in their investments. That is also why the SEC approved a summary prospectus, which requires disclosure in 'plain English' and in a succinct way: 'three or four pages'. The second reason is the clouding effect that one disclosure might have on another. For instance, there is one disclosure about the payment of a mortgage, the second is about the insurance and guarantee the creditor requires. So, the attention of an investor is somehow divided into two parts due to the two disclosures, and the understanding of one disclosure might obfuscate the understanding of the other. In the real financial dynamics, the disclosure would be innumerable in number, which would make the clouding effect more complicated. The more complicated the clouding effect, the less likely the investors in the financial markets are able to make sound decisions in an informed way.

22 See Chapter 1, Section 3.

23 European Commission, *EU Commission consultation paper, consultation reforming the structure of the EU banking sector* (2013), p. 2.

24 European Commission, *Commission staff working document impact assessment accompanying the document Proposal for a Regulation of the European Parliament and of the Council on structural measures improving the resilience of EU Credit Institutions and the Proposal for a Regulation of the European Parliament and of the Council on reporting and transparency of securities financing transactions, SWD/2014/030 final.* (January 29, 2014), pp. 8–11.

25 Viñals and others, *Creating a safer financial system: will the Volcker, Vickers, and Liikanen Structural measures help?* pp. 5–6.

2.2 Legislative progress in the EU and other economies

In the aftermath of the GFC, many jurisdictions have started reforming bank regulations. The bank structural reform is, among others, a critical part of their agenda, which denotes the separation of retail and commercial banking from investment banking and trading activities. So far, reforming structural separation has given rise to many heated discussions in major economies. In the EU, the rules are still in a legislation-making phase. But, in the US and the UK, detailed rules have been adopted (Box 3.1).

The High-level Expert Group drafted a structural reform proposal to the EC in October 2012.[26] In May 2013, the EC provided a follow-up consultation paper to the Liikanen Report, 'Reforming the Structure of the EU Banking Sector'.[27] The reform initiative is making progress to a certain extent.[28] On the contrary, the EU parliament was hesitant about reform, stating that although the Glass-Steagall Act 'helped to provide a way out of the worst global financial crisis occur[ing] in the US before the present crisis', there are still insufficient evidence in the financial industry to assess the effect of the separation rules in preventing the reoccurrence of crisis in the future.[29]

In December 2013, the European Commissioner Michael Barnier said in response to the newly adopted Volcker Rule in the US: 'we also have such plans in Europe, I confirm that we will present it in the coming weeks – at the beginning of January – a proposal on the structure of banks'.[30] The Commissioner's words were confirmed after one month. Following many sessions of consultation in the banking industry and analysing possible reform options, the EC adopted a 'proposal for a regulation on structural measures improving the resilience of EU credit institutions' in January 2014 (the BSR).[31]

Indeed, compared with the reforms in the EU, the US has already made substantive legislative progress on its structural reform. On December 10, 2013, The Federal Reserve System (FED), the Security Exchange Commission (SEC), and The Federal Deposit Insurance Corp (FDIC) approved a final rule (the 'final rule'),[32] implementing section 619 of the Dodd-Frank Act, which was commonly referred as the 'Volcker Rule'.[33] The long-awaited 'final rule' attracted extremely

---

26 Liikanen Erkki, *High-level Expert Group on reforming the structure of the EU banking sector*, pp. i–ii.
27 European Commission, *EU Commission consultation paper, Consultation Reforming the structure of the EU banking sector*.
28 Ibid, pp. 1–3. It gives a comprehensive analysis of current problems that the banking structural reform has to address and provides some options with regard to the scope and strength of structural reform.
29 Arlene McCarthy, *Report on reforming the structure of the EU banking sector (2013/2021(INI))*, *European Parliament Committee on Economic and Monetary Affairs*, pp. 7–8.
30 European Commission, *Commissioner Michel Barnier remarks following the ECOFIN Council meeting-on single resolution mechanism / bank recovery and resolution directive and deposit guarantee schemes package (MEMO/13/1133)* (December 11, 2013).
31 European Commission, *Proposal for a Regulation of the European Parliament and of the Council on structural measures improving the resilience of EU credit institutions,COM/2014/043 final* (January 29, 2014).
32 Prohibitions and Restrictions on Proprietary Trading and Certain Interests In, and Relationships With, Hedge Funds and Private Equity Funds (The Final Rule) (U.S).
33 The Dodd-Frank Wall Street Reform and Consumer Protection Act (U.S), section 619.

intense public debate. The final rule is 71 pages long, and the 'supplemental information', which is important for the understanding of the rule, is 900 pages long. It erects new hurdles for banks to commit trading activities and market-making activities.[34]

Compared with the EU, the UK has also made very promising legislative progress towards structural reform. It set up an Independent Commission on Banking (ICB) in June 2010, chaired by Sir John Vickers to review and make recommendations on the structure of the banking sector. It aimed to find out how to reform the structure of the banking sector to increase competition and at the same time maintain financial stability. Later, the ICB published its final report in September 2011 (the Vickers Rule).[35] Based on the ICB final report, the UK government published a White Paper in 2012, 'Banking Reform: Delivering Stability and Supporting a Sustainable Economy', which set out the proposals for reform of the banking sector.[36] The 'Banking Reform Act' was passed in December 2013. But many detailed separation and implementation rules have still not been laid down as yet.[37]

At the EU Member State level, many economies, such as France, Germany, Belgium, and the Netherlands have also been working on structural reform in the banking industry. In December 2012, the French Ministry of Finance presented a draft law proposal introducing a bank resolution framework and placing restrictions on certain 'speculative activities'.[38] The proposal requires banks to create a separate subsidiary to undertake speculative activities, which includes proprietary trading and acquiring financial operations and sponsoring leveraged investment trusts (e.g. hedge funds) and other similar investment vehicles. Subsequently, French law no. 2013-672 on the separation and regulation of banking activities was enacted on July 27, 2013. The reform generally relates to the separation of proprietary trading activities from vital banking activities and strengthening the powers of supervisory authorities and other regulatory agencies.[39] In addition, it also includes the creation of a new regime for the recovery and resolution of financial institutions.[40] Germany has also passed a new bill on bank structural reform. On June 7, 2013, the Act on Ring Fencing and Recovery and Resolution Planning for Credit Institutions and Financial Groups (Gesetz zur Abschirmung von Risiken und zur Planung der Sanierung und Abwicklung von Kreditinstituten und Finanzgruppen) was approved.[41]

34 Ryan Tracy and Stephanie Armour Scott Patterson, 'FDIC, FED, SEC vote to approve Volcker rule – FDIC, FED board vote unanimously to appove long-delayed rule for banks, SEC approves in a 3–2 vote', *Wall Street Journal*, http://online.wsj.com/news/articles/SB100014240527023 0356020457924973284159 2834, accessed November 21, 2014.
35 Independent Commission on Banking, 'Final Report, recommendations'.
36 HM Treasury, *Banking reform: delivering stability and supporting a sustainable economy* (June, 2012).
37 Banking Reform Act 2013 (UK).
38 Édouard Fernandez-Bollo, 'Structural reform and supervision of the banking sector in France', 2013 *OECD Journal: Financial Market Trends* 1.
39 French law no. 2013-672 of 26 July 2013 on the separation and regulation of banking activities.
40 Ibid.
41 Trennbankengesetz (GermanBankSeparationLaw) which is included in Article 2 of the Gesetz zur Abschirmung von Risiken und zur Planung der Sanierung und Abwicklung von Kreditinstituten und Finanzgruppen (Law concerning Separation of Risks and Restructuring and Winding-Up of Credit Institutions and Financial Groups), BGBl. 2013 I Nr. 47, 3090.

Box 3.1 The structural reform timeline

The timeline of the EU BSR

- Liikanen Report – Commissioner Michel Barnier announced his decision to set up a High-level Expert Group on reforming the structure of the EU banking sector (Chaired by Governor Erkki Liikanen) in November 2011. On October 2, 2012 the Group presented the 'Liikanen Report'.
- Proposal on banking structural reform – On January 29, 2014, the EC adopted the BSR proposal for regulations to prohibit the biggest banks from engaging in risky proprietary trading. It also gives national supervisors discretion to require those banks to separate certain potentially risky trading activities from their deposit-taking business if engagement in such activities compromises financial stability.
- After adopting the proposal, despite the difficulties in reaching an agreement on the regulation, the Committee on Economic and Monetary Affairs (ECON) and the Council presidency were actively continuing discussions on the BSR, with the support of the EC. It aimed to achieve agreement during 2015 (the proposal indicated in the Memorandum that it is expected to be adopted by June 2015, the prohibition on proprietary trading became effective on January 1, 2017, and the separation of trading activities becomes effective on July 1, 2018).[42]

The timeline of the US Volcker Rule

- Section 619 of the Dodd-Frank Wall Street Reform and Consumer Protection Act – On July 21, 2010, President Barack Obama signed the Dodd-Frank Act, Public Law 111–203, into law. The law aimed at promoting financial stability through various mechanisms including the Volcker Rule on prohibition of proprietary trading.
- Volcker Rule implementation – On December 10, 2013, the FED, the SEC, and the FDIC approved the 'final rule', implementing section 619 of the Dodd-Frank Act.
- Volcker Rule becomes effective by April 1, 2014; banking entities need to comply with it by July 21, 2015.[43] But the FED on December 18, 2014 announced that it would extend until July 21, 2016 the compliance of covered fund-related restrictions, and it is expected to further extend that to July 21, 2017. But the extension does not apply to proprietary trading prohibition.[44]

The timeline of the UK ring-fence rule

- ICB report – On September 12, 2011 the ICB published its final report on banking reform.
- HM Treasury published a White Paper in 2012, 'Banking Reform: Delivering Stability and Supporting a Sustainable Economy', which set out the proposals for reform of the banking sector, based on the ICB's recommendations.
- On December 18, 2013, the Banking Reform Act became law. The Banking Reform Bill received Royal Assent, becoming the Banking Reform Act and UK law. It introduced the 'ring-fence rule' for the deposits of individuals and small businesses, to separate the retail business from the trading floor and protect taxpayers when situations go wrong.
- Effective date – 2019, which is linked to the Basel III timetable.

---

42 According to the proposal, it was not impossible to have the rule adopted by June 2015. The Council eventually adopted a text on June 19, 2015 and the Member States are now preparing for legislation in the European Parliament. See Introduction, Section 4.1. See European Commission, *Proposal for a Regulation of the European Parliament and of the Council on structural measures improving the resilience of EU credit institutions,COM/2014/043 final*, p. 12. See also Hu Chen Chen, 'The structural reform for EU banks: does it work', *Nordic & European Company Law Working Paper 15-05* (2015).
43 See Order Approving Extension of Conformance Period.
44 Allen & Overy, 'Federal Reserve grants blanket extension of the Volcker Rule conformance period', www.allenovery.com/news/en-gb/articles/Pages/Federal-Reserve-grants-blanket-extension-of-the-Volcker-Rule-conformance-period.aspx, accessed March 11, 2015.

3 The purpose of the EC structural reform

An assessment of the EC structural reform would relate to the effectiveness and efficiency of new rules in achieving envisioned objectives. So, the analysis herein starts with the purposes of the reform.

3.1 The purposes of the Liikanen Report/BSR: a balance between stability and efficiency

The Liikanen Report was proposed to assess and evaluate the necessity of conducting a structural reform in the banking sector in the EU. As indicated in the executive summary, the objective of this report was to 'establishing a safe, stable and efficient banking system serving the needs of citizens, the EU economy and the internal market'.[45] In other words, there are two extremes in the spectrum of purpose: (i) to ensure financial stability, and (ii) to maintain efficient and fundamental financial services to serve the overall economy. Specifically, the report deems 'mak[ing the] banking group, especially their most vital parts safer and less connected to the trading activities; and to limit the implicit or explicit taxpayers guarantee for the banking groups' [46] as the central objectives of the separation reform.

The report further provides an even more detailed list of objectives of the structural reform in the summary, explaining how mandatory separation should be operated:[47]

(1) Limiting a banking group's risk-taking incentive and ability to take excessive risk with insured deposits;
(2) Preventing the coverage of losses incurred in the trading entity by the funds of the deposit entity, and hence limit subsidisation by the taxpayers;
(3) Avoiding the excessive allocation of lending from the deposit entities to other financial activities and entities;
(4) Reducing the interconnectedness between traditional banks and the shadow banking system to avoid the contagion effect; and
(5) Levelling the playing field in investment banking activities between banking groups and stand-alone investment banks.

With regard to the objectives, it should be noted that the mere protection of financial stability is not the full picture. Building an efficient banking system serving the needs of the overall economy is at the other end of the spectrum of objectives. A balance between different regulatory purposes would be desirable.

The need for regulatory balance can be seen from another regulatory consideration in the report: the 'competition' and 'competitiveness' section.[48] On the one hand, the proposal advocates enhancing consumer protection through more

45 Liikanen Erkki, *High-level Expert Group on reforming the structure of the EU banking sector*, p. 1.
46 Ibid, pp. 100–102.
47 Ibid, p. vi.
48 Ibid, p. 108.

transparency, effective disclosure, and more responsible market practice; on the other, it also has considerable regard to the competitiveness factor. Apparently, if structural reform were to be established in the EU, stringent regulation and supervision would bring about regulatory costs which would possibly affect the competitiveness of the EU banking industry, compared with other economies. After a reference to current regulation progress made in other jurisdictions, the report tentatively suggests that 'the proposals are balanced . . . if implemented, they would make it easier to manage, monitor and supervise. Tomorrow's banks would be less risky and more resilient, and the banking system as a whole would be more sustainable'.[49]

In the EC 2014 proposal, it points specifically to the objectives to be achieved for the credit institutions, which also indicate a balanced regulatory environment between stability and efficiency:[50]

(1) To reduce excessive risk-taking within the credit institution;
(2) To remove material conflicts of interest between the different parts of the credit institution;
(3) To avoid misallocation of resources and to encourage lending to the real economy;
(4) To contribute to undistorted conditions of competition for all credit institutions within the internal market;
(5) To reduce interconnectedness within the financial sector leading to systemic risk;
(6) To facilitate efficient management, monitoring, and supervision of the credit institution;
(7) To facilitate the orderly resolution and recovery of the group.

3.2 The purpose of separation: the Volcker Rule

Section 619 of the Dodd-Frank Act was enacted to deal with the structural problem in the US banking industry. It stipulates that to make recommendations and rules to implement the provisions, the Financial Stability Oversight Council (FSOC) should take the following variables into consideration:[51]

(1) Enhancing the safety and soundness of banking entities; and protecting taxpayers and consumers and enhancing financial stability;
(2) Limiting subsidisation by inappropriate transfer of federal subsidies from the FDIC covered institutions to unregulated entities;

---

49 Ibid.
50 European Commission, *Commission staff working document impact assessment accompanying the document Proposal for a Regulation of the European Parliament and of the Council on structural measures improving the resilience of EU Credit Institutions and the Proposal for a Regulation of the European Parliament and of the Council on reporting and transparency of securities financing transactions, SWD/2014/030 final*, art 2.
51 The Dodd-Frank Wall Street Reform and Consumer Protection Act (U.S), section 619.

(3) Reducing conflicts of interest between the self-interest of banking entities and non-bank financial companies supervised by the FED;

(4) Limiting activities that have caused or can reasonably be expected to cause undue risk in banking entities and nonbank financial companies supervised by the FED;

(5) Appropriately accommodating the business of insurance within an insurance company.

Although there are no further provisions in the 'final rule' about the purpose of the Volcker Rule, it is undeniable that the regulators also try very hard to balance regulation without risking the loss of competitiveness of the banking industry. This can be evidenced by the long list of exemptions of the 'prohibited activities'.[52] For instance, it has tried to exempt market-making activities and hedging activities from the prohibition on proprietary trading activities.[53]

3.3 The purposes of separation: the UK ring-fence rule

Although Vickers Rule in the UK is not the same as that in the EU and the Liikanen Report, but its purpose and its consideration may still be similar. In the introduction to the report, it points out the aims of the recommendations: (i) reducing probabilities of financial crisis in the future, (ii) maintaining the efficient flow of credit to the economy, and (iii) preserving the functioning of the payments system and guaranteed capital certainty and liquidity for small savers.[54] In terms of the retail ring-fence, the ICB states: 'the purpose of the ring-fence is to isolate those banking activities where continuous provision of service is vital to the economy and to a bank's customers'.[55]

The criteria that the ICB report suggests are as follow: (i) reduce complexity, make it easier to sort out both ring-fenced banks and non-ring-fenced banks, and eradicate taxpayers' subsidisation when banks get into trouble; (ii) protect core banking activities, insulate vital banking services on which households and SMEs depend from other risky activities in the financial system; and (iii) reduce other risk-taking incentives by the banks by curtailing government guarantees to reduce risks to public funds.[56]

From the main structure of the ICB report, its suggestions are based on the two variables: 'financial stability' and 'competition'. To enhance financial stability the ring-fence rule defines 'mandated services', 'prohibited services', and 'ancillary services'. To promote competition, 'barriers to entry' are provided through a new mandate. In addition, the recommendations also have regard to competitiveness. As indicated

---

52 Prohibitions and Restrictions on Proprietary Trading and Certain Interests In, and Relationships With, Hedge Funds and Private Equity Funds (The Final Rule) (U.S).

53 Ibid.

54 Independent Commission on Banking, 'Final Report, recommendations', p. 20.

55 Ibid, p. 35.

56 Ibid.

in the report, 'the package has been designed to address the dilemma facing the UK on how to maintain a globally competitive international financial services sector while securing greater domestic financial stability'.[57] The report suggests that the mere fact the UK banks would be adversely affected by the rules does not constitute a coherent reason to maintain the subsidisation in the banking industry, and that stronger banks and fewer costly bail-outs of the domestic banking system should be positive for the UK's reputation as a financial centre and attract more foreign investment.[58]

The 2013 Banking Reform Act further stipulates that the group ring-fencing purposes are to ensure: (i) the carrying on of core activities by a ring-fenced body is not adversely affected by the acts of other members of its group; and (ii) the ring-fenced body is able to carry on core activities and services even in the event of the insolvency of other members of its group.[59] The Prudential Regulation Authority (PRA) is required to ensure the objectives by focusing on two main aspects, resilience and resolution.[60]

The aim of the ICB's recommendations is to enhance 'financial stability' through the resilience of the banking industry so that the banks can withstand any possible future financial crisis by sorting out the risky activities from the ring-fenced entities. In the meantime, it aims to maintain the banking industry's effectiveness, efficiency, and competitiveness to the extent that it can provide all necessary banking services.[61]

4 The EU separation reform from a comparative perspective

There are at least two variables to be defined specifically: (i) which kinds of activities are to be restricted or prohibited (the scope); and (ii) to what extent should the separation rule be applied (the strength)? The rule needs to make sure the separation is strong enough to really prevent risks from transferring between different activities and avoiding subsidisation from the core retail financial services to other riskier businesses.[62] The answers to the two questions are the main battleground where controversies abound. What is widely agreed by many jurisdictions is merely admitting that the core retail financial services are less risky than other activities and that they should be protected. The depth and breadth of the reforms are highly controversial issues.

---

57 Ibid, p. 145.
58 Ibid, p. 146.
59 Banking Reform Act 2013, s 124(H)(4).
60 Prudential Regulation Authority, *The implementation of ring-fencing: consultation on legal structure, governance and the continuity of services and facilities – CP19/14* (October 2014), pp. 6–8.
61 Sullivan Cromwell, *The Independent Commission on Banking: the Vickers Report and proposals for the future of UK banking* (September 30, 2011).
62 European Commission, *EU Commission consultation paper, Consultation Reforming the structure of the EU banking sector*, pp. 2–5. With regard to addressing the structural reform problem in various jurisdictions, the paper raises three issues: which banks should the restriction be applied to; the scope of the separation rule to be applied; and the strength of the separation to be applied. See also Leonardo Gambacorta and Adrian Van Rixtel, Bank for International Settlements, *Structural bank regulation initiatives: approaches and implications* (2013).

(a) The scope. In the EC paper, it characterises the scope of separation into three groups, 'narrow trading entity and broad deposit bank', 'medium trading entity and medium deposit bank', and 'broad trading entity and narrow deposit bank':[63]

(1) The 'narrow trading entity and broad deposit bank' group. This means that narrow activities need to be separated from a broad deposit bank: only proprietary trading that is purely speculative and merely for the purpose of profit-making is separated from the deposit bank. The French separation rule, the German separation rule, and the Volcker Rule correspond to this group.

(2) The 'medium trading entity and medium deposit bank'. Based on the set of activities to be separated in the first group, it further includes market-making. Specifically, market-making denotes the purchase and sale of financial instruments for the bank's own account at prices defined by the market-makers. It aims to provide 'immediacy' to clients and investors by facilitating their requests to buy and sell more quickly. In this process, the ultimate goal for the market-maker is to 'buy low and sell high'. The Liikanen Report corresponds to this group.

(3) The 'broad trading entity and narrow deposit bank'. In the third group, the activities that need to be separated are expanded to the extent that the wholesale and investment banking activities are also separated based on the set in the second group. The set of activities to be separated includes underwriting, advisory services, brokerage services, derivatives transactions, and investing and sponsoring activities related to certain securitisation activity, in addition to proprietary trading and market-making. The Vickers Rule corresponds to this group.

(b) The strength. With regard to the second variable, the EC paper further classifies the strength of separation rule into three groups: (i) 'functional separation with economic and governance links restricted according to current rules'; (ii) 'functional separation with tighter restriction on economic and governance links'; and (iii) 'ownership separation'.[64]

Functional separation is also referred to as subsidiarisation, which denotes the separation of activities on a sub-group basis and includes some legal and economic separation requirements. Unlike the ownership separation, universal banking activities can still exist in a limited form under the subsidiarisation

---

63 European Commission, *Commission staff working document impact assessment accompanying the document Proposal for a Regulation of the European Parliament and of the Council on structural measures improving the resilience of EU Credit Institutions and the Proposal for a Regulation of the European Parliament and of the Council on reporting and transparency of securities financing transactions, SWD/2014/030 final*, pp. 28–29. See also European Commission, *EU Commission consultation paper, Consultation Reforming the structure of the EU banking sector*, pp. 5–6.

64 European Commission, *Commission staff working document impact assessment accompanying the document Proposal for a Regulation of the European Parliament and of the Council on structural measures improving the resilience of EU Credit Institutions and the Proposal for a Regulation of the European Parliament and of the Council on reporting and transparency of securities financing transactions, SWD/2014/030 final*, pp. 34–35.

model. The difference between the first group and the second group is that the latter applies more stringent link restriction rules.[65] The ownership separation, however, leaves no room for the existence of the universal banking model.

The ownership separation was adopted both in the Volcker Rule and the Glass-Steagall Act, where regulation requirements are to be implemented in the entire banking group together with intragroup and intergroup restrictions.[66] The Liikanen Report, the Vickers Rule, the French separation rule, and the German separation rule all correspond to the 'functional separation with tighter restriction on economic and governance links'.[67]

(c) **A map of current reforms in major economies.** According to the classification discussed above, the Liikanen separation rule corresponds to the group of 'medium trading entity and medium deposit bank' and 'functional separation with tighter restriction'. Accordingly, the Vickers Rule corresponds to the group of 'broad trading activities and narrow deposit bank' and 'functional separation with tighter restriction'. However, the Volcker Rule corresponds to the 'narrow trading entity and broad deposit bank' and 'ownership separation' (Table 3.1).[68]

4.1 The separation rule in the Liikanen Report

The High-level Expert Group drafted the proposal in 2012 to the EC; it is the predecessor of the BSR. Therefore, the analysis of it gives subsequent discussions a reference point.

4.1.1 Universal banking model and the Liikanen model's strength

(a) **The debate on the universal banking model.** The universal banking model encountered much criticism after the GFC in 2008 due to its huge underlying risks caused by the co-existence of retail-commercial banking activities, trading-oriented activities, and investment banking activities. Although different models

Table 3.1 Map of separation rule in major jurisdictions

Activities/strength	Functional with tighter requirements	Ownership separation
Narrow trading entity and broad deposit entity	Choice A: FR, DE Reform	Choice D: Volcker/BSR
Medium trading and deposit entity	Choice B: Liikanen Report	Choice E
Broad trading entity and narrow deposit entity	Choice C: Vickers/BSR	Choice F: Glass-Steagall

65 Ibid.
66 Ibid, p. 32.
67 Ibid, pp. 28–30.
68 Ibid, p. 34. see also infra Chapter 3, Section 4.2.

existed in different jurisdictions,[69] a universal bank generally includes at least two parts: the trading entity and the deposit entity. The two parts represent different activities with varied funding sources, profit outlook, and different risk potentials. The model acted as a destabilising factor in the run up to the GFC.[70] The reason was that the co-existence of a wide range of activities facilitated the exploitation of the innovation of structural debt products, added to the interconnectedness, accumulated different risks, increased cyclicality in the banking industry, and created huge bank resolution difficulties for regulators. By facilitating risk-taking incentives, the model drove the financial markets out of their equilibrium and made the market bubbles burst and precipitate a disastrous crisis.

On the other hand, there were also comments against the criticisms. A contrary opinion suggests that the universal banking model was, to a certain extent, more of a resilient factor than a precipitating factor in the run up to the GFC.[71] Among the advantages of the universal banking model, the most important one could be that this model allows a bank to utilise the economies of scope and diversify the main risks from different activities in the model. According to modern portfolio theory, the golden rule of investment is that you should never put all your eggs in the one basket.[72] The universal banking model in the pre-crisis era put the profit sources of the banking industry into different baskets, which in this context could be various geographically different branches, or varying business activities. It should be noted that risks are always very high in the banking industry and the need for diversification is imperative. Therefore, this argument seems also not unreasonable.

(b) Tolerance of the universal banking model in the Liikanen Report. In the report, the universal banking model is to be preserved, but not in the same way as it was in the pre-crisis era. Unlike the lack of regulation over the encompassing set of activities and services provided by banks, under the provisions of the Liikanen Report, a bank group is required to structure according to the bank holding company model, in which the entities conducting core banking activities and trading activities are separated on a sub-group basis.[73]

---

69 Gambacorta, *Structural bank regulation initiatives: approaches and implications.* In this working report, it classifies banks in contemporary times into four models: the investment bank, the investment banking-oriented universal bank, the commercial banking-oriented universal bank, and the commercial bank. The classification is done according to different funding sources and business orientations.

70 Emilios Avgouleas, *Governance of global financial markets: the law, the economics, the politics* (Cambridge, UK: Cambridge University Press 2012), pp. 129–130.

71 John Armour, 'Structural regulation of banking' (a preliminary draft of a chapter for a book, entitled *Principles of Financial Regulation*). http://web.law.columbia.edu/sites/default/files/microsites/law-economics-studies/john_armour_structural_regulation_working_22.06.2014.pdf, accessed May 29, 2015, pp. 5–7.

72 Robert A. Jarrow, David Lando and Fan Yu, 'Default risk and diversification: theory and empirical implications' 15 *Mathematical Finance* 1.

73 Liikanen Erkki, *High-level Expert Group on reforming the structure of the EU banking sector*, pp. v–vi.

That said, it also provides some restrictive criteria within the context of the universal banking model. Within the bank holding company, the risk exposures and transactions between the deposit entity and the trading entity are also restricted to the extent that any transaction should be conducted according to market-based terms.[74] In addition, intrabank exposure would not be allowed if the transactions being conducted would endanger either directly or indirectly the current capital requirement standards. The Liikanen Report also restricts the capacity of the deposit entity and trading entity in their dividend policy. The direct result is that paying a dividend is only permitted if capital requirements are met.

Additionally, to maintain the resilience of both the deposit entity and the trading entity, the Liikanen Report requires that each group entity be subject to the prudential requirements separately. These requirements include, but are not limited to, the capital requirement, non-risk weighted capital buffer, the liquidity requirement, and the leverage requirement in the CRR/CRD IV.[75] The major objective of the separation rule is to safeguard the deposit entity against the contagion effect of the trading entity and maintain its stability and safety.

4.1.2 The Liikanen model's scope

Trading activities, unlike traditional banking activities, are susceptible to market risk and systemic risk.[76] This is for many reasons, such as the leveraged financial structure of banks, and the complexity and interconnectedness of structured products.[77] The risk potentials of the trading entity and the deposit entity are really distinct and demand different measures and distinct regulatory treatments. The critical purpose of the separation is to transfer the core business of the whole group into a separated entity so that a de facto decoupling mechanism could be achieved and the failure of one part would not endanger the others and even allow time for the recovery of that failing part.

(a) **Mandatory separation.** With regard to the separation of trading activities from the commercial banking activities, the Liikanen Report tends to wipe out all the proprietary trading activities from the traditional bank entity. Furthermore, it carves out all assets, liabilities, and positions driven by market-making, which is a key proponent of relevant academic debates in the US. The reason is that market-making is deemed to be an important source of immediacy provision.[78]

In addition, exposures and sponsoring hedge funds, special investment vehicles, and private equity funds are supposed to be transferred to the trading entity. To deal with the interconnectedness issue, the trading entity is not

---

74 Ibid, p. vi.
75 Ibid, pp. vi–vii.
76 See supra Chapter 1, Section 3(d).
77 Avgouleas, *Governance of global financial markets: the law, the economics, the politics*, p. 36.
78 Liikanen Erkki, *High-level Expert Group on reforming the structure of the EU banking sector*, pp. v–vi. Darrell Duffie, 'Market making under the proposed Volcker rule', Rock Center for Corporate Governance at Stanford University Working Paper (106).

allowed to fund its activities through the deposit entity or provide traditional financial services.[79]

The report also provides a threshold for the separation to be applied. It suggests that mandatory separation is only necessary if the trading activities amount to a certain level of the total assets or the volumes of the trading activities can significantly affect the financial stability of the entity. The threshold is a two-step test: (i) whether the bank's trading positions exceed 15–25% of the bank's total assets or more than EUR100 billion: if the answer is yes, then it proceeds to step two; (ii) the competent supervisors then determine the need for separation.[80] On meeting the two-step test and threshold, the relevant activities should be transferred into a separated entity based on the competent supervisors' decision.

(b) Permitted activities. Except delineating the separation of certain activities, the Liikanen Report also provides an accurate set of permitted business activities in the deposit entity:[81]

> Lending to large as well as small and medium-sized companies, trading finance, consumer lending, mortgage lending, interbank lending, participation in loan syndications, plain vanilla securitization for funding purposes, private wealth management and asset management, and exposures to regulated monetary market funds. The use of derivatives for own assets and liability management purposes, as well as sales and purchases of assets to manage the assets in the liquidity portfolio, would also be permitted for deposit banks. Only the deposit bank is allowed to supply retail payment services. Provision of hedging services to non-banking clients . . . and securities underwriting . . . do not have to be separated.

The delineation of the permitted business for the trading entity is clearer and easier: it can do all other business other than that under the mandate of the deposit entity. In addition, it is not allowed to receive funds from the insured deposit entity.[82]

(c) Additional separation and link to resolution. The Liikanen Rule is designed to resolve the current structural problem in the banking sector. Two very prominent features of the structural problem are the complexity and interconnectedness problem and the resolvability problem.[83] It seems that mandatory separation focuses on the complexity and interconnectedness factor. However, dealing with interconnectedness is not directly helpful in tackling the resolvability problem.[84]

79   Liikanen Erkki, *High-level Expert Group on reforming the structure of the EU banking sector*, p. v.
80   Ibid, pp. v–vi.
81   Ibid, p. vi and pp. 101–102.
82   Ibid, pp. v–vi and p. 102.
83   See supra Chapter 1, Section 3(b)–(d).
84   See infra Chapter 5, Section 6.

Thus, the Liikanen Report also has regard to how the separation mechanism could be connected with resolution. The second tier of the separation rule in the Liikanen Report is an additional measure to deal with the structural problem according to the needs of assumptive resolution, and recovery and resolution planning (RRP), in cases where mandatory separation would be inadequate. The report indicates that to really eradicate the banking structural problem, a practical recovery and resolution mechanism is inevitable.

Therefore, apart from mandatory separation, the Liikanen separation also empowers the regulatory agencies to require additional separation to the extent that a bank could be resolved 'in a way that does not compromise critical functions, threaten financial stability, or involve costs to the taxpayers'.[85] Additional separation is to be carried out on a case-by-case basis according to the recovery and resolution examination conducted by the competent supervisor.[86]

4.2 The separation rule in the BSR (Box 3.2)

Following a series of public consultations on the Liikanen Report, the College of Commissioners had a heated discussion with regard to the rules in it. The European Commission's former president Barroso called for an impact analysis and assessment to decide the 'various possible options and their implications'.[87] On July 3, 2013, the European Parliament adopted an initiative report 'Reforming the structure of the EU banking sector' in which the European Parliament called on the EC to provide a principles-based approach for EU structural reform, ensure the continuity of the core banking business, ensure the trading activity does not receive implicit subsidisation, and ensure that the separated entities have different sources of funding.[88] The EC made the proposal in 2014.

Compared with the separation reform in the US and the UK, the EC proposal is approximately equivalent to a combination of the Volcker Rule and the Vickers Rule. However, it is quite different from the two and it is also distinct from the above Liikanen proposal. It departs from the Liikanen Report in two aspects: (i) the proposal includes a Volcker-style prohibition rule, but without a Volcker-style exception set; and (ii) it also has a Vickers-style ring-fence rule. But unlike the ring-fence rule in the UK, it is not mandatory in the proposal.

---

85 Liikanen Erkki, *High-level Expert Group on reforming the structure of the EU banking sector*, p. vii.
86 Ibid, p. vii and p. 103.
87 European Commission, *Commission staff working document impact assessment accompanying the document Proposal for a Regulation of the European Parliament and of the Council on structural measures improving the resilience of EU Credit Institutions and the Proposal for a Regulation of the European Parliament and of the Council on reporting and transparency of securities financing transactions, SWD/2014/030 final.*
88 Ibid, p. 6.

Box 3.2   Rules in the BSR

A Entity scope

(a) **The scope-size.** The EC narrows down the entities to which the regulation is to be applied to a size threshold: (i) the global systemically important institutions in the EU (G-SIIs), including all the branches and subsidiaries irrespective of location; and (ii) entities that for a period of three consecutive years have total assets amounting at least to EUR30 billion and has trading activities amounting at least to EUR70 billion or 10% of its total assets for three consecutive years (EU-SIIs).[89] But it should be noted that the size threshold is for the prohibition rule only.

(b) **The scope-entity: the whole bank group.** The BSR applies to (i) credit institutions established in the EU including all its branches irrespective of location; (ii) the EU parent, including all branches and subsidiaries irrespective of their location provided that one of the group entities is a credit institution in the EU; and (iii) the EU branches of credit institutions established in third countries.[90] However, the EU BSR rules will not apply to non-EU subsidiaries of EU banks and to EU branches of non-EU banks if the EC decides these entities are subject to equivalent regulation in the relevant jurisdictions.[91]

(c) **Model of separation.** The separation model in the BSR is approximately a combination of the Volcker's Rule and the Vickers' Rule. For entities above the size threshold, the prohibitive rule applies, while the ring-fence rule applies on a discretionary basis irrespective of size.

B Prohibitive rule

Unlike the ring-fence regulatory approach in both the Liikanen Report and that in other Member States indicated above, such as France, Germany, and Belgium, the regulatory approach in this part is a prohibitive approach.[92]

(d) **Prohibited activities: principles-based approach.** According to the BSR, proprietary trading means using own capital or borrowed money to take positions in any type of transactions.[93] It is trading 'for the sole purpose of making a profit for own account, and without any connection to actual or anticipated client activity or for the purpose of hedging the entity's risk as a result of actual or anticipated client activity', and the trading is to be done 'through the use of desks, units, divisions or individual traders specifically dedicated to such position taking and profit making, including through dedicated web-based proprietary trading platforms'.[94]

(e) **Exception 1** (related to market-making, hedging, underwriting). Due to the principles-based prohibition delimitation, the exception is not definitive except in excluding trading or hedging connected to actual or anticipated client activity.

(f) **Exception 2** (related to government bonds and liquidity management). The exception covers: financial instruments issued by Member States' central governments, use of its own capital in the cash management process, and exposures to cash or cash equivalent assets.[95]

(g) **Exception 3** (others): there are no further specific exceptions if not related to actual or anticipated client activities.[96]

C Ban on investment in funds

(h) **Prohibition.** With its own capital or borrowed money and for the sole purpose of profit-making for its own account: (i) acquiring or retaining units or shares of Alternative

---

89 European Commission, *Proposal for a Regulation of the European Parliament and of the Council on structural measures improving the resilience of EU credit institutions,COM/2014/043 final*, art 3(1).

90 Ibid, art 3(2).

91 Ibid, art 4(1).

92 See supra Chapter 3, Section 2.2.

93 European Commission, *Proposal for a Regulation of the European Parliament and of the Council on structural measures improving the resilience of EU credit institutions, COM/2014/043 final*, art 6(1).

94 Ibid, art 5(4).

95 Ibid, art 6(2).

96 Ibid, art 5(4).

Investment Funds (AIFs); (ii) investing in financial instruments whose performance is linked to shares or units of AIFs; or (iii) holding any units or shares in an entity that engages in proprietary trading or acquires units or shares in AIFs.[97]

(i) **Exception.** The definition of AIFs is related to the definition in the AIF Managers Directive (AIFMD).[98] The prohibition does not apply to (i) UCITS funds; (ii) closed-ended unleveraged EU funds, or non-EU funds if they are marketed in the EU; and (iii) qualifying venture capital funds, social entrepreneurship funds, and European Long Term Investment Funds (ELTIFs).[99] Unlike the Volcker Rule, there are no further exceptions. It also does not prohibit sponsoring activities.

B1 Ring-fence rule

The second part where the BSR differs from the Liikanen proposal is the ring-fence rule, which is comparable with the UK Vickers Rule. Different from the prohibition rule, it basically applies to all EU banks that are covered by the Deposit Guarantee Scheme Directive.[100] Similar to the prohibition rule, the provisions in this part also have an extraterritorial effect: they will be applied to the EU parent, and all of its subsidiaries and branches.[101] Although the coverage scope is very broad, compared with the Liikanen ring-fence rule, this rule is not mandatory, but contingent on the risk assessment decision of the competent authorities.[102]

(j) **Mandated activities.** Mandate activities include taking deposits eligible for deposit insurance, lending, retail payment services, financial leasing, issuing of other means of payment, and some other retail and commercial banking activities.[103]

(k) **Restricted activities.** In chapter III of the proposal, the competent authorities seem to have a very broad discretion in determining the risk assessment and the necessity to implement the ring-fence rule in particular institutions. A wide range of 'trading activities' would need to be assessed, apart from the above mandated commercial activities. The regulators would especially focus on market-making, investments in and acting as a sponsor for securitisation, and trading in derivatives other than those derivatives permitted as prudential management of own risk or provision of risk management services to customers.[104]

(l) **Exception: permitted activities.** The entities that are subject to the separation decision by the competent authorities can still commit to: (i) prudential management of risk, which is carrying out their trading activities to the extent of only prudentially managing its capital, liquidity, and funding; and (ii) provision of risk management services to its clients, which is selling certain derivatives to non-financial clients or financial entities for the purpose of hedging interest rate risk, foreign exchange risk, credit risk, commodity risk, or emissions allowance risk.[105]

(m) **Standard of ring-fence/link.** Since ring-fencing is not mandatory, in order to apply the rule, a condition needs to be met such that there is a threat to the financial stability of the core credit institution (CCI) or the EU financial system as a whole. That would be based on the discretion of the competent authorities according to the proposal.[106] The competent authorities are to carry out the risk assessment on a yearly basis and make the ring-fence decision using the following metrics: (a) the relative size of trading assets; (b) the leverage of trading assets; (c) the relative importance of counterparty credit risk;

(continued)

97 Ibid, art 6(1)(b).
98 Directive 2011/61/EU of the European Parliament and of the Council of 8 June 2011 on alternative investment fund managers and amending Directives 2003/41/EC and 2009/65/EC and Regulations (EC) No 1060/2009 and (EU) No 1095/2010[2011] OJ L174/1(AIFMD).
99 European Commission, *Proposal for a Regulation of the European Parliament and of the Council on structural measures improving the resilience of EU credit institutions,COM/2014/043 final*, art 6(3).
100 Ibid, art 9.
101 Ibid.
102 Ibid, art 10.
103 Ibid, art 8(1).
104 Ibid, art 10–12.
105 Ibid, art 11–12.
106 Ibid, art 10.

(continued)

(d) the relative complexity of trading derivatives; (e) the relative profitability of trading income; (f) the relative importance of market risk; (g) the interconnectedness; and (h) credit and liquidity risk arising from commitments and guarantees provided by the CCI.[107]

The trading activities being separated out can still be carried on by a group entity that is legally, economically, and operationally separate from the CCI. So, the ring-fence rule does not prevent the trading activities from being carried out elsewhere in the same banking group provided that the CCI and the trading entity meet the following separation standards:[108]

(1) A group containing the CCI and the trading entity shall be structured on a sub-consolidated basis, and among the two distinct sub-groups that are created, only one can contain CCIs;
(2) The CCI cannot hold capital instruments or voting rights in a trading entity unless the competent authorities decide such a holding is indispensable for the function of the group;[109]
(3) The CCI and the trading entity shall issue their own debt on an individual or sub-consolidated basis provided that this is not inconsistent with the resolution plan;[110]
(4) All contracts and other transactions entered into between the CCI and the trading entity shall be on a third-party basis;
(5) A majority of the members of the management body of the CCI and of the trading entity respectively shall consist of persons who are not members of the management body of the other entity;
(6) The name of the trading entity and the CCI shall be clear enough to avoid the public confusion with regard to whether it is a trading entity or a CCI;
(7) The capital, liquidity, leverage, and requirements as such in CRR/CRD IV shall be applied on an individual basis;
(8) The CCI shall not incur an intragroup exposure that exceeds 25% of the CCI eligible capital to an entity that does not belong to same sub-group as the CCI;[111]
(9) The exposure limits of 25% and 200% of the eligible assets that the CCI can incur to a financial entity and financial entities in total.[112]

D Other elements

(n) **Anti-circumvention rule.** The restriction and prohibition adopt a principles-based approach without giving a specific list of exceptions. There is no anti-circumvention rule provided.[113]
(o) **Discretion and flexibility.** The BSR provides the EC with no obvious flexibility to adapt to new changes or needs compared with that included in the Volcker Rule and the Vickers Rule.[114]
(p) **Connection to resolution.** In article 19, it requires that carrying out the separation, especially the ring-fence decision-making process should be in cooperation with resolution authorities.[115]

---

107 Ibid, art 9(2)
108 Ibid, art 13.
109 Ibid, art 13(5).
110 See generally Directive 2014/59/EU of the European Parliament and of the Council of 15 May 2014, establishing a framework for the recovery and resolution of credit institutions and investment firms and amending Council Directive 82/891/EEC, and Directives 2001/24/EC, 2002/47/EC, 2004/25/EC, 2005/56/EC, 2007/36/EC, 2011/35/EU, 2012/30/EU and 2013/36/EU, and Regulations (EU) No 1093/2010 and (EU) No 648/2012, of the European Parliament and of the Council [2014] OJ L 173/190/1 (BRRD).
111 European Commission, *Proposal for a Regulation of the European Parliament and of the Council on structural measures improving the resilience of EU credit institutions, COM/2014/043 final*, art 14.
112 Ibid, art 15.
113 See infra Chapter 3, Section 4.3(n) and Section 4.4(n).
114 See infra Chapter 3, Section 4.3(o) and Section 4.4(o).
115 BRRD, art 19.

4.3 US structural reform (Box 3.3)

Compared with the strength of separation reform in the EU where universal banking is still preserved, the case in the US is a little bit different. In the Dodd-Frank Act and the 'final rule', the trading activities are completely separated from the commercial bank and bank holding company.[116] Similar to the BSR prohibition rule, the US model corresponds to class D.[117]

4.4 The UK structural reform (Box 3.4)

The UK ring-fence rule has two dimensions, referred to in the Vickers Rule as the 'location' and the 'height'. Similar to the BSR ring-fence, it corresponds to group C in the separation rule world map.[118]

In summary, the above analysis of structural reform in the EU compared with that in the US and the UK from the perspective of application scope, the prohibitive rule, the ring-fence rule, and other elements provides the basic foundation for further analyses of the effectiveness and efficiency of the EU model in the following chapters.

---

116 The Dodd-Frank Wall Street Reform and Consumer Protection Act (U.S), section 619.
117 See supra Chapter 3 Section 4, Table 3.1.
118 see supra Chapter 3 Section 4, Table 3.1.

Box 3.3   The Volcker Rule

A Entity scope

(a) **Size limit.** There is no size limit for the Volcker Rule.

(b) **The scope-entity.** It covers all banking entities within a group controlled by the bank holding company, with the exception of (i) portfolio companies acquired under the merchant banking authorities; (ii) a covered fund that is allowed and is not itself a banking entity, e.g. the foreign public funds; and (iii) regulated insurance companies.[119]

(c) **Model-ownership separation.** The prohibition on proprietary trading and investing in or sponsoring hedge funds and private equity funds applies to specific defined entities:[120] (i) insured depository institutions by FDIC and entities that own them, such as a bank holding company or a savings and loan holding company; (ii) foreign banks or bank holding companies that have a US bank branch or subsidiary (section 8 of the International Banking Act of 1978); or (iii) any affiliate or subsidiary of the foregoing (as defined in the Bank Holding Company Act of 1956) (i.e. at least 25% of common control) institutions. The prohibition is to be carried out in the entire group, rather than on a sub-group basis. Therefore, the universal banking model is not allowed.

B Prohibitive rule

(d) **Prohibited activities.** The prohibition on proprietary trading means that the covered entities are not allowed to engage as principal in buying or selling any securities, derivatives, or futures or forward contracts, and any option on the foregoing products. The US rule basically includes trading for short-term profit-making.[121] Unlike the EU rule, it does not apply to trading physical commodities or 'spot' foreign exchange transactions.[122]

(e) **Exception 1.**[123] (i) Transactions in securities or other financial instruments in connection with underwriting are permitted provided that they do not exceed the reasonably expected near-term demands of clients, customers, or counterparties; (ii) similarly, market-making-related activities are also exempt from the prohibition provided that the market-maker inventory does not exceed expected near-term demands and the banking entity would enforce an internal compliance program; and (iii) the risk-mitigation hedging transactions are also permitted if the banking entities establish and enforce a compliance program and have reasonably designed policies and procedures regarding the positions, techniques, and strategies used for hedging.[124]

(f) **Exception 2.** (i)Transactions of the US government or agency obligations, obligations of government-sponsored enterprises (GSEs), obligations of any state or political organs, and foreign government obligations,[125] for example US Treasury debts or agency securities, debts issued by Fannie Mae or Freddie Mac; and (ii) transactions for liquidity management.[126]

(g) **Exception 3.** The final rule provides a lot of other exceptions:[127]

   (1) Securities lending and repo activities;
   (2) Clearing activities of banking entities that are members of clearing organisations;
   (3) Transactions to satisfy existing delivery obligations or reorganisation and rescue plans;
   (4) Transactions in securities or other financial instruments acting as agent for customers;

---

119 Prohibitions and Restrictions on Proprietary Trading and Certain Interests In, and Relationships With, Hedge Funds and Private Equity Funds (The Final Rule) (U.S), section 2(c)(2). See also The Dodd-Frank Wall Street Reform and Consumer Protection Act (U.S), section 619(d)(1)(F).
120 The Dodd-Frank Wall Street Reform and Consumer Protection Act (U.S), section 619.
121 Prohibitions and Restrictions on Proprietary Trading and Certain Interests In, and Relationships With, Hedge Funds and Private Equity Funds (The Final Rule) (U.S), section 3(b).
122 Ibid, section 3(c)(2).
123 The Dodd-Frank Wall Street Reform and Consumer Protection Act (U.S), section 619(d)(1) (A)–(J).
124 Prohibitions and Restrictions on Proprietary Trading and Certain Interests In, and Relationships With, Hedge Funds and Private Equity Funds (The Final Rule) (U.S), sections 4–5.
125 Ibid, section 6(a).
126 Ibid, section 3(d)(3).
127 Ibid, section 3(d) and section 6, The Dodd-Frank Wall Street Reform and Consumer Protection Act (U.S), section 619(d).

(5) Activities through an employee compensation scheme;
(6) Transactions in the course of collecting a previous contracted debt in good faith;
(7) Transactions in securities and other financial instruments conducted by a regulated insurance company, subject to compliance with applicable state insurance law;
(8) Proprietary trading activities conducted by non-US subsidiaries or branches of non-US banks or BHCs;
(9) Transactions in connection with investment in small business investment companies, which are designed primarily to promote public welfare.

The US separation rule also introduces restrictions on intragroup transactions. Generally speaking, all transactions must be done on an arm's length basis. It also imposes some restrictions on interaffiliate transactions.[128]

C Ban on investment in funds

(h) **Prohibition.** The Volcker Rule prohibits a banking entity from acquiring or retaining any ownership interest in or sponsoring a covered fund.[129]
(i) **Exception.** Different from the BSR, the closed ended funds, unleveraged funds, private equity, venture capital and ELTIFs are not excluded. However, it does exempt many entities as covered funds: (i) foreign public funds, (ii) wholly owned subsidiaries, (iii) joint ventures, (iv) acquisition vehicles, (v) foreign pension or retirement funds, (vi) insurance company separate accounts, (vii) bank owned life insurance accounts, (viii) loan securitisations, (ix) qualifying asset-backed commercial paper conduits, (x) qualifying covered bonds and registered investment firms, and (xi) Small Business Investment Companies (SBICs) funds.[130]

With regard to the prohibition on investment in funds, the final rule provides the following exceptions:[131]

(1) Ownership interests held by asset managers that organise and offer a covered fund to customers or issue asset-backed securities as securitiser;
(2) Underwriting and market-making in ownership interests of a covered fund;
(3) Acquiring and retaining ownership interests in a covered fund for the purpose of establishment or de minimis investment, subject to per-fund limits and aggregate limits;
(4) Ownership interests held to hedging some identifiable risks to the banking entity;
(5) The prohibition does not apply to bank entities that are not organised or controlled by a US banking entity.

[Elements **(j)** to **(l)** inclusive are not applicable and element **(m)**, standard of separation, is at arm's length under the Volcker Rule – see Table 3.2.]

D Other elements

(n) **Anti-circumvention rule.** The exception of prohibition is limited further by other restrictions, which act as an anti-circumvention rule. No transactions may be deemed permissible in the following situations: (i) involving or resulting in a material conflict of interest between banking entities and their clients or counterparties; (ii) resulting in a material exposure to high-risk trading strategies; or (iii) posing a threat to the safety and soundness of the banking entity.[132]
(o) **Discretion and flexibility.** The Volcker Rule provides certain flexibility to adapt to new changes by amending the rule or terminating identified aversion by order.[133]
(p) **Connection to resolution.** There are no relevant provisions.

128 The Dodd-Frank Wall Street Reform and Consumer Protection Act (U.S), section 608.
129 Prohibitions and Restrictions on Proprietary Trading and Certain Interests In, and Relationships With, Hedge Funds and Private Equity Funds (The Final Rule) (U.S), section 10.
130 Ibid, section 10(c).
131 Ibid, sections 11–13.
132 Ibid, section 7(a) and section 15(a).
133 The Dodd-Frank Wall Street Reform and Consumer Protection Act (U.S), section 619(e).

Box 3.4 The UK reform

A Entity scope

(a) **Size limit.** There is a size limit of £25 billion of core deposits for a UK deposit-taker.[134]
(b) **Entity scope.** It applies to UK incorporated banks and building societies.[135]
(c) **Model.** Similar to the Liikanen separation rule, the universal banking model is also preserved in the Vickers Rule. To carry out ring-fence separation and protect the deposit banks, the report also has due regard to the economies of scale and scope.[136]

B1 Ring-fence rule

The ring-fence separation rule classifies the bank's business activities into three sets: the 'mandated activities/required activities', 'prohibited activities', and the 'permitted activities/auxiliary activities'.[137]

[Elements (d) to (i) inclusive are not applicable under the Vickers Rule – see Table 3.2.]

(j) **Required activities within the ring-fenced entity.** It refers to activities that are of such vital importance that even a temporary disruption of them is not tolerable. It includes the taking of deposits from and provision of lending to individuals, and small and medium-sized enterprises (SMEs).[138]

(k) **Prohibited activities within the ring-fenced entity.** The Vickers Rule does not provide a definitive list of prohibited activities in the ring-fenced entity. Rather, it provides criteria whereby activities should not be allowed within the ring-fenced entity: (i) they are no integral to the provision of payment services to customers, or the direct intermediation between savers and borrowers within the EEA non-financial sector; (ii) they directly increase the exposure of the ring-fenced bank to the financial markets; (iii) they would significantly complicate the resolution; or (iv) they threaten the objectives of the ring-fence rule.[139]

But the Vickers Rule also provides a broad yet non-inclusive list of prohibited activities. This includes: securities trading; market-making; underwriting; exposures to relevant financial institutions subject to certain exemptions under specific conditions (trade finance, securitisation and covered bonds, conduit lending, repo transaction, ancillary exposures);[140] and ownership of non-EEA branches or subsidiaries.[141] It also excludes investing in hedge funds and private equity funds.[142]

(l) **Permitted activities.** According to the Vickers Rule, activities that are necessary for the provision of mandated activities are also permitted within the ring-fenced entity. Specifically, the ring-fenced entity is allowed to undertake activities beyond the provision of non-prohibited services to the extent that they are necessary for its core functions. For instance, risk management, liquidity management, and trade finance.[143]

---

134 The Financial Services and Markets Act 2000 (Ring-fenced Bodies and Core Activities) Order 2014, SI 2014/1960, section 12.
135 Independent Commission on Banking, 'Final Report, recommendations', p. 233.
136 Ibid, p. 12 and p. 68. Prudential Regulation Authority, *Consultation paper, The implementation of ring-fencing: consultation on legal structure, governance, and the continuity of services and facilities – CP19/14* (October 7, 2014), pp. 10–12.
137 Independent Commission on Banking, 'Final Report, recommendations', pp. 36–40.
138 Ibid, p. 235.
139 Ibid, p. 234.
140 The Financial Services and Markets Act 2000 (Excluded Activities and Prohibitions) Order 2014, SI 2014/2080, sections 14–19.
141 Independent Commission on Banking, 'Final Report, recommendations', p. 235.
142 To compare with the EU and UK (h)–(i), see Table 3.2.
143 Independent Commission on Banking, 'Final Report, recommendations', p. 236.

(m) **Standard of separation and link.** Although maintaining the universal banking model, it also imposes certain restrictions on the model: (i) group entities meeting regulatory requirements on a stand-alone basis, are separately subject to the prudential requirements; they need to have legal and operational independence; and (ii) the intragroup relationship is to be restricted to the extent that all transactions should be allowed but be conducted on an arm's length basis.[144]

D Other elements

(n) **Anti-circumvention.** There are no relevant provisions in the UK reform.

(o) **Discretion/flexibility.** The excluded activities are not allowed within the ring-fenced entity, except in special circumstances specified by the Treasury by order.[145] The Treasury can also further expand other activities as being excluded by order if it is necessary for the sake of protecting the continuity of the core services.[146]

(p) **Connection to resolution.** The Vickers Rule fully considers the need for different sets of rules to work together. Besides the structural ring-fence rule, it also includes other loss-absorbency rules, which would all be helpful in building a practical resolution regime. These rules include: (i) a higher capital requirement ratio (on a risk weighted basis) than that of the Basel III, with a complementary leverage ratio (on a non-risk weighted basis); (ii) primary loss-absorbency capacity, e.g. the large UK banking group should have primary loss-absorbency capacity of at least 17% of RWAs; (iii) bail-in provides a tool whereby the shareholders rather than the debtors would finally absorb the risks and losses of the financial group; (iv) depositor preference, by which the insured depositors have preferential rights in the insolvency and resolution process; and (v) the resolution buffer requirement.[147]

5 Conclusion: two attributes and two reforms

5.1 Trading activities and financial stability: non-linear relationship

After discussing the structure of the separation reform in the EU and providing a comparative analysis of the separation reforms in the US and the UK (Table 3.2), the next step is to explore whether the reform would bring safety and stability to the banking industry and solve the TBTF bank structural problem. But before that an unavoidable concern is whether there really is a perfect linear relationship between the separation of trading activities and the enhancement of financial stability. In other words, is the universal banking structure really the key function of financial safety and soundness? Do the bank structure and financial stability maintain a linear relationship?

A logical hypothesis is that were a structural reform to be adopted and implemented, banks would have a very healthy post-regulation structure. But they could still engage in a wide range of permitted yet risky activities and maintain many exposures to high-risk assets.[148] For instance, they could have a very high leverage rate, continue their reckless risk-taking behaviour and be closely interconnected

---

144 Ibid, p. 12.
145 Financial Services (Banking Reform) Act 2013 (c.33), section 142D(2).
146 Ibid, section 142D(4).
147 Independent Commission on Banking, 'Final Report, recommendations', p. 238.
148 According to the above separation rules in the three jurisdictions, trading activities would still be permitted, although the degree of tolerance is different. Except purely trading activities, some non-trading activities could also be very risky, such as market making and underwriting.

Table 3.2 The map of separation reforms from a comparative perspective

Factor/rule	US Volcker Rule	EU BSR-PR	EU BSR-RF	UK rule
a. Size	N/A	G-SIIs and EU SIIs (EUR30bn; EUR70bn/10%)	N/A	£25bn retail and SME deposits
b. Applied entity	Banking entities with exceptions: (i) Portfolio companies (ii) Allowed covered funds (iii) insurance companies (unlike EU)	EU banks; their EU parents; their subsidiaries and branches; subsidiaries and branches in the EU of banks in a third country		UK banks and building societies
c. Model	Ownership	Ownership	Ring-fence	Ring-fence
d. Prohibit	(i) Trading for short-term profit-making (ii) Not applicable to physical commodities or 'spot' foreign exchange (unlike EU)	(i) Own profit (ii) Not hedge and not client activity (iii) Through trading platforms	N/A	N/A
e. Exception 1 Market-making Hedging Underwriting	(i) Market-making: expected near-term demands (ii) Underwriting: expected near-term demands (iii) Hedging	Trading connected to client activity	N/A	N/A
f. Exception 2	(i) Domestic/foreign government obligations (ii) Cash management	(i) Government bonds (ii) Cash management	N/A	N/A
g. Exception 3 Others	(i) Repo (ii) Clearing (iii) Delivery obligations (iv) Agent for customers (v) Employee compensation plan (vi) A prior contracted debt (vii) Transactions conducted by insurance company (viii) Non-US entities (ix) Investment in small business investment companies	No other exceptions	N/A	N/A

h. Prohibition: funds	(i) Acquiring or retaining any ownership interest in or sponsoring a covered fund (ii) The closed ended funds, unleveraged funds, private equity, venture capital, and ELTIFs are not excluded (unlike EU)	Prohibit acquiring or retaining (directly or indirectly) shares or units of AIFs	N/A	Excludes investing in hedge funds and private equity
i. Exceptions: funds	Long list of exceptions to covered funds, e.g. foreign public fund. Exceptions: (i) Organising and offering a covered fund to customers or an issuing entity of asset-backed securities (ii) Market-making and underwriting (iii) Establishment of de minimis investment (iv) Hedging of employees' compensation risks (v) Non-US entities	(i) UCITS (ii) Close-ended funds (iii) VC, ELTIFs, social entrepreneurship funds	N/A	N/A
j. Mandated activities	N/A	N/A	Taking deposits, lending, and a short list of commercial banking – BRRD, art 8	(i) Taking deposits from individuals and SMEs (ii) Provision of loans to individuals and SMEs
k. Restricted activities	N/A	N/A	Wide range of activities except above-mandated activities	Broad definition of trading activities, including: Securities trading; market-making; underwriting; exposures subject to exemptions; ownership of non-EEA branches or subsidiaries etc.

(continued)

Table 3.2 (continued)

Factor/rule	US Volcker Rule	EU BSR-PR	EU BSR-RF	UK rule
l. Permitted activities	N/A	N/A	(i) Liquidity management (ii) Risk management services for clients	Services necessary for the provision of core services, e.g. liquidity management, risk management, trade finance
m. Standard of separation	Arm's length (Dodd-Frank Act, section 608)	N/A	Separation on a sub-group basis, with operational, legal, and economic standards	(i) Sub-group basis (ii) Arm's length
n. Anti-circumvention	Three principles: (i) Conflict of interest (ii) Material exposures to high-risk assets (iii) Threat to soundness of entities	No		No
o. Discretion and flexibility	The agencies have certain flexibility to amend rules	No		Treasury's flexibility to change by order
p. Connection to resolution	No	Article 19 Cooperation with resolution authorities		Detailed loss absorbency and bail in
q. Extraterritorial effect	Yes – section 2 'final rule'	Yes – art 3		Yes – ICB, p. 39

in the global financial markets. Eventually, failure of certain entities could still affect the economy as a whole due to the seemingly unavoidable contagion effect of the financial markets.[149]

This analysis is not unreasonable based on certain research conducted. A statistical research by the IMF tried to find out the correlation between trading activities and distress in the GFC. The research conducted a 'filter rule test' on 79 SIFIs across the EU, the US, and Asian countries, including investment banks, commercial banks, and universal banks. The research treated these sample banks with a high percentage of trading income as 'vulnerable banks', as identified by the filter rule. It also identified the total number of banks and the total number of 'vulnerable banks' which received official support in 2008. They then calculated the number of 'vulnerable banks' that received official support as a percentage of the total number of banks that received official support during the crisis in 2008. The result of the filter rule showed that both in the US and the EU, the majority of banks that received assistance during the crisis were institutions that were deemed 'vulnerable' (67%). Their trading income to total revenue ratios were very high. However, this was not the case in the Asian countries.[150]

Therefore, the different results in different geographical areas at least indicate that an assumptive linear relationship between the separation of trading activities and financial stability is not absolutely accurate. At least the statistics do not demonstrate this in the Asian countries. And it should be noted that Asia is also an area with many financial entities that account for a significant part of the international financial markets. However, positive correlation does exist between the susceptibility to distress and the importance of trading activities as revenue generators in the US and the EU banks.

5.2 Structural and cyclical attribute and reforms

This section further elaborates the point made at the end of Chapter 1 on the two attributes of the bank structural problem.[151] What are some other factors that are related to the vulnerability of banks in the structural problem? The IMF has provided some tentative answers. For example, the comparatively solid economic fundamentals in Asian markets may have played an important role in maintaining the resilience of financial markets; and the low exposure to poisonous securities-backed assets, such as RMBS and CDOs, made their banks safer. Two significant explanations were noted in the research:[152]

(1) Proprietary trading may be only one part of the structural problem; risk and vulnerability could also be triggered by other activities, such as market-making, investment banking, and hedging;

---

149 Gambacorta, *Structural bank regulation initiatives: approaches and implications*, pp. 4–5.
150 Chow, *Making banks safer: can Volcker and Vickers do it?* pp. 14–16.
151 See supra Chapter 1, Section 5 and Chapter 2, Section 5.
152 Chow, *Making banks safer: can Volcker and Vickers do it?*

(2) There is a need to ponder the question of whether the origin of the crisis is cyclical or structural.[153]

This analysis is convincing based on former statistical research. Therefore, the relationship between trading activities and financial stability is more complex than expected (not linear). A reasonable explanation is that apart from trading activities, there are probably other variables which have a causal relationship with the susceptibility of banks to distress and the occurrence of crisis. Proprietary trading is not the only activity where risk might be unleashed. The culprit could also include activities such as market-making.[154]

If the analysis were to go deeper, there is still a distinct possibility that risks could be accumulated due to the risk-taking inclination and the cyclical attribute of banking activities. Thus, the cyclicality attribute of the banking industry acts as the other variable causing banking instability. It acts as an endogenous source of risk that interacts with the structural attribute.

However plausible the IMF analysis might be, it indicates and deems the cyclical and structural attributes to be two completely different issues. That might not be exactly true. According to the behavioural analysis in Chapter 2 on how the cyclical attribute was maximised through the universal banking model, it is more reasonable to argue that the structural and cyclical variables constitute the two attributes of the structural problem.[155] The two attributes are interrelated and closely interact with each other. The universal banking model intensified the interaction between the two attributes.

If examining the structural problem of the banking industry and analysing it from a static perspective, it might be correct to say that the cyclical variable and structural variable are separate. But in the dynamic and complex financial markets, the two variables are inseparable. It should be noted that within the context of the universal banking model in the financial markets, animal spirits tend to intensify risk-taking incentives and that amplifies the influence of financial cyclicality on the development of economic bubbles. Then, however irrational the bubbles are, the behaviours of participants can affect each other and form a mutual reinforcement mechanism through 'persuasion and social influence' and other cognitive heuristics.[156] In the end, the cyclicality driven by behavioural factors would be a key crisis trigger and catalyst when negative signals appear in the markets.[157]

---

153 This IMF research on cyclicality from a statistical perspective corresponds with the cyclicality analysis in Chapter 2 of this volume, which, however, is explained from a behavioral perspective. See supra Chapter 2, Section 5.

154 See infra Chapter 5, Section 4.2. On the cost and benefit analyses of structural reform, we discuss how market making and hedging activities could be both beneficial and harmful.

155 Chapter 2 refers to how herding, wishful thinking, and heuristics as such are maximised through the universal banking model. See supra Chapter 2, Section 5.

156 Stefano DellaVigna, *Psychology and economics: evidence from the field* (2007). See also Financial Conduct Authority, *Financial Conduct Authority (2013), Applying behavioral economics in Financial Conduct Authority, Occasional Paper No.1.* (2013). See also Daniel Kahneman and Amos Tversky, 'Prospect theory: an analysis of decision under risk', *Econometrica: Journal of the Econometric Society* 263.

157 Robert J. Schiller, *Irrational exuberance* (2000), pp. 1–10.

It should be noted that the co-existence of activities under the universal banking model is the main channel for risk-taking, which constitutes the structural problem. In terms of the sources of risk, the banking structural attribute intensified the cyclical attribute, and the latter also further supported the former in return.

Financial markets are riskier as a result of the unhealthy chemistry between cyclicality and the universal banking structure that facilitates the former. The risks emanate not only from a single institution or even from all of the financial institutions, but rather from the complex dynamics of 'social influence' and collective heuristics in the markets by all entities and participants.[158]

In sum, the structural problem includes two attributes (Figure 3.1): (i) the structural attribute co-existence of commercial banking with investment banking and trading activities; and (ii) the pro-cyclical attribute, where the banking industry tends to be cyclically driven by behavioural factors and animal spirits.[159] The first attribute could possibly be tackled by the separation rule (Chapters 3–5). The second could possibly be addressed by resolution reform (Chapter 6).

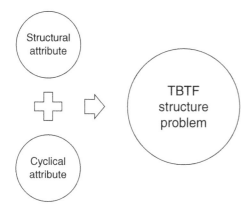

Figure 3.1 The TBTF and the structural and cyclical attributes

158 Avgouleas, 'Governance of global financial markets: the law, the economics, the politics', pp. 241–244.
159 DellaVigna, *Psychology and economics: evidence from the field.*

4 Banking structural regulation
Its implications and effectiveness

Chapter 3 mainly explores the denotation of the unsolved TBTF structural problem and the current regulatory progress in the EU and new legislations in other jurisdictions, such as the US and the UK. To achieve more or less similar objectives after the GFC, the approaches that have been employed are so different in each jurisdiction. Chapters 4 and 5 essentially focus on evaluating the EU BSR and make a case for a well-structured separation reform.

The two chapters refer to the effectiveness and efficiency of the BSR compared with the other two jurisdictions to find out what are the pros and cons of the BSR from a behavioural finance perspective and a comparative perspective. The two chapters attempt to discover whether the BSR can achieve its envisioned purposes and objectives.

1 Behavioural analysis and its normative implications

Chapter 4 mainly analyses the separation rules in the BSR from a behavioural perspective, i.e. market failure analysis.[1] But before that, the theoretical basis for applying behavioural analysis into financial regulation should be explained. Building on the behavioural analysis of investors' behaviours,[2] nudge theory advocated by Thaler and Sunstein suggests that legislative prodding is needed to direct the behaviour of people to overcome anomalies.[3] Nudging is defined as an 'aspect of choice architecture that alters people's behaviour in a predictable way without forbidding any options or significantly changing their economic incentives'.[4]

Compared with Thaler and Sunstein, George Akerlof and Robert Shiller go further by suggesting that behavioural analysis and the demonstration of

1 Financial Conduct Authority, *Financial Conduct Authority (2013), Applying behavioral economics in Financial Conduct Authority, Occasional Paper No.1.* (2013), p. 54.
2 Ibid.
3 Alina Maria Neaţu, 'The use of behavioral economics in promoting public policy', 22 *Theoretical and Applied Economics* 255.
4 Richard H. Thaler and Cass R. Sunstein, *Nudge: improving decisions about health, wealth, and happiness* (New Haven, CT: Yale University Press 2008).

bounded rationality require more government intervention.[5] The purpose of active government intervention is to guide people's behaviours and the decision-making process so that good human inclinations could be strengthened while some anomalies could be tamed.

Therefore, such a suggestion of more government intervention as advocated by George Akerlof and Robert Shiller provides a solid basis for applying behavioural analysis to the bank structural reform and turning it into more effective regulation.

1.1 Applying behavioural analysis in intervention: market failure analysis and cost benefit analysis

The Financial Conduct Authority (FCA) adopted a three-step approach in suggesting how behavioural economics could be applied to regulatory reform in the UK.[6]

First, spotting consumer harm caused by bias. Bias is rarely directly observable. The FCA suggests a set of indicators that could help to identify where the possibility of harming consumers may be particularly high due to mistakes caused by behavioural bias. These indicators provided by the FCA emphasise potentially problematic consumer and firm behaviours and product features.

Second, understanding the root cause of problems. The FCA suggests that they must investigate whether consumers are making mistakes, and if so which bias is the reason for it.

The third step is designing effective legal interventions to offset the influence of behavioural factors on the development of risks in the banking industry. The FCA provided some possible changes to the rules to provide better consumer protection in retail services, such as providing more information, changing the choice environment, controlling product distribution, and controlling product design.

As Chapter 2 identified, many behavioural factors played a significant role in the development of the TBTF structural problem. This corresponds to the first and second steps above. That leaves the third step, to design effective interventions to offset behavioural influence. In terms of separation reform, the BSR reform was introduced and analysed in Chapter 3, so what remains is to analyse whether the rules could be effective in tackling the problem in terms of offsetting behavioural influence.[7]

---

5 George A. Akerlof and Robert J. Shiller, *Animal spirits: how human psychology drives the economy, and why it matters for global capitalism* (Princeton, NJ: Princeton University Press 2010), pp. 2–10.

6 Financial Conduct Authority, *Financial Conduct Authority (2013), Applying behavioral economics in Financial Conduct Authority, Occasional Paper No.1*, pp. 9–11. The FCA also emphasises the challenges ahead of applying behavioural economic in financial regulation, 'we will have to tackle difficult questions like: what is in consumers' best interests, where should the limits to consumer responsibility lie, and how effective are less interventionist measures, such as nudges, or more interventionist measures, such as product banning? When choosing between different measures, or no intervention at all, we need to assess their costs and benefits, to the extent that this is practically possible'.

7 Ibid, pp. 42–48.

Therefore, we need to assess the BSR from the perspective of behavioural economics. After a behavioural analysis, regarding how to assess the effectiveness of rules in attaining designated purposes, the FCA suggests two approaches, among others: in particular the Market Failure Analysis (MFA) and the Cost Benefit Analysis (CBA). The FCA introduced an integrated analysis of the effect of a proposed rule, which includes an MFA and a CBA among others that suits a given situation. Furthermore, it says:[8]

> The crucial point arising from the MFA is that the option selected must correct the relevant market failures, including after firms have reacted to implementation of the option. Alternatively, if correction is impossible or not possible at an acceptable cost, the intervention must be designed to off-set the effects of the failures identified. The role of the CBA is to inform a decision on which of the options available is likely to secure the best balance of costs and benefits.

In this book, the two approaches will be conducted respectively in Chapters 4 and 5, because they correspond well with the effectiveness and efficiency assessment of the structural reform reflected in the latter's intended objectives (Figure 4.1).[9]

1.2 Controversies and conflicting considerations

In the aftermath of the GFC, the rationale of the BSR and other similar reforms was that the structural problem and the universal banking model were the key

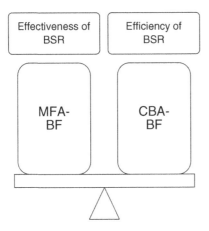

Figure 4.1 Effectiveness and efficiency of BSR

8 Ibid, p. 54.
9 See supra Chapter 3, Section 3.1.

culprits in the devastating banking failure.[10] Proponents mainly argued that the structural problem enabled the banking industry to blackmail governments and cause the moral hazard problem.[11]

But, there are also others who intensively contested that. These were essentially from the banking industry. It is undeniable that for the past decades, the banking industry has expanded at a perilous and unparalleled rate, and witnessed one of the most glorious ages of boom on the path to financial modernisation.[12] There is an accepted belief that the one-stop-shop services provided by the universal banks can best benefit the real economy against the backdrop of rapid growth in the global economy. Theoretically, it can maximise the ability of banks to perform their critical role in fostering the economy, accelerating the production of information for the markets, prompting pooling of money and provision of finance, facilitating economic transactions, strengthening the monitoring of investments, and managing risk through diversification.[13] They advocate that the universal banking model in the TBTF institutions not only exploits the economies of scale and scope, but also diversifies the hidden risks for banking institutions, which is highly necessary in the banking industry.[14]

That said, the above various dissents against the structural reform have not stopped the resolve of regulators towards the direction of tighter structural measures. The EU, the US, the UK, Germany, and France have all made progress in their respective processes of dealing with the risks in the universal banking model.[15] The current direction of reform is in stark contrast to the trend towards liberalisation seen in the past two decades around the world.

In terms of the impact of the reform, whether the envisioned purposes can be achieved needs to be assessed with regard to the BSR. As indicated in the EC proposal, by carrying out and implementing structural reform, regulatory agencies were intending to reduce excessive risk-taking and enhance the soundness and stability of this sector, while still maintaining the competitiveness of the banking industry.[16]

---

10 Édouard Fernandez-Bollo, 'Structural reform and supervision of the banking sector in France', 2013 *OECD Journal: Financial Market Trends* 1, pp. 1–4. See also supra Chapter 3, Section 4.1.1.

11 Matthias Lehmann Bonn, 'Volcker Rule, ring-fencing or separation of bank activities: comparison of structural reform acts around the world', LSE Legal Studies Working Paper No 25/2014 http://ssrn.com/abstract=2519935 or http://dx.doi.org/10.2139/ssrn.2519935, accessed May 15, 2015, pp. 3–4.

12 Liikanen Erkki, *High-level Expert Group on reforming the structure of the EU banking sector* (Final Report, Brussels, 2012), pp. 12–13. In the years before the financial crisis, the total assets growth of banks outran the growth in GDP. Statistics showed the total assets of monetary financial institutions in the EU was EUR 43 trillion in 2008, about 350% that of the total GDP.

13 Emilios Avgouleas, *Governance of global financial markets: the law, the economics, the politics* (Cambridge, UK: Cambridge University Press 2012), pp. 23–27.

14 Leonardo Gambacorta, and Adrian Van Rixtel, Bank for International Settlements, *Structural bank regulation initiatives: approaches and implications* (2013), pp. 1–5.

15 See supra Chapter 3, Section 2.2.

16 BRRD, art 1.

The Liikanen report and the EC proposals advocate enhancing financial stability and consumer protection by reducing risk-taking incentives, removing conflicts of interest, reducing interconnectedness, avoiding resource misallocation, and facilitating efficient supervision and resolution of the banking groups.[17] On the other hand, they also have due regard to competitiveness in the banking industry.

It should be noted that when considering the legal impact of structural reform, one must bear in mind the conflicting objectives between financial stability, and competition and competitiveness, especially within the context of conflicting views on the universal banking model. In terms of those conflicting views and conflicting objectives, the assessment of structural reform is characterised by many policy considerations and weighs varied interests against risks until a winning argument emerges in each case.

2 The EU BSR targets behavioural factors in the bank structural problem

This section concentrates on whether the BSR reform has regard to and is capable of containing the behavioural factors in the TBTF bank structural problem.

2.1 Animal spirits and the bank structural problem

According to BF theory, it is indisputable that behavioural factors have played a significant role in the process of the wax and wane of the economy, especially during times of historical crisis, including the recent GFC. This can be seen in Chapter 2, which focuses on analysing the causes of the GFC and the bank structural problem.[18] It shows how various behavioural variables affect decision-making of market participants, such as preferences, beliefs, and decision-making anomalies.[19] Their bias misled participants to act against their own best interests in the financial markets.[20]

Chapter 2 categorises identified behavioural factors into two groups: uncertainty and greed. These identified factors also correspond with the so-called 'animal spirits', a notion conceptualised by Robert Schiller. 'Animal spirits' denote a number of psychological factors influencing the path of the economy, shaping the landscape of the financial markets. Robert Schiller essentially identifies the following five factors:[21]

---

17 European Commission, *Commission staff working document impact assessment accompanying the document Proposal for a Regulation of the European Parliament and of the Council on structural measures improving the resilience of EU Credit Institutions and the Proposal for a Regulation of the European Parliament and of the Council on reporting and transparency of securities financing transactions, SWD/2014/030 final* (January 29, 2014), art 2.

18 Financial Conduct Authority, *Financial Conduct Authority(2013), Applying behavioral economics in Financial Conduct Authority, Occasional Paper No.1.*

19 See supra Chapter 2, Section 2.2.

20 Akerlof and Shiller, *Animal spirits: how human psychology drives the economy, and why it matters for global capitalism*, pp. 1–10.

21 Ibid.

(1) Confidence and amplifier. This refers to the excessively optimistic state of market participants that always plays an important role in most economic bubbles in history. In fact, it is also deemed to be a catalyst for economic crises.

(2) The concept of fairness. The abstract and intangible concept exists in people's sub-consciousness and significantly affects the decision-making process. The behavioural perspective of it refers mainly to situations where the fairness concept clouds people's judgement and directs them to make wrong decisions.

(3) The tendency for corruption and fraud. This represents the sinister part of human beings. It has always been vividly displayed in the development of economic bubbles as a catalyst or a precipitating factor to various economic crises.

(4) Money illusion. It represents people's confusion about inflation or deflation and its effects. The confusion tends to compromise people's ability to make sound judgements.[22]

(5) Social influence and story-telling. It is similar to the 'feedback loop' mechanism.[23] The tendency to follow others' examples compromises people's rational decision-making.

The behavioural analyses of the GFC and the TBTF structural problem in this book correspond to the BF theory by Robert Schiller.[24]

2.2 Behavioural factors, animal spirits, and historical continuity

Building on the analyses of the causal relationship between behavioural factors and the structural problem in large institutions in Chapter 2,[25] this section further substantiates the general link between behavioural factors and the occurrence of economic crises from an historical perspective.

A few other historical cases are referred to in order to analyse the continuity of the influence of behavioural factors on economic crises. It paves the way for arguments in Section 2.3: (i) the imperativeness of addressing behavioural factors in financial regulation; and (ii) the necessity to provide distinct ways to address them in the specific TBTF bank structural problem compared with addressing other crisis triggers that are based on the premise of efficient market hypothesis (EMH) and the rationality assumption.[26]

(a) The crisis in the 1890s. Historically speaking, the development of the economy showed that the occurrence of an economic crisis was always preceded

---

22 People are always confused about the meaning and relationship between 'nominal prices' and 'relative prices'.
23 See supra Chapter 2, Section 2.4.
24 See supra Chapter 2, Sections 2 and 3.
25 Daniel Kahneman and Amos Tversky, 'Prospect theory: an analysis of decision under risk', *Econometrica: Journal of the Econometric Society* 263.
26 Avgouleas, *Governance of global financial markets: the law, the economics, the politics*, p. 57.

by huge bubbles or overheated markets.[27] In the past several huge crises, the valuation of the stock markets in the pre-crisis era were all abnormally high.[28] The market optimism was largely because of the combined effect of wishful thinking and careless investment decision-making motivated by ignorance and greed.[29] The 1890 depression was by no means an exception. The S&P index increased for about 32% in just 17 months from December 1890 to May 1892. Then, it declined by 27% in the subsequent 14 months until July 1893 without any special material change of the market fundamentals.[30] The turmoil of the stock markets was plausible because bubbles in the markets would burst anyway, sooner or later.[31]

According to research by Robert Schiller, the trigger for the crisis was the Bank Purchasing Act, which allowed the redemption of legal tender paper money in gold or silver. Theoretically, there was no logical link between the run on the banks and the new Act. However, in practice, people somehow were haunted by a hunch that there might be no sufficient gold reserves at central government.[32] This baseless hunch grew into a market fear, and market fear developed into maniac withdrawal of investments. This exhausted all the gold deposits of the country and finally caused a deterioration in the overall market situation, which in turn caused the crisis.

It can be seen that the crisis trigger was bank panic. But from a behavioural perspective, the cause of the bank panic was just a baseless hunch that had absolutely no economic basis. In addition, other animal spirits also played an important role in the development of the panic and its subsequent crisis.[33] In the process of the crisis, there was a severe problem with deflation and a fall in consumer prices. This axiomatically put considerable pressure on firms' profit margins. When the establishment owners tried to cut wages, they were faced with the fiercest workers' resistance. The reason was that, on the one hand, people were uncertain about the relationship between the cut in nominal wages, and real wages triggered by the illusion of money; on the other hand, their resistance also came from a comparison of wages with other firms and wages in the pre-crisis era due to the consideration of 'fairness'.[34] Therefore, the money illusion and the consideration

27 Robert J Schiller, *Irrational exuberance* (2000), pp. 8–9.
28 Ibid.
29 Ibid, pp. 203–205. Robert Schiller, said that 'it's a serious mistake for the public figures to acquiesce in the stock market valuations we have seen recently, to remain silent about the implications of such high evaluations, and to leave all commentary to the market analysts who specialize in the nearly impossible task of forecasting the market over the short term'.
30 Akerlof and Shiller, *Animal spirits: how human psychology drives the economy, and why it matters for global capitalism*, pp. 59–60.
31 Schiller, *Irrational exuberance*, pp. 5–10.
32 Akerlof and Shiller, *Animal spirits: how human psychology drives the economy, and why it matters for global capitalism*, p. 59. Robert Schiller pointed out that the panic was totally unreasonable; the fact that people tended to withdraw their money from the banks due to some absurd reason was not understandable.
33 Ibid, pp. 59–60.
34 Ibid, p. 19.

of fairness made people prefer a shutdown rather than a reduction. The direct result was the record high unemployment rate of 18.4% in 1894, which did not fall below 10% until 1899.[35]

Hence, the points that can be made here are: (i) that the influence of behavioural factors on the development of the crisis was evident, such as the herding behaviour, social influence, and money illusion;[36] and (ii) there was a need to deal with the behavioural factors to ensure sound economic development.

(b) The 1930 Great Depression. After the 1890 crisis, the Fed was established to prevent the future relapse of a similar bank run and safeguard the banking system. However, it seems that it did not fulfil its duty properly. Following the over-heated economy in the 1920s, with a peacefully solid economic growth and stock market hike that peaked in 1929, the subsequent plummeting stock markets attacked both sides of the Atlantic. The unemployment rate rose to 25.6% in May 1933 in the US and to 26.6% in the UK.[37]

People wonder how the crisis happened in the first place and how the establishment owners and investors reacted to the over-heated economy. Current scholarship shows two points: (i) the initial trigger of the depression was the stock market crash in 1929 after its irrational exuberance; (ii) but the further catalyst of the crisis was the irrationality of market participants and the stubborn government's attitude to safeguarding the gold standard. The truth is that if the government had abandoned the gold standard sooner, the overall economy would have benefitted from the competitive lower interest rates and recovered more quickly.[38]

In the process of the crisis deteriorating into the Great Depression, behavioural factors played a very significant role. Just as the money illusion and fairness consideration led to record high unemployment in the 1890s, when deflation happened and the intention of business owners to cut wages to survive was shot down by fierce labour protests, a major reason was the confusion about the relationship between the cuts in nominal wages and the value of real wages. The direct result was that when the CPI dropped by about 27% in the early years of the Great Depression, nominal wages changed very little.[39]

On the other hand, the government did not initially intervene in the correct manner. When Robert Schiller referred to feedback theory, he said feedback could also occur in a downwards direction: 'as initial price declines discourage some investors, causing further price declines, and so forth'.[40] That fits very well with what happened in the Great Depression. When the government's regulation policy was focusing on increasing prices in the US through the National

---

35 Ibid, p. 60.
36 Kahneman and Tversky, 'Prospect theory: an analysis of decision under risk'.
37 Akerlof and Shiller, *Animal spirits: how human psychology drives the economy, and why it matters for global capitalism*, pp. 59–60.
38 Ibid, p. 60.
39 Ibid, pp. 68–70.
40 Schiller, *Irrational exuberance*, pp. 62–63.

Industrial Recovery Act (NIRA), it paid no attention to a more serious problem that led the stock market crash to become a prolonged and overall sluggish crisis. That was the crisis in confidence where no investors were willing to invest in any project even though the interest rate was very low. According to the public polls conducted by Fortune in 1941, about 90% of investors were concerned about some sort of radical economic revamp which would totally devastate their future investment returns.[41]

The points to be made here are: (i) behavioural factors and animal spirits contributed significantly to triggering and aggravating the Great Depression; and (ii) the periodically occurring crises and lack of deserved attention to behavioural factors tend to indicate that behavioural factors have shown and are still showing a strong historical continuity, especially if they are not given full attention in post-crisis regulatory reforms.

2.3 Targeting behavioural factors in the bank structural problem

The above analyses show that both the 1890s and 1930s crises originated from their respective previous irrational exuberance, ignited by a crisis of confidence in the markets and a burst of financial bubbles.

2.3.1 The imperative to tackle behavioural factors: from past to present

The imperative to tackle behavioural factors can be seen from analysing the interaction between the previous crises and governments' reactions.[42]

Still using the above crises as examples, the reason why the Fed was established was that the government was trying to learn a lesson from the 1890s crisis and established a central authority to safeguard the markets. With the establishment of the Fed, the central bank relies on 'its open market operation' and 'the discount window' regarding adjusting the money and credit supply to influence or control the markets. The adjustable interest rate to affect the supply of money could be an effective measure to deal with crises, and it turned out to have a great aspirin effect.[43]

However, facing the unprecedented Great Depression in the 1930s, pure aspirin seemed insufficient to tackle the systemic failure.[44] Thus, the new FDIC was established, created by the Banking Act of 1933, and operating as an independent agency to guarantee the safety of the financial markets alongside the Fed. By doing this there were now four channels available to protect the safety of the depository institutions: the general supervision by the Fed of the banking industry; the liquidity provision by the Fed; the FDIC deposit guarantee scheme; and the

---

41 Akerlof and Shiller, *Animal spirits: how human psychology drives the economy, and why it matters for global capitalism*, pp. 70–71.

42 Ibid, pp. 59–74.

43 Rok Spruk, 'Iceland's financial and economic crisis: causes, consequences and implications', *European Enterprise Institute Policy Paper*, pp. 7–12.

44 Banking Act of 1933, 48 Stat. 162, now repealed.

power of the FDIC to resolve problematic banks.[45] These measures turned out to be effective in maintaining the gradual growth of the economy thereafter. For example, with these measures at their disposal, the regulators successfully addressed the problem of the savings and loan crisis, the recession of 1991, and the recession in 2001.[46]

In the run up to the TBTF bank structural problem, things have changed in the past few years. Behavioural factors were playing an increasingly significant role in the development of economic bubbles, especially in the universal banking model.[47] There was a worldwide credit expansion and a low interest rate policy in the financial liberalisation process, and the extremely irrational exuberance of financial innovations made international financial markets become interconnected and vulnerable in an unprecedented manner.[48]

Behavioural factors loomed ever large in the 2008 GFC and the bank structural problem. This, to a certain extent, challenged the effectiveness of the regulatory tools, such as supervision, disclosure and transparency, and the resolution rule, which were deeply embedded in the EMH. How the current EMH-based measures are limited was evidenced by the Lehman Brothers' case, where the extant regulatory policies and measures could not deal with the systemic risk and spill over effect.[49] Although Richard Fuld expected the government bail-out with such confidence, the government had to abandon the rescue plan, appalled by the size of the failing bank.[50]

Therefore, despite progress having been made after the major reforms in financial regulation in a historical context responding to varied crises, it was still flawed in terms of not having regard to the ever-present behavioural factors, and hence could not minimise the occurrence of crisis driven by irrational exuberance. But, now we come to a time of change. The GFC reached an unprecedented scale and level of destructibility, and this shows the urgency with which the TBTF structural problem needs to be dealt with in terms of behavioural factors.[51]

2.3.2 The distinctiveness of measures to tackle behavioural factors

The initial government response after the 1930s crisis was a good example of how policies that lack any consideration of how to address behavioural factors would ended up being unsuccessful.

---

45 The Dodd-Frank Wall Street Reform and Consumer Protection Act (U.S), section 619. The bankruptcy and resolution were further established by the Dodd-Frank Act Title I and II.

46 Akerlof and Shiller, *Animal spirits: how human psychology drives the economy, and why it matters for global capitalism*, pp. 30–31.

47 See supra Chapter 2, Section 5.

48 See supra Chapter 1, Section 3(d).

49 See supra Chapter 1, Section 3.

50 Federal Deposit Insurance Corporation, 'The orderly liquidation of Lehman Brothers Holdings Inc. under the Dodd-Frank Act', www.fdic.gov/bank/analytical/quarterly/2011_vol5_2/lehman. pdf, accessed November 15, 2014. It recalls Fuld's calmness over the process of the credit crunch and the soliciting of potential buyout and strategic investors, and his final desperation after being informed of the no bail-out news.

51 See supra Chapter 1, Section 3.

Behavioural factors are distinctive compared with other precipitating factors within the context of the EMH and the rationality assumption. They are readily discernible, but it is pragmatically different to resolve them due to the fact that it is difficult to program or direct people's behaviour to be standard and rational even though researchers are aware of their bounded rationality.[52]

It should be noted that measures designed to contain behavioural factors need to be distinct when compared to conventional measures.[53] Government intervention and legal regulation of the financial markets is still mostly based on the assumption of EMH.[54] But here is where BF departs significantly from the EMH.

Thus, legal regulation also needs to be adjusted to cater for changing assumptions. Therefore, when assessing whether the BSR could contain behavioural factors, we need to examine whether the BSR can distinctively exert influence over behavioural factors, before considering its effectiveness and efficiency.[55]

2.3.3 Putting the normative paradox of behavioural analysis into perspective

It should also be noted that although behavioural factors affecting the performance of the financial markets are discernible in the GFC, the question of how to address them and tame the intangible factors is very difficult. That is also why Amos Tversky and Daniel Kahneman concluded that:[56]

> Alternative descriptions of a decision problem often give rise to different preferences, contrary to the principle of invariance that underlies the rational theory of choice. Violations of the theory are traced to the rules that govern the framing of the decision and to the psychological principles of evaluation embodied in prospect theory. Invariance and dominance are obeyed when the application is transparent and often violated in other situations, because these rules are normatively essential but descriptively invalid; no theory of choice can be both normatively adequate and descriptively accurate.

Therefore, although the expected utility theory and the EMH are normatively accurate, they could be descriptively wrong. However, although the BF theory is accurately descriptive, it can be difficult to normatively support a rule to address the problems reflected in its description.[57] All in all, the irrational assumption of investors and unpredictability of behavioural factors make it easy to discern them on an ex-post basis. But, it is pretty difficult to tackle them on an ex-ante basis, let

---

52 Amos Tversky and Daniel Kahneman, 'Rational choice and the framing of decisions', *Journal of Business* S251.
53 See infra Chapter 4, Section 2.4(a). It explains why there is a need for a distinctive structural reform rather than purely relying on a conventional price-based approach.
54 Burton G Malkiel, 'The efficient market hypothesis and its critics', *Journal of Economic Perspectives* 59.
55 See infra Chapter 4, Section 3 and Chapter 5.
56 Tversky and Kahneman, 'Rational choice and the framing of decisions'.
57 Ibid.

alone prevent and address them. It could be concluded that a descriptive analysis by BF could not be easily transformed into a normative legal solution.

Be that as it may, with regard to the TBTF bank structural problem, the very existence of a difficulty in applying BF still does not mean it is impossible. First, rules such as separation can reduce the influence of behavioural factors, although it is impossible to eradicate them.[58]

Second, the introduction of the AMH would tilt the scale, to a certain extent, in favour of applying BF in a normative way.[59] Although there might be a normative paradox here with regard to the behavioural analysis undertaken in Chapter 2, it should be put into perspective, especially with the modification of BF by the AMH.

2.4 The BSR: de-link the interaction between behavioural factors and the bank structural problem

The above analyses shed light on the theoretical challenges in applying behavioural findings normatively to the structural problem to bring about actual regulatory reform with distinctive measures. Keep that in mind and consider: (i) whether the structural reform is imperative; (ii) how the BSR is distinctive and thereby is better than price-based rules in taking behavioural factors into consideration; and (iii) whether the BSR has overcome that particular theoretical challenge.[60]

2.4.1 The inadequacy of the price-based approach and imperativeness for structural reform

To tackle the TBTF bank structural problem, the EU has adopted many price-based reforms as indicated in Chapter 3.[61] For instance, the capital requirements in CRDIV/CRR[62] were designed to address the capital inadequacy problem in the banking industry by requiring leverage ratios, higher capital ratios, and liquidity requirements. Additionally, the reform of the supervision system has also made great progress.[63] The EBU including the SSM has been proposed and gradually adopted.[64] The MiFID II, MiFIR, and UCITS have also stipulated a higher level of disclosure and enhanced consumer protection. In terms of the price-based reform within the context of behavioural analysis, and comparing it with the structural reform, it has at least two weaknesses.

---

58 Detailed analyses can be found below, see infra Chapter 4, Section 2.4.
59 See supra Chapter 2, Section 4.1.
60 Daniel Kahneman, 'Maps of bounded rationality: psychology for behavioral economics', *American Economic Review* 1449.
61 See supra Chapter 3, Section 1.2.
62 See CRD IV and CRR generally with regard to capital requirements.
63 European Commission, *Communication from the Commission to the European Parliament and the Council: A Roadmap towards a Banking Union, COM (2012) 510 final* (September 12, 2012).
64 As early as December 2012, great progress had already been made when Eurozone finance ministers agreed a plan to cede power to a common bank supervisor based on a Commission proposal on banking union in September 2012.

(a) It is inadequate in addressing fat-tail risk. The Basel III and CRD IV/CRR raised the capital requirements, and also made up for the RWA-based capital requirement weakness by adding the new capital conservation buffer, leverage ratio, liquidity coverage ratio (LCR), and the net stable funding ratio (NSFR).[65] But the main concern about these rules is whether they can successfully address systemic risk.

The answer to this question is probably negative. These requirements are trying to regulate the banking industry by taking the universal banking model and the co-existence of various activities for granted. The higher capital requirements may make the banks have a stronger shelter. However, they still mostly rely on the RWA calculation, which does not capture the fat-tail risk.

It has at least three disadvantages:

(1) As indicated by much current research, risk weighting has its merits; however, it has inevitable imperfections in practice. The risks weights attributed to the sovereign bonds turned out to definitely be inaccurate in the pre-crisis era; they were normally lower than the real market default risk.[66]

(2) The use of RWAs gave the wrong incentive to banks to manipulate the risk weights of assets so that they could minimise their capital requirement level. Statistics showed that in the run up to the crisis, the risk weights of the assets of the four largest banks in the UK decreased significantly, albeit increasing the leverage ratio. The truth was that the risk weights were deliberately manipulated to bypass compliance with the capital requirements.[67]

(3) There is no statistical evidence that current other non-RWAs-based requirements would offer banks sufficient loss absorbency capacity in a systemic crisis, such as the GFC.[68]

A good example with regard to the fat-tail risk is the investment losses that occurred in JPMorgan in a portfolio investment managed by its chief investment officer in 2012.[69] Trader Bruno Iksil (London Whale) accumulated outsized CDS positions, and an estimated loss of USD2 billion was announced after this event.[70] This event brought about many investigations to examine the firm's risk management mechanism and the internal control model. The results and the headlines in the media did not disclose the exact nature of the trading involved. But it was said to relate to CDX IG 9, a credit default swap index based on the default risk of US companies, the so-called 'derivative of a derivative'.

---

65 See generally CRD IV/CRR.
66 Independent Commission on Banking, 'Final Report, recommendations', p. 83.
67 Ibid, p. 98.
68 Ibid, pp. 112–114. See supra Chapter 1, Section 3(c).
69 Dawn Kopecki, 'JPMorgan pays $920 million to settle London Whale probes', Bloomberg, www.bloomberg.com/news/2013–09–19/jpmorgan-chase-agrees-to-pay-920-million-for-london-whale-loss.html, accessed November 20, 2014.
70 On July 13, 2012, the total losses were said to be USD5.8 billion, with an extra USD4.4 billion of losses in the second quarter. It was claimed by the firm that projected total losses were more than USD7 billion. See also, Arwin G. Zeissler and Andrew Metrick, 'JPMorgan chase London Whale G: hedging versus proprietary trading', *Yale Program on Financial Stability Case Study*, pp. 8–9.

As one of the most powerful financial entities in the world, JPMorgan definitely has its own self-sufficient internal risk control model, which must be in line with regulatory requirements including the required capital requirements. JPMorgan took all the necessary and critical principles into consideration, such as a reduction in the portfolio by assessing RWAs, maintenance of profits under the VaR model, and a having a higher default protection. But internal risk controls could not guarantee the safety of its investment. Its CEO Jamie Dimon admitted after the event that the investment strategy was 'flawed, complex, poorly reviewed, poorly executed, and poorly monitored'.

What happened in this case was that although it strictly complied with the risk control, it still ended up with a huge loss. A further audit on an ex-post basis discovered that the internal control and the risk management model were not adapted proportionally according to the increased complexity of its trading positions. Apparently, one of the most important triggers for the losses was the increasing complexity of the financial products and unsatisfactory modelling accuracy. Although a risk control model could capture many anticipated variables, the increasing market uncertainties and volatility accompanying the complexity still challenged the model's ability to control risk.[71]

Through the use of the non-risk-weighting-based leverage ratio, the objective of regulation is to avoid systemically important banks manipulating their risk weights. But even by adding the non-risk-weighted requirements such as the leverage ratio, they still do not directly target the risk-taking incentives and behavioural factors. Unfortunately, although fat-tail risk and systemic risk do not happen frequently, it is an actual and fatal threat to the overall economy because its occurrence is accompanied by a disastrous catastrophe, just like what happened in the GFC.[72]

(b) The price-based approach is insufficient to protect the CCI. This is because it does not directly correspond with many essential features in bank failures and the bank structural problem highlighted in Chapter 1, such as complexity and interconnectedness and the spill over effect. The contagion effect was one of the main issues in the TBTF bank structural problem that doomed the banking industry. In other words, the trading entity excessively exploited the low-cost wholesale funding sources and used them for business expansion in investment banking and trading activities. By so doing, the deposit entity provided implicit subsidisation to the trading activities.[73] When the failure happened, the risks materialising in the trading entities instantly spread to the CCIs. The price-based approach, however stringent it might be after the post-crisis reform, has a very limited impact in dealing with the contagion effect and interconnectedness problem.

---

71 José Viñals and others, *Creating a safer financial system: will the Volcker, Vickers, and Liikanen Structural measures help?* (New York: International Monetary Fund 2013), pp. 7–8.
72 Avgouleas, *Governance of global financial markets: the law, the economics, the politics*, pp. 346–347.
73 Liikanen Erkki, *High-level Expert Group on reforming the structure of the EU banking sector*, pp. 4–7.

In contrast, the structural reform (BSR) could as an imperative and distinctive measure deal with the TBTF bank structural problem. Its framework has due regard to factors such as complexity, interconnectedness, and resolvability.[74]

The following section tries to indicate how the BSR can exert influence on behavioural factors through its structural separation.

2.4.2 The BSR distinctiveness: de-link the behavioural factors and the structural problem

Compared with price-based measures, the BSR shows its distinctiveness and caters to the urgent need to minimise the influence of identified behavioural factors.[75] The BSR was initiated against a background of other regulatory measures, especially price-based measures. These measures are definitely helpful to enhance the safety and soundness of the banking sector to a certain extent. But the previous section proves their shortcomings.

Specifically, price-based measures can be of auxiliary and subsidiary help to the structural problem. A better-supervised and safer banking sector under enhanced price-based measures can of course promote the resilience of it to any problem, including the bank structural problem.[76] The truth is they do not address the structural problem exactly, in particular because they do not de-link the mutual interaction between the identified behavioural factors and the bank structural problem.

In contrast, the structural separation rule in the BSR intends to separate the deposit entity from trading activities in order to reduce the inclination for risk-taking and the moral hazard problem. It is an approach that is distinct from the price-based measures, and it can either intentionally or incidentally contain the behavioural factors.[77] According to Robert Schiller, the bounded rationality of market participants requires more regulatory intervention, and more specifically tailored regulation can reduce the misleading influence of anomalies.[78]

The BSR does not directly point out or show how behavioural factors could exert influence on fuelling bubbles and aggravating the structural problem. However, it does undermine the channel through which the misleading influence of behavioural factors is amplified: the co-existence of the deposit entity and the trading entity. As indicated in Chapter 1, it is the co-existence of different activities and the implicit subsidisation from the CCI to other risky activities that fuelled the risk-taking incentives, the interconnectedness of the banking sector, and the resolution problem.[79] According to Chapter 2, behavioural factors contributed significantly to these problems, but they mostly existed and exerted influence

74 Julian TS Chow, *Making banks safer: can Volcker and Vickers do it?* (New York: International Monetary Fund 2011).
75 See supra Chapter 4, Section 2.3.2.
76 Independent Commission on Banking, 'Final Report, recommendations', p. 110.
77 See supra Chapter 4, Section 2.3.2.
78 Akerlof and Shiller, *Animal spirits: how human psychology drives the economy, and why it matters for global capitalism*, pp. 167–177.
79 See supra Introduction, Section 1.1.

through trading activities and the trading entity.[80] It was mainly through the trading entity that the behavioural factors also affected the stability of the CCI.

Therefore, by restricting or prohibiting the trading activities, the BSR has two effective aspects to contain the behavioural factors in the structural problem, and put the normative paradox into perspective:

(1) It reduces the link and mutual interaction between behavioural factors and the trading entity. In fact, the role of the behavioural factors as a precipitating factor of bubble making and bubble bursts was only strengthened because of subsidisation due to the co-existence of activities.[81] Conversely, when co-existence is restricted or prohibited, subsidisation is controlled. The role of behavioural factors as a precipitating factor in the trading activities would therefore also be contained.[82]

(2) It de-links the behavioural factors and the CCI. The CCI is a traditionally safe entity engaging in only core financial services. The possibility of the CCI being exposed to highly risky activities and being affected by behavioural factors is very limited.[83] The fact that the CCI was lethally impacted in the GFC, which was significantly attributable to behavioural factors, was due to the co-existence of activities and the contagion effect from the trading entity. Conversely, without the co-existence of activities under the BSR, the link and possible contagion effect would mostly be contained.[84]

Having said that, it should also be noted that the BSR could not eliminate the influence of behavioural factors, such as wishful thinking, animal spirits, and the social influence on the development and accumulation of risks in the financial markets.[85] However, rather than ignoring behavioural factors as in the price-based approach, the BSR takes the behavioural factors into consideration by separating out the trading entity where behavioural factors tend to be amplified and have a bad influence on the CCI and the bank group as a whole.

Under the BSR, the risks triggered by behavioural factors could only happen in the restricted activities and entities and would not contaminate the CCI. Therefore, a failure of the trading entity is less likely to have as big a spill over effect as that in the GFC and probably would not be able to systemically disrupt the economy as a whole. By de-linking the connection between different entities, they would all be treated as independent units.

---

80 See supra Chapter 2, Section 2.2. All the identified behavioural factors are mostly referred to within the context of the trading entity and the universal bank, rather than the separated CCI.

81 See supra Chapter 1, Section 3(b). The interconnectedness feature in the banking sector denotes both the subsidisation from the CCI to the trading entity, but also the dependence on interbank wholesale funding. For more detailed analysis on the subsidisation, see also infra Chapter 5, Section 4.5.

82 For detailed analysis see infra Chapter 4, Section 3.2.1.

83 See supra Chapter 2, Section 2.2. The CCI did not directly interact with the behavioural factors in the GFC. For more detailed analysis on the safety of the CCI, see also infra Chapter 4, Section 3.

84 For detailed analysis, see infra Chapter 4, Section 3.2.1.

85 Steven L. Schwarcz, 'Systemic risk', 97 Geo LJ 193.

Thus, the role of the behavioural factors in the development of the economic bubble could be tamed and contained. Consequently, the risks in the trading entity could be well controlled; any remaining risks would also be ruled out in the CCI. In this way, banking safety and soundness and financial stability could possibly be enhanced.

3 MFA of the BSR: enhancement of safety

The previous section shows that the BSR could contain the link between behavioural factors and the structural problem. Building on this, this section analyses the BSR's effectiveness in bringing about safety and stability to the banking sector, especially to the CCI, through MFA.

3.1 Theoretical concern: fuzziness

As indicated earlier, the universal banking model tends to be a precipitating factor. It encourages risk-taking, distorts competition, increases complexity and interconnectedness, and exploits the economies of scope and scale.[86] The crackdown on the model tends to enhance financial stability and the safety and soundness of the banking industry.

Except for the strength of the reform, the scope of restriction or prohibition is essential for the reform's effectiveness.[87] This means it is of critical importance to define and delimit the boundary of the structural regulation reform and to distinguish the permitted activities and the prohibited activities.

It should be noted that the fuzziness between permitted and prohibited activities raises a theoretical concern about the reform's effectiveness.[88] The fuzziness here relates to the difficulties in reality to distinguish A activity from B activity. With this in mind, the approach of defining the scope of prohibition in the BSR is a principles-based one. Under the prohibition rule, proprietary trading, which is referred to as 'using own capital or borrowed money to take positions in any type of transaction . . . for the sole purpose of making a profit for own account', is prohibited.[89]

While it does not provide as long a list of exceptions as that in the Volcker Rule, it generally provides a principle as a possibility for exceptions: activities that are 'connected to actual or anticipated client activities'.[90]

For the principles-based rule, on the surface, it does not need to legally delimit the differences between trading activities and the usual exceptions, such as

---

86   United States Senate Permanent Subcommittee on Investigations, *Wall Street and the financial crisis: anatomy of a financial collapse* (Cosimo Reports 2011), pp. 15–45. See also Liikanen Erkki, *High-level Expert Group on reforming the structure of the EU banking sector*, pp. 32–38.

87   Fernandez-Bollo, 'Structural reform and supervision of the banking sector in France'.

88   H. Patrick Glenn, 'Comparative law and legal practice: on removing the borders', 75 Tul L Rev 977. Fuzziness refers to the logical difficulties in disentangling similar concepts. In this context we referred it as both the theoretical and practical difficulties in differentiating prohibited and permitted activities.

89   European Commission, *Proposal for a Regulation of the European Parliament and of the Council on structural measures improving the resilience of EU credit institutions, COM/2014/043 final* (January 29, 2014), art 5(4).

90   Ibid.

market-making, hedging, and underwriting. The reason is that it doesn't provide a detailed exceptions list. But in reality, the principles-based rule makes it even harder to actually carry out the rule in practice because of the ambiguity between trading and some possibly exempted activities.[91] The lack of explicit provision of exceptions only makes the fuzziness problem more serious.

In terms of the Volcker Rule, it adopted a different approach in defining the scope of prohibition by providing a long, detailed list of exceptions, such as transactions in US government obligations; market-making activities; hedging activities; and transactions for customers.[92] Therefore, in terms of prohibition, it leaves an explicitly clear open door for some activities.[93] Admittedly, even in the case of the Volcker Rule where the prohibition and exceptions are clearly defined, the implementation would still meet the practical challenges of ambiguity and fuzziness. A classic example is the practical difficulties in identifying real market-making activities and trading activities, the line between the two being so vague.[94]

Similarly, the UK ring-fence rule also provides a detailed list of restrictions and exceptions. But in the Vickers Rule, it excludes a broader scope of activities including market-making, underwriting, hedging, as well as investment banking. So, in terms of the broader scope, it would avoid the fuzziness problem to a certain extent.[95]

Therefore, as regards the effectiveness of the BSR in enhancing safety, a theoretical concern is the fuzziness problem and the difficulty in defining the boundary between prohibited activities and exceptions, e.g. distinguishing proprietary trading and market-making. The Vickers Rule, with a broader scope of prohibition, however, avoids this problem of fuzziness in a better way compared with the BSR and the Volcker Rule.

3.2 The protected part becomes safer

The fundamental purpose of the BSR is to enhance the safety and resilience of the banking industry while maintaining an efficient financial services sector to serve the overall economy.[96] So there always needs to be a balance between stability and efficiency. Efficiency will be discussed in the next chapter, but this section will focus on safety.

3.2.1 The prohibition rule and safety

If we look at the prohibition rule in the BSR, the proprietary trading activities and investment in AIFs would be prohibited. These activities cannot be committed

---

91 Ibid, art 3.
92 Prohibitions and Restrictions on Proprietary Trading and Certain Interests In, and Relationships With, Hedge Funds and Private Equity Funds (The Final Rule) (U.S), Sections 4–6.
93 The Dodd-Frank Wall Street Reform and Consumer Protection Act (U.S), section 619. See infra Chapter 5, Section 4.2.1.
94 Darrell Duffie, 'Market making under the proposed Volcker rule', Rock Center for Corporate Governance at Stanford University Working Paper 106, pp. 7–15.
95 Independent Commission on Banking, 'Final Report, recommendations', p. 234.
96 Liikanen Erkki, *High-level Expert Group on reforming the structure of the EU banking sector*, p. 1. See also European Commission, *Proposal for a Regulation of the European Parliament and of the Council on structural measures improving the resilience of EU credit institutions, COM/2014/043* final, p. 6.

even in the same banking group. It seems the prohibition rule is very stringent in promoting CCI safety.

The BSR prohibition rule has a very narrow application scope. It applies only to G-SIIs and EU-SIIs.[97] Unlike the detailed prohibition rule in the US with a long list of exemptions, the prohibition rule is principles-based: only proprietary trading for the sole purpose of profit-making and certain investments in AIFs would be prohibited. Although the rule only targets a very limited number of banks of global significance, when it applies, it applies to the whole banking group, as in the Volcker Rule. According to article 3, the prohibition rule applies to all the branches and subsidiaries of a group regardless of their location. It applies to non-EU subsidiaries of EU banks and to EU branches of non-EU banks unless relevant jurisdictions have equivalent requirements to the prohibition rule in the BSR.[98] Therefore, it ensures that prohibited activities would not exist in the entire banking group. Besides, it leaves no obvious room for non-EU arbitrage because of the extraterritorial effect of the rule.

Given the prohibition rule actually prohibits trading activities in the entire group and therefore prohibits the universal banking model, it could evidently achieve the purpose of providing a safer bank, especially a safer CCI.[99]

The reason is that the risks that triggered the bank failure, as discussed in Chapters 1 and 2, emanated mainly from the trading entity, and the behavioural factors only loomed largest with the universal banking model as its platform. And the behavioural factors mostly interacted with these causes and risks in the trading entity.[100]

A TRADING, BEHAVIOURAL FACTORS, AND SAFETY

First, the irrational overdependence of CRA ratings as a major micro cause of the TBTF bank structural problem, was mainly related to the trading of structural debt securities and other financial products, to which the preference bias was deeply related.[101]

Second, the 'originate-to-distribute model' was another major cause of the TBTF bank structural problem and was also only created to facilitate the production of the structural debt securities. Within the context of the model, the biased beliefs, such as overconfidence and overextrapolation, greatly contributed to the expansion of the derivative markets and the Ponzi scheme style boom of the structural debt securities.

Third, the complexity of the financial products and the overuse of financial innovation (a macro cause of TBTF structural problem), also only happened in

---

97 European Commission, *Proposal for a Regulation of the European Parliament and of the Council on structural measures improving the resilience of EU credit institutions*, COM/2014/043 final, art 3.

98 Ibid, art 21.

99 European Commission, *Commission staff working document impact assessment accompanying the document Proposal for a Regulation of the European Parliament and of the Council on structural measures improving the resilience of EU Credit Institutions and the Proposal for a Regulation of the European Parliament and of the Council on reporting and transparency of securities financing transactions*, SWD/2014/030 final, pp. 33–34.

100 See supra Chapter 2, Section 2.2.

101 Avgouleas, *Governance of global financial markets: the law, the economics, the politics*, and pp. 89–92. See supra Chapter 2, Section 1 on the macro and micro cause of the GFC.

the trading entity. The complexity of the products definitely took advantage of the decision-making bias of investors, such as framing, salient decision, and social influence.[102]

Fourth, another major macro cause was the loose monetary and financial liberalisation policies, as we indicated in the Lehman Brother's case and the Iceland case. These policies exerted the largest influence on bank expansion in the investment banking and trading entities. They were also somehow influenced by some irrational ignorance of human beings.[103]

Finally, as indicated by S&P, the industry's misaligned incentives and irrational risk-taking were driven by the urge for survival and were only maximised in the non-CCI entities if their expansion was subsidised by the CCIs.[104]

B SHADOW BANKING, TRADING, BEHAVIOURAL FACTORS, AND SAFETY

The trading activities were also closely related to shadow banking, which was another major channel of risks and behavioural influence (e.g. wishful thinking and overconfidence).[105] It is generally accepted that shadow banking fuelled the derivative markets and securitisation-related trading activities by providing credit to the markets through non-bank channels. This brought about huge risks in the run up to the GFC, and it contaminated the whole banking industry due to the way CCIs were interconnected with other risky entities and their implicit subsidisation link. When discussing shadow banking risk, the Financial Stability Board (FSB) advocated that:[106]

> Shadow banking . . . such intermediation, appropriately conducted, provides a valuable alternative to bank funding that supports real economic activity. But experience from the crisis demonstrates the capacity for some non-bank entities and transactions to operate on a large scale in ways that create bank-like risks to financial stability (longer-term credit extension based on short-term funding and leverage). Such risk creation may take place at an entity level, but it can also form part of a complex chain of transactions, in which leverage and maturity transformation occur in stages, and in ways that create multiple forms of feedback into the regular banking system.

A leveraged shadow banking that is dependent on maturity transforming can be vulnerable to 'runs' and thereby creates the contagion effect and amplifies the possibility of systemic risk. The shadow banking activities tend to heighten cyclicality by accelerating credit supply and asset price increases during a time of good economic foundation driven by market confidence. On the contrary, it could also

102 Steven L. Schwarcz, 'Regulating complexity in financial markets', 87 Wash UL Rev 211.

103 Jerome A. Madden, 'A weapon of mass destruction strikes: credit default swaps bring down AIG and Lehman Brothers', 5 Bus L Brief 15.

104 Andrew W. Lo, 'Reconciling efficient markets with behavioral finance: the adaptive markets hypothesis', 7 *Journal of Investment Consulting* 21.

105 Financial Stability Board, *Strengthening oversight and regulation of shadow banking: an overview of policy recommendation* (August 29, 2013), pp. i–ii.

106 Ibid.

precipitate decreases in asset prices when there is any negative event in the market that causes a sudden loss of confidence.

Therefore, all the above causes of the structural problem mostly happened in the trading entity and were closely related to and interacted with identified behavioural factors. In other words, the causes, risks, and their behavioural embodiments in the run-up to the GFC and the TBTF bank structural problem basically happened in non-CCI activities, i.e. the trading activities.[107]

By absolute prohibition of these activities in the entire group through the prohibition rule, the BSR definitely protects the banks from two aspects:

(1) It contains the risks in the trading entity. Due to the prohibition rule, the eradication of implicit subsidisation from the CCI to the trading entity would appease the risk-taking incentive in the trading entity.[108] The less risky trading entity would also probably rule out the possibility of any indirect contagion effect to the CCI.
(2) The CCI is protected from the above risks and the behavioural misleading influence in the trading entities. By prohibiting these activities from being conducted in the G-SIIs, although the prohibition rule does not eradicate the behavioural factors' influence on the creation of risks, it does minimise and remove the risks in the CCI so that they would be absorbed by the markets internally.

Thus, for sure the prohibition rule ensures the CCI is insulated from the risks hidden in the trading activities, and the protected part is safer.[109] By making the CCI safer, it is more resilient in any future market volatility stemming from either indigenous or exogenous factors.[110]

3.2.2 The ring-fence rule and safety

The ring-fence applies to all banks covered by the DGS irrespective of size. A broadly defined set of trading activities is required to be transferred into a separated entity on a case-to-case basis decided by the competent authorities. Unlike the prohibition rule, the prohibited activities, although not allowed to be in the CCI of a bank holding company or group, can still exist in another entity on a sub-group basis. The rule only applies according to the discretion of the competent authorities based on their assessment.[111]

A NON-NEGLIGIBLE POSITIVE IMPLICATIONS

Under the ring-fence, the extremely inclusive restricted trading activities include almost all other activities except for the short list of core banking activities.[112]

---

107   Ibid.
108   For the analysis on interconnectedness and subsidization, see also supra Chapter 1, Section 3(b).
109   Schwarcz, 'Regulating complexity in financial markets', pp. 236–256.
110   Financial Conduct Authority, *Financial Conduct Authority(2013), Applying behavioral economics in Financial Conduct Authority, Occasional Paper No.1*, pp. 54–55.
111   European Commission, *Proposal for a Regulation of the European Parliament and of the Council on structural measures improving the resilience of EU credit institutions, COM/2014/043 final*, art 10.
112   Ibid, art 8(1).

These non-CCI activities would be carried out in another separate group entity. The rule has at least two implications.

First, due to the inclusive scope of the restriction compared with that in the prohibition rule, the ring-fence would mostly transfer all significant and identifiable risks from the CCI to an independent trading entity in the same group as the CCI when it is deemed necessary by the competent authorities. As discussed earlier, the trading entity was the major source of risk, and the major platform where behavioural factors, such as preferences, beliefs, and decision-making bias, exerted their influence on market participants. Because of the scope, the risks being transferred would probably be even more inclusive than that under the prohibition rule.

Second, due to the less robust strength of restriction, the ring-fence itself does not deal with the behavioural factors as effectively as the prohibition rule. It only transfers the restricted activities together with their risks into a comparatively more independent entity rather than completely removing it from the CCI as under the prohibition rule. It severs, to a certain extent, the ties and links between the CCI and the trading entity. The ties are compromised to a large extent through legal, economical, and operational separation requirements.[113]

For many of the banks in the EU, retail deposits were still a very significant source of funding for their development.[114] By ring-fencing the CCI, it severs one of the most important sources of funding for trading entities. Without sufficient funding sources, asset bubbles would be less likely or more difficult to happen. Therefore, to some extent, it tames the behavioural factors, such as the overconfidence bias and the decision-making bias. However, as indicated in the Liikanen Report, retail deposits on the banks' balance sheets were becoming less and less important in some EU banks:[115]

> As regards non-equity funding, important developments occurred. Retail deposits grew roughly in line with EU GDP and did not allow bank balance sheet growth to outpace GDP growth. EU banks funded their rapid growth with funding in the interbank markets (unsecured) and wholesale repo markets (secured) instead.

Therefore, under the ring-fence, the effect on the banking sector and the protected part would be as follow:

(1) There is no doubt that by ring-fencing, the behavioural factors in the trading would be partly tamed. By restricting the subsidisation from the CCI to the trading entity, less risk-taking incentives would make the trading entity safer. On the other hand, the ring-fence reduces the interconnectedness of the banking sector and the intragroup relationship, which could minimise the contagion effect.[116] Therefore, the less risky trading entity would also lower the possibility of CCI volatility.

---

113 Ibid, art 13–15.
114 Liikanen Erkki, *High-level Expert Group on reforming the structure of the EU banking sector*, p. 15.
115 Ibid.
116 Ibid, pp. 14–15.

(2) Although not as effective as the prohibition rule due to the difference in strength, the ring-fence would for sure make the CCIs insulated from the risks hidden in trading activities and therefore the protected part would be safer when compared with the status quo and the pre-crisis era.[117] Mechanically speaking, the ring-fence can provide a buffer for the protected part. The ring-fence insulates the CCI from the trading entity that is the major source of risk and is a major platform where behavioural factors exert their influence.

B CONCERNS WITH REGARD TO RING-FENCE STRENGTH

Having said that, despite the broad scope of the restrictions, there are still concerns about the ring-fence. First, unlike the prohibition rule, the trading entity and the deposit entity under the ring-fence can still co-exist in the same group. This raises concerns that the insulation mechanism may not be sufficient to deal with certain situations, such as systemic risk and reputation risk.[118] Second, the ring-fence is not applied on a mandatory basis, but on a case-by-case basis according to the decision by competent authorities. Therefore, the above effects would largely be dependent on an effective supervision mechanism.[119]

3.3 The migrating of risks

After tightening the regulation of the universal banking structure, the trading activities would either be prohibited or separated from the CCI under the prohibition rule and the ring-fence. By so doing, the risks mainly emanating from the trading entities and the behavioural factors could be tamed to a certain extent. But, another practical concern is that these risky activities and behavioural factors might possibly migrate to other less restricted areas to evade regulation.

First, the ambiguous exemptions of the prohibition and restriction leave some room for migration. With regard to the prohibition rule, which applies to the EU and G-SIIs only, it would not tolerate the proprietary trading activities existing in the entities covered by the exemptions. But, the delimitation of the proprietary trading is a principles-based approach. It focuses on the purpose of own account profit-making, while not being connected to any client activities. But, unlike in the US, it does not provide a specific exceptions list to allow some less risky activities.[120] In reality, there must be some less risky activities that need to be exempted under this definition. In the absence of a detailed EU delimitation and exceptions list, it would leave the competent authorities with more discretion in practice. On the one hand, the existence of discretion by competent authorities would bring about uncertainties and ambiguity in implementation; but on the other, there is also the risk that the exemptions provided by the competent authorities might be inconsistent.[121]

---

117 Schwarcz, 'Regulating complexity in financial markets'.
118 Liikanen Erkki, *High-level Expert Group on reforming the structure of the EU banking sector.*
119 Wymeersch Eddy, 'The Single Supervisory Mechanism or "SSM", Part One of the Banking Union (2014)'. European Corporate Governance Institute (ECGI) – Law Working Paper No 240/2014, available at SSRN: http://ssrn.com/abstract=2397800 or http://dx.doi.org/10.2139/ssrn. 2397800, accessed March 23, 2015.
120 The Dodd-Frank Wall Street Reform and Consumer Protection Act (U.S), section 619.
121 Eilis Ferran and Valia S.G. Babis, 'The European single supervisory mechanism', University of Cambridge Faculty of Law Research Paper.

As regards the ring-fence, this rule is not mandatory. Therefore, it would be up to the competent authorities' decisions to assess whether certain activities would be a threat to the stability of the CCI or to the EU financial markets as a whole. It also only provides a very principles-based assessment approach based on a series of metrics: the relative size of trading assets, the leverage of trading assets, the importance of counterparty credit risk, the complexity of trading derivatives, the profitability of trading income, etc.[122] These are only general principles and variables to assess the risks; no concrete criteria have been defined so far. According to the rule, the European Banking Authority (EBA) would have the power to develop draft regulatory technical standards to direct how the metrics should be measured and specify the details of the metrics using supervisory data.[123] Be that as it may, the assessment process carried out by competent authorities might still leave room for discretion. Besides, there is the uncertainty and ambiguity problem between restricted activities and permitted activities, which also provides a possibility for regulatory arbitrage.

Second, were the BSR to be implemented, tightening regulation on the banks' structures would dwarf the regulation reform progress in the shadow banking system. This makes for the possibility of activity migration.

Compared with the increasingly regulated traditional banking area, shadow banking is still quite a regulation-free area. The EU has been very keen on regulating the shadow banking system awakened by the risks it unleashed in the GFC. The EC issued a 'Roadmap' for tackling the risks in shadow banking in a Communication on September 4, 2013.[124] The Communication proposed a series of new rules for money market funds' (MMFs) regulation and supervision reform in order to reduce risks. It also provided possible further actions in five priority areas to strengthen the reform. The Communication came less than a week after the FSB issued its 'final policy recommendations'.[125] That said, legislative progress on shadow banking reform has been very limited so far. And shadow banking is still a highly risky area.

The shadow banking activities created many evident risks in the GFC.

(1) Because of using repo to create short-term, money-like liabilities, it facilitated credit growth. But it also promoted the overuse of leverage and maturity transformation. That made the sector so vulnerable to a bank run.

(2) Securities financing tended to increase cyclicality of leverage and thus add instability to the markets exponentially.

(3) There was the risk of a fire sale of collateral securities. Following a certain counterparty default, creditors of repo financing and securities lending would sell collateral securities immediately. That would lead to sharp price falls and fire sales by other firms.[126]

---

122 European Commission, *Proposal for a Regulation of the European Parliament and of the Council on structural measures improving the resilience of EU credit institutions*, COM/2014/043 final, art 9.

123 Ibid, art 9(3).

124 European Commission, *Commission's roadmap for tackling the risks inherent in shadow banking* (press release) (September 4, 2013).

125 Financial Stability Board, *Strengthening oversight and regulation of shadow banking: an overview of policy recommendation*, pp. i–iii. See also Financial Stability Board, *Strengthening oversight and regulation of shadow banking: policy framework for addressing shadow banking risks in securities lending and repos* (August 29, 2013), pp. 4–17.

126 Financial Stability Board, *Strengthening oversight and regulation of shadow banking: policy framework for addressing shadow banking risks in securities lending and repos*, pp. 4–6.

Shadow banking includes the securitisation entities, MMFs, and investment funds providing credit, and they are all highly leveraged.[127] Shadow banking activities include a broad set of activities, such as securitisation, securities lending and repurchase transactions, which constitute an important source of finance for financial entities. Statistics shows that the EU still has a very large amount of shadow banking even after the GFC.[128]

Based on the less-regulated situation for shadow banking, the significance of it in the EU, and the risks inherent in it, the regulation reform on prohibition and the separation of trading activities might force banks to migrate their activities to the shadow banking arena.

Thus, eventually, the activity restriction rule might be faced with a migration challenge. For instance, migration may be related to the uncertainties on exempted client-related activities and shadow banking activities. Due to the broadly defined scope of shadow banking, migration to this sector might be a good approach to evade regulation and continue engaging in risky activities.[129] But if risks materialise in shadow banking, they could also contaminate the financial markets in a similar way to risks emanating from the pre-crisis universal banks. In addition, as indicated in the next section, migration to other markets and jurisdictions might also be a possibility.

4 Conclusion: safety and challenges

The lack of an international concerted action in bringing about structural reform could also create huge challenges and uncertainties for both the banking industry and its clients. For the EU BSR, the lack of concerted action also leads to the possibility of migration to other markets and jurisdictions.

The current international financial regulation framework is of a soft law context, which can be seen from the institutional nature of the IMF, the FSB, and the Bank for International Settlements (BIS).[130] The non-binding international regulatory framework has varying legal effects when it comes to different countries and jurisdictions. The Basel III capital requirement framework, for instance, sets only a basic framework for capital requirements, and it is not necessarily obligatory for all countries.[131] The direct consequence of the international incompatibility and inconsistency within the soft law context is the constant conflicts of rules and the arbitrage risk. Therefore, some risky activities can be transferred to less regulated jurisdictions. That would also distort the international competition environment. The same happens in the structural reforms.

---

127 European Commission, *Communication on shadow banking: frequently asked questions* (Brussels, September 4, 2013).

128 Ibid, p. 2. Statistics showed that in 2011 'Despite the fact that shadow banking assets have decreased slightly since 2008, the global figure in 2011 was €51 trillion. In terms of geographical distribution, the biggest share was concentrated in the United States (around €17.5 trillion) and in Europe (Eurozone with €16.8 trillion and the United Kingdom with around €6.8 trillion)'.

129 Chow, *Making banks safer: can Volcker and Vickers do it?* pp. 10–11. It also suggests that the proposals discussed in structural reform could be limited in terms of the capacity to reduce systemic risk if no corresponding reform is undertaken in the shadow banking industry.

130 Avgouleas, *Governance of global financial markets: the law, the economics, the politics*, pp. 213–217.

131 Basel Committee on Banking Supervision, *Basel III: International framework for liquidity risk measurement, standards and monitoring* (December 2010).

First, at the international level, the countries that have structural reform in progress include the US, the UK, Germany, France, Belgium, and the Netherlands. The BSR definitely has the extraterritorial effect, as it applies to all EU credit institutions and their EU parents, their subsidiaries and branches including in third countries. It also applies to EU bank subsidiaries and branches of banks established in third countries.[132] Such a broad scope of application is to ensure a level playing field for the banking industry. The Vickers Rule also has a similar extraterritorial effect.[133] In contrast, the US Volcker Rule has an even broader extraterritorial effect, with a similar scope to the BSR, as it also applies to foreign branches and subsidiaries of foreign banks or holding companies which have a local branch or bank subsidiary.[134]

Now that the structural reforms in the major economies all have extraterritorial effect, it is almost unavoidable that different rules in different jurisdictions will be in conflict with one another with regard to the regulation and supervision of banks. This is especially true for large cross-border banks. Besides, as analysed in Chapter 3, the regulation models in the three jurisdictions are very different from one another. That means there are three models in the three major economies, which has produced a lot of uncertainties for the banking industry and its customers.[135]

Second, even within the EU, a similar practical coordination problem does exist even after the adoption of the BSR, when a certain Member State has its own rules and regulations on bank structural separation. As a general rule, a regulation normally supersedes relevant Member State law. But on structural reform, to soften the conflict between different jurisdictions over the same legislative issue, the BSR proposal includes article 21, the 'grandfather clause'. This means that relevant Member State law that was passed before January 29, 2014 could still apply to credit institutions on the EC grant of derogation.[136] For instance, the structural reforms in the UK and Germany can still apply even after the adoption of the BSR. It would make the supervision mission even more difficult due to the possible lack of consistency. To think about a different but remotely related case, the cross-border resolution difficulties caused by different rules in different countries after the crisis significantly impeded the recovery and resolution process of large cross-border banks.[137]

Third, as regards other countries, especially emerging markets, there is also the concern that trading activities might migrate to emerging markets, which would also create market instability that would be large enough to threaten the safety of the international financial industry. Most of the emerging markets still have no plans for separation reform, because their developing financial markets have still

132 European Commission, *Proposal for a Regulation of the European Parliament and of the Council on structural measures improving the resilience of EU credit institutions, COM/2014/043 final,* p. 7.
133 Independent Commission on Banking, 'Final Report, recommendations', p. 39.
134 Prohibitions and Restrictions on Proprietary Trading and Certain Interests In, and Relationships With, Hedge Funds and Private Equity Funds (The Final Rule) (U.S), section 2.
135 Lehmann Bonn, 'Volcker Rule, ring-fencing or separation of bank activities: comparison of structural reform acts around the world', p. 15.
136 European Commission, *Proposal for a Regulation of the European Parliament and of the Council on structural measures improving the resilience of EU credit institutions, COM/2014/043 final,* art 21.
137 Avgouleas, *Governance of global financial markets: the law, the economics, the politics,* pp. 370–372.

not experienced the incredible movement of internationalisation and integration. For instance, in China, its financial integration and internationalisation pace is still very limited. Financial conglomeration development is still very slow. Thus, it will be unnecessary to provide very harsh structural separation regulations for such a developing market.[138]

Thus, either at the international level, or at the EU Member State level, or from the perspective of the emerging markets, varied structural regulations still exist widely. Although current progress has been made in major jurisdictions including the EU, their different strategies and approaches still create the huge challenge of inconsistency.[139]

With the diversity and differences together with the extraterritorial effects of each domestic rule, it is unavoidable that implementation conflicts will abound. The adverse effect would be provident in this case.

In summary, different rules in different jurisdictions would impede the development of an internal level playing field for the banking industry. The risky trading activities that are prohibited in one country might be conducted in other countries. Those who can take advantage of the diversification effects of various business activities would have the competition edge.[140] Banks may face more uncertainties. Some of them might suffer tightening separation rules and loss absorbency rules so that they would not need any bail-out scheme from government, while others might still receive implicit government guarantees.

In addition, from the perspective of customers and other bank clients, the diversity of structural rules would bring about confusion for them in making wealth management decisions.[141] The complexity of international regulations might make the banks suffer, but not necessarily more than their customers because complexity will obfuscate their decision-making. For instance, in deciding on the risk profile of a bank, customers could hardly know or understand that a highly regulated bank might have certain domestically prohibited risk exposures elsewhere in less regulated jurisdictions.

In sum, by conducting MFA, this chapter analyses the imperativeness, distinctiveness, and feasibility of the BSR to address the structural attribute of the bank structural problem, and it makes banks safer, although challenges still persist. Chapter 5 shifts to the CBA to analyse the efficiency of the BSR to address the structural attribute.

---

138 Zhan Heng Wealth Management, 'Report on shadow banking in China 2012', JRJ http://bank.jrj.com.cn/2013/01/14151714940440.shtml, accessed January 22, 2015.

139 Eilis Ferran, 'European Banking Union and the EU Single Financial Market: more differentiated integration, or disintegration?' University of Cambridge Faculty of Law Research Paper.

140 John C. Panzar and Robert D. Willig, 'Economies of scope', *The American Economic Review* 268.

141 Lehmann Bonn, 'Volcker Rule, ring-fencing or separation of bank activities: comparison of structural reform acts around the world', p. 17.

5 Banking structural regulation
Its efficiency

To deal with the structural landscape change in the banking industry, structural reform has been making progress in the EU.[1] The previous chapter conducted an MFA to discover whether the reforms would make the banking sector and the CCI safer. And the results seem to be promising albeit there are practical challenges, such as migration risk and a lack of concerted international action. The BSR could make the banks safer by targeting and containing the behavioural factors that appeared in the development of the TBTF bank structural problem and the GFC.[2] This chapter focuses on a CBA.[3] It further evaluates whether the BSR strikes a balance between stability and efficiency.

1 Structural reform: to preserve the pros and tame the cons of the universal banking model

There are widespread concerns about the costs of a structural reform like the BSR. The basis for these concerns is the rationale behind the emergence and development of the universal banking model. The driving force behind the change for banks was an urgent need to enhance their competitiveness and to ensure they survived amid the intensely competitive atmosphere that arose following the financial liberalisation policies around the world, including in the EU. This explanation is in accordance with Andrew Lo's opinion that market actors struggle not for optimal returns, but for survival within an evolving framework. They can be both rational and irrational according to their need for survival.[4]

---

1 Liikanen Erkki, *High-level Expert Group on reforming the structure of the EU banking sector* (Final Report, Brussels, 2012), pp. i–v.
2 Steven L. Schwarcz, 'Regulating complexity in financial markets', 87 Wash UL Rev 211.
3 Financial Conduct Authority, *Financial Conduct Authority (2013), Applying behavioral economics in Financial Conduct Authority, Occasional Paper No. 1.* (2013), p. 54.
4 Emilios Avgouleas, *Governance of global financial markets: the law, the economics, the politics* (Cambridge, UK: Cambridge University Press 2012), pp. 62–64, see also Andrew W. Lo, 'Reconciling efficient markets with behavioral finance: the adaptive markets hypothesis', 7 *Journal of Investment Consulting* 21. See supra Chapter 2, Section 4.1.

The emergence of various financial innovations driven by technology and investment theory advancements have eclipsed the profit margins of traditional banking activities, especially retail activities and services. This is why the universal banks that offered an all-encompassing set of services, including securitisation activities, gained such momentous strength.[5]

Besides, evidence about the pros and cons of the universal banking model is mixed, as shown in Chapter 3.[6] There is an obvious trade-off between the economies of scale and economies of scope and the risks brought about by them.[7] An OECD Report (2013) found that the universal banking model could act as a catalyst for real economic development, as was evidenced in France and Canada; and as a destabilising factor causing crises like what happened in Iceland, the US and the EU.[8] Canada is a vivid example of how the GFC was avoided by safe and sound policy-making and business operations. It shows that the universal banking model could also be used as a positive factor rather than being totally depicted as the culprit behind the GFC.[9]

As a matter of fact, the issue is not really about whether universal banking is positive or negative for the overall economy, but rather to which extent regulators should maintain its pros while at the same time taming its cons.[10] Hence, it seems fair to say that a structural reform of the banking industry should be undertaken by providing a reasonable strength and scope of separation to reduce financial instability without impeding those advantages of the universal banking model.

The lack of a theoretical absolute answer also leads to more room for policy considerations: considering and weighing different regulatory objectives and interests. This also makes a CBA more appropriate to give an economic perspective in terms of weighing different economic interests against the risks.

In addition, in terms of weighing different objectives and considerations, the current policy orientation should largely determine the extent and approach of any separation. Under the paradigm of a competitiveness-oriented regulatory regime in the pre-crisis era, the attention of market participants was fixated on the advantages of the universal banking model, and the merits of the economies of size and scope. However, with the inception of the GFC, the paradigm shifted, and what was more important was to restore the financial markets and economic confidence in the post-crisis era.[11]

---

5 Leonardo Gambacorta, and Adrian Van Rixtel, Bank for International Settlements, *Structural bank regulation initiatives: approaches and implications* (2013), pp. 1–4.

6 See supra Chapter 3, Section 4.1.1.

7 Avgouleas, *Governance of global financial markets: the law, the economics, the politics*, pp. 40–51.

8 Édouard Fernandez-Bollo, 'Structural reform and supervision of the banking sector in France', 2013 *OECD Journal: Financial Market Trends* 1, pp. 3–4.

9 Ibid.

10 See supra Chapter 4, Section 1.2.

11 Eilís Ferran, *The regulatory aftermath of the global financial crisis* (Cambridge, UK: Cambridge University Press 2012), pp. 111–112.

The paradigm shift can be demonstrated by various regulatory reforms after the GFC, such as the price-based reform.[12] This paradigm shift was also reflected in the transformation from an institutional reform towards a structural reform.[13] Both the Liikanen Report and the BSR reflect the strong motivation to reach a regulatory balance between conflicting considerations: 'stability' and 'competitiveness'.[14] Absence of either one would distort the making of an efficient market.[15]

Compared with Chapter 4 which focused on discussing stability considerations, a CBA focuses on balancing the relationship between stability and efficiency. This chapter analyses the pros and cons of the BSR. It aims to discover whether the rules could possibly achieve the envisioned objectives in an efficient way. When undertaking the BSR CBA, it also compares the BSR with the rules in other jurisdictions: the Vickers Rule in the UK and the Volcker Rule in the US.[16]

2 The costs and benefits of the BSR

Theoretically, it is desirable to undertake a very comprehensive CBA with regard to a new rule and its implementation. The reason is that the essence of economic thinking is to quantify all relevant factors and parameters to reach a comparatively definitive conclusion and to find out what would be the most efficient rule and how to achieve it (Table 5.1).

2.1 The quantitative difficulty

Be that as it may, quantitative analysis is not indispensable in reaching a conclusion, because of the various difficulties of undertaking it in different scenarios. There are many practical problems: the non-availability of necessary data, the inaccuracy of mathematical models to fully capture all variables in reality, and the uncertainty in identifying the effect of a rule on society.[17]

---

12 Julian T.S. Chow, *Making banks safer: can Volcker and Vickers do it?* (New York: International Monetary Fund 2011), p. 5.
13 Niamh Moloney and Jennifer G. Hill, *The regulatory aftermath of the global financial crisis* (Cambridge, UK: Cambridge University Press 2012), pp. 111–112. After the crisis, the world major economies reformed their regulatory agencies to strengthen financial supervision and surveillance to enhance international coordination.
14 Liikanen Erkki, *High-level Expert Group on reforming the structure of the EU banking sector*, p. 108. See also supra Chapter 3, Section 3.
15 European Commission, *Proposal for a Regulation of the European Parliament and of the Council on structural measures improving the resilience of EU credit institutions, COM/2014/043 final* (January 29, 2014), art 1.
16 Ryan Tracy and Stephanie Armour Scott Patterson, 'FDIC, FED, SEC vote to approve Volcker rule – FDIC, FED board votes unanimously to approve long-delayed rule for banks, SEC approves in a 3–2 vote, *Wall Street Journal*, http://online.wsj.com/news/articles/SB1000142405270230 3560204579249732841592834, accessed November 21, 2014. The US newly adopted rule was approved unanimously by the regulatory agencies. It signalled a new era of tough supervision and surveillance targeting the profitable trading activities in the universal banking model.
17 Independent Commission on Banking, 'Final Report, recommendations', pp. 139–140.

With regard to the desirability of quantitative analysis, Anat Admanti advocates that if one were not relying on quantitative analysis of the impact of different capital requirements on the economy, she would rely on crude benchmarks from other industries and banking history. Anat Admanti also provides an example where crude benchmarks rather than quantitative analysis could be of vital importance in determining the impact of a rule on society. Imagine a heavily laden truck driving through a residential area at a speed of more than 90 miles per hour, intimidating pedestrians and nearby residents, and honking its horn.[18] Now, if regulators were required to set a rule about speed restrictions, they wouldn't need to design a mathematical model, consider all relevant factors, calculate all the possible effects the rule could have on the community, and then quantify all of them to set a standard. Instead, some crude benchmarks could tell that 90 miles an hour is not a safe speed for such a truck to be passing through a residential community due to concerns over traffic accidents. Hence, driving slowly would be more socially desirable because it caters best to society's social needs with probably limited social costs.[19]

Notwithstanding the argument that quantitative analysis is not necessarily needed in a CBA, it is also quite obvious that a quantitative approach in banking regulation is almost improbable to conduct because of many practical difficulties.[20] These include:

(i)   The non-availability of data, which is a huge practical problem when it comes to the impact of structural reform on the industry. For instance, with regard to the prohibition of trading activities and the exception of market-making, not to mention the unlikely ability to differentiate the two accurately in reality, data on trading and market-making activities will very likely be unavailable.

(ii) The EC public consultation on the estimated impact of structural reform on banking groups' balance sheets, profits and losses, where there was a very limited number of banks that actually responded.[21]

(iii) It being very hard to tell the exact difference between private costs and public costs (to be discussed further in detail in the next section).[22] Even if the private costs can be established, the extent to which they will be transferred to public costs is almost impossible to calculate.

---

18 Anat R. Admati, 'The compelling case for stronger and more effective leverage regulation in banking', Rock Center for Corporate Governance at Stanford University Working Paper.
19 Anat R. Admati et al., *The leverage ratchet effect* (2013).
20 Independent Commission on Banking, 'Final Report, recommendations', p. 139.
21 European Commission, *Commission staff working document impact assessment accompanying the document Proposal for a Regulation of the European Parliament and of the Council on structural measures improving the resilience of EU Credit Institutions and the Proposal for a Regulation of the European Parliament and of the Council on reporting and transparency of securities financing transactions, SWD/2014/030 final* (January 29, 2014), p. 67.
22 See infra Chapter 5, Section 2.2.

(iv) Another analytical challenge, which is how to untangle the impacts and costs caused by the BSR and those which were implemented after the crisis, especially those that are relevant to the structural reform, for example the CRR and the BRRD. A quantitative analysis would first of all require an assumption to be made of the baseline to which the changes in BSR could then be added.[23]

Under this scenario, quantitative research on this topic is not only not essential but is also very likely to be improbable. It only acts as one perspective providing limited value to a comprehensive BSR analysis, but not necessarily the decisive role. Therefore, some inaccurate rough quantitative data on structural reform provided in other jurisdictions, such as in the UK, has only acted as one consideration among many others in the regulators' decision-making processes.[24]

2.2 Public costs vs. private costs

In the impact analysis of the EC, it differentiates public benefits and costs and private benefits and costs of the BSR.[25] The latter mainly refer to the benefits and costs of the BSR to the shareholders of the banks and the banking sector as a whole, while the former mainly refer to the benefits and costs related to a broad group of people – all relevant stakeholders – including bank customers, creditors, government finances, and the stability of the economy as a whole.

The CBA herein inevitably needs to discuss both the public and private benefits and costs. Therefore, the correlation between social costs and benefits and private costs and benefits needs to be accurately defined. It should be noted that the relationship between social costs and private costs is of significant importance within this context. The relationship is not necessarily linear or positively related. For instance, the structural reform is expected to increase private costs, such as funding costs and liquidity costs, but that does not necessarily mean there is an equivalent increase in social costs.

There are a few points to consider when looking at the correlation between social costs and benefits and private costs and benefits. First, there is the question of the impact of the transfer of costs. For instance, when subsidisation is decreased, the ratings of financial institutions might also decline. This means that the funding costs of banks will rise, but these will not be incorporated as an increase in social costs. The reason is that the reduction in government guarantees brings about fewer risks to taxpayers. Therefore, this process could be viewed

---

23 Independent Commission on Banking, 'Final Report, recommendations', p. 139.
24 Ibid.
25 European Commission, *Commission staff working document impact assessment accompanying the document Proposal for a Regulation of the European Parliament and of the Council on structural measures improving the resilience of EU Credit Institutions and the Proposal for a Regulation of the European Parliament and of the Council on reporting and transparency of securities financing transactions, SWD/2014/030 final*, pp. 39–40.

as a social benefit and private costs' redistribution. By doing so, the costs are transferred to the banks, but the overall costs to society do not increase.[26]

Second, other than the relationship in the transfer of costs, the correlation between the two seems to be convoluted, with both positive and negative connections in different scenarios. For instance, the BSR separates the former banking group into distinct entities committed to either core activities or trading activities. Each entity would have to comply with the capital requirements separately. In this scenario, banks would have more equities and fewer debts in their corporate finance structure. It is widely known that debt financing enjoys certain tax advantages when compared to equity financing. Therefore, the corporate finance structure change means that there would be more funding costs for the banks. However, that does not translate into higher social costs. Instead, governments would gain not only a higher tax yield, but it would also lessen tax distortion.[27] Therefore, this scenario provides an example of negative correlation.

However, another example could also indicate positive correlation.[28] As referred to in Chapter 4 on the migration risk of the BSR, restricted activities could migrate to either other less regulated sectors or to less regulated jurisdictions.[29] As a result, it is possible that many risky activities might end up in the shadow banking arena. Based on current shadow banking reforms, they still fall behind the reform schedule of the BSR. Therefore, such migration would also be dangerous for the banking sector. One lesson learned from the GFC was that the risks that were not properly transferred out of the banking sector backfired.[30] In this scenario, the increase in private costs might be directly connected to an increase in social costs. Therefore, social costs and private costs could also show a positive correlation.

To sum up, the point to be made on public and private costs is that when undertaking a CBA, it seems to be fair to focus more on the broader interests of society or the public interest. The reason is obvious. One of the main considerations and purposes of structural reform is to reduce public subsidisation of risky banking activities. Having said that, private costs also deserve due attention because of the complicated relationship.[31] But more importantly, the convoluted correlation between the two should not be ignored.

With regard to the CBA of structural reform, some might argue that the BSR proposal based on the Liikanen structural reform can reduce complexity and interconnectedness in banking and financial markets; that it can enhance the efficiency of supervision and resolution; and that it can deleverage the banks and

---

26 Independent Commission on Banking, 'Final Report, recommendations', p. 123.
27 Ibid, p. 133.
28 Ibid, p. 134.
29 See supra Chapter 4, Section 4.
30 See supra Chapter 1, Section 1 on the originate-to-distribute model and transferring of risk. Chapter 1 explains how the securitisation activities failed to move risks out of the banking sector.
31 See infra Chapter 5, Section 4.5.4.

provide them with less incentives for risk-taking, and thus have a positive effect on the global economy. Others argue that setting aside the benefits the reform could bring about, which are not without controversy in reality, it would incur many costs, such as high compliance and operational costs, and there would be less efficiency in bank service provision, less liquidity in the markets, regulatory arbitrage, and bring about difficulties in international coordination.

3 Possible benefits

Through the BSR, the main benefits of the structural reform are: significantly reducing the risks hidden in the current banking industry, reducing complexity, lessening interconnectedness, and enhancing the resolvability of banks.

3.1 Reducing complexity

As referred to in Chapter 1, complexity is one of the major features of the TBTF bank structural problem. The structural reforms and the BSR do possess the capacity and potential to deal with the complexity issue. Complexity mainly relates to the intricacies of the products including the complexity of the underlying assets of those structural securities traded in the financial markets, as referred to in Chapter 1.[32]

In the pre-crisis era, the underlying assets of securitisation products were extremely complex because they included a wide set of assets including various mortgages loans and many other financial assets. Issuers even used structured securitisation products as underlying assets to create more complicated structured products. For instance, they used structured debt securities, such as MBS, as underlying assets to securitise CDOs. Different assets require different risk management models, because they tend to be exposed to different default risks, interest rate risks, repayment risks, etc. The modelling of the structural debt securities based on various different underlying assets was extremely convoluted, such as the LEVELS model used for RMBS and CDO evaluations in the S&P case.[33] Therefore, the originate-to-distribute model added exponential complexity to the entire market.[34]

Apart from the complexity of underlying assets, the complexity of products can also be seen from the basic classification of many forms of mortgage-backed securities. The simple form issued by the SPV or SPE is MBS, which is backed by a mixed pool of assets including mortgage loans and other financial assets.[35]

---

32 See supra Chapter 1, Section 1.
33 *The United States of America v. S&P, 12 U.S.C. § 1833a, 18 U.S.C. § 1341*, see the complaint, pp. 48–55.
34 Schwarcz, 'Regulating complexity in financial markets'.
35 *The United States of America v. S&P, 12 U.S.C. § 1833a, 18 U.S.C. § 1341*, see the complaint, pp. 6–7. The typical approaches of credit protection in RMBS include subordination, over-collateralisation, and excess spread. The existence of various methods of credit protection makes product risk evaluation more difficult for investors.

A more complicated form is the CDO, which is backed by a mixed pool of mortgage loans, other financial assets, and existing structural debt securities and even credit derivatives.[36] The CDOs can be further categorised into cash CDOs, synthetic CDOs, and hybrid CDOs according to the different underlying assets. In the pre-crisis era, cash CDOs were collateralised by various pools of debt securities, including but not limited to RMBS. Synthetic CDOs, however, were collateralised by credit derivatives including CDS. Hybrid CDOs were collateralised by a combination of debt securities including RMBS and credit derivatives.[37]

Structural reforms, by separating out a wide set of prohibited activities, could transfer the complexity problem out of the CCI. In the Liikanen Report, it provides two levels of separation. First, the mandatory separation rule removes all proprietary trading activities from traditional banking activities and removes all assets, liabilities, and positions driven by market-making and investing in hedge funds and private equity funds.[38] But, it still permits these activities to be undertaken within the same banking group in other group entities, provided some intragroup restrictions are adhered to, such as the arm's length requirement for intragroup transactions.[39] The second level of separation is not mandatory, and it is only to be triggered if required for the recovery and resolution of the bank.

Building on the earlier analysis of the risks, the trading entity, and behavioural factors, the connection between the banking industry and these complex products was created through trading-oriented activities.[40] With two levels of separation, it would be fair to say that the degree of complexity could be significantly reduced for the CCI. Compared with the very narrow scope of prohibition in the Volcker Rule, the scope of separation in the Liikanen Report is much broader. That would make the complexity reducing effect more prominent. However, due to the fact that these separated activities would still be permitted in the holding company or elsewhere in the group, unlike that in the Volcker Rule, the complexity of the group is not obviously changed.

The BSR, however, made some other changes compared to the Liikanen Report. It departs from the Liikanen separation rule in two aspects: (i) it includes a Volcker style prohibition rule, which means the prohibited activities would not be permitted even within the banking group or the holding company; and (ii) it also includes a Vickers style ring-fence rule. However, unlike the ring-fence in the UK, the BSR ring-fence is not mandatory.[41] With the changes in the separation rule, the impact on complexity is also different both for the bank and the group.

36 Schwarcz, 'Regulating complexity in financial markets'.
37 *The United States of America v. S&P, 12 U.S.C. § 1833a, 18 U.S.C. § 1341*, see the complaint, pp. 8–9.
38 Liikanen Erkki, *High-level Expert Group on reforming the structure of the EU banking sector*, pp. v–vi.
39 Ibid, p. vi.
40 See supra Chapter 4, Section 3.2.1 on the how behavioural factors loomed large through trading activities.
41 European Commission, *Proposal for a Regulation of the European Parliament and of the Council on structural measures improving the resilience of EU credit institutions, COM/2014/043 final*, pp. 8–9.

3.1.1 Reducing complexity for the bank

Under the BSR, the degree of complexity reduction varies in different institutions. For the firms where the prohibition rule applies,[42] such as in the EU and G-SIIs, the CCI is prohibited from engaging in trading activities, and there is not even a detailed list of exceptions. Therefore, the complexity has been almost wiped out at the bank level because all the permitted activities in the CCI are nothing more than those core banking retail services. This includes only essential banking activities: lending to large-, small- and medium-sized companies, consumer lending, mortgage lending, interbank lending, participation in loan syndications, taking deposits eligible for deposit insurance, lending, retail payment services, financial leasing, issuing of other means of payment, and some other retail and commercial banking activities.[43]

Like the Volcker Rule, prohibiting the engaging in trading-oriented activities means the complexity in structural debt products that tend to unleash much operational risk, fat-tail risk, and potential systemic risk are excluded from the CCI.[44] Therefore, both the BSR prohibition rule and the Volcker Rule evidently reduce the complexity at bank level by complete separation of trading activities.

But the fact is, the prohibition rule only applies to a very limited number of banks that are in the EU or are G-SIIs. Given the existence of numerous large banks in Europe which are not deemed to be SIFIs, they have considerable size and their safety also has a significant influence on the industry and the overall economy. Therefore, the importance and effectiveness of the ring-fence rule also matters a lot.[45]

Contrary to the prohibition rule, the ring-fence rule focuses in particular on a broad set of activities, which could possibly bring instability to the banks or even the whole banking system. It requires activities to be separated from the CCI on a case-to-case basis through an assessment process by the competent authority. But after ring-fencing, these activities are still permitted to exist in the banking group on a sub-group basis. To apply this rule, the competent authority needs to make a decision based on some metrics, such as the relative size of trading assets, the leverage of trading assets, the relative importance of counterparty credit risk, and the relative complexity of trading derivatives.[46]

It should be noted that complexity is one of the major metrics by which the ring-fence is to be applied as determined by the competent authority. Therefore, when the decision is carried out, it would ipso facto reduce the complexity of the CCI. The ring-fence separation, just like that in the Vickers Rule, would also have a positive effect in reducing complexity, especially at the bank level.

---

42 Ibid, art 3.
43 Ibid, art 8, see also Liikanen Erkki, *High-level Expert Group on reforming the structure of the EU banking sector*, p. vi.
44 Schwarcz, 'Regulating complexity in financial markets'.
45 European Central Bank, *Report on financial integration in Europe* (April 26, 2014).
46 European Commission, *Proposal for a Regulation of the European Parliament and of the Council on structural measures improving the resilience of EU credit institutions, COM/2014/043 final*, art 9(2).

3.1.2 Reducing complexity for the bank group

Under the prohibition rule, the prohibited activities are not only prohibited in the CCI, but are not even permitted within the banking group or the holding company. The rule not only applies to credit institutions established in the EU (including all the subsidiaries and branches irrespective of location), but also their EU parents. Its effect extends to EU branches of credit institutions established in third countries. Provided that the universal banking model is not preserved, the complexity in the whole banking group would be reduced, as would happen within the CCI.

From that perspective, the prohibition rule would be more effective in reducing complexity in the banking group as a whole compared with the Liikanen Report where all the separated activities would remain within the banking group. In this regard, the BSR prohibition rule is similar to the Volcker Rule in terms of its strong effectiveness in reducing group complexity.[47]

On the contrary, unlike the Volcker Rule and the prohibition rule, the ring-fence rule is applied premised on preserving the universal banking model, which is similar to the Vickers Rule. Therefore, at the group level, not much has been changed. The complexity still exists, but it is transferred into a different compartment of the same banking group. The reduction in complexity is therefore not prominent at the group level through the ring-fence rule.

In addition, the ring-fence's complexity-reducing effect to the group is possibly even worse than under the Vickers Rule. The fact is the ICB ring-fence and the Liikanen ring-fence are mandatory, which makes the ring-fence applicable for all covered entities. However, the application of the ring-fence is dependent on the discretionary decision of the competent authority. The inconsistency and uncertainty of implementation is more likely to compromise the effectiveness of the rule.[48]

3.2 Reducing interconnectedness

The interconnectedness issue was deemed to be another major culpable feature in the run up to the GFC and the structural problem. The interconnectedness feature was reflected in two channels: intragroup links and interbank links.[49] Intragroup links includes relationships, such as the transfer of funds and other subsidisation mechanisms from the deposit-taking CCI

47   David R. Sahr, 'Does Volcker + Vickers = Liikanen? EU proposal for a regulation on structural measures improving the resilience of EU credit institutions', *Mayer Brown Legal Update*, www.mayerbrown.com/files/Publication/f6722a7a-b666-4384-931f-0f77d6424e37/Presentation/PublicationAttachment/1a249a85-3015-43eb-8389-26237a62e419/update_volcker_vickers_feb14.pdf, accessed November 25, 2014.

48   Eilis Ferran and Valia S.G. Babis, 'The European single supervisory mechanism', University of Cambridge Faculty of Law Research Paper.

49   European Commission, *Commission staff working document impact assessment accompanying the document Proposal for a Regulation of the European Parliament and of the Council on structural measures improving the resilience of EU Credit Institutions and the Proposal for a Regulation of the European Parliament and of the Council on reporting and transparency of securities financing transactions, SWD/2014/030 final*, p. 11.

to the riskier trading entity. The trading entity exploited the links with the deposit entity, thereby benefitting from lower funding costs and transferring the risks to the deposit entity accordingly.

Intergroup links were also another important channel where interconnectedness in the banking industry mounted, making banks more susceptible to market volatility. The interconnectedness in the banking sector could happen in a number of ways, typically through wholesale funding and borrowing and risk exposures in derivative markets.[50]

The interbank exposures through the derivative markets were actually quite common in the securitisation products boom.[51] With the increasing exposure to structural debt securities, the trading assets and other assets of the banks increased substantially relative to the banks' total assets. By so doing, banks inevitably became interconnected with one another.

3.2.1 Reducing intragroup links

Under the BSR prohibition rule, the CCI would be prohibited from being involved in trading activities, and that would apply to the whole banking group. Thus, this stringent prohibition would eradicate interconnectedness at the group entity level to the largest extent for the banks covered by this rule (the EU and G-SIIs). For instance, it would curb funding transfers and prevent risk contagion.

In contrast, the intragroup link reduction in the Volcker Rule is arguably even stronger. It does not have specific intragroup exposure restriction by itself, but through the Federal Reserve Act 23 B and the Dodd-Frank Act, Section 608, it also provides an arm's length standard for bank transactions with affiliates and imposes several restrictions on certain transactions, called the 'covered transactions'. [52]

As regards the ring-fence rule that is applicable to all banks irrespective of their size, the new separation on a sub-group basis and the detailed legal, operational, and economical requirements would also reduce the intragroup links significantly.[53] The Liikanen separation requires that the transfer of funds between the deposit entity and the trading entity be conducted on a market-terms basis and is restricted according to normal large exposure rules. By so doing, the exploitation of the lower funding costs and the subsidisation issue could be tamed. Building on that, the BSR ring-fence rule further strengthens the intraexposure rule by providing detailed requirements of separation standards. The ring-fence rule does not prevent the trading activities from being carried out elsewhere in the same banking group, provided that the CCI and the trading entity meet specific separation standards, such as debts on a sub-consolidated basis; transactions on

---

50 Ibid.
51 Liikanen Erkki, *High-level Expert Group on reforming the structure of the EU banking sector*, pp. 4–5.
52 The Dodd-Frank Wall Street Reform and Consumer Protection Act (U.S), section 608.
53 European Commission, *Proposal for a Regulation of the European Parliament and of the Council on structural measures improving the resilience of EU credit institutions, COM/2014/043 final*, art 13.

a third-party basis; management separation, etc.[54] It further stipulates the intra-group exposure restriction, that the CCI shall not incur an intragroup exposure that exceeds 25% of the CCI's eligible capital to an entity that does not belong to the same sub-group as the CCI.[55]

Through detailed restrictions, the interconnectedness reduction effect of the ring-fence rule could be even better than the Liikanen proposal.[56] Therefore, the aforementioned links, such as cross-shareholdings, liquidity management, and guarantee links, would all be significantly reduced.

Compared with what is stipulated in the Vickers Rule, the positive effect of the BSR ring-fence rule in reducing intragroup links may be similar. In the Vickers Rule, it also specifically stipulates that transactions should be done on an arm's length basis.[57]

3.2.2 Reducing intergroup interconnectedness

The intergroup relationship mainly concerns banks' exposures to short-term wholesale and interbank funding.[58] Many banks still largely rely on interbank and other wholesale funding markets even after the adjustments in post-crisis funding structures.

The prohibition rule has some positive effects on disincentivising the inclination for risk-taking and placing too much reliance on wholesale lending. Although there is not much detail in the rule limiting wholesale lending and interbank borrowing, that does not mean that the prohibition rule has no effect on reducing interbank interconnectedness. It should be noted that the exuberances of the wholesale funding markets and interbank exposures were accompanied by developments in the universal banking model, which was established to meet the financing needs for the development of the banks overall.[59] The fact that the model has been prohibited by the prohibition rule should ipso facto cool the overheated interbank exposures and hence reduce interconnectedness.

Therefore, as typical advocates for complete separation, the prohibition rule and the Volcker Rule have arguably similarly positive effects in reducing interbank interconnectedness.

In addition, on closer examination of the text of the BSR, the ring-fence rule not only stipulates an intragroup exposure limit, but also mentions the restriction on limiting interbank exposure: the CCI can incur some extra-group exposures to a financial entity (less than 25% of the CCI's eligible capital) and financial entities in total (less than 200% of the CCI's eligible capital).[60] So, the BSR ring-fence

---

54   Ibid.
55   Ibid, art 14.
56   Liikanen Erkki, *High-level Expert Group on reforming the structure of the EU banking sector*, p. vi.
57   Independent Commission on Banking, 'Final Report, recommendations', p. 236.
58   Liikanen Erkki, *High-level Expert Group on reforming the structure of the EU banking sector*, pp. 15–16.
59   Hyun Song Shin, 'Reflections on Northern Rock: the bank run that heralded the global financial crisis', *The Journal of Economic Perspectives* 101.
60   European Commission, *Proposal for a Regulation of the European Parliament and of the Council on structural measures improving the resilience of EU credit institutions, COM/2014/043 final*, art 15.

rule is more specific than the Liikanen Report. The latter does not set out detailed large intergroup exposure limits in this regard.

The BSR is definitely helpful in reducing interconnectedness through the ring-fence rule and using a system of intergroup limits. There are four channels by which connections between banks can lead to a contagion effect: (i) liquidity hoarding, meaning banks tend to hoard their liquidity in case of imminent or short-term volatility; (ii) counterparty risk, which refers to the situation where one bank fails triggering the failure of other banks that are its creditors; (iii) information contagion, which shows the spread of market diffidence; and (iv) fire sales and common creditors, which refers to when many banks have the same creditors; the failure of one bank will cause the withdrawal of funds by the creditors from the remaining banks.[61]

With the limit of exposures to one banking entity, and all banking entities in total for a CCI, interconnectedness and the contagion effect are contained to a particular level in all four channels. It is widely known that the nature of banks is such that they tend to rely on maturity transformation. Maturity transformation at reasonable level would actually benefit banks by lowering their costs.[62] As indicated by the case of Northern Rock, the reason why it went bankrupt was because of its excessive dependence on wholesale funds. As the fifth biggest mortgage bank, its ever-expanding mortgage business activities demanded more sources of funds rather than the traditional retail deposit-based funding. The bank started using wholesale funding, which was largely employed as an alternative to meeting the needs of business expansion and to fill the gap between short-term retail funding and long-term investment requirements.[63] Had the wholesale funding been used at a contained level, it would not have triggered such unexpected failure.

Thus, to some extent, a ring-fence can control intergroup exposures and risk contagion to a certain extent. With a direct interbank exposure limit, the effects of a reduction in interconnectedness seems arguably to be stronger than under the Vickers Rule in this regard.

3.3 Enhancing the resolvability of the banking industry

To a certain extent, it might be plausible to argue that provided there are benefits in reducing complexity and interconnectedness, the enhancement of resolution will be self-evident. As discussed in Chapter 1 on the four features of the TBTF structural problem, they converge into one issue to a certain extent: the resolvability difficulty of banks. In other words, it would be reasonable to argue that size, homogeneity and interconnectedness, ignorance of low possibility events, and the tremendous domino effect of failure all contribute to the resolvability problem.[64]

The resolvability of banks would be impeded by these factors. For instance, size is an important consideration of the TBTF bank structural problem: how can

61 Independent Commission on Banking, 'Final Report, recommendations', pp. 278–279.
62 Avgouleas, *Governance of global financial markets: the law, the economics, the politics*, pp. 96–100.
63 Shin, 'Reflections on Northern Rock: the bank run that heralded the global financial crisis'.
64 See supra Chapter 1, Section 3.

banks possibly be resolved when the size of the banking sector is more than ten times the GDP of a country?[65] In addition, the interconnectedness issue could aggravate the resolvability problem. What is more, there are many other factors impeding the resolution of banks, such as the procedural problem. The lack of an orderly liquidation procedure at the EU level and the international level turned out to be a huge obstacle to resolving banks in the GFC. The procedural issue gives rise to two problems. Initially, which country's law should be applied in regard to the whole resolution procedure; should the territorial approach or the universal approach be applied? Then, what kind of procedure is applicable? The fact is that some countries use corporate insolvency law, while other countries might use more specialised financial institution insolvency law.[66]

Given both the substantial resolvability problem and the procedural difficulties, structural reform also aims to enhance the resolvability of banks. The BSR could not by itself tackle the problem directly, but at least it could facilitate or simplify bank resolution.[67]

3.3.1 Enhancing the resolvability of the bank

If the banks were separated according to the Liikanen proposal, the complexity of banks would be reduced; the interconnectedness of banks and groups would also be contained to a certain extent. This is aligned with arguments in a BCBS report.[68] Various banking group structures and intragroup relationships are very useful in some circumstances: rating management, risk management, and operational management. On the other hand, the report suggests that these structures tend to increase complexity and the contagion effect in distressed banking groups because the safety and soundness of one entity is intertwined with the remaining entities in a particular group.[69] As a recommendation, the report suggests that regulatory agencies should consider imposing some regulatory incentives on institutions to encourage them to simplify their structures.[70] The Liikanen separation rule provides exactly the recommended incentives. In the Liikanen separation reform, the group structure, funding mix, and risk management of banks are simplified.

In addition, the Liikanen separation rule would definitely have a positive effect on the reducing the size and activities of the trading entity due to the curbing of subsidisation from the CCI. As discussed in the Northern Rock case, the reason

---

65 Eyvindur G. Gunnarsson, 'The Icelandic regulatory responses to the financial crisis', 12 *European Business Organization Law Review* 1.

66 Avgouleas, *Governance of global financial markets: the law, the economics, the politics*, pp. 252–253.

67 More detailed analysis will be conducted in Chapter 6. But it should be noted that the structural reform and resolution reform are supposed to be assessed together in terms of the structural problem because they both have a huge influence on resolvability.

68 Basel Committee on Banking Supervision, *Report and recommendations of the Cross-border Bank Resolution Group* (March 2010).

69 Ibid, pp. 29–30.

70 Ibid, p. 30.

why wholesale funding emerged was because of the activity expansion requirements of the bank.[71] So, wholesale funding thrived and subsidisation from the deposit entities fuelled the rapid expansion in universal banking.[72] Without this subsidisation, the overall size of the banks would be smaller compared to now and it would have been easier to resolve the banks when market volatility caused market failure.

It is also clear that the additional separation mechanism in the Liikanen Report is based on a resolvability assessment of the banks. In this regard, the practicality and possibility of resolution was given full consideration in the implementation of separation reforms under the Liikanen proposal. A well-tailored structural reform according to the needs of future possible resolution would definitely facilitate bank resolution procedures.[73]

If reducing complexity and interconnectedness and size are very significant for enhancing resolvability, the BSR rules could perform the task just as well, if not better than the Liikanen Report. Under the prohibition rule, the resolvability enhancing effect would be more prominent than in the Liikanen Report, because the CCI would be allowed to only engage in very narrowly defined critical banking services. Trading activities are completely eradicated from the entire group. In this scenario, the group structures referred to earlier for fund and liquidity management, risk management, and operational management are almost destroyed. In so doing, the resolvability of banks would definitely be enhanced.

Due to the similar approach in prohibiting the universal banking model, the resolvability enhancement effect of the prohibition rule is similar to the Volcker Rule. But the actual effect is also, to a certain extent, dependent on the scope of the exceptions. The US's long list of exceptions to prohibition was greatly criticised for compromising the separation effect.[74]

On the other hand, the resolvability enhancing effect of the BSR ring-fence rule would also be no less prominent than that in the Liikanen Report, because it applies to a broader scope of activities. The restriction basically includes all activities except the core activities defined in article 8.[75] The ring-fence separation is not carried out mandatorily but upon the discretional decision of the competent authority. It is to be carried about based on the competent authority's assessment of whether 'there is a threat to the financial stability of the CCIs and the Union financial system as a whole'. In addition, all the metrics on which the decisions are made, such as leverage, complexity, and counterparty risks, are all directly related to the resolvability of banks. To some extent, it could be said that the actual implementation of the ring-fence separation is also remotely related to the need for a possible resolution scenario. But, this connection is definitely not as strong in the Liikanen additional ring-fence rule.

71 Shin, 'Reflections on Northern Rock: the bank run that heralded the global financial crisis'.
72 Liikanen Erkki, *High-level Expert Group on reforming the structure of the EU banking sector*, p. 14.
73 Ibid, p. vii.
74 Fernandez-Bollo, 'Structural reform and supervision of the banking sector in France', pp. 3–5.
75 Chow, *Making banks safer: can Volcker and Vickers do it?*

Compared with the BSR ring-fence rule, it seems that the Vickers Rule is more specifically tailored to the needs of financial stability and resolution through the loss-absorbency rule. Thus, it might arguably have a stronger effect in promoting resolvability.

With regard to the tailored structural reform for future resolution, legislative progress in France is worthy of note. France is very prominent in this regard because it is intending to directly delineate a recovery and resolution plan and grant their regulatory authority, Autorité de Contrôle Prudentiel et de Résolution (ACPR), the power of recovery and resolution in their legislation.[76]

3.3.2 Enhancing the resolvability of the group

By excluding the existence of trading activities in the entire group, the prohibition rule under the BSR would not only definitely enhance resolvability at the bank level, but also enhance resolvability at the group level.[77] The Volcker Rule also has a similar effect. But the uncertainties about exceptions are still the same as at the bank level.

This is different from the Liikanen proposal, where although resolution-oriented structural separation does exist, it is to be applied only at the group entity level.[78] But at the group level, complexity and interconnectedness still persist although are relatively contained. Without containing the complicated bank structures, the sheer size of the banks would also still be a big impediment to resolution. Even if separation were to be achieved, the sheer size and its spill over effect in a resolution would still frighten regulatory agencies.[79] The resolution enhancement effect at the group level seems hardly to exist in this scenario.

It should be noted that for the ring-fence rule in the BSR, it is not only weaker in terms of separation compared with the prohibition rule but does not need to be applied mandatorily. Therefore, its effect on group resolution would be very limited. Due to the similar scope and strength of the ring-fence, the BSR ring-fence rule and the Vickers Rule have the same effect on group resolution.

3.3.3 Another concern

There is also a concern with regard to the resolution enhancement effect of the structural reform. Contrary to high expectations, the structural reform might actually hinder the orderly resolution of banks.[80] The rationale behind the separation rule is that it protects the CCI from the contagion effect of other riskier

---

76 French law no. 2013-672 of 26 July 2013 on the separation and regulation of banking activities
77 Emilios Avgouleas, *The reform of 'Too-Big-To-Fail' Bank: a new regulatory model for the institutional separation of 'casino' from 'utility' banking* (2010), pp. 37–40.
78 Liikanen Erkki, *High-level Expert Group on reforming the structure of the EU banking sector*, p. vii.
79 Basel Committee on Banking Supervision, *Report and recommendations of the Cross-border Bank Resolution Group* (March 2010).
80 John Armour, 'Structural regulation of banking' (a preliminary draft of a chapter for a book, entitled Principles of Financial Regulation) http://web.law.columbia.edu/sites/default/files/microsites/law-economics-studies/john_armour_structural_regulation_working_22.06.2014.pdf, accessed May 29, 2015, p. 7.

entities. But the recent widely accepted trend for bank resolution is to use the bail-in tool and adopt the Single Point of Entry (SPE) approach.[81]

Specifically, the effectiveness of the SPE relies on up-streaming the debts and down-streaming the capital at the group level to avoid a large-scale failure and the spill over effect. However, structural separation either through the prohibition rule or the ring-fence rule would require sub-group entities to meet capital requirements on a standalone basis. In this case, compliance with the separation rule appears to possibly be in conflict with the basis for the SPE and therefore requires due legislative attention.

4 Possible costs

As discussed earlier, possible benefits notwithstanding, structural reform would also bring additional costs to the industry and to society in various ways. This section focuses more on public costs, but also takes private costs into consideration as well.

As a minimum, the BSR probably has the following costs: (i) there would be implementation costs for the regulatory agencies, and compliance and operational costs for the banking industry; (ii) it might compromise the market-making function of banks; (iii) it might compromise the risk-hedging capacity in the banking industry; (iv) it could damage the benefits of diversification that existed in the pre-crisis banking industry; and (v) the tightening of regulations may reduce the efficiency of the banking industry, such as increasing the cost of borrowing for society, allowing less subsidisation, producing lower ratings for banks, and cause a risk of migration to other sectors in the economy which might be less regulated and cause an unnecessary externality effect.[82]

4.1 Implementation costs

The costs of structural reform are very complex, the most important of which are the implementation costs. Within this context, implementation costs basically refer to the costs necessary for the regulators to supervise compliance, the costs of compliance for the banking industry itself, and the operational costs after structural reform for the industry.

4.1.1 Differentiating between the restrictions and the exceptions

To actually carry out the BSR in the banking industry, it is imperative to delimit the prohibition rule and the ring-fence rule in a more detailed manner. A closer

81 Federal Deposit Insurance Corporation, *Resolution of systemically important financial institutions: the single point of entry strategy, Reg. 243, pp. 76614–76624* (December 18, 2013). See infra Chapter 6, Section 4.3.2.

82 European Commission, *Commission staff working document impact assessment accompanying the document Proposal for a Regulation of the European Parliament and of the Council on structural measures improving the resilience of EU Credit Institutions and the Proposal for a Regulation of the European Parliament and of the Council on reporting and transparency of securities financing transactions, SWD/2014/030 final.*

examination of the rules will find it is very hard to differentiate between prohibited and exempted activities. For instance, there is an extremely subtle difference between trading activities, and market-making and hedging in reality. In Chapter 3, we briefly mentioned that compared with the BSR prohibition rule and the Volcker Rule, the Vickers Rule has a broader scope of restriction, which seems to avoid the difficulties associated with differentiation to a certain extent.[83] This section analyses in detail the subtle differences between trading and hedging to demonstrate the difficulties of supervision and its costs.

A AMBIGUITY BETWEEN TRADING AND HEDGING

In the Liikanen Report, it separates proprietary trading without exempting market-making or hedging activities. That is different from the Volcker Rule where market-making and hedging are permitted in the protected entity. In the BSR prohibition rule, it applies a principles-based approach without a long list of exceptions (but it also does not preclude the necessity of excluding some activities that are connected to client activities). However, the ring-fence rule applies an extremely broad definition of 'proprietary trading' and specifically focuses on assessing the instability and threat brought about by a wide spectrum of activities apart from some traditional, core banking services.[84] Therefore, it seems the delimitation of difference is much more important for the BSR prohibition rule than the ring-fence rule due to their different scopes.[85]

The newly approved Volcker 'final rule' has also given full consideration to this fuzzy issue. But it does not provide a comprehensive differentiation of the two. In the 882 page preamble, it only provides that banks must make sure their hedging activities aim to diversify the underlying risks based on an analysis conducted by the banks of the appropriateness of the hedging instruments, strategies, techniques, and limits used. Therefore, although the Volcker Rule has a long and clear list of exceptions, it still doesn't provide a clear line between proprietary trading and hedging except as a general principle. To avoid the activities that banks are committing being banned, the banks have to prove their intent to mitigate the risk in their current positions.[86]

The difference between proprietary trading and hedging sounds very transparent. However, it is a very obscure issue in theory, not to mention applying its

---

83 The various scopes of prohibition and restriction make the difficulties of delimitation different. See supra Chapter 4, Section 3.1 on the scope of separation and the fuzziness issue in the UK ring-fence rule.

84 European Commission, *Proposal for a Regulation of the European Parliament and of the Council on structural measures improving the resilience of EU credit institutions, COM/2014/043 final*, art 8.

85 See Steve Denning, 'The Volcker rule make us safer, but not safe', Forbes, www.forbes.com/sites/stevedenning/2013/12/13/the-volcker-rule-makes-us-safer-but-not-safe/, accessed November 27, 2014.

86 See Scott Patterson, 'FDIC, FED, SEC vote to approve Volcker rule – FDIC, FED board votes unanimously to approve long-delayed rule for banks, SEC approves in a 3–2 vote', *Wall Street Journal*.

guiding legislation in reality.[87] To assess what would be the appropriate boundary when setting the rules in relation to the restriction on trading activities, a clear picture of the distinction between speculation and hedging, or the difference between proprietary trading and hedging, needs to be identified. As a matter of fact, many scholars are very sceptical with regard to whether the differences in proprietary trading and hedging are sufficiently informative to guide legislation (Box 5.1). This theoretical fuzziness could perhaps further complicate concerns about compliance costs.[88]

It should be noted that uncertainty about the scope of the rule itself would make implementation and compliance more difficult and more costly. In addition, the lack of specified exemptions in the BSR could also render implementation susceptible to inconsistency and regulatory arbitrage. Basically, it might leave the interpretation of the provisions on discretionary decision-making powers up to the competent authorities.[89]

Box 5.1   Hedging

Scholars have conducted much research with regard to determining what hedging actually is. For example, how often do investors hedge? What causes them to hedge? Ing-Haw Cheng and Wei Xiong conduct a two-step test to examine how hedgers commit to trading activities in the futures markets in agricultural products. In the first step they compare the intensity of trading activities with the volatility of agricultural product output, which answers the question of how often do hedgers trade in the futures markets. In the second step, they further explore why the hedgers hedge so often, and what is the driving force or the main reason that causes them to hedge so often.[90]

For the first part, they use a set of figures which plot the volatility of the percentage changes in producers' futures positions and the volatility changes in the output of the agricultural products. The statistics show that the volatility of the futures positions is several times larger than the output volatility from time to time. In addition, the research shows that the volatility does rise significantly during the planting season when the output volatility is extremely high. However, the changes in futures positions also increase when output uncertainties are declining. In summary, the futures position volatility is far higher than the agricultural output uncertainties.

Then, they explored the second question: what is the cause of very frequent hedging? Based on statistical research, it transpires that producers' short positions always show a pattern. The monthly changes in positions are positively correlated to the price changes of all commodities. Namely, if the price goes up, then investors increase their short positions; if the price goes down, then they decrease their short positions. Therefore, the relevant evidence shows that although the futures positions of the hedgers in the commodity markets try to mitigate the fluctuations in commodity price, the changes in the short positions seem to be almost completely unrelated to the output changes.[91]

---

87 Arwin G. Zeissler and Andrew Metrick, 'JPMorgan Chase London Whale G: hedging versus proprietary trading', *Yale Program on Financial Stability Case Study*, pp. 6–8.

88 See H Patrick Glenn, 'Comparative law and legal practice: on removing the borders', 75 Tul L Rev 977. The fuzziness of different concepts is the theoretical basis for the approach of comparison. But it also denotes the difficulty in differentiating similar concepts.

89 See Sahr, 'Does Volcker + Vickers = Liikanen? EU proposal for a regulation on structural measures improving the resilience of EU credit institutions, Mayer Brown Legal Update'.

90 Ing-Haw Cheng and Wei Xiong, 'Why do hedgers trade so much?' http://ssrn.com/abstract=2353218 or http://dx.doi.org/10.2139/ssrn.2353218, accessed December 12, 2014.

91 Ibid.

The evidence in Box 5.1 casts considerable doubt on the possibility of using the distinction between hedging and speculating to provide legislative guidance. Commercial hedgers, under the guise of mitigating risks, may actually regularly commit to trading activities either on purpose or driven by some heuristics.[92] Commercial hedgers are very likely to exploit their informational advantage and excessively engage in trading.[93]

B AMBIGUITY BETWEEN HEDGING AND TRADING IN STRUCTURAL DEBT SECURITIES

The above sub-section focuses on the futures markets in agricultural products. Commercial hedgers may commit to physical production or may be committed to both physical production and complicated trading activities. The purpose of trading is to offset risks in real economic activities, irrespective of how it is actually carried out in realty. But in the case of trading with regard to credit derivatives and structural debt securities where the institutional investors and sophisticated investors are the main players, the dynamics are a little more complicated.[94] The fact is that sophisticated investors may focus more on short-term investments, relying on their information advantage and various modern investment strategies and techniques.[95] Whilst pursuing short-term profits, the boundary between trading and hedging has become blurred. Within this context, the ambiguity between proprietary trading and hedging has become even more intangible. The different policy treatments of trading and hedging, which are based on different motives in the structural reforms, turn out to be extremely difficult to deal with in practice.[96]

(a) **Using the CDS product as an example.** The credit derivative products that were so prevalent in the run up to the GFC vividly reflected how the nominal hedgers could actually be speculators, and how the boundary between the two concepts is so vague when it comes to reality. According to Jerome A. Madden, 'a CDS is a derivative, a quasi-insurance product, that protects the insured against a company defaulting on its debt obligation'.[97] Emilios Avgouleas defined the CDS as 'a swap in which two parties enter into an agreement whereby one party pays the other a fixed periodic amount for the life of

92 Ibid, p. 11.
93 Arwin G. Zeissler, Daisuke Ikeda and Andrew Metrick, 'JPMorgan Chase London Whale A: risky business', *Yale Program on Financial Stability Case Study*, pp. 8–10.
94 Ibid, pp. 8–12.
95 Jerome A. Madden, 'A weapon of mass destruction strikes: credit default swaps bring down AIG and Lehman Brothers', 5 Bus L Brief 15, pp. 16–17.
96 Darrell Duffie, 'Challenges to a policy treatment of speculative trading motivated by differences in beliefs', 43 *The Journal of Legal Studies* S173, pp. 180–181.
97 Madden, 'A weapon of mass destruction strikes: credit default swaps bring down AIG and Lehman Brothers', p. 15.

the agreement. The other party makes no payments unless a specified credit event occurs'.[98] Thus, should the defined credit event happen, the party who pays the premium can turn to the seller of the credit protection product and receive payment when the swap is terminated. In the whole cycle of the legal relationships, one of the most important points is the definition of the credit event, which typically includes material default, bankruptcy, etc.

In terms of the hedging issue at question here, what matters is figuring out the default rate of the underlying securities of the CDS, and the real hedging effect.

It should be noted that for most institutional investors, they tend to use CDS to hedge risks in their current debt positions. Pimco CEO, Mohamed El-Erian, said CDS are good products, 'they are an integral part of good risk management, they allow you to position the portfolio in a much more refined process'.[99] But this is not quite true in reality. In the run up to the GFC, most large banks had excessive exposures to structural debt products, such as CDOs and RMBS, because the originate-to-distribute model turned out to be so successful in helping the banking sector exploit the booming housing market. The motive of these banks was that as long as the housing market kept going higher, these mortgage-related products would always be profitable.

This conflicting situation makes us wonder: assuming the bankers intended to hedge the risks, were they really hedging in reality? Is it possible that they were either really hedging risk as they intended or were they sometimes carelessly engaging in pure trading based on speculation? If the suspicions are proven, this would substantiate the view that the differences between speculative trading and hedging are not sufficiently distinct to support the different policy treatments in a structural separation reform.[100]

For credit derivatives transactions, it is plausible to say that many intended hedges are actually so speculative that they amount to pure trading. This can be substantiated by the complexity of structural debt securities underlying the swap products in the GFC. As is widely known, complexity made it virtually impossible to really assess the risks of these assets, not to mention using them to hedge other risks.[101] First, as indicated earlier on reducing complexity, the underlying assets of the structural debt securities were very tied up with a wide range of assets including mortgages loans, other financial assets, RMBS products, and credit derivative products.[102] Second, the complexity was further magnified by credit protection, or 'subordination'.[103] Structural debt securities normally have a hierarchy of

---

98   Avgouleas, *Governance of global financial markets: the law, the economics, the politics*, pp. 48–50.
99   Ben Levisohn, 'Are you exposed to credit default swap', *Bloomberg Business Week*, www.business-week.com/stories/2008–09–24/are-you-exposed-to-credit-default-swaps, accessed November 27, 2014.
100 Cheng and Xiong, 'Why do hedgers trade so much?'
101 See supra Chapter 4, Section 2.4 on the complexity issue.
102 See supra Chapter 5, Section 3.1.
103 See supra Chapter 5, Section 3.1 on credit protection.

cash flows and loss absorbency between tranches. Investors who get the senior tranches, which have the highest credit rating and lowest interest rates, are paid first in the event of default. The investors who purchase the junior tranches with a lower credit rating and higher interest rates are paid after the senior tranches if failure happens. The originator can also group the products into different categories according to their safety levels, say classifying RMBS into prime RMBS and non-prime RMBS. The latter could further be classified into alt-A, second lien, and subprime loans.[104]

The direct result of the complexity of structural debt products made it virtually impossible to assess the risk and undertake risk control of trading positions related to these products.[105] Therefore, it is difficult to see how CDS can actually be used as a form of risk hedging.[106] In terms of the complexity and its negative effects, an article in the *Wall Street Journal* suggests:

> So-called multi-sector CDOs, in particular, were exceptionally complex, involving more than 100 securities, each backed by multiple mortgages, auto loans or credit card receivables. Their performance depended on tens of thousands of disparate loans whose value was hard to determine and performance difficult to systemically predict.[107]

In addition, a massive reduction in the value of assets could happen in transactions related to structural debt securities and credit derivatives. If a credit event happens, such as the market deteriorating noticeably and the insured value declining, it may give the counterparty a right to demand more collateral. The demand for more collateral may cause the downgrade of the insurers' credit rating, which would in return cause demands for more collateral, and so forth.[108] This was exactly what happened in the GFC.[109]

What is more, another very important factor that added to the risk uncertainties surrounding the CDS products in the GFC was the unlimited number of buyers of these products. To engage in relevant transactions, investors do not need to have an insurable interest.[110] The direct result of this rule was that

---

104 *The United States of America v. S&P, 12 U.S.C. § 1833a, 18 U.S.C. § 1341.* See the complaint.

105 Ibid, see the complaint, pp. 48–55. The update of the CDO evaluator indicated the difficulties of risk evaluation for these securitisation products.

106 Arwin G. Zeissler and Andrew Metrick, 'JPMorgan Chase London Whale C: risk limits, metrics, and models', *Yale Program on Financial Stability Case Study*, pp. 4–6.

107 Serena Ng Carrick Mollenkamp, Liam Pleven and Randall Smith, 'Behind AIG's fall, risk models failed to pass real-world test', *Wall Street Journal*, http://online.wsj.com/news/articles/SB122538449722784635, accessed November 27, 2014.

108 Madden, 'A weapon of mass destruction strikes: credit default swaps bring down AIG and Lehman Brothers', pp. 16–17.

109 Liikanen Erkki, *High-level Expert Group on reforming the structure of the EU banking sector*, p. 5.

110 Richard Portes, 'Ban naked CDS', *Economist's view*, http://economistsview.typepad.com/economistsview/2010/03/ban-naked-cds.html, accessed November 27, 2014. Normally the precondition for buying insurance is that the buyers have insurable interests. CDS requiring no such insurable interests are called naked CDS.

any entity that had no relationship whatsoever with a certain debt obligation could enter into a CDS transaction to bet on certain securitisation products where others might not be able to fulfil their responsibilities. Together with the housing bubble and the lax monetary policy, this special insurance mechanism fuelled the unprecedented spike in the CDS markets. Statistics showed that by 2006, the market was approximately USD30 trillion in size, and then further increased to USD60 trillion in 2008, which was more than four times the GDP of the US.[111]

Therefore, the above variables on the unprecedented complexity of securitisation products, the prominent propensity for value destruction, and the unlimited number of buyers, all substantiate the very strong speculative aspect of hedging activity relating to credit derivatives, especially in the pre-crisis era. The fall of AIG was a telling example. It was discovered that there were devastating pitfalls in AIG's risk assessment model for their credit derivative products. When Gordan and Cassano designed the model, they assumed that AIG would never have to pay for the real default debts. However, they did not assess the potential collateral call by counterparties and how this could have a catastrophic effect on AIG. The fact was that the rescue required to stop the collateral call eventually cost AIG USD85 billion, which was mainly funded by a government bailout. 'Had the federal government not stepped in to save AIG from bankruptcy, AIG would have defaulted on $440 billion in CDS contracts'.[112]

(b) Ambiguity between trading and hedging adds to implementation costs. To sum up, the above analysis provides substantial evidence to cast doubt on the existence of a clear delimitation of proprietary trading and hedging activities in reality. It challenges, to a certain extent, the approach of employing different policy treatments for trading and hedging based on motives.[113]

What happened in the GFC was that the CDS used for hedging turned out to be merely speculative. And these only added to the securitisation bubble. Thus, any exposures to these products in the name of hedging risks turned out to be mere trading activities based on speculation.[114] There is actually some occasional evidence to show that the banking sector actually knew of the speculative bubble in the securitisation business and exploited it. For example, Mr Gordan commented on his risk model:

---

111 See Madden, 'A weapon of mass destruction strikes: credit default swaps bring down AIG and Lehman Brothers', pp. 15–16.

112 Ibid.

113 Duffie, 'Challenges to a policy treatment of speculative trading motivated by differences in beliefs', p. 181.

114 Zeissler, Ikeda and Metrick, 'JPMorgan Chase London Whale A: risky business', pp. 10–12.

[m]odels are guided by a few, very basic principles, which are designed to make them very robust and to introduce as little risk as possible. We always build our own models. Nothing in our business is based on using a publicly available model.[115]

Based on this analysis, it seems the Liikanen Report made the right choice in terms of not differentiating hedging and trading based on motives by prohibiting both of them. Compared with the Liikanen separation, the BSR prohibition rule cannot avoid this problem of fuzziness due to the principles-based approach of defining 'trading activities' and the implicit exceptions.[116] The same fuzziness problem also happens in the Volcker Rule, albeit there is a detailed but complicated delineation of trading and risk management. The prohibition rule will add to the uncertainties and ambiguity in implementation and hence considerably increase implementation and supervision costs.[117]

Similarly, the ring-fence rule and the Vickers Rule still partly rely on the ambiguous distinction between trading and risk management, so implementation costs are also not going to be negligible. But the broad scope reduces the need for differentiation and makes the costs slightly smaller than those of the prohibition rule.

4.1.2 Adjustment and compliance costs

Compliance costs refer mainly to the fact that banking groups have an obligation to separate their capital to comply with regulatory requirements on a standalone basis.[118] To really separate banks could be very complicated and involve a lot of adjustment costs.

To begin with, costs are even more considerable given the fact that the universal banking model has had a long history and is deeply entrenched in the banking industry in the EU.[119] This is not the same as the situation in the US where the orientation for legislation has been oscillating between two extremes: separation and dismantling separation. From the co-existence of commercial banks and investment banks before the 1930s to the Glass-Steagall Act, from the Bank Holding Company Act to the Gram-Leach-Billey Act,[120] policy orientation in the

---

115 Carrick Mollenkamp, 'Behind AIG's fall, risk models failed to pass real-world test', *Wall Street Journal*.
116 Glenn, 'Comparative law and legal practice: on removing the borders'.
117 Ibid.
118 European Commission, *Commission staff working document impact assessment accompanying the document Proposal for a Regulation of the European Parliament and of the Council on structural measures improving the resilience of EU Credit Institutions and the Proposal for a Regulation of the European Parliament and of the Council on reporting and transparency of securities financing transactions, SWD/2014/030 final*, p. 41.
119 See supra Chapter 1, Section 3(a).
120 Richard Scott Carnell, Jonathan R. Macey and Geoffrey P. Miller, *The Law of Banking and Financial Institutions* (Netherlands: Wolters Kluwer Law & Business 2009), pp. 10–30.

US has been going back and forth between co-existence and separation.[121] The universal banking model that is deeply embedded into the financial niches in the EU adds to the compliance costs.

In addition, apart from the historical obstacles, another equally significant obstacle is the practical difficulties in the decoupling process. The structure of a bank holding company is very complex with banking entities, non-banking entities, operational affiliates, non-operational affiliates, branches, etc. There are many different structural models for the co-existence of commercial banking activities and other activities.[122] In the 'HoldCo funded' model, for instance, the holding company holds all bank and investment business. A part of the external funding, including equities, capital instruments, and unsecured debts, is raised at the holding company level. Business activities, CCI activities, and trading activities are undertaken at the main bank level. In another model, such as the 'Big Bank' model, the holding company has a bank with a large balance sheet that is almost empty. Funding is often raised primarily at the bank level, and assets are held in the bank itself or in its subsidiaries. Therefore, the diversity of banking structural models also makes compliance and adaptation costs very expensive in reality.[123]

What is more, another adjustment obstacle would be that the industry might be reluctant to comply and even exert pressure on not complying with the BSR rule, especially given the fact that many other economies are still lagging behind in regard to this reform.[124] After the Volcker Rule was adopted, the regulatory agency in Japan wrote a consultation letter to the Fed and argued that the prohibition of proprietary trading had had a big adverse effect on Japanese government bonds. The reason was that the prohibition of trading activities together with the subtlety between trading and market-making made many US-based dealers have to exit the Japanese markets. That adversely affected the liquidity of Japanese government bonds and distorted the price due to the absence of the price discovery mechanism in market-making. Similar things also happened to US government bonds and the European sovereign debts.[125] Although the Volcker 'final rule' subsequently exempted the trading of US government bonds and foreign governments' bonds, the price discovery mechanism for trading and market-making activities was still adversely affected.[126] When compared with these adverse effects, it is likely that the compliance obstacles would be considerably larger.

121 See supra Chapter 1, Section 3(a).
122 Liikanen Erkki, *High-level Expert Group on reforming the structure of the EU banking sector*, p. 137.
123 Ibid, pp. 137–138. There are many other structural models. For instance, the 'Global Multi-Bank' model, in which the holding company holds several banks incorporated in different jurisdictions, which are restricted as a result of their interconnectedness. Some debts could be raised at the holding company level, but some of the subsidiary banks would also raise external financial debts. So, this group is structured as mutually independent.
124 Jan Schildbach and others, 'Universal banks: optimal for clients and financial stability'.
125 Darrell Duffie, 'Market making under the proposed Volcker rule', Rock Center for Corporate Governance at Stanford University Working Paper (106), pp. 4–5.
126 Prohibitions and Restrictions on Proprietary Trading and Certain Interests In, and Relationships With Hedge Funds and Private Equity Funds (The Final Rule) (U.S), section 6(a).

With regard to the international disparity in regulation, it should be noted that the concept of structural separation is still not familiar to the emerging markets, which makes their reluctance to comply even stronger due to considerations of competitiveness.[127] The separation of deposit entities and trading entities presumed that the relevant jurisdiction would have a well-developed and liquid secondary capital market on which most of the firms could rely. However, that is not the case for many emerging markets. The financial markets in these countries normally have a limited scale, a low percentage of direct financing, a suboptimal market mechanism, and an unbalanced structure of stock markets and bond markets.[128] For instance, the capital markets in China are limited. At the end of 2006, the value of securities accounted for only 22% of its total financial assets, which was in stark contrast with the data in other countries: 82% in the US, 71% in the UK, and 62% in Japan. Although this had increased to 37% by 2007, that was still very small compared with the rest of the world. In addition, for most of the developed economies, most of their external financing for corporations is basically from equity or bond markets rather than direct loans. However, this was not the case in China, the proportion of direct financing being only a small proportion of the total financing scale. From 2001 to 2007, the ratios were: 9.5%, 4.1%, 3.0%, 4.5%, 2.1%, 8.4%, and 22.0% respectively. Although this has increased in past years, it is still very minute compared with other developed countries. In 2006, funds raised by direct financing accounted for only 15.1% of all non-financial institutions' external financing, with bank loans accounting for all of the remaining part.[129]

Therefore, given this disparity in international regulation of the structural problem, compliance with the BSR raises concerns about the competitiveness of the banking sector in the EU against other relevant economies.

Given the historical and practical difficulties, the compliance costs of the BSR would seem to be significant. As regards concerns over competitiveness, similar to the Volcker Rule and the Vickers Rule, both the prohibition rule and the ring-fence rule have a European and an extraterritorial effect.[130] To a certain extent, international disparity in regulation and lack of coordination add to the compliance costs.

---

127 See supra Chapter 4, Section 4 on the pace of financial internationalisation in the emerging markets.

128 China Securities Regulatory Commission, *China Capital Markets Development Report* (Beijing: China Financial Publishing House 2008), pp. 255–258.

129 Ibid. See also China Banking Regulatory Commission, 'China Banking Regulatory Commission 2013 Annual Report'.

130 European Commission, *Proposal for a Regulation of the European Parliament and of the Council on structural measures improving the resilience of EU credit institutions, COM/2014/043 final*, art 3(2).

4.1.3 Operational costs

Operational costs refer to the costs that have to be borne by banks after the separation process because the former universal banks have to be operated on a stand-alone basis.[131] After the separation of the deposit entity from the trading entity, the operational costs for the banks may be higher than those in the pre-crisis era. For instance, management systems might also have to be separated. Similarly, administrative systems might also have to be changed accordingly.

For those institutions covered by the prohibition rule – the EU and G-SIIs – the increase in these operational costs would undoubtedly be very prominent because of the elimination of trading activities in the entire banking group. On the other hand, the costs should also not be overexaggerated because after complete separation, the bank would no longer need to operate various activities within the same group. The former costs of items such as risk management and monitoring the co-existence of activities will be no longer necessary. Therefore, it seems unlikely that operational costs will increase considerably under the BSR prohibition rule and the Volcker Rule.

With regard to the ring-fence rule, it requires separation on a sub-group basis, and it still permits the existence of the universal banking model. It specifically defines many standards on legal, economic, and operational links. For instance, the majority of the management board of CCIs will not be members of the management board of other entities, and vice versa.[132] By so doing, it seems that the operational costs would be at least as high as under the prohibition rule. Therefore, both the Vickers Rule and the BSR ring-fence rule would increase operational costs. But they would not be so prominent because it is hard to say to what extent the operational costs on a sub-group basis would be higher than those in universal banks with an unlimited co-existence of activities. In addition, although the definition of trading activities is very broad, its application is not mandatory, which could mitigate the inefficiency it might bring about in this regard.

4.2 Market-making costs

Operating under BSR rules, market-making costs refer mainly to detrimental effects on the efficient transaction of securities and the price discovery mechanism.[133]

---

131 European Commission, *Commission staff working document impact assessment accompanying the document Proposal for a Regulation of the European Parliament and of the Council on structural measures improving the resilience of EU Credit Institutions and the Proposal for a Regulation of the European Parliament and of the Council on reporting and transparency of securities financing transactions, SWD/2014/030 final*, p. 41.

132 European Commission, *Proposal for a Regulation of the European Parliament and of the Council on structural measures improving the resilience of EU credit institutions, COM/2014/043 final*, art 13(8).

133 Duffie, 'Market making under the proposed Volcker rule', p. 22.

4.2.1 Market-making costs in theory

(a) **Market-making and the rationale.** Proprietary trading normally refers to the activities conducted by trading entities as principal through the purchasing and selling of financial instruments for the purpose of making profits from the price difference between the transactions.[134] Thus, it is a buying low and selling high transaction. During the GFC, proprietary trading mostly happened through the purchase of structural debt securities, such as CDOs, and other credit derivatives, such as CDS. Fundamentally speaking, market-making activities are also a kind of proprietary trading. The only difference is that they can also act as a mechanism to provide immediacy to the markets and investors.[135]

Normally speaking, for investors in the capital markets, either sophisticated or unsophisticated investors, those who intend to sell and other potential counterparties who intend to buy cannot easily be matched by themselves due to the size of transaction costs and the information asymmetry.[136] Therefore, rather than identifying investors and counterparties by themselves, the market-making mechanism was created by market-makers to absorb clients' demands or supplies of assets into their own inventories as principal. Then, they can provide immediacy to any potential investor who wishes to transact with them.

In the US, market-makers can transact many products including government bonds, municipal bonds, corporate bonds, OTC derivatives, mortgage-related securities, commodities, currencies, etc.[137] The market-makers play a significant role in the financial market transactions both in the US and the EU. The envisioned function is to contain financial instruments' price volatility so that any demand for a transaction can be met at the best price.

As explained earlier, what the market-makers do through market-making activities is to absorb clients' supplies of, or demands for, assets into their own inventories in the hopes of trading these positions at different prices to generate profits. This trading behaviour makes both the market-makers and the investors better off. For the market-makers, it represents another highly profitable business. For the investors, it decreases the transaction costs and enhances transaction efficiency by instantly identifying potential counterparties.[138] That efficiency made it so popular that in the pre-crisis era, a majority of transactions in the OTC markets were transacted with market-makers. Even compared with the exchanges, market-makers still maintained the same advantage in transactions.[139]

---

134 European Commission, *Proposal for a Regulation of the European Parliament and of the Council on structural measures improving the resilience of EU credit institutions, COM/2014/043 final,* Art 5(4).

135 Darrell Duffie, 'The failure mechanics of dealer banks', *The Journal of Economic Perspectives* 51, pp. 5–6.

136 Paul M. Healy and Krishna G. Palepu, 'Information asymmetry, corporate disclosure, and the capital markets: a review of the empirical disclosure literature', 31 *Journal of Accounting and Economics* 405.

137 Duffie, 'Market making under the proposed Volcker rule'.

138 Yakov Amihud and Haim Mendelson, 'Dealership market: market-making with inventory', 8 *Journal of Financial Economics* 31, pp. 34–35.

139 Duffie, 'The failure mechanics of dealer banks', pp. 6–8

To further the efficiency in rebalancing the market-maker's inventory, a mechanism of dealer-to-dealer trades or interdeal brokers was established.[140] In practice, many investors would request quotes from a market-maker or several market-makers, which may lead them to trade with one particular market-maker. The market-makers could adapt or change their inventories through interdealer networks to further enhance transaction efficiency. Thus, this mechanism further strengthened the ability of market-makers to facilitate the immediacy provision function.[141] This was far better than the situation where one investor in the capital markets had to wait for another investor as the counterparty before a trade could be done.

On the other hand, like proprietary trading, market-making also played a not insignificant role in the run up to the GFC. Reinhart and Rogoff argued that the root cause of the GFC was the default of loans, the over-extension of credit to subprime mortgagers in the US, too much sovereignty debts in the EU, and all of them happening within the banking sector.[142] It is undeniable that excessive trading of securitisation products based on debt was also a precipitating factor in the mortgage crisis and made it deteriorate into an incredible overall crisis.[143]

(b) Market-making and its risks. Although it seems that market-making could make both the investors and the market-makers better off, providing immediacy can be a very risky behaviour due to several factors.[144]

First, there is always the concern about inventory imbalances. Through absorbing the supply shock or demand shock, the inventory of a market-maker could be substantially above a set level if the anticipated market changes do not materialise. What needs to be done is to try to reduce a part of the positions it has absorbed to reach a relative inventory balance either through selling these positions to ultimate investors or amending these positions through the dealer-to-dealer markets. But as a result of risk-taking incentives, unbalanced inventories were not unusual before the GFC.

Second, trade frequency and size are normally huge. Based on reliable expectations of a price recovery, the trading activities of a market-maker could, at times, be both extremely large in size and sparsely spaced out. As the inventory positions grow larger and larger in either short or long positions, the liquidity and market risks would put pressure on the market-makers. Should special losses happen, it would further reduce the market-maker's ability and willingness to provide further liquidity.[145]

Due to these concerns, market-makers would have to be wary about inventory risk management and need to adjust it immediately according to market conditions, including their expectations for their financial instruments, their asset

---

140 Duffie, 'Market making under the proposed Volcker Rule', pp. 16–17.
141 Sanford J. Grossman and Merton H. Miller, 'Liquidity and market structure', 43 *The Journal of Finance* 617.
142 Carmen M. Reinhart and Kenneth Rogoff, *This time is different: eight centuries of financial folly* (Princeton, NJ: Princeton University Press 2009), pp. 49–67.
143 Avgouleas, *The reform of 'Too-Big-To-Fail' bank: a new regulatory model for the institutional separation of 'casino' from 'utility' banking*, pp. 22–25.
144 Duffie, 'Market making under the proposed Volcker rule'.
145 Duffie, 'The failure mechanics of dealer banks', p. 6.

types, the volumes of capital they currently allocate into the market-making business, the reversion rates in their short and long positions, etc. If there is any signal showing a rising risk in warehousing the market-making positions in the balance sheet, they might need to be more meticulous in absorbing the supply or demand shocks to prevent the balance sheet from deteriorating. But if risks do arise, the market-maker's functions of providing immediacy and liquidity would be affected, which could have an adverse effect on the markets.[146]

Although market-making tends to provide immediacy and enhance transaction efficiency, its distinction compared with pure proprietary trading can be subtle in terms of predicting the future prices of assets in the hope of huge profits.[147]

Despite so much hidden risk in these activities, market-making activities do make market participants better off in two ways: (i) it provides a valuable immediacy function to the markets and largely reduces transaction costs; and (ii) it constitutes a very efficient price discovery mechanism and contains excessive volatility of asset prices.[148] Market-makers also have a strong motive to engage in the business driven by the expectation of high returns. Without the possibility of huge profits, it would be very irrational for all those market-makers to conduct their business given the hidden risks could be extremely large, abnormal, and idiosyncratic. The fact is the profits they expect could well be proportionately commensurate with the risk they bear. Generally speaking, the profits come from two aspects: anticipated changes in market price, and the net effect of bid-offer spreads.[149]

4.2.2 Market-making costs of the BSR

In the Liikanen separation, there is no differentiation between proprietary trading and market-making in two particular areas. The first area includes two parts:[150] the non-risk weighted capital requirements for trading activities, and the Basel risk-weighted requirements and separation of banking activities according to an evaluation of the recovery and resolution plans.[151] The two parts contain both a price-based approach and a structural-based approach. The rule requiring the separation of banking activities provides no explicit provision that market-making activities should be exempted from the separation rule. As regards the second area, the main difference is to change the conditional separation to a mandatory separation.[152]

But compared with the Liikanen separation rule, the Volcker Rule in the US explicitly exempts the market-making activity. The prohibition is premised on

---

146 Duffie, 'Market making under the proposed Volcker rule'.
147 Duffie, 'Challenges to a policy treatment of speculative trading motivated by differences in beliefs'.
148 Duffie, 'Market making under the proposed Volcker rule', pp. 4–5.
149 Ibid, p. 14.
150 Liikanen Erkki, *High-level Expert Group on reforming the structure of the EU banking sector*, p. 95.
151 Ibid.
152 Ibid, p. 96.

recognising the rationale of the market-making activity. It admits that although market-making could bring about instability and volatility to the banks and the entire industry, it has, to a certain extent, one irreplaceable advantage: providing immediacy and efficiency to the markets.[153] Giving due consideration to the fact that the trading activities of market-makers could both be extremely large in size and sparsely spaced out, and that the liquidity and market risks would be destabilising factors, the US regulators tend to think that the immediacy provision advantage pre-empts the concern over possible risks.[154] Therefore, for the Volcker Rule, the market-making costs might be comparably limited, largely due to the ambiguity between trading and market-making in practice.[155]

The BSR inherits the legacy of the Liikanen Report to a certain extent in regard to how to treat market-making. In the prohibition rule, it adopted the principles-based approach to define trading activities; it only exempts client-related activities, which allows a vague but theoretical possibility of exempting market-making. Thus, compared with the Volcker Rule's clear and detailed definition of market-making and its exceptions, the market-making costs in the EU prohibition rule might be more prominent.

In the ring-fence rule, however, the market-making activity is particularly targeted to ensure the safety and soundness of the bank and the stability of the whole industry, despite the general exception of risk management services to customers.[156] Therefore, the effects of curbing market-making through the use of the ring-fence rule, similar to Vickers Rule, might be more evident than that of the prohibition rule.[157]

4.2.3 Market-making costs by the BSR in practice

Therefore, for the BSR, under the prohibition rule and the principles-based proprietary trading definition in Article 6, the CCI could still possibly commit to market-making by meeting the clients' activities' requirement.[158]

But under the ring-fence rule, Article 9 almost rules out the possibility of market-making. The only permitted possible market-making activities according to

---

153 Prohibitions and Restrictions on Proprietary Trading and Certain Interests in, and Relationships with Hedge Funds and Private Equity Funds (The Final Rule) – Supplementary information, pp. 151–153.

154 Prohibitions and Restrictions on Proprietary Trading and Certain Interests In, and Relationships with Hedge Funds and Private Equity Funds (The Final Rule) (U.S).

155 Prohibitions and Restrictions on Proprietary Trading and Certain Interests in, and Relationships With, Hedge Funds and Private Equity Funds (The Final Rule) – Supplementary information, p. 152. Many commenters hold different views and believe that the definition of market-making in the final rule has been wantonly narrowed down.

156 European Commission, *Proposal for a Regulation of the European Parliament and of the Council on structural measures improving the resilience of EU credit institutions, COM/2014/043 final*, art 12.

157 Ibid, art 9

158 Ibid, art 6.

Article 12 are for risk management and selling derivatives to clients.[159] But the fact is, given the earlier analysis of the subtle differences between market-making and trading, such general principles and exceptions would probably mean it would be difficult to actually create a tolerable space for an efficient market-making function, especially within the context of the competent authority's discretion and its inconsistency. In this case, the market immediacy provision function would be seriously affected. The adverse influence would be very evident, as discussed next.

First, the extremely limited market-making activities would increase execution costs and transaction costs of the investors and make market participants suffer losses because of price volatility. As a matter of fact, the reason why the US regulatory agencies exempted US government securities is that they were afraid that the prohibition on the trading of government bonds would lower the price of the securities and make the government suffer as an issuer.

As referred to earlier, a related scenario is that after the adoption of the Volcker Rule, the Japanese Financial Services Agency wrote to the US regulatory agencies to consult about the trading in Japanese government bonds, insisting that the restriction of proprietary trading was having an adverse effect on the trading of these securities. Their basic argument was that the increase in transaction costs as a result of the prohibition would have an adverse effect on the liquidity of the bonds.[160]

Second, due to the diminishing provision of immediacy, the price discovery mechanism would also be undermined. Formerly, the market-making activity can act as a price buffer.[161] For instance, if there were some adverse market signals, many investors would probably try to reduce their positions of relevant securities. This behaviour would cause a further deterioration in market confidence. Then, low market confidence would further urge people to sell more of their positions, and so forth.[162] This is how crises can sometimes happen unexpectedly. If market-making activities remain with the banks, the absorption of supply and demand shocks by market-makers could act as a buffer against price volatility and facilitate real price discovery. Therefore, if a price change is not caused by a fundamental change in economic performance, but by some accidental event, the price buffer can help the markets to regain equilibrium.[163] Research shows that US Treasury bond prices were seriously distorted during the financial crisis when market-makers were absent, especially around 2008 at the beginning of the GFC.[164]

Third, given the fact that market-making activities are of significant importance to the markets and considerably profitable, the prohibition and separation

159   Ibid, art 12.
160   Duffie, 'Market making under the proposed Volcker rule', p. 5. See supra Chapter 5, Section 4.1.1(b).
161   Grossman and Miller, 'Liquidity and market structure'.
162   Financial Conduct Authority, *Financial Conduct Authority (2013), Applying Behavioral Economics in Financial Conduct Authority, Occasional Paper No. 1.*
163   Grossman and Miller, 'Liquidity and market structure'.
164   David Musto, Greg Nini and Krista Schwarz, 'Notes on bonds: liquidity at all costs in the great recession', Unpublished working paper, University of Pennsylvania.

would probably lead to migration.[165] Since the CCI is now not allowed to commit to market-making activities and proprietary trading, financial institutions would have to stop providing the services. But some might move these restricted activities to other entities or to exempted entities or even move them out of the European countries.[166] Within the EU, because of the existence of discretion in implementing the ring-fence rule by the competent authority, in practice there would be inconsistency and a lack of coordination that would persist in the future with regard to the market-making policy. For the prohibition rule, due to the stricter prohibition strength, it is also likely that market-making would be forced to migrate to other unregulated areas to avoid the rule.[167] Theoretically, non-bank firms, insurance companies, and hedge fund institutions could undertake some market-making activities. They are supervised by a less regulated system in terms of capital requirement, liquidity, and transparency requirements.[168]

As a matter of fact, even compared with the BSR, the market-making exemption as provided in detail in the US, was still widely criticised.[169] Many commenters claim that the agency's definition of market-making is actually bona fide market-making, the scope of which has been wantonly narrowed down. For those commenters, market-making is inherently a genre of proprietary trading that might be susceptible to many uncertainties: market volatility risk, future price miscalculation, the pressure of the prolonged period of time over which a position should hold, the unpredictability of timing and client demand. In their opinion, in terms of the merits of market-making, the narrow definition of market-making in the rule tends to impede the significant function of it.[170]

Thus, it can be seen that the BSR has its limits from both the prohibition rule and the ring-fence rule aspects for not clearly defining and delineating the boundary between proprietary trading and market-making. Lack of a clear delimitation of the rule and its exceptions would probably severely sabotage the immediacy provision function of the market-makers.

4.3 Hedging costs

Hedging in the banking sector mainly refers to the pooling of different activities and assets to contain the risks for the banks.[171]

---

165   See supra Chapter 4, Section 3.3.
166   José Viñals et al., *Creating a safer financial system: will the Volcker, Vickers, and Liikanen structural measures help?* (New York: International Monetary Fund 2013).
167   See supra Chapter 4, Section 3.3.
168   European Commission, *Commission's roadmap for tackling the risks inherent in shadow banking (press release)* (September 4, 2013), see also European Commission, *Communication on shadow banking: frequently asked questions* (Brussels, September 4, 2013).
169   Prohibitions and Restrictions on Proprietary Trading and Certain Interests in, and Relationships With, Hedge Funds and Private Equity Funds (The Final Rule) – Supplementary information, pp. 152–153.
170   Ibid, pp. 142–144. Duffie, 'Market making under the proposed Volcker Rule', p. 3. See supra Chapter 5, Section 4.1.1.
171   Edward I. Altman and John B. Caouette, 'Credit-risk measurement and management: the ironic challenge in the next decade', 54 *Financial Analysts Journal.*

4.3.1 Hedging in theory

As indicated earlier, arguably many would say that in the run up to the GFC, as the typical tool used in risk hedging, the CDS were actually just a tool for gambling.[172] Imagine a transaction in CDS products, unlike other insurance products it does not require an insurable interest for investors to buy the products. Therefore, anybody who does not have a clue about what a CDS actually is and what the underlying assets of the structural debt securities are, could turn out to be a buyer of CDS products betting on the rise or fall of the relevant assets. Lynn Stout gave a clear explanation of this costless speculative transaction of derivatives:

> The speculator who buys houses in the spot market must pay property taxes, fix leaking roofs, and make sure lawns are mowed. In contrast, derivatives betting can be virtually costless, at least until the bet comes due. In an interest rate swap, for example, one party bets that interest rates will rise by agreeing to make fixed payments tied to today's interest rate, while the other bets that interest rates will fall by agreeing to make payments tied to future interest rates. Because the parties to the swap are merely exchanging bets as consideration, unless and until interest rates actually change, betting does not cost either party anything.[173]

Nevertheless, it is also undeniable that in many cases traders in derivatives transactions also intend to hedge against risks because banks have inherent uncertainties with regard to capital, liquidity, and funds, and they are inclined to conduct maturity transformation. The trading of derivatives, such as credit derivatives products, was also used to hedge risks.[174] In this scenario, different scopes in restrictions and different strengths of separation between the CCI and the trading entity might somehow impede the hedging effect to a certain extent.

As a matter of fact, it is fair to say banks need hedging activities to offset their risky business. Edward Altman explained the necessity of risk hedging for banks, that instead of holding their loans, 'they are increasingly willing to consider transacting their assets in counterparty arrangements whereby the credit-risk exposure is shifted with the reduction in total risk of the original lender'.[175] This means that the supply of derivatives actually takes on the task of essentially reducing total bank risk to a containable level.

---

172 See supra Chapter 5, Section 4.1.1(a). It refers to the abuse of CDS products.
173 Stout Lynn, 'Derivatives and the legal origin of the 2008 credit crisis', 1 *Harvard Business Law Review* 1. As indicated by the essay, it would not be fair to argue that there would have been no financial crisis but for the existence of the structural debt products and market speculation, but the correlation of speculative investment in derivatives market and the crisis was absolute.
174 Madden, 'A weapon of mass destruction strikes: credit default swaps bring down AIG and Lehman Brothers'.
175 Edward I. Altman and John B. Caouette, 'Credit-risk measurement and management: the ironic challenge in the next decade', pp. 2–3.

Theoretically, the development of the credit derivatives markets could significantly contribute to financial stability within the banking industry, because banks tried to transfer credit risk outside them through the origination and securitisation activity. Well-managed exposures to these derivatives products envisioned for risk reduction would also help to hedge banks' original risks. Therefore, these exposures could make banks safer.[176]

The significance of hedging can be substantiated by empirical research. For instance, the British Bankers' Association (BBA) surveys (1999/2000 and 2001/2002) showed that many banks in the London market argued that credit derivatives transactions were more significant in reference to active portfolio and asset management than in reference to complying with relevant bank regulation rules.[177]

Premised on the presumption of the hedging capacity of derivative products, many researchers were actually concerned about how to prevent the prevailing transactions of derivatives becoming a two-edged sword: both a factor for shifting risk and a potential threat to bank stability. The concern was not without foundation. First, banks' ability and technology required to measure internal risk were not perfect in reality.[178] Second, research showed that when banks had quick and convenient access to a large set of derivatives to manage and hedge their risks, it also created the incentive for more risk-taking in an aggressive way.[179] Risk-taking and overextension of credit, which was supposed to be a concern for banks, became more attractive when the underlying risks could easily be shifted and transferred through derivatives trading. To some extent, this argument can be partly substantiated by some empirical research. The BBA's surveys indicated that market demand for securitisation products with sovereign debt as underlying assets declined prominently from 35% in 1997 to 17% in 2004, while the demand for products with corporate debts as underlying assets increased significantly from 35% to 57% in the same period.[180]

4.3.2 Hedging costs of the BSR

In the BSR, the hedging exception is not provided in detail under the prohibition rule except in the principles-based definition. The principles-based approach still leaves room for exempting hedging activities according to Article 5(4).[181] Besides, it seems to give banks a degree of flexibility by not establishing a finite set of non-prohibited activities. However, compared with the Volcker Rule's definitive

---

176 Norvald Instefjord, 'Risk and hedging: do credit derivatives increase bank risk?' 29 *Journal of Banking & Finance* 333, pp. 334–335. See also Edward I. Altman, 'Credit risk measurement and management: the ironic challenge in the next decade'.

177 Instefjord, 'Risk and hedging: do credit derivatives increase bank risk?' p. 334.

178 Jeremy Berkowitz and James O'Brien, 'How accurate are value-at-risk models at commercial banks?' *Journal of Finance* 1093.

179 Instefjord, 'Risk and hedging: do credit derivatives increase bank risk?'

180 Ibid, p. 335.

181 BSR, art 5(4).

exceptions and its clarity, it would also clearly contribute to uncertainty as to the extent to which it would compromise hedging activities.[182]

The hedging exception is specifically referred to in the ring-fence rule of the BSR. But it should be noted that the ring-fence provisions are directed to focus generally on risky activities, including market-making, investing in and acting as sponsor of covered funds, and trading in derivatives. With regard to hedging, it is only permissible as prudential management of own risk according to Article 11 of the BSR.[183] The prudential management of risk exception permits some specific derivatives trading which demonstrably reduces or significantly mitigates identifiable risks of individual or aggregated positions of the CCI.[184] In addition, the remuneration policy applicable to bank staff should aim to prevent any residual and hidden proprietary trading, reflect the legitimate hedging objectives of the CCI, and not be based on the profits of such activities.

According to Article 11, apparently the EC has considered the two-edged attribute of the derivatives transaction: it aims to restrict trading activities. On the other hand, it also provides certain exceptions to cater for the necessity of risk hedging for banks. The hedging exception is similar to the UK rule, which provides a general exception, but not much explanation or delineation of it. In contrast, for the hedging activity exception, the Volcker Rule defines at least the individually based internal compliance procedures, demonstrably reducing identifiable risk and remuneration policy in a very comprehensive manner. The US agencies believe that the clarity would bring better certainty of implementation.[185]

Thus, the ring-fence rule could cause the costs of hedging to rise considerably, probably more than the prohibition rule, because of the broad scope of its restrictions and because of the uncertainties in the permitted discretion of the competent authority to differentiate between the two activities. But the hedging costs in the prohibition rule are also non-negligible due to the principles-based approach and the fuzziness problem. The Volcker Rule, in comparison, might perform better in reducing hedging costs as a result of its clearly defined exceptions.

4.4 Diversification costs

Diversification is intertwined with the issue of the economies of size and scope. The discussion here focuses on the diversification effect of business lines and banking activities, especially in the TBTF institutions. Many researchers and legislative assessments and comments believed that structural reform would compromise the

182   Sahr, 'Does Volcker + Vickers = Liikanen? EU proposal for a regulation on structural measures improving the resilience of EU credit institutions', *Mayer Brown Legal Update*, pp. 6–7.
183   BSR, art 11.
184   European Commission, *Proposal for a Regulation of the European Parliament and of the Council on structural measures improving the resilience of EU credit institutions, COM/2014/043 final*, art 11.
185   Prohibitions and Restrictions on Proprietary Trading and Certain Interests in, and Relationships With, Hedge Funds and Private Equity Funds (The Final Rule) – Supplementary information, pp. 330–356.

diversification effect, i.e. the economies of scope and size in the banking industry.[186] With regard to the diversification effect under the BSR, it needs closer examination due to its complex approach to separation.

It was found that a bank of considerable size in the pre-crisis era usually had a universal banking model, providing a wide range of services. On the contrary, those relatively small-sized publicly funded financial institutions did not necessarily use the universal banking model.[187] The underlying fact is that by employing the universal banking model, banks could have a particular competitive edge in many aspects, such as organising and managing its own portfolios to diversify its risks. And competitive advantage tends to make banks larger still. The economies of scale and scope tend to be intertwined with one another.

4.4.1 The economies of scale for TBTF institutions

The economies of scale have always been a frequent topic of discussion and research in the history of modern economy. Specifically, when it comes to the context of the TBTF institutions, a more concrete question is: are the efficiency and economies of scale in TBTF institutions substantial enough to mitigate the social costs and risks the size brings to the banking sector?

Supporters of the economies of scale argue that banks could benefit from a reduction in single unit operating costs of financial entities.[188] Since banks provide financial services to their clients in the markets, the cost saving effect for banks would be transferred to customers rather than accrue to banks alone. In this scenario, economies of scale do exist in the banking industry.

According to Robert DeYoung, obtaining comprehensive statistics on the efficiency and costs of a larger scale bank are not practically possible because it involves so many immeasurable uncertainties. The first problem is that the current statistical techniques used to measure the economies of scale can only represent accurately the average companies in a particular industry.[189] However, the performance of average companies does not necessarily speak for the banking industry as a whole, not to mention the TBTF institutions. The banking sector has witnessed the most unprecedented merger and consolidation process since the late 1990s. Statistics showed that until March 2010, three of the largest US banks (the Bank

---

186 Independent Commission on Banking, 'Final Report, recommendations'.

187 Liikanen Erkki, *High-level Expert Group on reforming the structure of the EU banking sector*, pp. 56–57. It refers to the existence of the cooperative and savings banks in European countries. Research shows that cooperative and savings banks were built to facilitate regional economic development rather than seeking highest profits. So, even in the prevailing trend of the universal banking model transformation, the cooperative and savings banks still insisted on their business model. It turned out their performance showed more stability than that of the TBTF institutions.

188 Loretta J. Mester, 'Scale economies in banking and regulatory reform', Federal Reserve Bank of Philadelphia papers, www.minneapolisfed.org/publications_papers/pub_display.cfm?id=4535&, accessed December 2, 2014.

189 Robert DeYoung, 'Scale economies are a distraction', The Region, Federal Reserve Bank of Minneapolis, p. 2.

of American, JPMorgan Chase, Citibank) had assets of over USD2 trillion each and ten times the assets of the 13th largest bank in the country.[190] Thus, the scale expansion in this industry was not proportionate to most other industries. The same trend also happened in the EU, or even more severely because of the deeply rooted universal banking model in this region.[191] Therefore, with such examples at hand, just one or two of the largest banks could easily distort any measure of efficiency of the economies of scale in the large banks.

Second, the operational model of large banks is quite different from that of small banks. They are not only different in size but also in business model. A BIS report (2013) gives an explanation of the totally different income components in investment banks, investment banking-oriented universal banks, commercial banks, and commercial banking-oriented universal banks.[192] Therefore, to generalise about the economies of scale might also seem to be inappropriate.

Third, the inaccuracy of market forces in allocating financial resources in a free market could also be a problem.[193] Theoretically, market force theory argues that market forces drive the merger and consolidation process in the banking industry. Otherwise, probably the consolidated companies would turn out to be inefficient and consumers and clients would finally give up on the banks. But, such market force theory ignores another variable, which is the guarantee of public funds to these TBTF institutions. As a result of this, the possible inefficiencies of scale would be masked by the performance enhancing illusion of the public guarantee. The direct result is that shareholders and clients would knowingly disregard the inefficiency of the banks because these banks can still bring profits to them.[194]

Due to the aforementioned reasons, it is hard to know to what extent economies of scale exist and at what level they reach an optimal size without causing unnecessary costs. Relevant research shows different results. According to Berger and Mester with their data up until 1995, 20% of bank costs could be saved due to economies of scale.[195] In addition, they found that for the size range from less than USD50 million to more than USD10 billion, economies of scale substantially existed.[196] McAllister's and McManus' research showed that banks could have economies of scale for a size of more than at least USD500

190 Loretta J. Mester, 'Scale economies in banking and regulatory reform', Federal Reserve Bank of Philadelphia papers', p. 8. See also United States Senate Permanent Subcommittee on Investigations, *Wall Street and the financial crisis: anatomy of a financial collapse* (Cosimo Reports 2011).
191 Ferran, *The regulatory aftermath of the global financial crisis*, pp. 65–68.
192 Gambacorta, *Structural bank regulation initiatives: approaches and implications*, pp. 6–8.
193 Barr Rosenberg, Kenneth Reid and Ronald Lanstein, 'Persuasive evidence of market inefficiency', 11 *The Journal of Portfolio Management* 9.
194 DeYoung, 'Scale economies are a distraction', pp. 5–6.
195 Allen N. Berger and Loretta J. Mester, 'Inside the black box: what explains differences in the efficiencies of financial institutions?' 21 *Journal of Banking & Finance* 895.
196 Loretta J. Mester, 'Scale economies in banking and regulatory reform', Federal Reserve Bank of Philadelphia papers, p. 3.

million of total assets.[197] Other research indicates that commercial banks whose assets exceed USD50 billion would have proportionately higher operating costs than those of smaller banks. Thus, it seems that the size accommodating economies of scale have been various and growing, but what is uncertain is whether the economies still exist in the current banking system with many banks being unparalleled in size.

Theoretically, there are several grounds for the economies of scale, and that applies to the banking industry and even to the TBTF institutions. First, they need lower operating costs. A bigger size can allow a bank to concentrate all its resources in operating its business, and thereby reducing its production and operating costs. Lower costs can be reflected in lower prices, which would turn out to be beneficial for both the banks and their clients. Second, the economies of scale derive from a better diversification effect. With a bigger size, the risk-taking potential would be well managed and diversified through appropriately managed portfolios. Better diversification could reduce risks, such as liquidity risk and credit risk. Third, in the consolidation process and financial internationalisation process, these large and significant banks play a more and more important role in promoting international banking, especially in the banking industry in the EU.[198]

On the other hand, the advantages of scale are also accompanied by inefficiencies. According to Loretta J. Mester, apart from a better diversification effect, there is another negative effect of a large bank: the risk-taking effect.[199] Specifically, the scale effect could be overexploited or might be abused to a certain extent. Market force theory assumes that the market has driven the consolidation and merger process in the industry. If the consolidation were no longer efficient to the markets, the shareholders would vote against their banks by withdrawing their investment. However, the situation is different in TBTF institutions. Since these banks can gain implicit public guarantees, this makes them less exposed to the risk of bankruptcy. Thus, shareholders and investors in these banks would not give up on their banks even if the larger scale brought no further efficiencies. Without the risk of bankruptcy, these banks have more and more incentive for risk-taking.[200] In addition, from the perspective of antitrust, if a firm has too much concentrated market share, which is the current situation of the TBTF institutions, it is very likely that they will abuse their position of power in the concentrated market.[201]

---

197 Patrick H. McAllister and Douglas McManus, 'Resolving the scale efficiency puzzle in banking', 17 *Journal of Banking & Finance* 389, pp. 390–391.
198 European Central Bank, *Report on financial integration in Europe*, pp. 97–98.
199 Loretta J. Mester, 'Scale economies in banking and regulatory reform', Federal Reserve Bank of Philadelphia papers, pp. 3–4.
200 Ibid.
201 Financial Conduct Authority, *Financial Conduct Authority (2013), Applying behavioral economics in Financial Conduct Authority, Occasional Paper No. 1*. See also United States Senate Permanent Subcommittee on Investigations, *Wall Street and the financial crisis: anatomy of a financial collapse*, pp. 5–12.

The point to be made here is that despite the quantitative uncertainties and possible inefficiencies brought about by large scale, the economies of scale in the banking industry are well established to a certain extent.

4.4.2 The economies of scope

To consider whether the BSR separation rule could have a negative impact on diversification, the economies of scope are also inextricably intertwined. The issue to be discussed is to what extent the wide scope of services could enhance the diversification effect.

IMF research sampled seven G-SIBs, including five US banks and two UK banks. It plots a picture showing the confidence bands for the volatility-adjusted return ratios and showed that the retail business was the most profitable, followed by the wholesale business, and then the trading business. By operating all three business segments, banks were able to diversify their risks even during the period of the GFC.[202]

But with regard to the empirical effect of diversification, it is hard to reach a conclusion. Compared with the above point, there is also incompatible research about the efficiency of different business models in the banking industry. In an IMF (2013) paper, it provided a chart plotting the total losses from write down and credit default swaps in banks with the universal banking model and those with the investment bank model. It drew the conclusion that no bank model clearly fared better than another, and the universal banking model did not perform better in the GFC.[203]

A possible explanation is that business model is not the only key function of bank failure, rather other fundamental factors exist, such as the risk-taking incentive in the industry, the leveraged balance sheets, the over-reliance on short-term wholesale funding, the homogenisation of business activities, etc. Thus, practically speaking, whether the diversification effect could happen is contingent on many factors.[204]

Be that as it may, at least there are some advantages to a wide variety in activities, which are well accepted.[205] First, the wide scope brings lower costs. Just like economies of scale, wide scope also brings about lower operational costs for bank products through the provision of one-stop-shop services. In other words, if banks attract one customer with one service, and the customer feels satisfied about it, this feeling can act as a feedback to encourage the customer to purchase more relevant services. The feedback would be strengthened over time

202 Viñals et al., *Creating a safer financial system: will the Volcker, Vickers, and Liikanen structural measures help?* pp. 21–22.
203 Ibid, pp. 12–13.
204 Ibid, p. 13.
205 Financial Stability Oversight Council, *Study of the effects of size and complexity of financial institutions on capital market efficiency and economic growth* (January 2011), pp. 38–46.

and constitute a social influence cycle.[206] Therefore, the typical positive feedback loop paves the way for lowering product marketing costs and increasing bank revenues.[207]

Second, economies of scope denote diversification of risks. The capacity to combine different businesses and activities in the universal banks could bring about benefits of diversification, albeit there is some controversial and contrary empirical evidence.[208] By providing various products and managing business activities with different risk potentials and different return cycles, the universal banking model corresponds to the definition of diversification. It minimises risks by filling up its basket with assets of both positive and negative correlations, to create a state of risk-offsetting. Thus, operating risks could be minimised.[209]

Third, the universal banking model also allows banks to share information and operations, such as IT systems, between the retail bank and the investment bank.[210] Therefore, the operational cost savings are also evident.

However, setting these advantages aside, the basic disadvantages that come with the wide banking scope are also evident. To begin with, it brings the problem of complexity. A traditional bank has only services, such as deposit taking, extension of credit, and providing payments. But in a universal bank, there is a wide set of activities being undertaken: traditional banking activities, investment banking, underwriting, wealth management, insurance, derivatives transactions, etc. Complexity would not only make the financial products too complicated to understand for customers but would also make it difficult to comply with transparency standards. Most importantly, it brings about difficulties of supervision and regulation.[211]

In addition, the all-encompassing set of activities causes problems of conflicts of interest. For instance, there is always a prominent conflict of interest problem when engaging in both underwriting and trading activities. For a universal bank, such a model provides an incentive to buy or sell the securities it underwrites to exploit profits.[212]

What is more, risk-taking incentives are more evident in universal banks. It should be noted that there is a difference between costs absorbed by the public and costs absorbed by the private sector.[213] If the business scope is very broad,

---

206 Daniel Kahneman, 'Maps of bounded rationality: psychology for behavioral economics', *American Economic Review* 1449.
207 Robert J. Schiller, *Irrational exuberance* (2000), pp. 40–44.
208 Independent Commission on Banking, 'Final Report, recommendations', pp. 273–275.
209 Harry M. Markowitz, *Portfolio selection: efficient diversification of investments*, vol. 16 (New Haven, CT: Yale University Press 1968).
210 Independent Commission on Banking, 'Final Report, recommendations', pp. 136–137.
211 Schwarcz, 'Regulating complexity in financial markets'.
212 European Commission, *Commission staff working document impact assessment accompanying the document Proposal for a Regulation of the European Parliament and of the Council on structural measures improving the resilience of EU Credit Institutions and the Proposal for a Regulation of the European Parliament and of the Council on reporting and transparency of securities financing transactions*, SWD/2014/030 final, p. 40.
213 See supra Chapter 5, Section 2.2

the size of the banks makes them TBTF; they have more incentives to undertake risk-taking business irresponsibly because the public might absorb the costs.[214]

Due to the above disadvantages, the universal banking model also tends to give rise to extra risks to banks and the entire industry. The diversification effect might exist on a stand-alone basis for a bank. However, for the ecology of the whole banking industry, the prevalence of the universal banking model makes all large institutions have more or less similar business lines without much diversity. In this manner, diversification on a case-by-case basis would possibly be devoured by the eradication of diversity in the whole system. Along with the conflicts of interest and the inclination for risk-taking, the homogeneity could unleash devastating power to the bank sector. That is also why the failure of Lehman Brothers instantly had such an appalling effect around the world.[215]

The point to be made here is that despite the conflicting empirical evidence and the possible disadvantages, there are also certain well-established grounds for economies of scope in the banking sector.

4.4.3 The corresponding costs of the BSR

The economies of size and economies of scope are intertwined, and they are the basis on which the diversification effect relies. Based on the earlier analyses, it seems that even without separation reform, the diversification effect is not completely guaranteed; it still depends on many factors and is susceptible to many pitfalls. Much research conducted supports neither strict separation nor unrestricted co-existence.[216] The BSR's complex approach of separation seems not to be in conflict with such research.

As regards economies of scale, it was taken into consideration by the Liikanen Report both in the mandatory separation and the conditional separation provisions. Under mandatory separation, there is a size threshold reflected by a two-step test: (i) the banks' trading positions exceeding 15–25% of the bank's total assets or having total assets of more than EUR100 billion; and (ii) the competent authority deciding the extent of the separation to be carried out. According to McAllister and McManus's research, the banks could have economies of scale for a size of up to at least EUR500 million of total assets.[217] Other research shows that commercial banks whose assets exceed EUR50 billion would have higher operating costs than those of smaller banks. The threshold of trading to assets ratio (15–25%) and the size of EUR100 billion are not exactly aligned with

214   Federal Deposit Insurance Corporation, 'The orderly liquidation of Lehman Brothers Holdings Inc. under the Dodd-Frank Act', www.fdic.gov/bank/analytical/quarterly/2011_vol5_2/lehman.pdf, accessed November 15, 2014.

215   Madden, 'A weapon of mass destruction strikes: credit default swaps bring down AIG and Lehman Brothers'.

216   Financial Stability Oversight Council, *Study of the effects of size and complexity of financial institutions on capital market efficiency and economic growth*, p. 47.

217   Cf. supra Chapter 5, Section 4.4.1 on the size range of the economies of scale.

statistical research; it is actually a higher threshold than research has shown.[218] Thus, it might be fair to say the report is cracking down only the inefficiency aspect of behemoth banks; it might not be detrimental to the economies of size generally speaking.

In the BSR, the threshold for the application of the prohibition rule is for G-SIIs and entities that for a period of three consecutive years have had total assets amounting to at least EUR30 billion and trading activities amounting to at least EUR70 billion or 10% of its total assets. Compared with the Liikanen Report, the threshold is different, but no lower in terms of the asset level. Thus, the detrimental effect to the economies of scale might not be obvious. In contrast, the Volcker Rule is applied indiscriminately to all banks. In this scenario, the detrimental effect could be non-negligible.

For the BSR ring-fence rule, its application is equally applied to all banks. By contrast, the admission level in the Vickers Rule is £25 billion of mandated deposits.[219] But, be mindful that compared with the UK, the indiscriminate application of the BSR ring-fence rule is based on the discretion of the competent authority rather than on a mandatory basis. Therefore, the detrimental effect to the economies of scale seems also not to be very prominent.

With regard to the economies of scope, the Liikanen Report's mandatory separation rule tends to wipe out all proprietary trading activities and the acquisition of or investing in hedge funds, special investment vehicles, and private equity funds. In the prohibition rule of the BSR, the scope is even broader than this and is based on its very inclusive definition of proprietary trading being everything except client-related activities.[220] In comparison, the equally strictly applied Volcker Rule has more detailed exceptions. Thus, it seems that there is a negative influence on the economies of scope by the prohibition rule, arguably more in the BSR than the Volcker Rule where the effect might be negligible because the diversification effect through the narrowly defined proprietary trading activities turns out to be limited at the outset.

In the ring-fence rule, although it still preserves the universal banking model, the broad scope of definition of restricted activities would still make the negative influence non-negligible. Activities such as market-making and investment banking, which are known to be useful for diversification, are specifically targeted by the ring-fence rule.[221] Similarly, the Vickers Rule's broad restriction carried out in all banks means it can also possibly compromise the economies of scope in a non-negligible way. But this negative influence does not seem to be very intense for the following reasons.

218 McAllister and McManus, 'Resolving the scale efficiency puzzle in banking'.
219 Independent Commission on Banking, 'Final Report, recommendations', p. 236.
220 European Commission, *Proposal for a Regulation of the European Parliament and of the Council on structural measures improving the resilience of EU credit institutions*, COM/2014/043 final, art 5–6.
221 Duffie, 'Market making under the proposed Volcker rule', pp. 2–4.

First, the analysis of the advantages shows that the separation rule could reduce complexity, interconnectedness, and enhance resolvability in the EU.[222] These merits tackle the negative effects of the banks' wide scope of activities, but are not necessarily correlated to the positive effects of this wide scope. Additionally, the scope restriction in the ring-fence rule is not mandatory in the EU. Rather, it is to be decided and implemented on a case-by-case basis according to the need for stability of the banks and the whole banking industry. Third, the ring-fence approach is deemed by many researchers, including the Vickers Report, to be retaining a part of the diversification effect.[223]

Therefore, research indicates that there is a possible negative influence on the economies of scale and scope of the universal banks due to the BSR. But that is also subject to some possible theoretical controversies.[224]

4.5 Less implicit government guarantees and liquidity

It is debatable whether the above-mentioned costs, such as hedging costs and diversification costs, are private costs or public costs,. But, what is beyond doubt is that these costs have at least some public aspect to them.[225] This section discusses reducing implicit government guarantees and also considers the liquidity costs. Both are basically private costs because they are closely related to the banking industry as a whole, not to the overall economy.[226]

4.5.1 Reducing implicit government guarantees

With the advent of the structural reform, many market participants take the view that the new rules will have the effect of substantially reducing the implicit government guarantee.[227] In this scenario, the banks' funding costs will be much higher, especially for activities that are outside the permitted scope.

---

222 European Commission, *Commission staff working document impact assessment accompanying the document Proposal for a Regulation of the European Parliament and of the Council on structural measures improving the resilience of EU Credit Institutions and the Proposal for a Regulation of the European Parliament and of the Council on reporting and transparency of securities financing transactions, SWD/2014/030 final.* pp. 39–40. Viñals et al., *Creating a safer financial system: will the Volcker, Vickers, and Liikanen Structural measures help?* p. 17.

223 Independent Commission on Banking, 'Final Report, recommendations', pp. 297–300.

224 Financial Stability Oversight Council, *Study of the effects of size and complexity of financial institutions on capital market efficiency and economic growth,* pp. 46–47.

225 European Commission, *Commission staff working document impact assessment accompanying the document Proposal for a Regulation of the European Parliament and of the Council on structural measures improving the resilience of EU Credit Institutions and the Proposal for a Regulation of the European Parliament and of the Council on reporting and transparency of securities financing transactions, SWD/2014/030 final.* pp. 41. See also Independent Commission on Banking, 'Final Report, recommendations', pp. 136–137.

226 Independent Commission on Banking, 'Final Report, recommendations', p. 123.

227 Viñals et al., *Creating a safer financial system: will the Volcker, Vickers, and Liikanen structural measures help?*

There are many worries with regard to decreasing implicit government guarantees.[228] Moody stated that the ring-fence proposal in the UK would reduce the assumption of systemic support included in its rating for the senior debts of major UK banks. JPMorgan analysts said that the ring-fence reform would be a transformational factor and most likely lead to a reduction in the sector's ratings.[229]

The private benefit of the implicit guarantee to the banks has three aspects: (i) banks tend to rely on maturity transformation and have outstanding amounts of debts, and thus they are very susceptible to credit risk; (ii) it provides higher recognition of safety towards bank debts because creditors feel reassured by government support; and (iii) the premium that investors would otherwise have demanded is included in the credit risk of banks.[230] By researching Moody's ratings for the four largest UK banks, the Vickers Report shows that the rates for assets with support were clearly higher than the rates without the support.[231]

4.5.2 Less provision of liquidity

Because of the nature of banks, they are supposed to provide finance to the economy as a whole. To maximise their profit margin, it is natural for them to largely rely on maturity transformation, which is using short-term debts to pay off long-term assets.[232]

In terms of bank funding structure, it would be fair to say that the structural reform would have a material impact on liquidity in the banking sector. The separation rule would allow less room for maturity transformation, and both the trading entities and non-entities alike would have to depend more on long-term debts to replace short-term debts and deposits. As an alternative, they would have to hold more liquid assets, such as government debts, to replace illiquid loans to risky borrowers.[233]

In addition, as indicated in the ICB report, the ring-fence rule would curb the ability of retail deposits to fund assets except loans to the public and the non-financial private sector.[234] With such restrictions, the deposits of retail banks are trapped to a certain extent. Instead of being investing in profitable assets, they would only be used for investing in low-risk assets, such as government bonds or central government balances.

Therefore, it seems obvious that there is a negative impact from structural reform in terms of reducing maturity transformation and trapping deposits. But there is also research that suggests structural reform and subsidiarisation would not have a substantial influence on liquidity in terms of the level of interest rates

---

228 Independent Commission on Banking, 'Final Report, recommendations', pp. 135–136.
229 Ibid.
230 Ibid, pp. 293–294.
231 Ibid.
232 See supra Chapter 1, Section 3(a) on transformation of bank funding mix.
233 Independent Commission on Banking, 'Final Report, recommendations', p. 276.
234 Ibid, p. 277.

at which corporate and sovereign debts can fund themselves.[235] The research showed that ten-year Spanish government bond yields have doubled from 3.5% in 2006 to 7.5% in July 2012. The bid and offer spreads on sovereign bonds of Germany, France, the UK, and large companies were already at a negligible level before broker-dealers in universal banks started to perform significantly in this area from 2002. Its conclusion was that the ability of market-makers to influence interest rate levels is relatively limited. But it should be noted that contrary evidence could not negate the reduction in the effects of maturity transformation and deposit trapping by structural separation.

4.5.3 The BSR's influence on government guarantees and liquidity

As regards the BSR prohibition rule, the elimination of the universal banking model, as in the Volcker Rule, would definitely reduce the implicit government guarantee significantly. Rating agencies could directly reflect this.[236] Similarly, the trapping of deposits and the curbing of maturity transformation would also be significant due to the absence of universal banking.

The pre-crisis funding mix of banks could substantiate these evident costs.[237] Before the GFC, there was a paradigm shift in funding sources in the banking industry from being dependent on deposit funding to increasingly relying on wholesale funding.[238] However, the retail funding was still a very important part in the funding mix and the most stable source of funding by which the banks could mitigate their market risks. According to the Liikanen Report, in the European banks, deposits accounted for a significantly important part of funding, with the deposit-funding ratio varying from 15% to 60%.[239] This figure further proves the importance of the deposit funding source to the banking operation.

Given the reliance on the deposit funding mix, in the BSR prohibition rule, prohibiting deposits from being a funding resource for trading activities and other investment banking business would make the funding costs higher. Some would then argue, given that the importance of deposit funding has decreased, probably the adverse effect on the funding costs would be mitigated to a certain extent. This argument is based on the assumption that wholesale funding markets would not be affected by the separation reform. However, the truth is that due to the decrease in liquidity and funding from deposits to subsidise the trading entity, all trading entities would have to turn to other alternative funding channels. The wholesale channel would be one of the best remaining alternatives.

235 European Commission, *Commission staff working document impact assessment accompanying the document Proposal for a Regulation of the European Parliament and of the Council on structural measures improving the resilience of EU Credit Institutions and the Proposal for a Regulation of the European Parliament and of the Council on reporting and transparency of securities financing transactions, SWD/2014/030 final*, pp. 72–73.
236 Independent Commission on Banking, 'Final Report, recommendations', pp. 135–136.
237 See supra Chapter 1, Section 3(a).
238 Liikanen Erkki, *High-level Expert Group on reforming the structure of the EU banking sector*, p. 14.
239 Ibid, p. 47.

Thus, changing supply and demand dynamics would probably make the funding costs higher than the previous level.[240]

With regard to the BSR ring-fence rule, it maintains the universal banking model by the approach of subsidiarisation and thus retains the advantages of government guarantee and liquidity flow to a certain extent. Therefore, the corresponding costs might be less evident compared with the prohibition rule. This argument is also supported by the ICB opinion on the retaining effect of the ring-fence rule compared with an absolute separation.[241]

4.5.4 Private costs can feed into public costs

According to the above section, structural reform of all kinds would affect implicit government guarantees and liquidity to a certain extent. Instead of being solely private costs, they would also feed into the wider economy and public funds through three ways:[242] (i) by increasing the private costs to banks these would be passed onto consumers through changes in banks' lending and saving spreads; therefore, consumers would reduce consumption and their investments, which would cause a decrease in GDP; (ii) for those costs that are absorbed by banks, they would be transformed into decreases in banks' profits, which would bring about a reduction in tax receipts in government funds; and (iii) costs suffered by banks would be directly passed onto government funds because of the equity investments it may hold in the banks (Figure 5.1).[243]

5 Competitiveness concerns

To assess the reform by the CBA, after the analyses of benefits and costs, another factor to be assessed is the competitiveness of the banking sector. As referred to in Chapter 3 on the purposes of the structural reform, it includes not only curbing the risks in the TBTF bank structural problem to enhance financial stability and efficiency, but also the consideration of competitiveness.[244] A similar balanced consideration of a structural reform is also reflected in the Vickers Rule and the Volcker Rule.[245]

The competitiveness consideration is mainly assessed within the international context, i.e. to what extent the BSR would affect the competitiveness of EU banks

240 Anshu Jain, 'Challenges and opportunities for universal banks', Frankfurt am Main, CFS Colloquium.
241 Independent Commission on Banking, 'Final Report, recommendations', p. 293.
242 European Commission, *Commission staff working document impact assessment accompanying the document Proposal for a Regulation of the European Parliament and of the Council on structural measures improving the resilience of EU Credit Institutions and the Proposal for a Regulation of the European Parliament and of the Council on reporting and transparency of securities financing transactions, SWD/2014/030 final.* pp. 70–77. See Chapter 5, Section 2.2.
243 HM Treasury, *Banking reform: delivering stability and supporting a sustainable economy* (June 2012), paras 59–67.
244 See supra Chapter 3, Section 3.1 on the purpose of the EU structural reform.
245 See supra Chapter 3, Sections 3.2 and 3.3 on the purposes of the US and UK structural reforms.

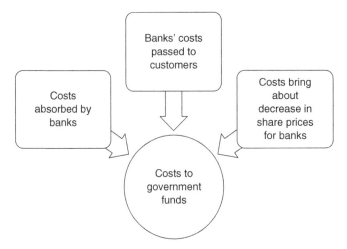

Figure 5.1 Affects of structural reform on implicit government guarantees

compared with their non-EU competitors.[246] The above analyses have compared the BSR and the US and UK reforms in many respects. A tentative point to be made here is that the fact there are many similarly motivated, yet differently constructed, reforms at least indicates that the concern over competitiveness should not be overexaggerated within the context of global prevailing reforms. [247]

Besides, there are some jurisdictions which have even more robust rules than the BSR in some respects. For the Vickers Rule in the UK, apart from the ring-fence separation suggestions, it also has a special pillar about enhancing loss-absorbency requirements for UK banks. Some countries have also indicated their intention to go beyond the Basel framework of capital requirements.[248] Switzerland, for instance, decided to require a higher level of capital for its two largest banks (Credit Suisse and UBS).[249]

With regard to the prohibition rule in the BSR, due to the harsh prohibition of trading activities in the G-SII and EU-SIIs, and the vaguely defined exceptions, it might compromise much of the efficiency brought about by the universal banking model. Therefore, the effect of a reduction in competitiveness as a result of the prohibition rule is significant, and probably more so than in the Volcker Rule.

For the ring-fence rule, it was argued in the ICB report that it can retain the advantages of universal banking while enhancing stability and resolvability when compared with an absolute separation.[250] Therefore, to a certain extent, the

246 Liikanen Erkki, *High-level Expert Group on reforming the structure of the EU banking sector*, p. 108.
247 But the diversity of regulation does bring about more implementation uncertainty in reality. See supra Chapter 4, Section 4 on difficulties with international coordination.
248 Independent Commission on Banking, 'Final Report, recommendations', pp. 237–238.
249 Liikanen Erkki, *High-level Expert Group on reforming the structure of the EU banking sector*, p. 108.
250 Independent Commission on Banking, 'Final Report, recommendations', p. 309.

BSR ring-fence rule could retain some of the advantages of the universal banking model for EU banks.

6 Conclusion: balance, challenge, and what next

EU structural reform needs to strike the right balance between stability and efficiency. It should also not impede the competitiveness of the banking sector in the EU. As indicated in the executive summary of the Liikanen Report, the objective of this reform is to 'establishing a safe, stable and efficient banking system serving the needs of citizens, the EU economy and the internal market'.[251] The need to strike a balance can be seen from another regulatory consideration in the report: 'competition' and 'competitiveness'.[252]

Table 5.1 Comparison of rules

Building on Chapter 4, MFA: BSR brings about bank safety and stability, albeit with challenges; Chapter 5 conducts the CBA

CBA	Volcker Rule	BSR-prohibition rule	BSR-ring-fence rule	Vickers Rule
I Benefit/effectiveness				
Complexity				
A Banks	A: √√	A: √√	A: √	A: √
B The group	B: √√	B: √√	B: ××	B: ×
Interconnectedness				
A Intragroup links	A: √	A: √	A: √	A: √
B Intergroup links	B: √	B: √	B: √√	B: √
Resolvability				
A Banks	A: √?	A: √?	A: √?	A: √√?
B The group	B: √?	B: √?	B: ×	B: ×
II Costs				
A Implementation	√√	√√	√	√
B Compliance costs	√	√	√	√
C Operational costs	×	×	√	√
Market making costs	×	√	√√	√√
Hedging costs	×	√	√√	√√
Diversification costs				
A Scale	√	×	×	×
B Scope	×	√	√	√
Government guarantee and liquidity costs	√√	√√	√	√
III Competitiveness	√	√√	√	√

Behavioural factors: partly contained

Strongly positive: √√; positive: √; marginal: ×; no impact: ××; not applicable: N/A; uncertain: ?

251 Liikanen Erkki, *High-level Expert Group on reforming the structure of the EU banking sector*, p. 1.
252 Ibid, p. 108.

In the BSR, it points out specifically the objectives to be achieved: to reduce excessive risk-taking; to remove material conflicts of interest; to avoid misallocation of resources; to reduce interconnectedness within the financial sector leading to systemic risk; and to facilitate the orderly resolution and recovery of the group.[253] This set of objectives also shows a balance between banking stability and efficiency of resource allocation by the banking sector.

6.1 BSR effectiveness

In Chapter 4, we discovered that these objectives can, to a certain extent, be achieved by the BSR separation reform. The separation rules are effective from the behavioural perspective to tackle with the structural attribute of the TBTF bank structural problem on an ex-ante basis: it targets the structural pitfalls and it contains the behavioural factors in the GFC.

Specifically speaking: (i) it reduces the link and mutual interaction between behavioural factors and the trading entity by minimising subsidisation from the deposit entity to the trading entity due to the co-existence of activities;[254] and (ii) it de-links the behavioural factors and the CCI by avoiding the contagion effect.[255]

6.2 BSR efficiency and the challenges

Chapter 5 focuses mainly on the CBA analysis on the BSR. The cost benefit analysis indicates the reduction of complexity, reduction of interconnectedness, and enhancement of resolvability. By the two tiers of the prohibition rule and the ring-fence rule, the BSR is capable of accommodating many benefits from both the Volcker style prohibition and the Vickers' style subsidiarisation.[256] From the analyses on the costs of implementation, hedging, market-making, diversification, and liquidity, the BSR is able to retain substantial advantages from the universal banking model.

To decide between Choice C or Choice D (see Table 3.1) is a rather difficult one in terms of their respective balances between benefits and costs.[257] Therefore, the choice in practice is really more a political matter than a technical one. Therefore, the two-tiered rules in the BSR would possibly bring about a balanced interest for the EU banking industry.

---

253 European Commission, *Proposal for a Regulation of the European Parliament and of the Council on structural measures improving the resilience of EU credit institutions, COM/2014/043 final,* art 2.

254 See supra Chapter 4, Section 3.2.2 on the de-linking of the connection between behavioural factors and trading activities.

255 See supra Chapter 4, Section 3.2.2.

256 See supra Chapter 5, Section 4, Table 5.1.

257 European Commission, *Commission staff working document impact assessment accompanying the document Proposal for a Regulation of the European Parliament and of the Council on structural measures improving the resilience of EU Credit Institutions and the Proposal for a Regulation of the European Parliament and of the Council on reporting and transparency of securities financing transactions, SWD/2014/030 final,* p. 65.

That said, there are also significant challenges lying ahead for the reforms. Among others, the following are very prominent.

First, the disparity in the separation rules within the international context brings about uncertainties for the banking sector and clients.[258] Second, the immense challenges in delineating the various subtly distinct activities in both the prohibition rule and the ring-fence rule. In terms of delineation, the principles-based approach in the BSR makes the challenge even more provident.[259] Third, for the ring-fence rule, another practical challenge is how to maintain consistency in terms of the competent authority determining the separation decision on a case-by-case basis.[260]

6.3 Cyclicality attribute and what next

Building on the merits of the BSR, it can significantly reduce complexity and interconnectedness, curb excessive risk-taking and conflicts of interest, etc. The BSR is capable of achieving most of the objectives envisaged. Thus, it could deal with the structural attribute to a certain extent on an ex-ante basis. But it does not address the cyclical attribute, which is also inextricably related to behavioural factors and leads to the resolvability problem. In addition, there are no provisions under the BSR that are connected to the possible future framework for the resolvability problem to deal with the TBTF structural problem on an ex-post basis.[261]

In contrast, the Liikanen Report actually provides for an additional separation based on the needs for future possible resolution. Therefore, under the Liikanen Report, the cooperation between structural separation and resolution might be better. Similarly, in regard to the Vickers Rule, it also provides for loss absorbency requirements in addition to ring-fencing. Therefore, it might also perform better than the BSR with regards to cooperation with a future resolution framework.

The need for a resolution framework to be connected to the separation reform in relation to the TBTF structural problem can also be substantiated through relevant argument. In commenting on the effectiveness of the Volcker Rule, Steve Denning argued that 'the Volcker rule make us safer, but not safe'.[262] He attributed the TBTF bank structural problem and the GFC totally to the reckless investment propensity and cyclicality of bank activities. He advocated that 'bad profits' categorised by Fred Reichheld are attributable to the problem.[263] After

---

258 See supra Chapter 4, Section 4 on uncertainties brought about by not concerted actions.
259 Duffie, 'Challenges to a policy treatment of speculative trading motivated by differences in beliefs', pp. 180–181.
260 Matthias Lehmann Bonn, 'Volcker Rule, ring-fencing or separation of bank activities: comparison of structural reform acts around the world', LSE Legal Studies Working Paper No 25/2014, http://ssrn.com/abstract=2519935 or http://dx.doi.org/10.2139/ssrn.2519935, accessed May 15, 2015, p. 14.
261 See supra Chapter 3, Section 4.2(p).
262 Steve Denning, 'The Volcker rule made us safer, but not safe', Forbes.
263 'Bad profit' denotes the following behaviour: price gouging, which is unusual ways to levy hidden charges on customers, particularly customers who are vulnerable; gaming the system, such as betting against securities that they themselves had created; zero-sum proprietary trading in derivatives; extraordinary increases in executive compensation that are inversely related to the firm's long-term financial performance.

pointing out the direct trigger of instability, he then proposed a return to the real economy of finance so that the function of finance would not digress from the trail of serving the needs of the real economy.[264]

Different from the argument in Chapter 2 on the cause of the TBTF bank structural problem,[265] Steve Denning's opinion focuses on the cyclicality attribute of banking activities. It may not be entirely descriptively true due to its underestimation or ignoring of the structural attribute, but it is of great importance in terms of emphasising the cyclicality aspect of the TBTF bank structural problem.

The cyclicality, defined as the reckless and irresponsible investment propensity and risk-taking inclination in the banking industry, is deemed to be another attribute of the TBTF bank structural problem.[266] The existence of the cyclicality problem denotes the resolvability problem of banks and demands an effective reform of banking resolution.

In sum, the BSR might be able to address the TBTF structural problem to a certain extent, but the problem cannot be completely resolved merely by the structural separation reform. Disregarding the cyclicality variable, even if the CCI were protected in the future through structural separation, a similar or less severe crisis could still happen for two reasons: (i) the strength of the separation might not be sufficiently robust to minimise the negative links between the CCI and the trading entity; and (ii) there are still bankruptcy and failure risks for banks anyway, especially because of banks' tendency towards cyclicality. For instance, financial innovations might still diverge from the needs of the real economy; liquidity might still flow to speculative business rather than being committed to creative economic activities; and the tendency towards cyclicality might still exert influence on bubble-making in the banking sector. Therefore, the crisis could happen again, not necessarily in the CCI, but in other separate yet remotely related parts of the banking sector. In such a case, it could still devastate the economy as a whole.[267]

Thus, the next step besides with the BSR structural separation reform is to take the cyclicality attribute into consideration through an EU resolution reform. The BSR could be seen as an ex-ante regulatory reform to prevent the recurrence of the TBTF bank structural problem from the perspective of the structural attribute; a resolution mechanism is imperative to provide an ex-post problem-solving mechanism in terms of the pro-cyclical attribute.[268]

---

264 Steve Denning, 'The traditional economy is an economy of tired old firms, still focused on pushing products at customers and struggling to find opportunities to invest: this economy is in steep and fundamental decline . . . The Financial Sector has achieved profitability through practices that have caused increasingly serious financial crises: it needs to be reconnected to the real economy . . . Meanwhile, the emerging creative economy comprises firms focused on adding real value in goods and services for real people. It is the genuinely flourishing real economy of the future'.

265 See supra Chapter 2, Section 1 on the macro cause and the micro cause, and Section 2 on behavioural factors.

266 Chow, *Making banks safer: can Volcker and Vickers do it?*

267 Avgouleas, *Governance of global financial markets: the law, the economics, the politics*, pp. 53–61.

268 Financial Stability Board, *Recovery and resolution planning for systemically important financial institutions: guidance on developing effective resolution strategies*, July 16, 2013.

6 Resolving bank failures in the EU

1 Tackling the bank structural problem: the next step

Following the previous three chapters where the structural attribute and corresponding BSR have been discussed, this chapter analyses the pro-cyclicality attribute and its possible solutions. Namely, this chapter focuses on the cyclical attribute and the BRRD resolution regime and the SRM.

1.1 Cyclicality attribute and unavoidable failures

The IMF identification of the cyclicality attribute of the structural problem is aligned with the OECD's argument in its working paper.[1] When analysing the structural reform in France in comparison with that in the EU and the US, the OECD referred to the complementary plan to set up a new institution, *Conseil de la Stabilité Financière* (Financial Stability Board), to undertake the macro prudential supervision in order to deal with the cyclical problem of its banking industry. The working paper indicates that the rationale for this is that inherent cyclicality tends to create more risks and exacerbate negative market circumstances and trigger failures.[2]

As explained in Chapter 2, behaviour factors, such as wishful thinking, social influence, framing, could all act as amplifiers of cyclicality in the banking sector.[3] And cyclicality tends to lead to greater risk-taking and failures.

To give a concrete example, among all the cyclicality aspects of the industry, the VaR risk model is at the forefront.[4] It was incorporated into the Basel regime. The operation of VaR depends on two flawed hypotheses: the past asset price volatility shows continuity into the future; and the variations are distributed around a mean (following a bell curve).[5]

---

1 See supra Chapter 3, Section 5.2 on the two attributes of the bank structural problem.
2 Édouard Fernandez-Bollo, 'Structural reform and supervision of the banking sector in France', 2013 *OECD Journal: Financial Market Trends* 1, pp. 6–7.
3 See supra Chapter 2, Section 2.2.
4 Iman Anabtawi and Steven L. Schwarcz, 'Regulating systemic risk: towards an analytical framework', 86 Notre Dame L Rev 1349. For detailed analysis about the pitfalls of the model, see supra Chapter 1, Section 3(c).
5 Tim Morrison, *The risks of financial modeling: VaR and the economic meltdown*, 2009.

Specifically, there are several evident weaknesses that make it a problematic risk evaluation model resulting in increasing failures in the banking sector:[6] (i) it focuses more on the defaults of assets, which are less frequent events, rather than on the more frequently changing asset prices, although they are equally material to endanger the safety and soundness of the banking institutions which have such asset exposures; and (ii) it fails to capture the fat-tail risk, the so-called 'black swan' or low probability risk.[7]

In addition, it fails to capture some endogenous risks, in other words, the risks emanating from the irrational behaviours of the participants within the financial markets in response to various market situations. Nevertheless, it was the endogenous risks, to a certain extent, that triggered the contagion and domino effect in the GFC. It was not correct that the VaR model should have ignored the feedback effect among different financial entities and participants in the financial markets.

The flawed VaR model is an embodiment of the cyclicality attribute. Cyclicality factors tend to justify financial innovations no matter how risky they might be. Therefore, cyclicality facilitated risk-taking and brought about failure risks in the TBTF bank structural problem and the GFC. Such a scenario could recur in the future.

1.2 Cyclicality and necessity for resolution mechanism

The cyclicality attribute tends to amplify the behavioural factors and hence contribute to economic irrational exuberance.[8] To a certain extent, it was exploited in the 2000s to amplify the economies of size and scope.[9]

As indicated in Chapter 4, structural separation can address directly the first attribute of the TBTF bank structural problem, i.e. the coexistence of varied activities; however, it cannot be of much help in resolving the second attribute.[10] The structural separation scheme, according to Chapters 4 and 5, can be of direct and appreciable use to significantly reduce complexity and interconnectedness, but it can only enhance resolvability in a limited manner.[11] The risk of bank failure can still exist due to many factors, such as the behavioural influence, the inclination for risk-taking or any other variables relevant to the cyclicality attribute of the industry.[12]

Provided that certain bank failings would still be unavoidable, the remaining question in the TBTF bank structural problem is how should the resolution

---

6 Emilios Avgouleas, *Governance of global financial markets: the law, the economics, the politics* (Cambridge, UK: Cambridge University Press 2012), pp. 243–245.
7 See supra Chapter 1, Section 3(c) on VaR model.
8 Avgouleas, *Governance of global financial markets: the law, the economics, the politics*, p. 245.
9 Andrew Ross Sorkin, *Too Big to Fail: the inside story of how Wall Street and Washington fought to save the financial system – and themselves* (Harmondsworth, UK: Penguin 2010), pp. 10–50.
10 See supra Chapter 5, Section 6.3.
11 Ceyla Pazarbasioglu et al., *Creating a safer financial system* (2013), pp. 23–24.
12 Julian TS Chow, *Making banks safer: can Volcker and Vickers do it?* (New York: International Monetary Fund 2011) pp. 15–16.

mechanism be constructed to secure orderly liquidation when necessary. In the long run, a practical and efficient way to tackle failing banking institutions needs to be available when risks underlying the tendency to cyclicality materialise or even escalate into terrible systemic crisis.[13]

In the Liikanen Report, it is indicated that although the resolution framework would contribute to ensure the orderly winding down of banks, in reality the complexity and interconnectedness still created huge challenges on the path towards resolution.[14]

Specifically, the essential question to be answered in this chapter is: will the current resolution rules in the BRRD and the SRM be sufficient to address the remaining resolvability issues in the TBTF bank structural problem within the context of the BSR reforms?

2 Special case of bank failure in the bank structural problem

In terms of dealing with the bank failure problem, an inescapable question is whether the bailout alternative is more efficient in tackling distressed banks or whether the bankruptcy alternative makes stakeholders better off in the situation of insolvency.[15] Among the initial responses to the onslaught of the GFC, especially in the early phase of the crisis, governments' rescue schemes of failing banks were mostly dependent on the bailout alternative. In reality, government helped to facilitate the merger between Bear Stearns and JPMorgan. In the AIG case, the Federal Reserve Bank made a substantial direct loan to AIG to facilitate the rescue operation.[16] These cases seem to partly justify the need for bailout in banking crises.

But it should also be noted that bankruptcy is also deemed to be a conventional option that could possibly address failing banks. As Timothy Geithner commented on the rescue of failing banks, the US government is faced with the choice of either letting Lehman fail and causing catastrophic damage to the financial system or risking a huge amount of taxpayers' money and winding the bank down slowly.[17] The final choice was that the federal government refused to offer

13 Amandeep Rehlon and Dan Nixon, 'Central counterparties: what are they, why do they matter, and how does the bank supervise them?' *Bank of England Quarterly Bulletin* Q2. The article gave a comprehensive introduction to the CBA of introducing CCP for OTC transactions. It also pointed out that while CCPs must hold a prudent level of pre-funded sources, it remains possible that these sources might not be sufficient. This would threaten the viability of the CCP in the absence of plans to manage and to recover from any dire situation.

14 Liikanen Erkki, *High-level Expert Group on reforming the structure of the EU banking sector* (Final Report, Brussels, 2012), pp. 15–19.

15 Stefano Micossi, Jacopo Carmossi, and Fabrizia Peirce, *On the tasks of the European Stability Mechanism* (Brussels: Centre for European Policy Studies 2011), pp. 1–2. The establishing of the ESM and the signing of the IGA signalling the significance of bail out in dealing with the GFC in the EU.

16 United States. Congress. Senate. Committee on Homeland Security and others, *Wall Street and the financial crisis: anatomy of a financial collapse* (Cosimo Reports 2011), p. 45.

17 Kenneth Ayotte and David A. Skeel Jr, 'Bankruptcy or bailouts', 35 J Corp L 469.

a bailout and direct rescue plan, and let it file for chapter 11 bankruptcy instead. That also turned out to be a comparatively successful case in terms of maintaining market stability after triggering the bankruptcy procedure.

It is true that in the early phase of the GFC, both bailout and bankruptcy were deployed to deal with bank failing. But, bailout was largely criticised because it would drag taxpayers' funds into risk and danger, and hence bring about or exacerbate the moral hazard problem.[18] Bankruptcy, however, seems to avoid the similar moral hazard problem triggered by bailout as an alternative method of tackling failing banks. But it was also widely criticised for its prominent short-comings, such as ending the failing bank as a going concern; its long timeframe severely dissipating the value of the firm's assets; its insufficiency to deal with the systemic failure; and its disruptive effect in a crisis.[19] Most importantly, due to the interconnectedness of the banking sector, bankruptcy has a spill over impact on other directly or indirectly related entities.[20]

Thus, it has been argued by many that the story of dealing with distressed banks has been a hard trade-off between letting shareholders take the losses in bankruptcy (causing a systemic spill over effect) and preventing the occurrence of systemic risk at the cost of letting innocent taxpayers foot the bill.[21]

2.1 Bailout as an option

There were successful cases of bailout in the GFC, such as the rescue of Bear Stearns. The US government even guaranteed the merger between Bear Stearns and JPMorgan. Even the most fervent advocates of bankruptcy cannot deny some merits of bailout, such as the speedy rescue of TBTF institutions with sufficient funds backed by governments, which are normally not available by any other means.[22] When there is a bank failure, especially a systemic failure, there would always be the huge problem of liquidity crunch and credit crunch. Thus, the pro-vision of liquidity is absolutely a prominent advantage.[23]

That is partly why the bailout plan was implemented in the AIG case, as the Fed pointed out in its press release. Given the circumstances, a disorderly failure of AIG would undoubtedly have added to the financial market's volatility. It would also have led 'to substantially higher borrowing costs, reduced house-hold wealth, and materially weaker economic performance'. An article from the *New York Times* pointed out the imperativeness of the bailout:[24]

18 Jeffrey A. Miron, 'Bailout or bankruptcy', 29 Cato J 1.
19 Sorkin, *Too Big to Fail: the inside story of how Wall Street and Washington fought to save the financial system – and themselves*, pp. 20–30.
20 Miron, 'Bailout or bankruptcy'.
21 William K. Sjostrom, 'The AIG bailout', 66 *Washington and Lee Law Review* 943.
22 Avgouleas, *Governance of global financial markets: the law, the economics, the politics*, pp. 250–251.
23 See Sjostrom, 'The AIG bailout'.
24 Edmund L. Andrews, 'Fed's $85 Billion Loan Rescues Insurer', *New York Times*, www.nytimes.com/2008/09/17/business/17insure.html?pagewanted=all&_r=0, accessed Feburary 25, 2015.

If A.I.G. had collapsed – and been unable to pay all of its insurance claims – institutional investors around the world would have been instantly forced to reappraise the value of those securities, and that in turn would have reduced their own capital and the value of their own debt. Small investors, including anyone who owned money market funds with A.I.G. securities, could have been hurt, too.

To discuss the merits of bailout, distinguishing between illiquidity and insolvency is of critical importance. When a firm is at the brink of bankruptcy and seeking a rescue loan, it is in a state of illiquidity. However, it is not necessary in an insolvency that the value of its liabilities exceeds its total assets.[25] Thus, if a bank were only slightly illiquid while apparently solvent, a short-term government credit extension would be perfectly enough to deal with the illiquidity while guaranteeing the repayment to the taxpayers in the short term.[26] In this case, bailout could be both an efficient and primary solution to a distressed bank.

However, what happens to distressed banks is not the same on every occasion. Rather, for the distressed banks related to the TBTF bank structural problem, they had a very prolonged liquidity problem and were obviously insolvent with the value of their liabilities vastly exceeding the total value of their assets.[27] Banks were overreliant on maturity transformation, so it was very difficult for them to obtain new assets to roll over old debts. This was especially true when the liquidity markets encountered problems, which hindered further maturity transformation.[28] Under this circumstance, bailout seemed to be imperative to avoid a domino failure effect, but it also had many prominent negative consequences.

First, based on the size of the large banks, especially the TBTF institutions, a failure could cause astronomical direct costs to taxpayers' funds if a bailout program were to be implemented.[29] In the pre-crisis era, due to an overreliance on maturity transformation, most distressed banks had over-leveraged balance sheets. They were excessively dependent on either continuously available short-term liabilities or wholesale liquidity markets to finance their long-term assets. But this dependence was not always practical and safe. If any shortage in liquidity happened in the banks, it made it pretty difficult to roll over their debts. This would have forced them to conduct fire sales of their assets and easily push the banks to the brink of insolvency.[30]

---

25 Douglas W. Diamond and Raghuram G. Rajan, 'Liquidity shortages and banking crises', 60 *The Journal of Finance* 615. It discussed the interaction and relation between illiquidity and insolvency.
26 Ayotte and Skeel Jr, 'Bankruptcy or bailouts', pp. 483–484.
27 Security et al., *Wall Street and the financial crisis: anatomy of a financial collapse.*
28 Liikanen Erkki, *High-level Expert Group on reforming the structure of the EU banking sector*, pp. 14–15.
29 Financial Stability Board, *2013 update of group of global systemically important banks (G-SIBs)*. (Basel, November 2013).
30 Avgouleas, *Governance of global financial markets: the law, the economics, the politics*, pp. 96–100.

This was exactly what happened in the crisis: the failures of Bear Stearns and Lehman Brothers, the defaults on derivatives and the spill over effect suddenly depleted the liquidity in the markets and caused a credit crunch. In these two cases, any rescue plans would have been of gargantuan size. For instance, due to the liquidity problem of AIG, the original loan to rescue them was of an unprecedented size of USD85 billion.[31] Similarly, in the Dexia bailout case, on 30 September 2008, Dexia increased its capital by EUR6.4 billion, of which France and Belgium subscribed EUR3 billion each and Luxembourg subscribed EUR376 million.[32] Plans such as these meant a huge transfer of risk from the falling banks to taxpayers' funds.

Next, many scholars are concerned about the moral hazard problem that accompanies any bailout measure.[33] By implementing a bailout plan, it basically means that the bankers would have less or no incentive to take necessary measures or precautions against possible risks as they could rely on an expected bailout. This is why people argued that when bankruptcy procedures were triggered for Lehman Brothers, the firm could not have been any worse prepared. Its managing body actually totally believed that the US government would not let it fail following the precedence of the bailout of Bear Stearns.[34]

Furthermore, bailout tends to provide a bad incentive to the banking sector. For potential acquirers of a distressed bank, they would not have much incentive to finish a deal in the early phase of a distress or search for other possible alternatives to minimise losses to the firm. Instead, they would be carelessly waiting for the situation to deteriorate so that they could argue for taxpayer funding assistance as a precondition for any deal to be made. Bad incentives also exist in terms of managing the bank. The bank's board would certainly prefer to wait for a public bailout, assuming that the government could not afford the costs of letting the bank fail.[35] Without any risk of bankruptcy, the bank would tend to leverage their balance sheets and engage in risk-taking. Obviously, according to company financial structure theory, the higher the leverage ratio of a firm, the more profits it could gain if there were no bankruptcy risk.[36]

Last, carrying out a bailout scheme would cause a distortion in corporate governance.[37] For instance, with regard to the resolution procedure in the EU, when the resolution authority decides to trigger the procedure, it would appoint

---

31 Thomas C. Baxter, *Factors affecting efforts to limit payments to AIG counterparties* (2010). Eventually, the government extended the maturity of the loan to five years from two and increased the amount of committed funding to USD150 billion.

32 This was only the first rescue. There were second and third rescues which cost taxpayers' funds even more. See Avgouleas, *Governance of global financial markets: the law, the economics, the politics*, p. 251.

33 Ayotte and Skeel Jr, 'Bankruptcy or bailouts', p. 485.

34 Yalman Onaran and John Helyar, 'Lehman's last days', *Bloomberg Markets*, January 20. Against the backdrop of a high expectation of bailout from Lehman Brothers, the refusal of funding provision by the Treasury Secretary Paulson triggered desperation in the firm.

35 Ayotte and Skeel Jr, 'Bankruptcy or bailouts', p. 485.

36 Guy Fraser-Sampson, *Private equity as an asset class* (New York: John Wiley & Sons 2011), pp. 15–29.

37 Miron, 'Bailout or bankruptcy'.

a special manager to replace the management body of the institutions under resolution.[38] The BRRD stipulates that Member States should ensure that the special manager has the qualifications, ability, and knowledge required to carry out relevant functions.[39] But in the bailout procedure, it is more an administrative role. The managing replacement choice is likely to be influenced by factors other than optimal corporate governance considerations. Compared with resolution, the bailout procedure lacks any necessary transparency and predictability in terms of corporate governance.

2.2 The desirability of bankruptcy

When it comes to the bankruptcy option, a distressed banking institution is normally referred to as an entity that is no longer viable or likely to be no longer viable, and thus has no reasonable prospect of recovery.[40]

2.2.1 Bankruptcy as an option

Just like the distress of any other firm, a few common problems would also arise in a distressed bank. First, there is the debt overhang problem, which essentially means that the failing firm is so leveraged that it has to give up even profitable investments because it has no access to funds to continue financing them.[41] Although it might be true there is a profitable investment plan, the precondition to carrying out the investment plan would be to finance it in stages, such as issuing equities or debts. However, the benefits of any new investment would probably go to existing creditors rather than new investors. The seemingly profitable investment might only be sufficient to subsidise previous creditors instead of bringing new investors profits as was envisaged.[42] Therefore, in the debt overhang problem, the existing debts deter new investment.

The second problem that is frequently encountered in distressed banks is the creditor run problem.[43] Banks are normally extremely dependent on maturity transformation to finance their business operations.[44] In the run up to the GFC,

---

38 Directive 2014/59/EU of the European Parliament and of the Council of 15 May 2014, establishing a framework for the recovery and resolution of credit institutions and investment firms and amending Council Directive 82/891/EEC, and Directives 2001/24/EC, 2002/47/EC, 2004/25/EC, 2005/56/EC, 2007/36/EC, 2011/35/EU, 2012/30/EU and 2013/36/EU, and Regulations (EU) No 1093/2010 and (EU) No 648/2012, of the European Parliament and of the Council [2014] OJ L 173/190/1 (BRRD), art 35.

39 Ibid, art 35(1)–(2).

40 Ibid, art 32.

41 Owen Lamont, 'Corporate-debt overhang and macroeconomic expectations', *The American Economic Review* 1106, pp. 1106–1107.

42 Stewart C. Myers, 'Determinants of corporate borrowing', 5 *Journal of Financial Economics* 147.

43 Hyun Song Shin, 'Reflections on Northern Rock: the bank run that heralded the global financial crisis', *Journal of Economic Perspectives* 101.

44 Hyun Song Shin, 'Reflections on modern bank runs: a case study of Northern Rock', 23 *Journal of Economic Perspectives* 101.

most EU banks had highly leveraged balance sheets due to the overuse of maturity transformation.[45] Banks borrow money on a short-term basis and invest it into long-term less liquid assets.[46] For instance, they would invest in structural debt securities and issue loans to entrepreneurs, homeowners, and institutional investors to gain long-term profits. The short-term liabilities and funding they relied on were not only from deposits but also interbank borrowing and the wholesale repo markets.[47] The dependence on wholesale funding was especially evident in the shadow banking area where large-scale maturity transformation happened frequently.[48]

Such leveraged balance sheets means excessive dependence on either continuously available short-term liabilities to finance the long-term assets or the unhindered functioning of liquid markets for the sale of assets if necessary.[49] In reality, however, there is the huge possibility that a shortage of funding might happen due to different kinds of factors such as temporary market volatility. In this case, banks would lack money to repay their short-term liabilities. If they cannot find other funding alternatives, they would have to conduct a fire sale of assets. The fact is, a fire sale would always dissipate the value of all relevant assets, which in return adds to the pressure for the banks to sell more to secure more funding. It would also urge relevant counterparties to withdraw funds from the banks and hence trigger a crisis in market confidence.[50] Eventually, a normally insignificant temporary volatility in the markets would be sufficient to trigger a seriously deleterious funding crisis in the entire industry due to a crisis in confidence.[51]

Faced with the above two problems, with many powers and tools at its disposal, bankruptcy would seem to have some undeniable advantages in dealing with bank failures, and these advantages happen to provide some redress for the disadvantages of bailout (moral hazard and non-transparency/violation of rule of law).[52]

First, in addressing these common problems in distressed banks, bankruptcy, such as that adopted by the major economies, has the advantage of providing many corresponding measures in a very transparent way according to the rule of law (this merit is especially marked in relation to the special resolution, which will be discussed in detail next).[53]

---

45 Liikanen Erkki, *High-level Expert Group on reforming the structure of the EU banking sector*, pp. 14–15.
46 Avgouleas, *Governance of global financial markets: the law, the economics, the politics*, pp. 96–101.
47 Liikanen Erkki, *High-level Expert Group on reforming the structure of the EU banking sector*, pp. 14–16.
48 Avgouleas, *Governance of global financial markets: the law, the economics, the politics*, p. 99.
49 Markus K. Brunnermeier and Lasse Heje Pedersen, 'Market liquidity and funding liquidity', 22 *Review of Financial Studies* 2201
50 Ibid. See also Avgouleas, *Governance of global financial markets: the law, the economics, the politics*, pp. 100–101.
51 Shin, 'Reflections on modern bank runs: a case study of Northern Rock'.
52 Miron, 'Bailout or bankruptcy'.
53 See infra Chapter 6, Section 2.3.

For instance, in US bankruptcy procedures, there are three very noteworthy features in response to a distressed firm: (i) the refinancing plan, 'Debt in Possession Financing' (DIP), allows a distressed firm to issue senior claims which have priority over other creditors,[54] meaning that they are not concerned about the risk of subsidising former creditors, which makes DIP a very practical measure to deal with the debt overhang problem; (ii) automatic stay of assets (this does not include derivatives, which bring about controversies on the effectiveness of bankruptcy to curb short-term creditor run) is helpful to deal with a bank run – it essentially temporarily suspends the convertibility of debts to shield the firm's asset holders from any efforts to collect debts,[55] and provides a necessary period of time to liquidate the firm in an orderly manner or keep it as a going concern; (iii) the rule of selling assets free and clear of liens and other liabilities is also of great help for liquidation in an orderly manner – it makes it easier for a distressed firm to find a buyer because the buyer would not be concerned about the possible entanglement of liabilities of the distressed firm,[56] and the proceeds of the sale would be distributed to creditors through the reorganisation plan.

A telling example of the transparency and effectiveness merits of bankruptcy is the Lehman Brothers case. It turned out to be a comparatively successful bank bankruptcy case especially in terms of the swiftness with which the acquisition was completed. The fact was that Lehman Brothers could not have been worse prepared for the bankruptcy procedure where swiftness and efficiency are of the essence.[57] The reason was that after the bailout of Bear Stearns, the managing bodies of Lehman strongly believed that they would also receive a bailout because the government was concerned about the disruptive effect the failure would cause. Although the bailout did not materialise as expected, the implementation of the bankruptcy turned out to be comparatively efficient and successful despite the subsequent spill over effect. Three days after filing for bankruptcy on September 15, 2008, Lehman Brothers made a deal to sell its North American investment banking business to Barclays. The court quickly approved this, by which Lehman Brothers received a USD450 million DIP loan to fund the operation from Barclays.[58] This case indicates that the lack of swiftness might not necessarily be a big concern when carrying out a bankruptcy of a failing bank.

Second, the bankruptcy procedure is helpful in curbing moral hazard, which is a disadvantage of bailout. If a bank is likely to be resolved through bankruptcy in reality, creditors and stakeholders cannot presume that they will be supported by public funds in distressed circumstances. Thus, taking the failure risk into consideration, banks would tend to be more prudent when engaging in risk-taking and

---

54 11 U.S. Code § 364.
55 11 U.S. Code § 362(a). In the situation of bank failure, the bankcruptcy rule on stay of assets prevents counterparties from terminating their contracts or selling assets, but it does not apply to derivatives. Arguably, this exception actually makes the bank more vulnerable to run and value dissipation.
56 11 U.S. Code § 363.
57 Jerome A. Madden, 'A weapon of mass destruction strikes: credit default swaps bring down AIG and Lehman Brothers', 5 Bus L Brief 15.
58 Ayotte and Skeel Jr, 'Bankruptcy or bailouts', p. 481.

avoid the opportunistic thinking offered by Modigliani and Miller's proposition on corporate capital structure.[59] The management body would be more likely to supervise and monitor the operations of the failing bank very meticulously and try as hard as possible to exhaust any available alternatives to contain the situation.[60] Thus, the risk of moral hazard could be avoided to a certain extent.

Third, in a normal bankruptcy procedure, the relevant parties of the failing firm would be responsible for the decision on when to trigger the process. Because they have sufficient information and interests in relation to the firm, they would have adequate incentives to trigger the procedure. This could be especially true for the creditors of the failing firm.[61] However, in a bailout, the supervisory authority might tend to be reluctant to file proceedings because that would automatically mean admitting its failure in supervision.[62]

Therefore, compared with bailout, bankruptcy does have some merits in dealing with bank failures (including the bank run and debt overhang problems). Opponents still argue that the bankruptcy procedure would possibly trigger an immediate dumping of assets, which would exacerbate the situation of failing banks and cause unnecessary value dissipation.

Most importantly, it would also trigger the ripple effect of default and cause market diffidence.[63] That would be contrary to the envisaged purposes of bankruptcy: an orderly liquidation and value preservation.

In sum, bankruptcy has many advantages, such as a standardised and transparent procedure, special measures and tools in dealing with a bank run, and minimising the moral hazard problem. It turns out to be a comparatively efficient option to deal with distressed banks. However, it might still not be efficient enough, especially with regard to the speed of carrying out the procedure and the spill over effect.[64]

2.2.2 Bailout vs. bankruptcy: not an either-or choice

As discussed in the previous section, bankruptcy could provide special mechanisms to deal with liquidity and bank run problems. By employing relevant

---

59 See Stephen A. Ross, Randolph Westerfield, and Bradford D. Jordan, *Fundamentals of corporate finance* (New York: Tata McGraw-Hill Education 2008), pp. 409–417. It is argued by Modigliani and Miller that a firm's overall cost of capital cannot be reduced as debt is substituted for equity. Although debt seems to be cheaper than equity, as the debt increases, the remaining equity risk increases, which means the cost of capital will also increase. But if we eliminate the factor of risk increase, i.e. the failure risk increase, then the highest level of leverage is preferred for firms.

60 Thomas H. Jackson and David A. Skeel Jr, 'Dynamic resolution of large financial institutions', pp. i–ii.

61 David A. Skeel, 'Single point of entry and the bankruptcy alternative', *Across the Great Divide: New Perspectives on the Financial Crisis* 14, pp. 11–12.

62 Valia Babis, 'European bank recovery and resolution directive, recovery proceedings for cross-border banking groups', University of Cambridge Faculty of Law Legal Studies Research Paper Series, Paper No 49/2013, pp. 16–19.

63 Avgouleas, *Governance of global financial markets: the law, the economics, the politics*, pp. 100–101.

64 Ayotte and Skeel Jr, 'Bankruptcy or bailouts', p. 476.

bankruptcy tools, the demand and size of any refinancing could be smaller than in a government bailout due to the preservation of the value of the failing bank and the value of the bank's assets.[65] Additionally, under the bankruptcy rule, the priority of the DIP creditors, the pre-bankruptcy creditors, and the shareholders are determined by clear and transparent bankruptcy rules.[66] Thus, the predictability of recovery and distribution of proceeds would be more transparent in a bankruptcy procedure than in a bailout.

Building on this, the question to be answered is whether to choose bankruptcy or bailout. The discussion above shows that despite their respective merits, the bailout option is mainly criticised for causing the moral hazard problem and imposing an unfair burden on innocent taxpayers. However, opponents of bankruptcy criticise it for its possible systemic risk and spill over effect.[67] Therefore, many have concluded that the choice between the two is a trade-off between providing government rescue to prevent systemic failure at the cost of taxpayers and using bankruptcy procedures to avoid moral hazard in spite of the possible occurrence of systemic risk.[68]

But in reality, this trade-off seems to be dubious; the either-or choice of bailout or bankruptcy is also dubious. The dire consequences of systemic risk are very real. For instance, Lehman had a substantial amount of short-term commercial paper before it filed for chapter 11 bankruptcy in 2008. This paper was mostly held by MMFs. Normally speaking, this paper is quite safe and has a very high credit rating. However, when Lehman filed for chapter 11 bankruptcy, the paper holders soon became unsecured creditors.[69]

But the problem of making a case for bailout is would the bailout solution have avoided the resulting disruptive systemic failure? In other words, if a bailout had been carried out instead of bankruptcy in Lehman's case, would it have prevented the crisis that followed? Although a precise answer could not be given without accurate statistical research, some data analyses by researchers have cast sufficient doubt on a positive answer.

David Skeel looked across the four main indices with regard to the daily reactions towards the filing for the Lehman Brothers' bankruptcy and the AIG rescue plan. The result was that the reaction to the AIG bailout news was no smaller in magnitude than that of the Lehman Brothers' bankruptcy news.[70] The inconsistent responses of the VIX and TED indexes indicated there is no conclusive answer for the question posed above.[71]

---

65 Ibid.
66 11 U.S. Code § 364.
67 Miron, 'Bailout or bankruptcy'.
68 Ayotte and Skeel Jr, 'Bankruptcy or bailouts', p. 490.
69 Onaran and Helyar, 'Lehman's last days'.
70 The VIX (an index of market volatility, the so-called 'fear index') witnessed a higher percentage increase after the Lehman news. The TED spread (an indicator of credit market risk), however, showed a higher percentage increase after the AIG news.
71 Ayotte and Skeel Jr, 'Bankruptcy or bailouts', p. 490.

Thus, the trade-off between providing bailout to avoid systemic consequence and providing bankruptcy to avoid moral hazard might not be valid in reality. As a matter of fact, the bailout and bankruptcy choice is not an either-or choice. Bankruptcy, when properly used, could lead to a successful outcome, such as in the Lehman case. Bailout, on the other hand, appropriately conducted on the right occasion could turn out to be efficient. Some researchers have even argued that with hindsight, an amalgamation of a bailout and bankruptcy in the AIG case could have ended up with a better result. For instance, the government could have provided guarantees for securities such as CDS, while letting the firm through the bankruptcy procedure at the same time.[72]

As a matter of fact, bankruptcy neither deals with nor exacerbates systemic risk. For instance, in the US bankruptcy procedure, it excludes derivatives and other financial contracts from automatic stay due to the special nature of these contracts, in the hope of preventing market maniacs from continuously circulating these products. On the contrary, it could not deal with the market fear as envisaged, as the dumping of these contracts by the counterparties still happened.[73]

To sum up, to a certain extent, the provision of bankruptcy together with the availability of government bailout as a backup in certain situations is probably better than making an either-or choice. The designing of rules to tackle bank failures should also take necessary any bailout into consideration.

2.3 The desirability of a special resolution for bank failures

The previous section shows that bankruptcy has the advantage of transparency, predictability, and a curbing of moral hazard. However, it tends to have a disruptive effect. Thus, a special resolution regime seems to be necessary to make up for the weaknesses.[74]

2.3.1 Special resolution

The special resolution regime in the EU will be discussed in detail in the next section.[75] But in this section, a succinct reference to the resolution regime is mainly for the purposes of explaining the relationship between resolution and ordinary bankruptcy. The BRRD basically set up a range of resolution tools in three different phases: preparatory and preventative measures, early intervention, and resolution. Banks will have to prepare ex-ante recovery plans and update them

---

72 L.Z. Oliver Hart, 'Economists have abandoned principle – twelve months ago nobody could have imagined government interventions we now take for granted', *Wall Street Journal*, www.wsj.com/articles/SB122826736608874577?mod=_newsreel_2, accessed December 22, 2014.
73 Shmuel Vasser, 'Derivatives in bankruptcy', *The Business Lawyer* 1507. See also 11 U.S. Code § 362(a).
74 Eva HG Hüpkes, 'Insolvency: why a special regime for banks?' 3 *Current Developments in Monetary and Financial Law*.
75 See infra Chapter 6, Sections 3–4.

periodically so that they have at their disposal necessary measures to restore their financial positions in case of a significant deterioration in their financial structure. Resolution authorities will be required to prepare resolution plans for each bank, in which they would prepare the actions that could be taken if conditions for resolution were to be met.[76]

In addition, to ensure an orderly and swift liquidation without disrupting the systemic financial order, the resolution authorities are armed with four main resolution measures: the sale of the business, the establishment of a bridge institution, asset separation, and a bail-in tool.[77] What is more, all Member States are required to set up their own resolution funds on an ex-ante basis so that the aforementioned resolution tools can be applied in an effective way.[78]

This suggestion for a special resolution regime might be supported by at least three factors through a close examination of TBTF bank failure, such as the Lehman Brothers failure. Initially, the significantly important function played by banks makes any disruption to their relevant critical services intolerable for society as a whole, even for a single second. These banks take deposits and then extend credit in order to finance commerce. Furthermore, they provide access to the payments system for households and government agencies and legal persons. By credit intermediation and flow of capital through payment and settlement systems, banks are still the major liquidity source for most financial and non-financial entities even though direct finance through the capital markets is very mature.[79] Investment banking and underwriting services are also of critical importance because they provide firms with other alternatives to finance their activities by selling debts or other securitised products.[80] Any destruction of access to the banking system, even temporarily, would significantly hurt the overall economy.

Second, the capital structure of banks and their overall size make the winding-up process extremely convoluted and susceptible to short-term creditor run. The banking industry conducts much of its business operations based on maturity transformation, which is providing long-term loans to investors using short-term deposits or repo debts. Most of the banks tend to be leveraged and interconnected.[81]

---

76 Council of the European Union, *Council adopts rules on bank recovery and resolution* (May 6, 2014).
77 Ibid.
78 Directive 2014/59/EU of the European Parliament and of the Council of 15 May 2014, establishing a framework for the recovery and resolution of credit institutions and investment firms and amending Council Directive 82/891/EEC, and Directives 2001/24/EC, 2002/47/EC, 2004/25/EC, 2005/56/EC, 2007/36/EC, 2011/35/EU, 2012/30/EU and 2013/36/EU, and Regulations (EU) No 1093/2010 and (EU) No 648/2012, of the European Parliament and of the Council [2014] OJ L 173/190/1 (BRRD), art 102–103.
79 Avgouleas, *Governance of global financial markets: the law, the economics, the politics*, pp. 23–29.
80 Michael. Schillig, 'Bank resolution regimes in Europe: recovery and resolution planning, early intervention, resolution tools and powers', vol. 24, no. 6, *European Business Law Review* 751, pp. 4–7.
81 Frank J. Fabozzi, Franco Modigliani, and F.J. James, *Foundation of financial markets and institutions* (Hoboken, NJ: Pearson 2010), pp. 22–24.

Third, a bank failure may easily cause a spill over effect and a problem of lack of coordination, which bankruptcy is incapable of addressing.[82] Many large banks has central cash and funding for the financial group as a whole, and the failure of the hub could trigger the failure of the other branches. And due to the interconnectedness of the banking sector, the spill over effect could happen in the entire global banking sector.

Besides, the sheer behemoth size of banks tends to make governments shudder at any possibility of a banking failure. Taking these factors into account, the need for a special resolution (with administrative style efficiency) rather than bankruptcy (with its apparent disadvantages) seems to be more urgent.[83]

2.3.2 Merits and demerits of resolution vs. bankruptcy: is an amalgamation desirable?

Building on the above analysis, when it comes to the merits of the special resolution regime like that in the EU, it can be seen that a specially tailored resolution process for solving the failure of banks has several advantages compared with either bailout or bankruptcy.[84]

First, it has comparatively more adequate funds to tackle failing banks. As referred to above, the essential problem of a distressed bank is that due to the overuse of maturity transformation and the leveraging of their balance sheets, once a shortage of short-term funding occurs, it would instantly put pressure on the liquidity of the bank and ignite the contagion effect. The resolution fund requirement, which requires the setting aside of funds in accordance with a mathematical formula,[85] provides a comparatively easily available funding source compared with bankruptcy. It is widely known that the funding in bankruptcy procedures relies mainly on new lending from the markets and the liquidity of the failing bank's assets, which can prove unlikely in the case of a run on the bank.[86]

Second, with many resolution measures and tools at their disposal, such as separation, transfer of assets, selling of assets, and bail in, it can prompt a comparatively speedy resolution process and minimise the possibility of triggering systemic failure.[87] Due to the function of the 'living will', banks would tend to be well prepared for recovery. Besides, the resolution authorities, when armed

---

82 Skeel, 'Single point of entry and the bankruptcy alternative', pp. 4–6.
83 Schillig, 'Bank resolution regimes in Europe: recovery and resolution planning, early intervention, resolution tools and powers', pp. 4–5.
84 Ibid.
85 BRRD, art 102.
86 Jackson and Skeel Jr, 'Dynamic resolution of large financial institutions'. In the US, for instance, the FDIC is authorised to borrow up to 10% of the consolidated assets of the distressed bank at the time a failing bank is taken over, and 90% of its consolidated assets are available for repayment in the process of resolution. See also Dodd-Frank Act, section 210.
87 Kenneth E. Scott, 'A guide to the resolution of failed financial institutions: Dodd-Frank Title II and proposed chapter 14'.

with these provided measures and powers, are in a good position to direct a fast and efficient liquidation.

Third, a special resolution mechanism could design specially tailored rules to facilitate cross-border cooperation and coordination among EU Members or between EU Members and third countries. For instance, the group-level resolution authorities are required to establish a Resolution College to carry out relevant tasks and ensure coordination and cooperation among EU Members.[88] A mechanism such as this, despite some remaining shortcomings, partly addresses the long-seated cross-border resolution difficulty in the EU.[89] Difficulties in cooperation happen to be evident weaknesses of bankruptcy.

However, special resolution also has some disadvantages when compared with bankruptcy. Initially, it might lack the incentive to trigger the process. As part of the process of resolution activation, the resolution authority has a great deal of control. In the EU resolution framework, the activation of the procedure starts either upon receipt of the communication from the competent authority or upon the resolution authority's own initiative. But due to the fact that both the competent authority and the resolution authority lack stakes in the failing bank, they would not have sufficient incentive to initiate the procedure in a timely manner.[90] Rather, being the regulatory agencies, they might be reluctant to admit the fact of a bank distress.[91]

In addition, it lacks transparency compared with a normal bankruptcy procedure. For instance, the resolution authority has large discretion in determining whether to write down or convert relevant capital instruments when necessary into shares or other instruments of ownership of the new entities.[92] For most of the commercial banks, this concern is not very serious, because most of the debts they own are the liabilities of insured deposits. But for other trading-oriented financial institutions, which have a large range of various liabilities, the regulatory discretion is a serious risk worthy of concern.[93] Although the creditors and shareholders

---

88 Directive 2014/59/EU of the European Parliament and of the Council of 15 May 2014, establishing a framework for the recovery and resolution of credit institutions and investment firms and amending Council Directive 82/891/EEC, and Directives 2001/24/EC, 2002/47/EC, 2004/25/EC, 2005/56/EC, 2007/36/EC, 2011/35/EU, 2012/30/EU and 2013/36/EU, and Regulations (EU) No 1093/2010 and (EU) No 648/2012, of the European Parliament and of the Council [2014] OJ L 173/190/1 (BRRD), article 88.

89 Avgouleas, *Governance of global financial markets: the law, the economics, the politics*, p. 246.

90 Jonathan R. Macey and Geoffrey P. Miller, 'Kaye, Scholar, Firrea, and the desirability of early closure: a view of the Kaye, Scholar case from the perspective of bank regulatory policy', 66 S Cal L Rev 1115.

91 Skeel, 'Single point of entry and the bankruptcy alternative', p. 11. see also Schillig, 'Bank resolution regimes in Europe: recovery and resolution planning, early intervention, resolution tools and powers', pp. 21–22.

92 BRRD, art 59.

93 Jackson and Skeel Jr, 'Dynamic resolution of large financial institutions', p. 443. According to statistics in the US, about 93% of the liabilities of banks with assets between USD100 million and USD500 million are deposits. Thus, for these banks, the FDIC is not just the decision-maker in the process of orderly liquidation, but also the major creditor.

could resort to the 'no worse off' principle by arguing that the resolution process has incurred more losses than it would have done in a normal insolvency proceeding, the resolution authority could easily refute it by arguing that the creditors would have received little or nothing in a real liquidation.[94]

Therefore, comparing the pros and cons of bankruptcy with those of special resolution, it seems that this is not an absolute either-or choice either. Instead, one could argue, if there were no concern about systemic risk, bankruptcy could be the optional choice to deal with a distressed bank due to the nature of transparency and legitimacy. The special resolution, although not as transparent as bankruptcy, would be the prime option to deal with a distressed bank whose failure would cause systemic consequences.

This argument is aligned with the opinion of Thomas Jackson and David Skeel. Even the most fervent advocate of special resolution has to admit that bankruptcy is appropriate as a presumptive mechanism for resolving the distress of all but SIFIs. Thomas Jackson and David Skeel tend to believe that bankruptcy is appropriate for normal commercial banks, and resolution is apt for banks of systemic importance or SIFIs.[95] To a certain extent, David Skeel even argues for a case of bankruptcy, with some elements from the resolution mechanism added in.[96]

As sensible as David Skeel's opinion sounds, the point to be made here is, for the distressed banks in the TBTF bank structural problem, special resolution proceedings might be more desirable due to the concerns about systemic risk, but the merits of bankruptcy in transparency and predictability should also not be overlooked.

The fact is it is hard to have different legal policies based on a classification of SIFIs and non-SIFIs. Non-SIFIs can equally cause a negative spill over effect due to their interconnectedness problem. Besides, the comparatively neutral stance on the choice between bankruptcy and special resolution is contingent on the lack of systemic risk.

In sum, now that the contagion and domino effect are apparently prevalent in the banking industry and prove to be unquestionable – they fall exactly within the bounds of the TBTF structural problem – the resolution procedure seems to be more appropriate in this situation.[97]

3 The EU resolution reform and a reference to the US and UK reforms

According to the BRRD, to effectively make the resolution mechanism applicable and practical, each Member State ought to designate one or more resolution authorities if necessary under special circumstances, and arm them with the

---

94 Ibid.
95 Ibid.
96 Skeel, 'Single point of entry and the bankruptcy alternative', pp. 15–18.
97 Avgouleas, *Governance of global financial markets: the law, the economics, the politics*, pp. 134–135.

necessary tools and powers to implement the resolution process in covered entities.[98] It should be noted that unlike any resolution procedure in a single jurisdiction, the resolution authorities apply the procedure at the Member State level to highly integrated and internationalised institutions. The fact that there are different resolution authorities could pose serious challenges to the practicality of a real resolution.[99]

3.1 The current reform and progress in the EU

To be a justified resolution authority, it should be a public administrative authority or authorities with administrative powers, which could possibly be national central banks or competent ministries. To properly function as a national resolution authority (NRA), Member States should require that the authority has necessary expertise, resources, and capacity to implement the resolution action with swiftness and flexibility to meet the envisaged objectives. The resolution authorities should, during the process of implementing the resolution and recovery process, cooperate in a very close way with the competent authorities, especially in some areas such as preparation of a recovery and resolution plan.[100]

Given the complexity of banking institutions' operating structures, this resolution scheme has a very broad and inclusive scope; it is applicable to the recovery and resolution of the following entities:[101]

(1) Institutions (credit institutions and investment firms) that are established in the Union;
(2) Financial holding companies, mixed financial holding companies and mixed-activity holding companies that are established in the Union;
(3) Parent financial holding companies in a Member State, Union parent financial holding companies, parent mixed financial holding companies in a Member State, Union parent mixed financial holding companies;
(4) The financial institution established in the Union that is a subsidiary of a credit institution or investment firm, or of a company referred to in point (2) or (3);
(5) Branches of institutions that are established outside the Union.

3.1.1 Three steps: preparation, early intervention, and resolution

The BRRD established a wide set of instruments and measures to tackle a bank failure in three stages: recovery and resolution planning, early intervention, and the resolution procedure.[102]

---

98 BRRD, art 3.
99 Financial Stability Board, *Key attributes of effective resolution regimes for financial institutions* (London: Financial Stability Board 2011), pp. 1–3.
100 BRRD, art 3(4).
101 BRRD, art 1.
102 European Commission, *EU Bank Recovery and Resolution Directive (BRRD): frequently asked questions* (Brussels, April 15, 2014).

Step 1: Ex-ante recovery and resolution plan.[103] The Member States should make sure that each covered entity draws up and maintains a recovery plan both at the institution and group level. A recovery plan mainly includes ex-ante measures to be taken to restore the function of a firm in case any financial deterioration circumstance happens in the future.[104] In addition, the resolution authorities are required to draw up a resolution plan for each covered entity both at institution level and at group level. A resolution plan is mainly about how to deal with financial deterioration situations which might lead to distress or failure of firms.[105] If obstacles are identified during the recovery and resolution planning process, the competent authorities or the resolution authorities can direct the institutions to take appropriate measures, such as making changes to their funding strategy and governance structure.[106]

It should be noted that the group-level recovery plan and resolution plan are both to be decided on a joint decision basis by relevant authorities. Consolidating supervisor and NCAs of subsidiaries decide the former; and the latter is decided by the group-level resolution authority and resolution authorities of subsidiaries.[107]

Step 2: Early intervention is a procedure to deal with possible future crisis. The Member States should make sure that the competent authorities have relevant early intervention powers to tackle the instantly changing financial situation of an institution, such as deteriorating liquidity situation, the default or likely default of loans, over-interconnected exposures, and increasing level of leverage.[108]

This step includes mainly the following powers: implement one or more of the arrangements or measures in the recovery plan, convene a meeting of shareholders to adopt urgent reforms, require the problem institution to draw up a plan for the restructuring of debts with its creditors according to the recovery plan, require change of business strategy, require change of operational and legal structure of the institution, and remove or replace management body in the failing institutions.[109]

Step 3: The resolution procedure. As a matter of fact, the resolution mechanism is the most indispensable part of tackling bank failure in the TBTF bank structural problem. The objectives of it are[110] to ensure the continuity of critical functions of banks; to avoid a significant adverse effect to the financial system, to protect public funds by minimising the reliance on taxpayers' money; and to protect depositors' and clients' assets.[111] The conditions for carrying out the resolution are clearly defined in the BRRD; the resolution authority would trigger the

---

103 Andreas R. Dombret and Patrick S. Kenadjian, *The Bank Recovery and Resolution Directive: Europe's solution for 'too big to fail'?* (Berlin: De Gruyter 2013).
104 BRRD, art 5 and art 7.
105 BRRD, art 10.
106 BRRD, art 6(3)–(6).
107 BRRD, art 8 and art 13.
108 BRRD, art 27.
109 Ibid.
110 BRRD, art 31.
111 Ibid.

resolution mechanism when the conditions are met, i.e. when the firm is failing or likely to fail, while there is no reasonable prospect that any possible private measures could be of help to tackle the situation, and carrying out of the resolution would be in the best interests of public welfare.[112]

3.1.2 Four resolution measures (tools)

There are four essential measures at the disposal of the resolution authorities to carry out the resolution process, which Member States would have to transpose into national law according to the BRRD:[113]

(1) Sale of assets. Just like in a normal bankruptcy procedure, the firm being resolved should try its best to maximise the interests of all related parties. The sale of the firm's assets is, among other things, a very important tool to pay off its debts while avoid imposing a burden on public funds.[114]

(2) Asset separation tool. In the resolution process, the resolution authorities have the power to separate certain assets and transfer them to a publicly held asset management vehicle to avoid unnecessary value dissipation of assets in crisis.[115] The condition is that a normal liquidation of the assets tends to bring about adverse market effect, and that such transference is necessary for the proper functioning of the firm and maximising the liquidation proceeds.[116]

(3) The bridge institution tool. When a resolution process begins, a bridge company can be set up to protect the value of the assets in an institution and maintain the continuity of critical functions required by society.[117]

(4) Bail-in tool. It is a new tool that originated mainly in Europe.[118] It is basically a tool that allows banks to write down or convert some debts into equities so that the bank can mainly absorb the losses and minimise the externality of the recovery and resolution process.[119] It also stipulates further the minimal requirement for own funds and eligible liabilities (MREL).[120]

Bail-in is a very original tool designed for the sake of orderly liquidation of banks in distress without triggering much adverse effect in the financial markets. Its rationale is that the losses of the failing banks should never be absorbed by the

---

112 BRRD, art 32.
113 BRRD, art 63. See also Council of the European Union, *Council adopts rules on bank recovery and resolution* (May 6, 2014). Council adopts rules on bank recovery and resolution [Press release].
114 BRRD, art 38.
115 BRRD, art 42.
116 BRRD, art 42(3).
117 BRRD, art 40.
118 Jim Brunsden and Rebecca Christie, 'German push to accelerate bank bail-ins joined by Dutch', Bloomberg, www.bloomberg.com/news/2013-02-04/german-push-to-accelerate-bank-bail-ins-joined-by-dutch-finns.html, accessed December 5, 2014.
119 BRRD, art 43.
120 BRRD, art 45.

depositors or the taxpayers in principle. Only in rare and extreme conditions should this happen and only if it is necessary for the protection of overall financial stability. Thus, the suggestion of the bail-in tool is to tackle the failing banks through a new approach, where the losses have to be absorbed to the largest possible extent by the shareholders and the creditors through some ex-ante prepared bail-in instruments. Although resolution financial arrangements would be set up at the Member State level, the precondition for its activation is that shareholders and creditors have absorbed 8% of the total losses.[121] Therefore, the Directive gives the resolution authorities the power of write down or conversion of capital instruments.[122]

Some types of liabilities can be permanently excluded from bail-in including: covered deposits and secured liabilities, liabilities to employees of the failing institution, commercial claims relating to goods and services critical for the functioning of the institution, liabilities arising by virtue of holding of client assets, liabilities arising by virtue of a fiduciary relationship, liabilities owned to systems or operators of systems with a remaining maturity of less than seven days, and interbank liabilities with an original maturity of less than seven days.[123]

Besides the mandatory exclusion, NRAs have discretion in deciding extra exclusions. They are granted the power to exclude, or partially exclude, liabilities for reasons including: liabilities that cannot be bailed in within a reasonable time; to ensure the preservation of critical functions; to avoid any contagion effect; and to avoid any value destruction from harming creditors.[124]

The conversion and write down action in carrying out a bail-in would follow similar priority rules of the allocation of losses in insolvency. Equities have to be reduced completely before any debt claim is subject to reduction. After reduction of equity instruments, the resolution authority will impose losses evenly on holders of subordinated debts, and then evenly on senior debt-holders if necessary.[125]

3.1.3 The resolution financial arrangement

According to the Directive, all Member States are required to set up their own independent resolution financial arrangements on an ex-ante basis so that the aforementioned resolution tools can be applied effectively. In fact, the effectiveness of an orderly liquidation and resolution process for banks is mostly dependent on the success of the resolution financial arrangement in providing sufficient funds for failing banks.[126] The resolution financial arrangement has the following requirements:

---

121 BRRD, art 44(5).
122 BRRD, art 43.
123 BRRD, art 44(2), see also Council of the European Union, *Council adopts rules on bank recovery and resolution* (May 6, 2014).
124 BRRD, art 44(3). See also ibid.
125 BRRD, art 48. See also European Commission, *EU Bank Recovery and Resolution Directive (BRRD): frequently asked questions*.
126 Council of the European Union, *Council adopts rules on bank recovery and resolution*.

(1) The standard: according to the Directive, any Member State would phase in setting up a fund with the size of at least 1% of all the covered deposits of all the credit institutions in the State before 2024.[127] The finance arrangement includes many sources: ex-ante and ex-post contributions, alternative funding means, and borrowing between different financing arrangements.[128]

(2) The threshold: for Member States, the resolution authorities could use the resolution financial arrangements to cover bank losses and for bank recapitalisation. But a threshold has to be met: 8% of the total liabilities of the resolution bank must have been imposed on shareholders and holders of other ownership instruments.[129]

(3) Contribution by institutions: each bank should make contributions to the resolution financial arrangement, being pro rata to the amounts of its liabilities; however, the contribution of the financial arrangement can never exceed 5% of the bank's total liabilities.[130]

(4) Minimum requirements for own funds and eligible liabilities for each institution (MREL). The resolution financial arrangement is theoretically responsible for the resolution of all covered institutions, but it is only triggered after losses have been partly absorbed by the failing institution itself. To make sure there is adequate liquidity to effectively carry out the resolution process, the Directive provides that NRAs should ensure that institutions meet minimum requirements for own funds and liabilities at all times. The standard is to be determined according to many criteria, such as its special situation, business model, and the need to ensure orderly liquidation using all resolution tools.[131]

(5) Exception for setting up of resolution financial arrangements. The Directive Article 102 normally requires each Member State to set up its own resolution arrangement through a fund which is controlled by the resolution authority. However, a Member State may set up its own financial arrangement which is not through a fund controlled by the resolution authority. The condition is that the financial arrangement should at least be equal to that amount under Article 102, and the Member State's resolution authority is entitled to the equivalent amount.[132]

(6) Exception for the resolution financial arrangement: state aid. The assumption for setting up the resolution financial arrangement is to internalise the losses of excessive risk-taking by banking institutions and to avoid externality. However, according to the Directive, under exceptional circumstances, the public equity support tool and temporary public ownership tool are also allowed under EU state aid law.[133]

---

127 BRRD, art 102.
128 BRRD, art 102–107.
129 BRRD, art 5(a).
130 BRRD, art 44(5).
131 BRRD, art 45.
132 BRRD, art 99.
133 BRRD, art 56.

Therefore, the Directive also provides for the possibility of government financial stabilisation tools as the last resort when necessary. The tools are only available if one of the following conditions is met: (i) the application of resolution tools would not suffice to avoid a significantly adverse effect to the financial system; (ii) the application of resolution tools would not suffice to protect public interests where liquidity assistance from the central banks has been given to the institution; and (iii) the application of resolution tools would not suffice to protect public interest where public equity support has been given to the institution.[134]

It should also be noted that the EU resolution progress also includes another parallel and comparatively pro-EU resolution legislation, the SRM as a pillar of the EBU (the SSM, the SRM, and DGS).[135] The framework under the SRM is both parallel and different from the BRRD, as it tries to provide a more effective resolution for significant institutions at the EU level.[136]

3.2 The resolution mechanism in the US and the UK

The GFC brought to the spotlight the lack of an efficient resolution regime for failing institutions. Thus, the major economies all came up with new mechanisms to wind down financial institutions for future use.[137]

The US, through the adoption of the Dodd-Frank Act, set up the Orderly Liquidation Agency (OLA) and procedure to resolve the failing banks. In the UK, however, through the legislation of the Bank Reform Act 2009, it set up the Special Resolution Regime (SRR) to wind down failing banks.[138] Chronologically speaking, due to the earlier time in which these reforms were conducted, they came to be known as 'the first generation of resolution'.[139]

As the resolution reform moved forward, there was further new progress in the US and the UK. On December 12, 2012, the Bank of England (BOE) and FDIC issued a joint paper advocating for a Single Point of Entry resolution approach (SPE) to resolve globally active and systemically important financial institutions. The US adopted the SPE resolution approach in the December 2013 FDIC notice, 'Resolution of systemically important financial institutions:

---

134 BRRD, art 56(4).
135 European Commission, *Communication from the Commission to the European Parliament and the Council: a roadmap towards a banking union*, COM (2012) 510 final (September 12, 2012), pp. 1–5.
136 The rules under the SRM will be discussed in detail in Section 4.3.5 of this chapter. See Regulation (EU) No 1024/2013 of October 15, 2013 conferring specific tasks on the European Central Bank concerning policies relating to the prudential supervision of credit institutions [2013] OJ L 287/63 (SSM Regulation), art 6(4).
137 Stijn Claessens et al., *A safer world financial system: improving the resolution of systemic institutions* (Geneva: International Center for Monetary and Banking Studies 2010), pp. 57–82.
138 Bank Act 2009 (UK), s1.
139 John Armour, 'Making bank resolution credible', pp. 2–3.

the single point of entry strategy'. SPE refers to a resolution strategy where the resolution is conducted at the top parent firm or at the holding company level by a single resolution authority.[140] As regards the UK, more detailed bail-in rules are provided in schedule 2 of the Financial Services Act 2013. With the enactment of the BRRD Directive in 2014, the UK issued the Bank Recovery and Resolution Order (Order 2014 No. 3348 and Order No. 3329), and the UK resolution mechanism since then has been highly influenced by the EU mechanism.[141]

In the subsequent section, a brief introduction to the US and UK rules will be provided, and further comparative detailed analyses will be done afterwards. The analysis of the EU resolution will include a comparison with the EU and US reforms where necessary. The reason is that the US rules show more marked differences compared with the EU resolution, while the UK domestic rules have been hugely adjusted in accordance with the BRRD. Therefore, a comparison between the EU and the UK will not always serve the objectives of our analysis.

3.2.1 The FDIC and US resolution regime

The FDIC was originally set up to provide deposit insurance to all banks and saving associations. It also carries out the responsibility of the liquidation of any insured entity and the disposition of assets of such entity.[142] To protect the safety and soundness of the insured deposits, FDIC was given the right to pursue the depositors' claims against troubled banks, and thus was entrusted with the power to monitor the insured banks instead of depositors.

To deal with the distressed banks, there are three options of receivership under the FDIC resolution and liquidation regime:

(1) The FDIC can act as a receiver, to be in charge of the liquidation of distressed banks. Insured depositors would be paid by the insurance fund without suffering from the losses of the entity. The FDIC has many tools at its disposal, such as selling of assets to meet the need for liquidity.[143]
(2) The FDIC can also arrange another solution, where it finds another entity to assume and pay off the debts. The entity is also called a transferee bank. The transferee assumes all the assets of the entity and then pays off the debts and depositors instead of the FDIC to ease the pressure on public funds.[144] In this way, the transference of assets can be very swift, and the FDIC can also internalise the liabilities within the banking industry without any further externality effect of imposing losses on the public fund.

---

140 For details on SPE, see infra Chapter 6, Section 4.3.2.
141 Bank Recovery and Resolution Order 2014 (Order No. 3329) and (Order 2014 No. 3348).
142 12 U.S. Code § 1811 – Federal Deposit Insurance Corporation.
143 12 U.S. Code § 1811 (d)(2)(E).
144 12 U.S. Code § 1811 (d)(2)(G).

(3) The third solution is to set up a bridge company. It happens mainly if an instant liquidation is not available and while a transferee is being found. Technically, the FDIC transfers the assets to a bridge company, which is operated by the FDIC.[145] The FDIC would also make immediate repayment to depositors and be responsible for the liabilities the failing entity is exposed to. Eventually, the business would either be sold to private purchasers or be liquidated.

A very special part of the Dodd-Frank Act is that it provides two sets of rules to deal with failure: (i) the Title I bankruptcy proceeding, which requires all covered entities to prepare living wills to prove to the regulators that they are resolvable under the bankruptcy code; and (ii) Title II resolution proceedings – in case the bankruptcy procedure is not effective enough under circumstances where systemic stability is endangered, especially where a SIFI is about to fail, the Dodd Frank Act also provides Title II, by which the OLA conducts swift resolution of covered firms.[146]

The resolution rules in Dodd-Frank were criticised for many reasons, such as not addressing bank run and the spill over effect.[147] Thus, the FDIC 2013 Notice on SPE adopted more specific resolution and recapitalisation strategies and fund arrangements to make up for the Dodd-Frank insufficiencies.[148]

3.2.2 The SRR and the UK resolution regime

The UK has, through the Bank Act 2009, adopted the 'special resolution regime' (SRR) to wind down failing banks, including three stabilisation tools, the bank insolvency procedure, and the bank administration procedure.[149] The three stabilisation options are:[150]

(1) Private sector purchase. The BOE would transfer some or all of the businesses of the failed entity to a private sector purchaser through share or property transfer instruments.
(2) Bridge bank. All or some of the businesses of the distressed bank are transferred to a bridge company owned by the BOE where a private purchaser is not available.
(3) Temporary public ownership, where the Treasury will make one or more share transfer orders in which the transferee is either a nominee of or owned by the Treasury.

---

145 12 U.S. Code § 1811 (m), (n).
146 See generally the Dodd-Frank Wall Street Reform and Consumer Protection Act (U.S), section 619, Title I–II.
147 Skeel, 'Single point of entry and the bankruptcy alternative', pp. 4–6.
148 Federal Deposit Insurance Corporation, *Resolution of systemically important financial institutions: the single point of entry strategy, Reg. 243*, pp. 76614–76624 (December 18, 2013).
149 Bank Act 2009 (UK), s1.
150 Bank Act 2009 (UK), ss11, 12, and 13.

The SRR also includes a series of rules for waiving normal property rights to facilitate the transfer of the assets. It stipulates that a transfer can take effect by virtue of the instrument despite any restrictions in contract and other law with regard to property rights. The restrictions include any restriction, inability or incapability affecting what can be assigned and any requirement for consent.[151] In addition, the Banking Act 2009 even includes a clause which enables the Treasury to amend the law by order for the purpose of making the powers under this legislation to be used effectively to ensure the realisation of the resolution objectives.[152] That would definitely be helpful in dismantling any substantive restriction on the transfer of assets.

There are two critiques of the resolution powers, which might also be related to the following discussion in regard to the design of the resolution mechanism in the EU. First, the waiver of property rights contradicts Article 1 of the first protocol to the European Convention on Human Rights, which says possession shall not be deprived except in cases of public interest and under special conditions.[153] The critique suggests that after the transfer of assets, the shareholders are not adequately protected and compensated. But this argument ignores the fact that under statute, the shares would be valued on the grounds that no government support is guaranteed, and that the shares would be worthless after paying off the depositors and creditors. Thus, it is by no means the case that shareholders would be worse off due to the transfer.

Second, the waiver of property rights is in conflict with financial collateral termination rights. The argument suggests that the transfer is in conflict with EU law, which enables the counterparty to terminate existing positions on the event of default.[154] However, even the EU has already proposed modifying the financial collateral Directive to facilitate the resolution.[155]

In the 2013 Financial Services Act, the bail-in tool was also enacted to enhance the resolvability of banks.[156] Furthermore, asset management vehicles were also added in the 2014 Bank Recovery and Resolution order. Asset management vehicles can only be used in conjunction with other resolution tools (transfer to private sector purchaser, transfer to bridge bank, or the bail-in tool).[157] It is used to remove certain parts of assets in order to ensure that the rest of the business under resolution can continue to function, or to improve the performance of the remaining business.

3.2.3 The scope of the resolution

In the first instance, the FDIC only applied the resolution to deposit-taking institutions. However, the Dodd-Frank Act extended it to non-bank entities of

---

151 Banking Act 2009 (UK), s34.
152 Banking Act 2009 (UK), s75.
153 *SRM Global Master Fund LP v The Comissioners of HM Treasury [2009] EWCA Civ 788.*
154 Directive 2002/47/EC on Financial Collateral Arrangements [2002] OJ L 168/43, as amended by Directive 2009/44/EC [2009] OJ L146/37.
155 BRRD, art 63.
156 Financial Services Act 2013, s2.
157 Bank Recovery and Resolution Order 2014 (Order No. 3329), s19.

systemic risk through the OLA. In the UK, the situation is also similar, in that the Banking Act 2009 originally only applied to deposit-taking institutions. However, the Financial Services Act extended its application to large investment firms.[158]

From the scope point of view, this is similar to the BBRD; the recovery and resolution procedure can be applied to institutions (credit institutions and investment firms that are established in the Union) and to holding companies, parent holding companies, subsidiaries of these companies, and branches established outside the EU.[159]

Most importantly, the EU's broad scope of application can best eradicate the possibility of an adverse effect due to the failure of any of the covered entities. Besides, its scope is not restricted to SIFIs. That is an advantage compared to the Dodd-Frank Title II resolution, which applies only to SIFIs. This has been strongly criticised by scholars.[160] Opponents might argue that some of the covered entities might not be significant enough to trigger any adverse effect through their failures.[161] But this argument cannot be true after closer examination. Many entities might not fall within the definition of SIFIs, but the influence of the failure of an institution is hard to assess in advance because it might well be interconnected with other firms and cause a spill over effect.[162] At the end of the day, the widespread failure of a number of non-significant firms might be equally horrible and devastating compared with the failure of a single SIFI.[163]

3.3 Considerations of the resolution reform and its possible complementary role

The enactment of BRRD is based on many considerations in the post-crisis era. Among them, lack of resolvability and lack of coordination (due to the concerns of integration, size, and interconnectedness) are the essential ones. These considerations also fall into the denotation of the TBTF bank structural problem: the cyclicality attribute and the lack of resolvability, which is also the remaining issue after discussion in Chapters 4 and 5 on the structural attribute.[164] Hence, before undertaking a detailed analyses of the specific rules of resolution in the BRRD, a tentative conclusion can be drawn that the resolution scheme is possibly complementary to the structural separation reform in dealing with the TBTF bank structural problem.

---

158 Financial Services Act 2012 (UK), s101.
159 BRRD, art 2.
160 David Skeel, *The new financial deal: understanding the Dodd-Frank Act and its (unintended) consequences* (New York: John Wiley & Sons 2010), pp. 8–10.
161 Schillig, 'Bank resolution regimes in Europe: recovery and resolution planning, early intervention, resolution tools and powers'.
162 See supra Chapter 1, Section 3(b).
163 Schillig, 'Bank resolution regimes in Europe: recovery and resolution planning, early intervention, resolution tools and powers'.
164 Chow, *Making banks safer: can Volcker and Vickers do it?*

3.3.1 Interconnectedness considerations

The EU banking industry in the pre-crisis era was characterised as highly inter-connected.[165] The direct result was that it was more likely to affect the overall economic stability of the Union if certain banks encountered problems of insolvency. This was what actually happened in the crisis, and hence one of the reasons why the BRRD was proposed and enacted, to make banks less interconnected and less exposed to one another in terms of risks and to strengthen resolvability in general.[166]

The resolution mechanism in the BRRD, to a certain extent, might be complementary to the structural separation rules in reducing the interconnectedness. Examining the BSR closely, it does not address the intergroup exposure problem completely. The ring-fence separation only stipulates the intragroup exposure, but it does not necessarily ensure the safety and soundness of banks.[167] In this regard, resolution rules can be complementary to the structural rules by providing an exit channel and acting as admonishment to reckless risk-taking and interconnectedness.

3.3.2 Integration considerations

The enactment of the BRRD happened against the backdrop of bank failures in the highly integrated banking sector, which corresponds to the denotation of the structural problem. As indicated by the recital of the BRRD, banking integration has been intensified in an unprecedented manner, especially since the late 1990s. The Euro-pass has basically made integration one of the most prominent attributes of the EU banking sector.[168] The European Central Bank has conducted thorough research on this topic about the integration of the EU banking area. It assessed the integration of the banking sector through both the price indicator and the quantity indicator.[169] Its conclusion is that up until 2014, the integration of the EU banking sector was still not as intensive as that in the pre-crisis area, based on the banking service price disparity and quantity disparity in the distressed and non-distressed areas. It also reminds us that the extent of integration of the banking sector in the EU was very high in the pre-crisis era.[170]

The prevalent concern about overintegration in the banking sector also paved the way for the structural separation reform, but the resolution reform initiative goes one step further than mere structural separation. The reason why a resolution scheme is needed is because the EU financial banking industry is so

---

165 See supra Chapter 1, Section 3(b).
166 BRRD, recital (1).
167 European Commission, *Proposal for a Regulation of the European Parliament and of the Council on structural measures improving the resilience of EU credit institutions,COM/2014/043 final* (Jan 29, 2014), art. 13.
168 BRRD, recital (3).
169 European Central Bank, *Report on financial integration in Europe* (April 26, 2014).
170 Ibid.

integrated and internationalised that it makes the failure of cross-border institutions have an adverse effect on financial markets at the Union level.[171]

3.3.3 Lack of resolvability

Except for integration and interconnectedness, the main consideration in the enactment of the BRRD is the lack of a practical and efficient bank resolution procedure.[172] This also corresponds with the TBTF structural problem and the remaining resolvability issue. The GFC has shown that there was an apparent lack of effective supervision and regulation of banks to reduce their risk of failure. The supervision of the banks is still confined within national borders, which increases the risk of banks failing.[173] On the other hand, when failure actually occurred in the GFC, there was a lack of an effective resolution mechanism for the failing banks. The active international soft law framework present at the time had no meaningful role in bank resolution, as can be seen from the case of the failure of the Icelandic banks and the disappointing rescue of Fortis Bank.[174] In the 'Icesave dispute', it was this problem that forced the Union to preserve overall economic stability at the cost of taxpayers' funds.[175]

Even with the help of the structural separation mechanism, the resolvability problem still persists.[176] The building of the resolution framework could complement the structural separation reform. It would build up a necessary liquidity provision mechanism and a resolution fund framework to facilitate the recovery and resolution process. It would also give the resolution authority enough powers and tools to tackle bank failures when necessary.

3.3.4 Lack of coordination and harmonisation

The building of the resolution mechanism under the BRRD aims to deal with the lack of resolution coordination problem, eradicate the obstacles of regulatory inefficiency and inconsistency under the fragmented Member States' rules, and ensure the integrity of the internal market.[177] Thus, whether the coordination mechanism would be strengthened is a major standard against which to assess the effectiveness of the regime in the following sections.

---

171 Council of the European Union, *Council adopts rules on bank recovery and resolution* (May 6, 2014). Council adopts rules on bank recovery and resolution [Press release].
172 BRRD, recital (1)–(3).
173 See Avgouleas, *Governance of global financial markets: the law, the economics, the politics*, p. 247. The international regulators, such as BCBS and IMF in the current governance framework lack the standard setting function, monitoring of compliance, and the supervisory capacity.
174 It should be noted that the disappointing rescue happened in EU, an area with the highest extent of harmonisation of national banking law. So, this reflects the desperate need for a new resolution framework, see ibid, p. 248.
175 *Case E-16/11 [2013] EFTA Surveillance Authority v Iceland, not yet reported.*
176 This problem is discussed in the Chapter 5, Section 3.3.2.
177 BRRD, recital (9) and recital (10).

Given that many banks are operated internationally, however, regulation and supervision has still mostly been at the Member State level. When insolvency happened in the GFC, every Member State applied different rules and procedures to the failing firms. This resulted in a huge impediment to an orderly liquidation process. Even with the EU having the highest level of regional harmonisation of banking regulation and supervision, there was no practical procedure for resolution at the Union level.[178] Besides, it has also been shown by the GFC that the normal corporate insolvency procedure is not enough to deal with such systemic failure, because it could not ensure swift intervention, preservation of the critical part or function of the banks, or safeguard overall financial stability.[179]

The building of the resolution mechanism under the BRRD would provide the resolution authorities with enough powers to effectively deal with bank failures. It also aims to harmonise the Member States' resolution rules to the largest possible extent and avoid the conflicts between Member States that tend to impede orderly resolution process.

The BRRD is of such importance because it could possibly address the remaining problem of the lack of resolvability.[180] It provides a framework and platform to actually tackle the disorder of failing banks and the resulting crisis in confidence. It denies overlooking the possibility of future bank failings and requires all banks to prepare recovery and resolution plans on an ex-ante basis. It tries to focus especially on intervention and resolution since bank failure will always, to a certain extent, be unavoidable.

Through the provisions of the recovery and resolution plan, the Directive can also cooperate with the BSR on enhancing the effectiveness of ring-fencing banking activities.[181] For example, a resolution plan which considers how core activities could be separated from other risk activities to ensure continuity in crisis, might intensify the strength of separation rules.[182] On the contrary, if the exit mechanism for banks is not ready, then the effectiveness of all the other reforms would possibly be compromised.[183]

4 A practicality analysis of the EU resolution mechanism

With regard to dealing with the remaining resolvability problem,[184] the above section analyses the progress that has been made in the EU and other major economies in developing new resolution schemes. This section focuses on a specific discussion on whether the EU resolution reform progress will be

---

178 BRRD, recital (4).
179 See supra Chapter 6, Section 2.3.
180 Chow, *Making banks safer: can Volcker and Vickers do it?* p. 16.
181 BRRD, art 10(7).
182 BRRD, art 10(7)(c).
183 BRRD, recital (6).
184 European Central Bank, *Report on financial integration in Europe*, pp. 30–36.

able to deal with the remaining cyclicality attribute of the TBTF bank structural problem in practice, and whether it can tackle the lack of resolvability problem effectively, especially within the context of promoting cross-border cooperation.

4.1 The motivation of the BRRD corresponds with the FSB standard

With the adoption of the resolution regime in the BRRD, more comprehensive analyses need to be done to look at the feasibility of it. It should be noted that the assessment of such rules will always be tangled up in so many unpredictable factors, such as implementation; the cooperation with relevant rules, i.e. the EU SSM within the context of EBU; the political resolution to fight against the structural problem; and the cyclicality attribute, among others.[185] In the EU context, the evaluation of this new set of rules might be more convoluted due to an extra significant factor: the ever-lasting power struggle between the EU and its Member States in relation to the harmonisation of resolution.

The assessment herein aims at hopefully providing a meaningful perspective on the new resolution regime's effectiveness in dealing with the lack of resolvability issue of the TBTF structural problem within the context of promoting international coordination. But it should also be noted that many further concrete implementation rules or technical rules are still to be designed. Thus, the real effect of the regime is yet to be seen, to a certain extent.

The reform endeavours made in the EU resolution correspond with the endeavours in the international community. Among others, one of the landmark initiatives was the FSB's paper in October 2011 which provided a guide to resolution regime, 'The key attributes of an effective resolution regimes for financial institutions'.[186]

In general, the FSB paper suggests that the establishment of the bank resolution scheme should on the one hand set up some ex-ante requirements to make the banks resolvable, and on the other, facilitate rapid and swift bank liquidation when it is actually necessary for this to happen. It strongly emphasises that it is of critical significance to prevent any adverse effect on the core function of banks or the financial sector as a whole.[187] Assessing and evaluating the practical effectiveness of the newly established resolution mechanism under the BRRD, the guidelines provided by the FSB could well be a significant reference or set of criteria. Therefore, they would definitely shed some light on the discussion in the following sections.[188]

---

185 Eilis Ferran and Valia S.G. Babis, 'The European single supervisory mechanism', University of Cambridge Faculty of Law Research Paper, pp. 11–12.
186 Financial Stability Board, *Key attributes of effective resolution regimes for financial institutions*, pp. 2–3.
187 Ibid.
188 Ibid.

To be specific, the FSB provided some features in detail on an effective resolution regime, which should also be borne in mind in subsequent analyses: [189]

(1) Resolution planning: providing ex-ante planning for orderly resolution;
(2) Continuity preservation: ensuring continuity of systemically important financial services and banking functions;
(3) Depositor preference: protecting depositors and insurance policy holders and ensuring the rapid return of segregated client assets in coordination with the relevant insurance schemes and arrangements;
(4) Self loss absorbency: allocating losses to firm owners (shareholders) and unsecured and uninsured creditors, respecting the hierarchy of claims and not relying on public solvency support;
(5) Speed and transparency: avoiding unnecessary destruction of value, seeking to minimise the overall costs of resolution in home and host jurisdictions, and providing speed and transparency and predictability through legal and procedural clarity;
(6) Cooperation and coordination: providing a mandate in law for cooperation, information exchange, and coordination domestically and with relevant foreign resolution authorities before and during a resolution;
(7) Ensuring that non-viable firms can exit the market orderly and thereby enhance market discipline and provide incentives for market-based solutions.

Many critical features are reflected in the BRRD. To start with, it provides for a recovery and resolution plan both at institution level and at group level before the provisions of resolution. In addition, the objectives of the resolution mechanism are to ensure continuity of critical functions to protect depositors' and clients' assets, and to protect public funds and avoid any significant adverse effect on the financial system.[190]

What is more, it also provides a series of principles governing resolution, including self-absorbency of losses, management liability, equal treatment, and the no-worse-off principle.[191] Following the rules on resolution tools and procedure, it specifically provides for a series of rules with regard to cross-border resolution cooperation among the EU members and between the EU members and third countries.[192]

Thus, similarly to the FSB guide, the BRRD resolution regime also sets out the critical features that would be essential for a resolution regime including

---

189 Other features include rules such as scope of resolution, resolution authority, set-off, safeguard, crisis management groups, institution-specific cross-border cooperation agreements, resolvability assessment, access to information, and information sharing. Their implementation is deemed to be capable of ensuring authorities resolve banks in an orderly manner without taxpayers being exposed to losses.
190 BRRD, art. 31.
191 BRRD, art. 34.
192 BRRD, art. 87–93.

resolution powers; safeguarding of property rights; funds for resolution; legal framework for cross-border cooperation; recovery and resolution planning.[193]

In principle, the structural design and rationale behind the resolution scheme under the BRRD seems to be consistent with the FSB standards on an effective resolution mechanism. Starting from the next section further detailed analyses will be conducted with these principles as reference.

4.2 The recovery scheme and its effectiveness

Under the BRRD regime, the recovery framework is a critical part in the three-step special resolution regime: preparation, early intervention, and resolution. The reason is that when carrying out the BRRD framework, the effectiveness of the recovery framework can in practice reduce the possibility or necessity of applying an actual resolution process.[194]

4.2.1 Intragroup support

There is evidence that intragroup finance could be of significant importance to some extent for banks when there is a liquidity crisis or similar event. Thus, it is deemed to be an alternative option for bank recovery.[195]

In the BRRD, there are detailed provisions about intragroup resolution, including the pre-conditions for applying the intragroup finance, the controversial rules on joint decision-making processes among NCAs,[196] how a proposed agreement should be approved,[197] and the specific procedure to implement an approved agreement.[198]

Although the adoption of intragroup support shows significant progress, in practice the decision-making of intragroup support is still a joint decision system that is dependent on the approval of the consolidating supervisor and joint decisions between the relevant NCAs. That might compromise efficiency in reality due to practical reasons, especially under the context of using intragroup support to restore market confidence.[199] In addition, it has at least the following weaknesses: (i) there are also limits to intragroup support in the EC proposal regarding structural reform;[200] (ii) it is very difficult to balance the group's interest and group

---

193 Financial Stability Board, *Key attributes of effective resolution regimes for financial institutions*, pp. 2–3.
194 For a more detailed analysis of the recovery mechanism, see Hu Chen Chen, 'The recovery framework in the BRRD and its effectiveness (May 19, 2015). *Nordic & European Company Law Working Paper* No. 15–04. Available at SSRN: http://ssrn.com/abstract=2610594 or http://dx.doi.org/10.2139/ssrn.2610594.
195 DG Internal Market and Services, *Working document, technical details of a possible EU framework for bank recovery and resolution* (6 January 2011).
196 BRRD, art 20.
197 BRRD, art 21.
198 BRRD, art 24–25.
199 Schillig, 'Bank resolution regimes in Europe: recovery and resolution planning, early intervention, resolution tools and powers', pp. 25–27.
200 European Commission, *Proposal for a Regulation of the European Parliament and of the Council on structural measures improving the resilience of EU credit institutions, COM/2014/043 final*, art 14.

entity interests if the regulation does do not allow group interests to pre-empt group entity interests;[201] (iii) there are many other relevant constraints regarding applying intragroup support, such as the capital requirements, structural requirements, etc;[202] and (iv) the competent authorities have the right to object when it comes to the implementation of any intragroup support.[203]

4.2.2 Recovery and resolution plans

In addition to the above intragroup support mechanism, the BRRD also provides that the banks in the EU are required to prepare so-called 'living wills' as an ex-ante mechanism to deal with potential bank failure.[204]

According to the BRRD, banks are required to prepare both recovery and resolution plans in the EU. Banks make recovery plans, both at the institution level and the group level.[205] A group recovery plan prepared by the Union parent undertaking itself needs to be assessed by the consolidating supervisor, competent supervisors for subsidiaries, and the competent supervisors for the significant branches. The assessment decision-making is made on mostly a joint decision basis between a consolidating supervisor and the relevant NCAs.[206] In addition, the resolution authorities, either the group resolution authorities (together with resolution authorities of subsidiaries) or the institution's resolution authorities (in consultation with relevant supervisors), shall prepare resolution plans to provide resolution measures, both at the institution level and group level.[207] Similar to the group recovery plan assessment process, the group resolution plan is also subject to decision-making made mostly on the basis of a joint decision.[208]

From the perspective of effectiveness, the assessment process and decision-making process is a very evident weak point.[209] For example, the joint decision requirement by the consolidating supervisor and the competent supervisors, on the one hand, means there is a risk of a lack of coordination among relevant supervisors;[210] on the other hand, this decision-making process definitely relies on the effectiveness of the supervision mechanism (the SSM in the EU), which is still yet to be tested due to its many shortcomings.[211]

---

201 DG Internal Market and Services, *Working document, technical details of a possible EU framework for bank recovery and resolution*, art C4.
202 BRRD, art 23(1)(g)–(h). The discretion of NCAs will also be discussed further when analysing the effectiveness of the SSM in Section 4.4.1 of this chapter.
203 BRRD, art 24–25.
204 Dombret and Kenadjian, *The Bank Recovery and Resolution Directive: Europe's solution for 'too big to fail'?*
205 BRRD, art 5 and art 7.
206 BRRD, art 8.
207 BRRD, art 10 and art 12.
208 BRRD, art 13.
209 BRRD, art 8.
210 Emilios Avgouleas, Charles Goodhart, and Dirk Schoenmaker, 'Bank resolution plans as a catalyst for global financial reform', 9 *Journal of Financial Stability* 210, pp. 215–216.
211 Ferran and Babis, 'The European single supervisory mechanism', pp. 4–6. For more details see also Section 4.4.

In addition, except for the weakness of the decision-making process, the implementation of Recovery and Resolution Planning (RRP) still faces many other challenges, such as the complexity of the banks ('perhaps the most depiction-difficult corporations')[212] and the lack of a determined political resolution.[213]

4.2.3 Early intervention

Early intervention is applied to banks which are on the brink of a rapidly deteriorating financial situation, and, therefore, they are breaching or are likely to breach the prudential requirements.[214]

The BRRD stipulates a detailed map of early intervention and expands the powers of early intervention, for example demanding that the legal or operational structure of the firm be changed.[215] BRRD also provides a specific procedure for the implementation of the early intervention and triggering of the process, either at the EU group undertaking level or at the institution level. The decision should be made either by the consolidating authorities or the competent authorities,[216] but when it is to be used in more than one institution, then the decision would also made based on mostly a joint decision mechanism with the assistance of the EBA on request.[217]

Such a mechanism lacks a consolidated intervention at the group level, and therefore the consistency and coordination problem still exists in reality. In addition, similarly to the effectiveness of the RRP, the effectiveness of early intervention will also be dependent on the supervision mechanism, but the fact is that the SSM has been criticised for different weaknesses and flaws.[218]

4.2.4 The recovery framework still has its disadvantages

The fall of banks like Lehman Brothers left huge challenges for the regulators.[219] The recovery framework is equally as critical as the following resolution mechanism as an ex-ante measure.

It is true progress to have established such a recovery framework, but the practical effects of the recovery framework are yet to be seen, depending on the way it is to be implemented and the introduction of more concrete supplementary rules in

---

212 See Robert J. Schiller, *The subprime solution* (Princeton, NJ: Princeton University Press 2008), pp. 39–49. See also Henry T.C. Hu, 'Too complex to depict: innovation, pure information, and the SEC disclosure paradigm', 90 Tex L Rev 1601.

213 Schillig, 'Bank resolution regimes in Europe: recovery and resolution planning, early intervention, resolution tools and powers', p. 22.

214 Avgouleas, *Governance of global financial markets: the law, the economics, the politics*, p. 407. See also CRD IV, Article 102, the measures included in CRD III, art 136(1).

215 BRRD, art 27(1)(a)–(h).

216 BRRD, art 30(2)–(3).

217 BRRD, art 30(6).

218 Wymeersch Eddy, 'The Single Supervisory Mechanism or "SSM", Part One of the Banking Union (2014)'. European Corporate Governance Institute (ECGI) – Law Working Paper No 240/2014, SSRN: http://ssrn.com/abstract=2397800 or http://dx.doi.org/10.2139/ssrn.2397800, accessed March 23, 2015, pp. 25–44.

219 Skeel, 'Single point of entry and the bankruptcy alternative', pp. 5–7.

the future. To sum up, to address the post Lehman challenges, it still has some disadvantages: first, in the recovery framework where the Member States still reserve the main power over decision-making and implementation, the lack of coordination between different regulators/supervisors would still cast strong doubts on its practicality. What is more, in the aftermath of the crisis, firms and Member State regulators would not necessarily have strong incentives in being involved in procedures such as intragroup support and recovery and resolution planning. Last, the recovery framework and its effectiveness would mostly depend on the effectiveness of the supervisory mechanism under the SSM; therefore the current shortcomings of the SSM would also impact the effective operation of the recovery mechanism.

4.3 Assessing the European Multiple Point Entry approach

Except for the recovery and resolution planning framework, the EU BRRD corresponds with the bank resolution endeavours in the international community and the suggestions of the FSB in its 'Key Attributes' in its resolution framework: the establishment of resolution power and tools, the building of international coordination mechanism, the maintaining of market discipline, etc.[220]

Generally speaking, the BRRD requires all EU Member States, not just those in the eurozone, to make sure their NRAs have, at their disposal, a set of necessary common tools and powers which would enable them to conduct an orderly resolution of entities within their domains.[221]

Due to the consideration of cross-border issues in the resolution process, it also provides a framework to improve cooperation and coordination between relevant NRAs to avoid conflicts and enhance consistency and efficiency. In the scope of the Directive, it also empowers the NRAs to resolve branches of banks based in third countries in particular circumstances.[222] Thus, the Directive also includes provisions on the cooperation between the EU resolution authorities and the resolution authorities of third countries.[223]

In the post-crisis era, the Directive is a good representative and embodiment of the resolution reform paradigm shift from bail out to resolution and to self-insurance bail-in.[224] The following sections analyse the effectiveness of the new resolution framework.

4.3.1 The EU fragmented resolution mechanism in the BRRD

In the wake of prevailing bank failing, Member States' governments were the major players to tackle the problem because there was no Union-level mechanism on resolution.

---

220 Financial Stability Board, *Key attributes of effective resolution regimes for financial institutions*, pp. 2–3.
221 BRRD, art 3.
222 BRRD, art 1.
223 BRRD, art 93.
224 BRRD, art 43–58.

A INEFFICIENCIES IN UNION-LEVEL RESOLUTION AFTER THE CRISIS

After the GFC, Member State governments carried out bailouts, such as in the Fortis case. Belgium, the Netherlands, and Luxembourg concentrated their respective intervention on the parts of the group that were most important for their markets. There was inefficiency and a very limited cooperation mechanism to maintain effective coordinated actions.[225]

After a couple of failed interventions, such as in the Kaupthing Singer & Friedlander case, the Member States decided to introduce their own resolution schemes.[226] The UK was the first one with the enactment of the Bank Act 2009, inspired by the FDIC Improvement Act (FDICIA) of 1991. Germany also adopted a new Restructuring Act in 2011, introducing a new restructuring regime for German banks which would enable the 'Bundesanstalt für Finanzdienstleistungsaufsicht' (Bafin) to have more powers in intervention and restructuring of failing banks so that the losses would not be borne by the taxpayers.[227]

The basic problem of the Member State-based intervention and resolution mechanism is the lack of sufficient cross-border coordinated action. The critical functions banks play, their special financial structure, and their extent of inter-nationalisation require them to be resolved in a coordinated manner to avoid adverse effects arising in the international financial markets.[228] While the business of universal banks is operated at the global level and on a cross-border basis, the lack of a special resolution procedure to deal with their failures in a unitary or coordinated manner is lethal to the banking industry when distress happens.[229] In the crisis in the EU, in the absence of a unitary resolution mechanism, every Member State dealt only with their own bank failures, while ignoring the importance of collective action. This led to unavoidable disruptive externalities within the given context of an extremely integrated European banking industry.[230] Thus, the banking crisis escalated into a severe sovereign crisis and then into the overall economic crisis.[231]

225 Avgouleas, *Governance of global financial markets: the law, the economics, the politics*, p. 251.
226 KSFIOM Depositors Action Group, 'HM Treasury June 2012: events leading up to the failure of Kaupthing Singer & Friedlander Limited. Extracts from HM Treasury's report on the failure of KSF (UK)', www.ksfiomdag.com/news-menu/newsflash/1244-hm-treasury-june-2012-events-leading-up-to-the-failure-of-kaupthing-singer-a-friedlander-limited, accessed December 30, 2014.
227 Trennbankengesetz (German Bank Separation Law), which is included in Article 2 of the 'Gesetz zur Abschirmung von Risiken und zur Planung der Sanierung und Abwicklung von Kreditinstituten und Finanzgruppen' (law concerning separation of risks and restructuring and winding-up of credit institutions and financial groups), BGBl. 2013 I Nr. 47, 3090.
228 Hüpkes, 'Insolvency: why a special regime for banks?', see also Schillig, 'Bank resolution regimes in Europe: recovery and resolution planning, early intervention, resolution tools and powers', pp. 4–7.
229 Avgouleas, *Governance of global financial markets: the law, the economics, the politics*, p. 253.
230 The EU banking industry was highly interconnected and integrated due to the universal banking model as well as the great reliance on wholesale funding sources; see Liikanen Erkki, *High-level Expert Group on reforming the structure of the EU banking sector*, p. 13. See also European Central Bank, *Report on financial integration in Europe*, pp. 30–36.
231 Rosalind Z. Wiggins, Natalia Tente, and Andrew Metrick, 'Cross-border resolution: Dexia Group', pp. 8–9.

Therefore, the following analyses of the resolution will be conducted mainly from the perspective of whether the new rules establish a unitary or internationally coordinated resolution mechanism.

B THE BRRD: A MEMBER STATE-BASED RESOLUTION REGIME WITH COORDINATION

Even since 2010, the EC has proposed an EU framework for a bank resolution fund.[232] In this proposal the power would still be left with the Member States'. But it would ensure that common tools in Member State resolution authorities could be used in a coordinated manner to allow for prompt action in the event of a bank failure, to protect the overall financial system and ensure a level playing field.[233] Different from any other Member State resolution reform, or reforms by other jurisdictions, the EC has to fight for cross-border bank resolution at the Union level.

However, the political obstacles for this are huge. The reluctance of Member States to give up their sovereignty in bank resolution to the Union forced the EC to fight merely for more coordination and harmonisation in resolution on the consensus that the basic resolution powers would still be reserved within the Member States' mandate.[234]

The EC had been pushing through a legislative project to harmonise resolution powers across the EU Member States in a gradual process until the BRRD was finally adopted in April 2014. The following analysis shows that as harmonisation-oriented legislation for a Member State-based resolution regime, its efficiency is in serious doubt in reality,[235] although it can make a contribution to the coordination of bank resolution in the EU.

(a) **Multiple resolution authorities.** The BRRD requires that each Member State shall designate one or more resolution authorities if necessary under special circumstances.[236] A justified resolution authority would normally be a central bank, a competent ministry, a public administrative authority, or an authority entrusted with administrative powers. Thus, all the NRAs are supposed to cooperate in terms of international banks.

To ensure the designated resolution authorities' competency in carrying out the resolution function in a more efficient way, the Directive also stipulates that Member States can require the competent authorities to cooperate closely with regard to the preparation, planning, and implementation of any resolution.[237] Although the resolution would be implemented at the Member State level rather

---

232 European Commission, *Communication from the Commission to the European Parliament, the Council, the European Economic and Social Committee and the European Central Bank: Bank Resolution Funds, COM(2010) 254 final* (May 26, 2010)

233 Ibid.

234 Ibid.

235 George S. Zavvos, and Stella Kaltsouni, 'The Single Resolution Mechanism in the European Banking Union: legal foundation, governance structure and financing'. This paper was published as a separate chapter in Matthias Haentjens and Bob Wessels (eds), *Research Handbook on Crisis Management in the Banking Sector* (Cheltenham, UK: Edward Elgar 2015).

236 BRRD, art 3.

237 BRRD, art 3(3).

than the EU level, a decision taken by the resolution authority should take into account the impact of an ongoing resolution on all other Member States where the institution or group operates so that any negative effects can be minimised.[238]

(b) **Three steps to resolution and the multiple point of entry.** According to the resolution regime in the BRRD, it starts with multiple point entry in a three-step process. As alluded to above, the three steps it offers to tackle failing banks are: recovery and resolution planning; early intervention; and resolution. Each step is to be maintained and carried out on a multiple point entry basis.[239]

First, recovery and resolution plans should be prepared both at the institution level and the group level.[240] The Directive specifically emphasises that a union undertaking should also set up a group recovery plan and submit it to the consolidating supervisor.[241] That group recovery plan shall identify measures not only for the union parent undertaking, but also for each of its subsidiaries. This means that, at the end of the day, when the measures are implemented, they are to be carried out on a multiple point basis.[242] Resolution plans should also be prepared both at the institution level and the group level by the resolution authorities.[243] The plans should identify measures not only for the group undertaking, but also for its subsidiaries, parent-holding entities either in the EU or in Member States, and branches in third countries.

The second step in the BRRD, early intervention, is also to be maintained and carried out on a multiple point entry basis.[244] The decision of an early intervention for a Union parent undertaking is to be decided by the consolidating supervisor; however, NCAs can decide on its subsidiaries' early intervention. Were the intervention to be carried out in more than one institution in the same group, a joint decision would be needed.[245]

The third step is resolution and its cross-border coordination mechanism, which is still within the reserved mandate of Member States. The Directive empowers the resolution authorities to trigger the resolution mechanism when the conditions are met. That is, an institution is failing or likely to fail, while there is no reasonable prospect that any possible private measure could be of help to tackle the situation, and the resolution would be in the public benefit.[246] It also empowers the NRAs to resolve all relevant subsidiaries, parent holding companies, and even branches of the institution based in a third country. For the sake of cross-border issues in the resolution process, it provides the mechanism of the

---

238 BRRD, art 3(7).
239 Financial Stability Board, *Recovery and resolution planning for systemically important financial institutions: guidance on developing effective resolution strategies* (July 16, 2013), pp. 17–18.
240 The analysis of the recovery framework in detail is presented in Section 4.2.
241 BRRD, art 7.
242 Ibid.
243 BRRD, art 12.
244 BRRD, art 27.
245 BRRD, art 29(4).
246 BRRD, art 31 and art 32.

Resolution College to improve cooperation and coordination between relevant NRAs to enhance consistency and efficiency in both recovery and resolution.[247]

With regard to third countries, it also provides the mechanism of the European Resolution College to enhance coordination between Member States' resolution authorities and resolution authorities of third countries where a third country parent undertaking has union subsidiaries or branches established in more than two Member States.[248] Apart from this, according to Article 218 of Treaty on the Functioning of the European Union (TFEU), the EC shall advocate proposals to the Council for the negotiation of agreements with third countries on cooperation.[249]

If these measures were to be carried out, they would be implemented involving all the group entities, subsidiaries, branches, and parent holding companies. Thus, with such multiple points of entry in planning and resolution, unitary action in reality seems to be extremely difficult within the international context.

(c) **Resolution tools.** The tools offered in the BRRD seem to correspond with the features of an efficient resolution mechanism provided by the FSB: that losses are to be internally absorbed.[250] However, the employment of these tools on a multiple point of entry basis would still face the problem of a lack of coordination between each unit. This would compromise the effectiveness of a resolution, especially in an internationalised firm.[251]

There are four resolution tools provided in the Directive: (i) the sale of the business; (ii) the bridge institution; (iii) the asset separation tool; and (iv) the bail-in tool.[252] In terms of efficiency, the bail-in tool is of critical importance. The purpose of the bail-in tool in the Directive is to tackle the failing bank problem in accordance with a new international trend. That is, if neither the taxpayers nor the depositors absorb the losses, they might have to be absorbed to the largest extent possible by the shareholders and the creditors, which could make the banking system self-insured.[253]

With regard to the self-insurance bail-in tool, what is noteworthy is that it introduces the MREL requirement to ensure there are sufficient bail-inable assets in an institution. It is required that each firm should maintain a minimum requirement for own funds and eligible liabilities. The minimum requirement is calculated by the quantity of the firm's own funds, which is a percentage of the firms' liabilities and its own funds. The requirement would be determined based on many factors:[254] the need to ensure that the firm could be resolved properly by the resolution tools including the bail-in tool to meet the resolution objectives;

---

247 BRRD, art 88.
248 BRRD, art 94.
249 BRRD, art 93.
250 Jim Brunsden and Rebecca Christie, 'German push to accelerate bank bail-ins joined by Dutch'.
251 Financial Stability Board, *Key attributes of effective resolution regimes for financial institutions*, p. 9.
252 BRRD, art 37.
253 BRRD, art 43.
254 Ibid.

the firm has sufficient eligible liabilities for the application of the bail-in tool so that the losses could be properly absorbed; the firm's size; and the firm's business model, among others.[255]

But it should be noted that the minimum requirement laid down should be complied with on a multiple point entry basis, which is at both the consolidated level and the subsidiary level. At both levels, the consolidating authority and the resolution authorities for the subsidiaries should reach joint decisions, in the absence of which respective decisions could be made at the EBA's discretion upon request.[256]

(d) **Resolution financial arrangement – Member State level.** According to the Directive, all Member States are supposed to set up their own independent resolution funds on an ex-ante basis so that the aforementioned resolution tools and powers can be applied in an effective way. But the Directive allows any Member State to set up its own financial arrangements that are not controlled by the resolution authority, provided that NRAs are still entitled to an amount no less than the required level.

Before any comment on the sufficiency of the resolution fund (1% of total deposits before December 31, 2024), the noteworthy part is that the operation of the financial arrangement is still at the Member State level through both the ex-ante and ex-post contributions.[257] The only cooperation possible between different resolution authorities is through the rule about borrowing from different financing arrangements.[258]

From the Member State-based resolution authorities to the multiple point basis in the application of the resolution tools, and from both the institution and the group level of recovery and resolution plans to the Member State-based financial arrangements, it is undeniable that the BRRD lacks many necessary features of an effective SPE (Single Point of Entry) resolution mechanism. Instead, it shares most of the features of a MPE (Multiple Point of Entry) resolution mechanism.[259] Its complicated cross-border relations are still a big challenge to the framework's efficiency.

Building on this discussion of the EU resolution framework and its fragmented features, the following section analyses the theoretical differences between SPE and MPE, and suggests the desirability for an SPE strategy in the EU.

4.3.2 The choice between SPE and MPE

The current resolution strategy includes basically two kinds: SPE and MPE.[260] There are many current scholarships analysing the advantages and disadvantages

---

255 BRRD, art 45.
256 BRRD, art 45(7)–(10).
257 BRRD, art 103 and art 104.
258 BRRD, art 106.
259 Financial Stability Board, *Recovery and resolution planning for systemically important financial institutions: guidance on developing effective resolution strategies*, pp. 14–19.
260 Paul L. Davies, 'Resolution of cross-border banking groups', pp. 2–4.

of each one. Some might advocate a case-to-case choice between them according to different situations and suitability analyses. Before any conclusion can be reached, a detailed analysis on the two approaches is needed.[261]

As a resolution strategy, SPE denotes the following features: (i) the application of a resolution plan at the top parent firm or at the holding company level by a single resolution authority; (ii) the resolution would be with only one single resolution authority – normally, it would be the one in charge of the consolidating supervision; (iii) the measures to be taken are usually bail-in, write down, and conversion of unsecured debts at the top parent and holding company level; and (iv) the result, if the Loss Absorbency Capacity (LAC) is sufficient, is that it would keep the operational units from being disrupted so that each of them could continue functioning as a going concern.[262]

In contrast, the MPE strategy takes a different approach to resolving a failing bank:[263] (i) the resolution procedure applies to all different units of the firm; (ii) the subject of the resolution is more than one authority in different jurisdictions, so the firm would be broken up into several parts to a certain extent and the group would be split on a national or regional basis or according to different business lines, for example; (iii) the measures used for the resolution process would be tools such as the bail-in tool, bridge company, transfer of business, etc. and they would not necessarily be the same in different parts of the failing firm; and (iv) the result, due to the existence of more than two authorities being in charge of the resolution plan, would be that it would be necessary to ensure that a coordinated mechanism is put in place to avoid conflicts and inconsistencies.

With regard to the choice and the suitability of the two approaches, many advocate that there is really not an absolute either-or choice, rather they are two ends of a complicated spectrum.[264] Their advantages and disadvantages would depend on the circumstances and conditions of the firm. For instance, if most of the debt exposures in the group were located in the top parent undertaking, and there were also not many obstacles to impede the implementation of resolution, then SPE would be the best way forward because there is no need to drag the whole group into resolution. However, if a group has a more disintegrated structure with more independent parts and the LAC in the group level is also not sufficient to absorb the losses, then MPE would be a better option.[265]

---

261 Financial Stability Board, *Recovery and resolution planning for systemically important financial institutions: guidance on developing effective resolution strategies.*
262 Ibid.
263 Bank of England and Federal Deposit Insurance Company, *Resolving globally active, systemically important, financial institutions, a joint paper by the Federal Deposit Insurance Corporation and the Bank of England* (December 10, 2012), pp. 9–10.
264 Financial Stability Board, *Recovery and resolution planning for systemically important financial institutions: guidance on developing effective resolution strategies.*
265 Ibid, pp. 12–13.

According to the analyses of the FSB, SPE would be suitable under the following situations:[266] (i) the top parent or holding company would be subject to resolution; the operational subsidiaries and their affiliates that should remain unaltered would need to be identified; (ii) there are sufficient resolution tools and powers at their disposal, such as the write down of the equity and debts of the parent or holding company, or the conversion of the debts of the parent and holding company into the equities of the recapitalised entity; (iii) there is sufficient LAC available at the top or holding company level to facilitate resolution without causing unnecessary instability; (iv) losses that are incurred by subsidiaries could be effectively transferred to the top parent or holding company level where the LAC locates, and there are no practical impediments to the write down or conversion of the LAC of the parent, and the LAC should be of a high quality – for instance, it should not be concentrated within other financial firms, where write down and conversion could cause further instability; (v) there is a financial structure with up-streaming losses and down-streaming capital, and there are no legal, regulatory, accounting, and tax impediments to prevent the parent company from assuming the losses of the operating subsidiaries or down-streaming resources generated through bail-in at the parent company level to such subsidiaries; and (vi) home and host authorities cooperate with each other in regard to the implementation of the resolution, whereby host authorities identify the conditions under which they would be prepared to refrain from taking action and rely on the home authorities to implement an SPE resolution.[267]

The MPE strategy, however, is suitable under the following conditions and situations according to the analyses by the FSB:[268] (i) it is possible to identify the points at which resolution is likely to occur, and the operational subsidiaries and their affiliates that should remain unaltered should also be included in the resolution considerations; (ii) there are sufficient resolution tools and powers at their disposal, such as the write down of equities and debts, or the conversion of debts, such that the MPE strategy can identify the methods that are likely to be used at each point of entry to resolve that entity and any sub-group beneath it; (iii) instead of losses being absorbed at the parent and holding company level, each legal entity that has been identified as subject to a separate resolution action should have sufficient LAC to cover its own losses in resolution and those of the subsidiaries below it; (iv) group entities are able to fund themselves on a stand-alone basis, which requires all entities to be financially more independent than under SPE; (v) group operations have independent infrastructure, IT, employees, or other critical services without relying on other group entities; (vi) local operations have sufficient independent legal and operational structures, i.e. effective stand-alone governance and management arrangements;[269] and (vii) home and

---

266 Ibid.
267 Davies, 'Resolution of cross-border banking groups', pp. 10–15.
268 Financial Stability Board, *Recovery and resolution planning for systemically important financial institutions: guidance on developing effective resolution strategies.*
269 Ibid.

host authorities at their points of entry into resolution have the required resolution powers and operational tools to carry out their resolution strategies and coordinate their actions with one another to avoid conflicts and competition for assets between different proceedings.

B PREFERENCE IS DIFFERENT FROM SUITABILITY

In terms of choosing between the two, the choice seems to be contingent on circumstances and facts. In other words, it seems that the answer of suitability is more neutral and conditionally depends on the situation.[270] Be that as it may, the concept of preference is different from suitability. The former refers to choice-making based on a given situation, but the latter refers to the ideal choice based on a controllable situation. It implies the preferred option, not necessarily the situation-suitable one. What should be considered here is preference rather than suitability. And the answer of preference could be different, if the situation is controllable.[271]

Should all the conditions permit, and through a comparison within an isolated context, SPE would be more preferable because it smartly avoids the cross-border coordination problem by unitarily applying the resolution procedure at the group level and leaves the remaining units unaltered to the greatest possible extent. Therefore, if regulatory agencies were to give some regulatory incentives and enough legal prodding, or come up with some requirements to let most firms intentionally fall under the conditions of SPE resolution ex-ante, then SPE would be a better choice should resolution conditions be met in the future.[272]

In Switzerland, the Swiss Financial Market Supervisory Authority (FINMA) believes that SPE is the best suitable resolution approach for its two systemically important banks. The two banks are globally active as highly integrated institutions with concentrated funding and a wide scope of business lines. To be prepared for resolution should the conditions be met, both banks have subordinated and senior unsecured debt at the parent level. These equate to 30 to 40% of their risk weighted assets, on top of its 19% capital ratio once the Swiss capital regime for these banks is fully phased in by 2019.[273]

---

270 Institute of International Finance, *FDIC's Notice and Request for Comments on the Resolution of Systemically Important Financial Institutions: The Single Point of Entry Strategy (FR Docket No. 2013–30057)* (February 18, 2014). Apart from the FSB's neutral position on the preference of SPE and MPE, the IIF also suggested in the comments that the SPE approach should not be the exclusive resolution approach. But, it also insisted that clarity on the preferred path could help firms and investors in dealing with risk on the occasion of a failure.

271 Davies, 'Resolution of cross-border banking groups'. Paul Davies holds the view that 'only in the case of an actual multinational bank failure will the power or weakness of the SPE model become fully apparent'. He does not negate the merits of SPE, but suggests the preferred approach is MPE based on the argument that the notorious low trust and lack of international coordination problem cannot be overcome overnight.

272 Bank of England and Federal Deposit Insurance Company, *Resolving Globally active, systemically important, financial institutions, a joint paper by the Federal Deposit Insurance Corporation and the Bank of England*, p. 14.

273 FINMA, *Resolution of global systemically important banks-FINMA position paper on Resolution of G-SIBs* (August 7, 2013), p. 7.

4.3.3 The SPE in the US and the UK: good examples

To handle the banks' failure crisis and implement the FSB's 'Key attributes of effective resolution regimes for financial institutions' in 2011, and the FSB's 'Recovery and resolution planning for systemically important financial institutions: guidance on developing effective resolution strategies' in 2013, many jurisdictions have come up with new reform initiatives and even legislation. Compared with the former bailout and non-satisfactory bankruptcy cases in the EU and the US, such as Dexia and Lehman Brothers, SPE is a totally new resolution strategy.[274]

This new strategy is to set up a mechanism so that the losses of failing firms could ultimately be absorbed by the shareholders and unsecured creditors to avoid externality due to the failing of banks. On the one hand, the strategy is intended to swiftly resolve the failing banks while preserving the critical functions and services that they normally offer to the financial markets and the real economy, thereby minimising systemic risk; on the other, it ensures that the financial stability would be successfully maintained during this process.[275]

The main features and conditions under which carrying out an SPE is suitable are discussed above. In summary, there are three points underpinning the new SPE strategy in a resolution:[276]

(1) The resolution should be done on a top-down basis, applying the resolution tools to the top of a group by a SRA, instead of applying the resolution tool to many different parts of the group by two or more resolution authorities in a possibly difficult coordinated manner.
(2) The recapitalising measures: the SPE's efficient way of addressing the losses in a firm is to write down a part of the equities of shareholders and convert unsecured creditors' assets into equities at the group level.
(3) To support the resolution and its measures, normally a bail-inable capital structure and backup fund should be ready.

The result would be that the operating subsidiaries on a cross-border basis would be basically and mostly intact so that the authorities could successfully preserve their continuity and let them provide critical services and functions as usual.[277]

In an overview of the major economies, it seems both the US and the UK have made some progress in adopting the SPE approach with the aforementioned features. In the UK, ever since the outbreak of the GFC, the Bank Reform Act

---

274 Basel Committee on Banking Supervision, *Report and recommendations of the Cross-border Bank Resolution Group*, (March 2010). pp. 10–14.
275 Bank of England and Federal Deposit Insurance Company, *Resolving Globally active, systemically important, financial institutions, a joint paper by the Federal Deposit Insurance Corporation and the Bank of England*, pp. 1–5.
276 Ibid.
277 Banking Act 2009(UK), ss9 and 13.

2009 has empowered the BOE with tools and mandates to resolve any failing deposit-taking institutions. It would basically transfer a part of the failing firm to a private sector purchaser or a bridge company.[278] In the Financial Service Act 2013, it expanded the application of the resolution procedure in the Bank Reform Act 2009 for non-deposit-taking institutions to include investment banks and financial market infrastructures.[279]

Such a mechanism was also established in the US with the adoption of the Dodd-Frank Act and a series of further FDIC reforms regarding the mandate of the OLA established under Title II of the Act to allow orderly liquidation of banks.[280] This greatly enhanced the ability of regulators to address the failure of banks in a future crisis, similar to what happened in 2008.[281]

A THE RESOLUTION APPROACH IN THE US

On December 10, 2013, the FDIC proposed for public comment a notice on its SPE strategy for resolving SIFIs that are failing or likely to fail.[282] The notice is a follow-up reform to the establishment of the OLA under Title II of the Dodd-Frank Act. The Notice seconded the FDIC's original stance towards the SPE strategy made in 2012 in its joint paper issued with the BOE.[283]

Title I of Dodd-Frank Act requires all covered firms to prepare 'living wills', to arm themselves with ex-ante measures on how they would be resolved orderly and efficiently under the Bankruptcy Code or other applicable insolvency rules in the event of a material crisis. By Title I, the statute makes bankruptcy the preferred resolution mechanism in the event of a bank failure, but it also admits that a SIFI might not be resolvable only by applying the bankruptcy procedure without posing an adverse effect and systemic risk to the entire economy. Therefore, in Title II, it provides the resolution mechanism as a backup resort.

In Title II of the Dodd-Frank Act, it basically empowers the FDIC to have the necessary measures to resolve a firm at its disposal. The FDIC would appoint a receiver for a qualifying firm in default or likely to default.[284] Furthermore, it pointed out that 'all financial companies put into receivership under this title shall

---

278 Banking Act 2009(UK), ss9 and 13.
279 See generally Financial Services reform 2013.
280 See Federal Deposit Insurance Corporation, *Resolution of Systemically Important Financial Institutions: The Single Point of Entry Strategy, Reg. 243*, pp. 76614–76624. The FDIC's 'Request for Comments' notice was publicised through the Federal Register, by which the FDIC adopted what has come to be known as the SPE approach to implement the OLA and its resolution procedure under Title II of the Act.
281 Bipartisan Policy Center, *Too Big to Fail: the path to a solution* (May 2013), pp. 23–33.
282 Federal Deposit Insurance Corporation, *Resolution of systemically important financial institutions: the single point of entry strategy, Reg. 243*, pp. 76614–76624.
283 Bank of England and Federal Deposit Insurance Company, *Resolving Globally active, systemically important, financial institutions, a joint paper by the Federal Deposit Insurance Corporation and the Bank of England*, pp. 3–4.
284 12 U.S.C. §§ 5382. Dodd-Frank Act, section 203.

be liquidated, no taxpayer funds shall be used to prevent the liquidation of any financial companies under this title', and 'the taxpayer shall bear no losses from the exercise of any authority under this title'.[285]

Specifically, it stipulates that the FDIC would act as the receiver of the top parent of a financial group under the condition of failure. The mechanism includes the following main features underpinning the resolution strategy: (i) a bridge company would be set up; the FDIC would transfer assets into the bridge financial holding corporation, and then, by receiving funding from the top parent company of the financial group, its main subsidiaries would be basically kept intact. Thus, they can probably still function normally and provide the critical financial services and critical functions to the real economy;[286] (ii) in order to recapitalise the firm and restructure the debts, the FDIC would focus on the insubordinate debts or even senior unsecured debts to secure capital sources, the claims of the debt holder partly being converted into equities;[287] and (iii) in the case where instant capital is not available, the Dodd-Frank Act also provides access to the Orderly Liquidation Fund (OLF) for the failing bank and the Bridgeco, either through a direct cash infusion from the OLF, or through the guarantee of new debt obligations issued by the Bridgeco.[288]

The SPE strategy is expected to achieve two goals, which it turned out to be capable of doing.[289] The first is to carry out the Dodd-Frank mandate of dealing with unresolvable banks. To achieve this end, the management of the covered failed bank may be replaced; shareholders would be wiped out; creditors would bear the losses; and taxpayers would bear no losses. The second goal is to prevent a disruptive effect on the entire financial system.[290]

B THE RESOLUTION APPROACH IN THE UK

The provisions in the Bank Act 2009 and the Financial Service Act 2013 also provide a top-down resolution process. The BOE and FDIC joint paper issued on December 10, 2012, 'Resolving globally active, systemically important, financial institutions' explicitly accepted the SPE strategy.

The SPE approach focuses on resolution and restructuring measures. Based on the UK legislative reforms, there is not necessarily a bridge company to be set up, although it is also an option for resolution. Normally the equity

---

285 12 U.S.C. § 5384. Dodd-Frank Act, section 204(a).
286 Dodd-Frank Act, section 210(h).
287 Federal Deposit Insurance Corporation, *Resolution of systemically important financial institutions: the single point of entry strategy, Reg. 243*, pp. 76614–76624.
288 Dodd-Frank Act, section 210(h). See also Jeffrey N. Gordon and Wolf-Georg Ringe, 'Bank resolution in the European Banking Union: a transatlantic perspective on what it would take', Oxford Legal Research Paper Series Paper No 18/2014.
289 H. Rodgin Cohen (Sullivan & Cromwell LLP), 'SPOE resolution strategy for SIFIs under Dodd-Frank,' http://blogs.law.harvard.edu/corpgov/2014/01/17/spoe-resolution-strategy-for-sifis-under-dodd-frank/, accessed January 20, 2015.
290 Skeel, 'Single point of entry and the bankruptcy alternative'.

and debt securities would be transferred to a trustee before a valuation can be reached, the conclusion of which would be to determine the extent to which the losses should be absorbed in order to recapitalise the firm.[291] The trustee would hold the securities. When the valuation process is completed, the extent of the losses to be incurred by the firm would be determined, and the recapitalisation requirement would also be decided. Once the recapitalisation requirement has been determined, there would be an announcement on the bail-in terms to the securities' holders. This would be the preparatory process for the write down and conversion.

Debt securities would be written down and unsecured debts would be converted into equities. The loans from the parent to its subsidiaries would normally be written down to ensure the subsidiaries remain viable. Eventually, after the write down and conversion process, the equities from the trustee would be transferred to the original creditors.[292]

If the firm does not have enough debts at the holding company or parent bank level to be converted in the recapitalisation process, the DGS would also be brought into play.[293] If market-based funding is not available, temporary funding may be able to be provided by the authorities to meet the firm's liquidity needs. However, the funds could only be accessible on a fully collateralised basis.

The SPE in the UK also concentrates on minimising the cross-border coordination risk and maintaining financial stability. Unlike the US capital structure of financial holding companies characterised by equities and large amounts of unsecured debts of various maturities (which will be discussed in detail below), the financial holding company at the top in the UK often does not have a significant proportion of the group's unsecured debts. Thus, the SPE strategy also means that the UK groups should restructure so that more debts are issued by holding companies.[294]

After the adoption of the BRRD, as a member of the EU, the UK is obliged to transpose it into UK law. Thus, from this perspective, the UK resolution regime would largely be influenced by the EU resolution regime.[295]

4.3.4 The SPE and its advantages compared with the MPE in the EU

From the above analyses, it can be discovered that although the EU, the US, and the UK share some similarities with regard to the resolution powers and tools (bridge company, bail-in, sale of assets), the strategy in the EU is different. This can directly impact the effectiveness of the resolution mechanism. Compared

---

291 Banking Act 2009 (UK), ss12, 30, and 31.
292 Banking Act 2009: revised special resolution regime code of practice, s5.
293 Banking Act 2009 (UK), s169.
294 Bank of England and Federal Deposit Insurance Company, *Resolving globally active, systemically important, financial institutions, a joint paper by the Federal Deposit Insurance Corporation and the Bank of England*, pp. 9–13.
295 Financial Services and Markets, The Bank Recovery and Resolution (No. 2) Order 2014, 2014 No. 3348.

with the MPE in the BRRD, considerable progress has been made in the US and the UK with regard to setting up the SPE frameworks for recovery and resolution in their respective legislations.

According to the key attributes of the FSB, there are many elements which are imperative for the effectiveness of a resolution regime, such as resolution powers, resolution tools, and a framework for cooperation.[296] In this section, the advantages and disadvantages of both strategies will be discussed.

A THE CONCERNS OVER THE EU MPE

Apart from lacking resolution authorities, powers, and tools to resolve failing banks, the failure of banks like Lehman Brothers left at least two critical issues which are not addressed by the EU MPE strategy.[297]

The first concern is the susceptibility of derivatives and short-term credit to run.[298] When financial distress emerges, short-term credit is susceptible to run, and it can trigger a destructive influence on valuations. Market confidence can be destroyed as a result of any unprepared liquidation. It could finally trigger concerns about systemic risk. In fact, AIG's inability to stop such a run was a major factor in its chaotic liquidation. That is why the FSB deems avoiding unnecessary destruction of value to be one of the core features of a successful resolution regime.[299]

With the EU resolution mechanism under the BRRD in place, the value destruction effect can still be very likely to happen for two reasons: (i) not enough protection for the short-term funding; and (ii) the non-concentrated location of the LAC.[300]

First, unlike the US rule, the protection for the short-term creditor is not sufficient in the BRRD. The US rule protects the group of unsecured creditors, relating to derivatives and other short-term debts, but mostly restructures the long-term debts.[301] By the adoption of the SPE strategy, the FDIC reserves the power to change ordinary priorities and make the protection of short-term debts more predictable. The FDIC's discretionary powers allows room for disparate

---

296 Financial Stability Board, *Key attributes of effective resolution regimes for financial institutions*, pp. 1–2.

297 Federal Deposit Insurance Corporation, 'The orderly liquidation of Lehman Brothers Holdings Inc. under the Dodd-Frank Act', www.fdic.gov/bank/analytical/quarterly/2011_vol5_2/lehman.pdf, accessed November 15, 2014. The two concerns are also briefly referred to in Section 2.3.1.

298 Skeel, 'Single point of entry and the bankruptcy alternative', pp. 4–6. See also supra Chapter 6, Section 2.3.1.

299 Financial Stability Board, *Key attributes of effective resolution regimes for financial institutions*, pp. 1–2.

300 Jeffrey N. Gordon and Wolf-Georg Ringe, 'Bank resolution in europe: the unfinished agenda of structural reform', in Danny Busch and Guido Ferrarini (eds), *The European Banking Union* (2015); European Corporate Governance Institute (ECGI) – Law Working Paper No 282/2015; Columbia Law and Economics Working Paper No 507, p. 9.

301 Skeel, 'Single point of entry and the bankruptcy alternative', p. 10.

treatment provided that such action is necessary to continue operations essential to the receivership or the bridge financial company, or to maximise the possibility of recovery. Such a decision needs to be made by the board of directors of the FDIC. Each creditor affected by such treatment must receive at least the amount he/she would have received if the FDIC had not been appointed as the receiver. This alleviates any anxiety over a possible bank run.[302]

In the BRRD, the protection of creditors is different. Insured deposits (up to EUR100,000), are protected by deposit guarantee schemes.[303] Deposits that exceed the insurable amount may be given priority over other unsecured credit claims under the 'deposits preference' principle. In contrast, many other sources of short-term funding of a bank or its financial affiliates are not given special protection. If a bank finds itself in a negative, this could directly ignite the investors' fury and trigger a bank run.

Second, the LAC is to be positioned at the subsidiary level, based on the FSB guidelines on the features of the MPE.[304] This is exactly the same as in the BRRD, in that requirements such as MREL need to be complied with at both the group level but also at the subsidiary level, so that each institution or subsidiary could be independently resolved if necessary.[305] It should be noted that such an arrangement to place not just capital but also subordinated debt on the balance sheet at the subsidiary level rather than the group parent level creates a lot of extra difficulties for coordinating a resolution. Such a strategy is highly unlikely to facilitate efficient resolution in reality.[306]

Other concerns over the failure of the banks, such as Lehman Brothers, that could have been more effectively addressed in the BRRD are the spill over effect and the cross-border issue, especially the issue of cooperation.[307] Strengthening cooperation is also another critical feature of an effective resolution regime stressed by the FSB in 2011.[308] It turned out that some of the most destructive consequences of Lehman's failure happened outside the US. Because of the loss of quick access to funds in Lehman's cash scheme, several subsidiaries in Asia failed, which also triggered the failures of several hedge funds after Lehman's London subsidiary was placed in trustee custody.[309] In the BRRD, the existence of the Resolution College and the European Resolution College is not sufficient to be an efficient cooperation mechanism, neither can it lead to unitary actions in resolution.[310] Thus, the provisions of

302 Federal Deposit Insurance Corporation, *Resolution of systemically important financial institutions: the single point of entry strategy, Reg. 243*, pp. 76614–76624, p. 76622.
303 BRRD, art 109.
304 Financial Stability Board, *Key attributes of effective resolution regimes for financial institutions*, pp. 7–16.
305 BRRD, art 45.
306 Jeffrey N. Gordon and Wolf-Georg Ringe, 'Bank resolution in the European Banking Union: a transatlantic perspective on what it would take', pp. 3–11.
307 Skeel, 'Single point of entry and the bankruptcy alternative', see also supra Chapter 6, Section 2.3.1.
308 Financial Stability Board, *Key attributes of effective resolution regimes for financial institutions*, pp. 1–2.
309 Skeel, 'Single point of entry and the bankruptcy alternative', p. 6.
310 BRRD, art 89 and art 91.

resolution based on the MPE strategy would leave the spill over effect and the coordination problem still in existence.

The FSB does not suggest a clear preference between the SPE strategy and the MPE strategy. But it also points out that the MPE strategy could be a successful one for banking groups that operate in distinct units, with little integration between them. Only under that situation could they be resolved successfully. The FSB suggests that the MPE strategy is 'suitable for firms with a decentralised structure and greater financial, legal, and operational separation along national or regional lines; with sub-groups of relatively independent, capitalised, and separately funded subsidiaries'.[311] However, that is not the case for European banks, as they operate in the single market in a highly integrated way.[312]

B THE SPE STRATEGY CAN REMOVE THE CONCERNS

That said, based on the guidelines by the FSB's publications 'Key attributes of effective resolution regimes for financial institutions' in 2011, and 'Recovery and resolution planning for systemically important financial institutions: guidance on developing effective resolution strategies' in 2013, the SPE strategy has been advocated and adopted in the US and the UK. Based on the key features provided by the FSB, the SPE does have the following features that are intended to address the above two essential concerns (Figure 6.1).[313]

(a) **The measures at disposal to restructure failing entities.** In a top-down SPE resolution approach, the resolution entry point would be the top of a firm, the parent undertaking. Thus, the remaining units in the group, such as other operational subsidies and branches would be kept intact to preserve their continuity to a certain extent. In order to achieve that aim, it is quite imperative that there are sufficient restructuring measures at their disposal to tackle the losses at the top level, such as selling part of the group, breaking the group into different parts or closing some parts which are not essential to the function of the group and the provision of critical services.[314]

In the US legislation, for instance, the major consideration underpinning the resolution is the effective governance of the bridge financial corporation and the new corporation into which the bridge company would be transferred. The SPE strategy provides for the payment of creditors' claims in the receivership mainly

---

311 Financial Stability Board, *Recovery and resolution planning for systemically important financial institutions: guidance on developing effective resolution strategies*, pp. 1–2 and p. 13.

312 The issue of integration in the banking industry in the EU is discussed in Section 3.3.2.

313 Financial Stability Board, *Recovery and resolution planning for systemically important financial institutions: guidance on developing effective resolution strategies*, pp. 14–16. See also generally Financial Stability Board, *Recovery and resolution planning: make the key attributes requirements operational (Consultative Document)* (November 2012).

314 Bank of England and Federal Deposit Insurance Company, *Resolving globally active, systemically important, financial institutions, a joint paper by the Federal Deposit Insurance Corporation and the Bank of England*, p. 9.

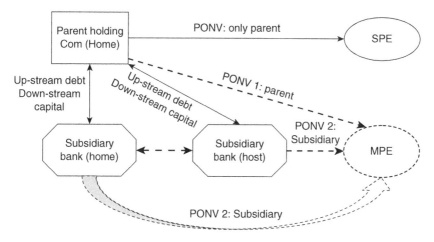

Figure 6.1 SPE strategy

through conversion: claims in exchange for securities in the NewCo.[315] There would be a newly appointed CEO for the company,[316] the shares would be written down, and the creditors would be converted into equity holders of the new firm. It is possible that the firm would be restructured after the FDIC starts the receivership. For example, the receiver could simplify it and make it less systemically significant. Through this process, the creditors, including the short-term creditors that are vulnerable to a bank run, can be protected in the best way.

In the UK legislation, however, normally the assets would be transferred to a trustee.[317] The extent to which it would be restructured would depend largely on the extent of the losses of the firm. If the losses only happen in one single business line, the restructuring is comparatively limited. If, however, the losses happen in different business lines, then the restructuring measures should be more systemic and comprehensive.

(b) The provision of the bail-in instrument. Bail-in is the essential part of the SPE resolution regime.[318] To make it effective, the pre-condition is that in the financial structure of the failing firm, there should be at least sufficient loss-absorbency capital available at the top level. That would not be a problem in the US due to the fact that most of the structures of US firms have the feature that the holding company owns the equities and most unsecured debts.[319] But that is not the same in the UK, where the holding company does not account for the most part of the debts in the group. Thus, for the regulatory and resolution concerns, there should be some legislative

---

315 Federal Deposit Insurance Corporation, *Resolution of systemically important financial institutions: the single point of entry strategy, Reg. 243*, pp. 76614–76624.
316 Dodd-Frank Act, section 204(h)(2)(B).
317 Banking Act 2009 (UK), s12 and ss30–31.
318 See supra Chapter 6, Section 3.1.2(4).
319 Bank of England and Federal Deposit Insurance Company, *Resolving globally active, systemically important, financial institutions, a joint paper by the Federal Deposit Insurance Corporation and the Bank of England*, p. 6.

changes in the future to rationalise the financial structures of firms.[320] In spite of this little shortcoming, the point to be made here is that through bail-in, the resolution process could, to a certain extent, internalise the losses of a failing bank.

(c) The stability of the financial markets. For all the choices of resolution strategy and approaches to be adopted, one of the most important objectives and considerations would always be enhancing financial stability.[321] A disorganised and protracted resolution process could be totally disastrous to the financial system as a whole and the overall economy. That has been proven by the disruptive effect of the Lehman Brothers' and Bear Stearns' collapses. To ensure financial stability, the failing firm should be able to safeguard its critical business and functions so they can be provided regularly without any disruption. The SPE applied in the US and the UK has the following two advantages.

The first advantage is that the internalisation of losses of the failing banks is made possible.[322] In the SPE approach there are two pillars ensuring the stability of market.[323] First, there is the mechanism of the up-streaming losses and debts (Figure 6.1). In other words, the losses of the subsidiaries could be absorbed at the top parent level of the financial group so that the business operation at the subsidiary level would not be affected. To recapitalise the firm and absorb the losses, the resolution authority could write down some of the shares and convert some unsecured debts into equities in a bridge company or the new firm to which the bridge company would be transferred. Another pillar is the down-streaming of capital and liquidity (Figure 6.1). In order to ensure the stability of the financial markets without giving rise to any disruptive effect, the SPE ensures that it is accessible for the subsidiaries to get capital from the top level to recapitalise and restructure them efficiently.

The prevailing Bank holding company model in the US is well suited to these conditions, in terms of both the up-streaming loss and equity and the down-streaming capital and liquidity. Thus, the subsidiaries of the failing firm would be kept intact, if the holding company or parent undertaking were to absorb all the losses. The advantage is described in the FDIC-BOE joint paper:[324]

> The strategies remove the need to commence foreign insolvency proceedings or enforce legal powers over foreign assets . . . Liquidity should continue to be down streamed from the holding company to foreign subsidiaries and branches. Given minimal disruption to operating entities,

320 Ibid, p. 13.
321 Financial Stability Board, *Key attributes of effective resolution regimes for financial institutions*, pp. 1–2.
322 Davies, 'Resolution of cross-border banking groups', pp. 2–4.
323 Financial Stability Board, *Recovery and resolution planning for systemically important financial institutions: guidance on developing effective resolution strategies*, p. 15.
324 Bank of England and Federal Deposit Insurance Company, *Resolving Globally active, systemically important, financial institutions, a joint paper by the Federal Deposit Insurance Corporation and the Bank of England and FDIC* (December 10, 2012), p. 11.

resolution authorities, directors, and creditors of foreign subsidiaries and branches should have little incentive to take action other than to cooperate with the implementation of the group resolution. In particular, host stakeholders should not have an incentive to ring fence assets or petition for a preemptive insolvency – preemptive actions that would otherwise destroy value and may disrupt markets at home and abroad.

Gordon and Ringe pointed out that the feature of the prevailing holding company structure in the US is critical to the successful implementation of an SPE.[325] They also pointed out that the emergence and prevalence of the Bank Holding Company (BHC) structure is not an ex-ante regulatory arrangement. Instead, it is a historical coincidence derived from the former regulatory mechanism.

As indicated in Chapter 1 about the liberalisation process, after the Great Depression in the twentieth century, the activities banks were allowed to engage in were narrowly defined.[326] Thus, the post-crisis crackdown on banks (mostly the Glass-Steagall Act) excluded them from committing to securities' underwriting or other investment bank activities.[327] These restrictions imposed on banks prompted them to find ways to bypass the regulations.[328] The emergence of the BHC served this objective very well. When analysing the development of the BHC and its intent to evade law, Jonathan Macey said that:[329]

> Like chain banking, group banking circumvented rules against branch banking. But group banking had three important advantages over chain banking. It provided better access to capital markets because the holding company could sell investors its own securities. It facilitated entry into nonbanking lines of business, directly, or through subsidiaries, because the holding company could engage in activities impermissible for banks themselves. It also facilitated centralised management because the holding company could oversee and guide the operations of all its subsidiaries.

A parent holding company could buy out banks in a particular geographic area, and through the subsidiaries within the group, it could provide equivalent activities (restricted activities). If the BHC structure was created to bypass regulation in the first place, the Bank Holding Company Act legitimated the BHC structure after constant lobbying by the industry. It stipulated that permitted subsidiaries of the BHC structure are supposed to be 'closely related to banking'.[330] Later, amid the background of the historical merger between Travellers Group and Citicorp

325 Jeffrey N. Gordon and Wolf-Georg Ringe, 'Bank resolution in the European Banking Union: a transatlantic perspective on what it would take', pp. 18–19.
326 The liberalisation process in the US and the UK is discussed in Chapter 1, Section 3(a).
327 See Banking Act of 1933, sections 16, 20, 21, and 32.
328 Richard Scott Carnell, Jonathan R. Macey, and Geoffrey P. Miller, *The law of banking and financial institutions* (Netherlands: Wolters Kluwer Law & Business 2009), pp. 16–27.
329 Ibid, pp. 17–18.

(a banking company), the Glass-Steagall restrictions were finally completely dismantled by the Gramm-Leach-Billey Financial Services Modernization Act of 1999.[331]

The second advantage is market confidence. Now that the failing financial group can be recapitalised in an orderly manner, the losses can basically be absorbed by shareholders and creditors. Thus, the counterparties would be mostly relieved as they would not have many incentives to trigger the termination right according to the default clause on the occasion of a resolution.[332] Likewise, there is also less possibility that depositors and short-term creditors would rush to collect debts and cause a bank run due to the fact that their concerns would be eradicated by the orderly resolution of the failing bank.

(d) Minimisation of cross-border coordination risk. The resolution process of a financial group can also be more complicated due to the cross-border factor. The good thing about the SPE strategy is the nearly total avoidance of any home and host coordination issues (Figure 6.1). As discussed earlier, there is the mechanism for the up-streaming of losses and the down-streaming of capital which could make it possible for the subsidiaries and the operating parts other than the holding company to be kept intact. That would definitely lessen the coordination risk on a cross-border basis. But even at the holding company level, there is still the possibility that the measures taken to recapitalise the firm would be related to home and host country coordination. The 'key attributes' of the FSB suggested many coordination mechanisms to enhance coordination, such as the institution-specific cooperation agreements (COAGs) and the crisis management group (CMG) requirement.[333] Thus, the coordination issue under the SPE would be minimised.

4.3.5 The SRM resolution framework: the MPE and its weaknesses

Building on the BRRD MPE resolution framework in the EU, this section focuses on the closely related and pro-EU resolution framework under the SRM regulation. The SRM is consistent with the BRRD, but it adopts a centralised decision-making process and is applicable only to significant institutions in the Euro area.[334] From the perspective of the EU, it also has a political wish to press on with the Union-level unitary regulation and supervision to break the definite link between sovereignty and a bank resolution mechanism.

---

330   See Bank Holding Company Act of 1956, Pub. L. No. 511, 70 Stat. 133. See also Avgouleas, *Governance of global financial markets: the law, the economics, the politics*, p. 69.

331   See Gramm-Leach-Billey Financial Services Modernization Act, Pub. L. No. 106–102, 113 Stat. 1338 (1999).

332   Bank of England and Federal Deposit Insurance Company, *Resolving globally active, systemically important, financial institutions, a joint paper by the Federal Deposit Insurance Corporation and the Bank of England*, p. 10.

333   Financial Stability Board, *Key attributes of effective resolution regimes for financial institutions*, pp. 13–14.

334   SRM regulation.

The EU legislators understand that resolution progress on the path to regulatory reform in the aftermath of the GFC is significantly important to deal with the TBTF bank structural problem, but they also lack sufficient resolution and concerted Member State incentives to build a unitary resolution framework. To harmonise the resolution mechanism in the EU, the EC proposed setting up the EBU in 2012 in an attempt to try to shift power from the Member State level to the Union level with regard to the regulation of the banking industry. Arguing for the necessity of the EBU, it said:[335]

> Coordination between supervisors is vital but the crisis has shown that mere coordination is not enough, in particular in the context of a single currency and that there is a need for common decision- making. It is also important to curtail the increasing risk of fragmentation of EU banking markets, which significantly undermines the single market for financial services and impairs the effective transmission of monetary policy to the real economy throughout the Euro area. The EC has therefore called for an EBU to place the banking sector on a more sound footing and restore confidence in the Euro as part of a longer-term vision for economic and fiscal integration.

Thus, in 2012, the EC proposed the building of a Single Supervision Mechanism (SSM) as a start of the EBU.[336] In March 2013, the European Parliament and the Council reached agreement with regard to the SSM and then the new SSM regulation was enacted, assigning the ECB the task of European bank supervision.[337] The SSM will be discussed further in the next section with regard to how it could impact the effectiveness of the resolution regime,[338] but this section will focus on the resolution mechanism.

Within the EBU proposal, other than the SSM, there is another important pillar to the RRP – the Single Resolution Mechanism (SRM) – which is deeply entrenched in the new EU regime (including three pillars: SSM, SRM, and DGS).[339] The discussion here with regard to the SPE and the MPE approaches aims to establish a self-insured banking industry which can absorb the losses by itself. The DGS would not be directly relevant and will not be discussed in detail in the book in this regard.

---

335 European Commission, *Communication from the Commission to the European Parliament and the Council: A Roadmap towards a Banking Union, COM(2012) 510 final*, p. 3. This legislative proposal was the first important step which signalled a huge improvement in enhancing financial stability and confidence in Europe.

336 European Commission, 'Proposal for a Council Regulation conferring specific tasks on the European Central Bank concerning policies relating to the prudential supervision of credit institutions, COM(2012) 511 final'.

337 Regulation (EU) No 1024/2013 of 15 October 2013 conferring specific tasks on the European Central Bank concerning policies relating to the prudential supervision of credit institutions [2013] OJ L 287/63 (SSM Regulation).

338 See infra Chapter 6, Section 4.3.6.

339 Rishi Goyal and others, *A banking union for the Euro area* (New York: International Monetary Fund 2013).

By establishing the EBU, the EC hopes that ensuring bank supervision and resolution across the Euro area would reassure citizens and the markets that a common, high level of prudential regulation is consistently applied to all banks. Besides, even if banks get into distress, the public should have the confidence that ailing banks would be restructured or wound down in an orderly manner while minimising costs to the taxpayers. The SSM and SRM will help build the necessary trust between Member States to support an orderly resolution of failing banks.

The SRM is applicable to the following entities: (i) credit institutions established in a participating Member State; (ii) parent undertakings established in a participating Member State and subject to the ECB consolidated supervision; and (iii) investment firms and financial institutions established in a participating Member State and covered by the ECB consolidated supervision.[340] According to Article 7(2), it de facto applies to: (i) 120 systemically important bank groups, deemed 'significant' in the EU, and (ii) about 200 'cross-border' groups in the participating area.[341]

A concise outline of the SRM for the EU financial entities is that: (i) a single resolution authority-single resolution board (SRB) would be established, which is empowered with all necessary tools and powers to carry out efficient resolution at the EU level rather than at Member State level;[342] (ii) the critical part of resolution powers and tools is the recapitalising capital available, to be achieved by a European Single Resolution Fund (SRF) being at the SRB's disposal, which would be financed by the financial sector through both ex-ante and ex-post levies based on the resolution fund in each Member State according to the BRRD requirements;[343] the regulation also provides for voluntary borrowing between resolution financial arrangements, alternative funding means, and access to financial facilities to support the SRF;[344] and (iii) there would be sufficient institutional and governance frameworks set up which would allow operational capacity and independence, and accountability.[345]

The SRM decision-making mechanism involves many players. The SRM involves a great concession of sovereignty in the banking regulations of Member States. Thus, it is not surprising that from the outset, there have been heated discussions and controversies with regard to many practical issues on the decision-making mechanism. For instance, rather than establishing a unitary resolution authority, Germany and France advocated a 'college' of NRAs instead of an EU decision-maker.[346] The Parliament and the Council approved the SRM regulation in July 2014.[347] The current decision-making mechanism of the SRM is a compromise,

---

340 SRM Regulation, art 2.
341 SRM Regulation, art 7(2).
342 SRM Regulation, art 5.
343 SRM Regulation, art 67–71.
344 SRM Regulation, art 72–74.
345 SRM Regulation, art 18–19. See also Jeffrey N. Gordon and Wolf-Georg Ringe, 'Bank resolution in the European Banking Union: a transatlantic perspective on what it would take', pp. 19–33.
346 Ibid, p. 28.
347 SRM Regulation.

which is related to many players including the ECB, the SRB (including members of Member States, the ECB, and the EC), the EC, and the Council.[348]

Subsequent to the above discussion on the pros and cons of the SPE and the MPE, and the situation in the BRRD with reference to the rules in the Dodd-Frank Act and the UK, the next section will analyse whether the SRM mechanism will change the dynamic of the resolution regime in the EU and hence facilitate tackling the cyclicality attribute of the TBTF bank structural problem.

B THE LEGITIMACY OF THE SRM AND ARTICLE 114 TFEU

The EC proposed establishing the SRM based on Article 114 TFEU, which is a classic basis for the establishment of new rules on the functioning of the internal market. Based on EU case law, Article 114 can only be applied as a basis 'where it is actually and objectively apparent from the legal act that its purpose is to improve the conditions of the establishment and functioning of the internal market'.[349] In fact, other than the possibility of relying on Article 114, the EU framework does not include any explicit legal basis for the establishment of EU agencies (except Article 352 TFEU, upon which many agencies have been established in practice, but it requires a unanimous vote in the Council).

Things have changed since the 'short-selling case' (case C-270/12) in which the conferral of powers on an EU agency was based on Article 114 TFEU.[350] The case was brought by the UK against the Council and the European Parliament seeking the annulment of Article 28 of the Regulation on short-selling and certain aspects of credit default swaps. The rule vests the European Securities and Markets Authority (ESMA) with certain powers to intervene or ban short-selling in Member States' financial markets in the event of a 'threat to the orderly functioning and integrity of financial markets or to the stability of the whole or part of the financial system in the Union'.

Advocate General Jääskinen delivered the opinion on September 12, 2013 when the negotiations for the establishment of the SRM were in progress. He made a case against Article 114 TFEU as the basis of the banning of short-selling, in which he claimed:[351]

> The reliance on Article 114 TFEU as the sole legal basis for Article 28 of Regulation No 236/2012 is not supported by the Court's case law because the conferral of decision making powers under that article on ESMA, in substitution for the assessments of the competent national authorities, cannot

---

348 SRM Regulation, art 18.
349 *Case 380/03 Germany v Parliament and Council, [2006] ECR I-11573*, paras 80–81. See also *Case C-270/12. United Kingdom of Great Britain and Northern Ireland v European Parliament and Council of the European Union [2014]*, para. 113.
350 *Case C-270/12.United Kingdom of Great Britain and Northern Ireland v European Parliament and Council of the European Union [2014]*.
351 See *Opinion of Advocate General Jääskinen delivered on 12 September 2013 Case C 270/12*, para. 37.

be considered to be a measure 'for the approximation of the provisions laid down by law, regulation or administrative action in Member States which have as their object the establishment and functioning of the internal market' within the meaning of Article 114 TFEU.

However, this interpretation was finally refuted by the Court argumentation, which ruled that Article 28 of Regulation No 236/2012 satisfies all the requirements laid down in Article 114 TFEU (approximation of law and improve the function of the internal market). In the final decision it insisted that:[352]

> Accordingly, the EU legislature, in its choice of method of harmonisation and, taking account of the discretion it enjoys with regard to the measures provided for under Article 114 TFEU, may delegate to a Union body, office or agency powers for the implementation of the harmonisation sought. That is the case in particular where the measures to be adopted are dependent on specific professional and technical expertise and the ability of such a body to respond swiftly and appropriately.

According to these criteria, the existence of the need for professional and technical expertise can justify conferring of new powers on EU agencies according to Article 114. In that case, specific professional technical expertise on bank resolution under the SRM could meet the condition. Thus, the conferral of power on the SRM seems to fall within the scope of Article 114.[353]

To justify the dependence on Article 114 as the legal basis, the statutory requirement is to prove 'measures for the approximation of the provisions laid down by law, regulation or administrative action in Member States which have as their object the establishment and functioning of the internal market'. First, the establishment of the SRM definitely falls into the denotation of 'approximation measures'. In recital 10, it points out clearly that the objective of an integrated resolution framework is to address the uncoordinated and non-harmonised Member States' resolution procedures.[354] In addition, it definitely meets the purposes of improving the conditions of 'functioning of internal market'. In recital 12, it specifically indicates that:

> Ensuring effective and uniform resolution rules and equal conditions of resolution financing across member states is in the best interests not only of the member states in which banks operate but also of all member states in general as a means of ensuring a level competitive playing field and improving the functioning of the internal market.[355]

---

352 *Case C-270/12. United Kingdom of Great Britain and Northern Ireland v European Parliament and Council of the European Union/2014/*, para. 105.
353 Steven L. Schwarcz, 'Regulating complexity in financial markets', 87 Wash UL Rev 211.
354 SRM Regulation, recital (10).
355 SRM Regulation, recital (12).

Therefore, the conditions for using Article 114 as the legal basis seem to be met both from the interpretation of statute and recent case law.[356] But there are still weak points as to the legitimacy of the SRM. Specifically, to what extent could it promote orderly bank resolution in the EU as a whole internal market?

The answer to this question is related to the scope of the SRM. According to SRM Article 2, it covers three kinds of entities:[357] (i) credit institutions; (ii) parent undertakings; and (iii) investment firms and financial institutions. They are covered by the ECB supervision or consolidated supervision of parent undertakings.

From the perspective of covered banks, the SRM scope is almost the same as that of the SSM. It includes only significant credit institutions and cross-border groups in the Euro area.[358] Thus, an obvious weakness will be its lack of sufficient capacity to promote the internal market. For a mechanism envisaged as promoting harmonisation of regulation and strengthening the functioning of the internal market, it excludes a significant part of the entities in the EU from its scope. It seems reasonable because it is the non-Euro countries that refused to join the Euro area in the first place, where provision of the SRM to them might provide an incentive for free-riding.

Having said that, it could be seen from the provision of the SRM that it tries its best to accommodate the interests of the EU as a whole including those non-participating countries. For example, in recital 12 of the SRM, it not only points out that the SRM benefits both Members and non-Members in many aspects, but also indicates that an orderly resolution of covered banks can eradicate the spill over effect from failing banks from the covered Member States to non-participating Member States. In addition, the SRM also encourages the cooperation between the SRB and non-participating Member States by 'concluding memoranda of understanding describing in general terms how they will cooperate with one another in the performance of their tasks under the BRRD'.[359]

Based on this analysis, it is reasonable to say that the SRM has sufficient legitimacy in relying on Article 114 TFEU. However, it is also fair to say that its scope seems to constitute an impediment to an efficient SPE resolution from the outset.[360]

---

356 Eilis Ferran, 'European Banking Union: imperfect, but it can work', University of Cambridge Faculty of Law Research Paper, pp. 17–21. Be that as it may, Article 114 has a weak legitimacy basis compared with Article 127 TFEU for the SSM, but both of them are flawed as they are unable to provide delegation of policy discretion to the relevant agencies due to the *Meroni*'s rule. That directly leads to inefficient decision-making by both the SRB (needs endorsement from the EC and the Council) and the Supervisory Board of the ECB (needs approval from the Governing Council); these two points are discussed in detail in Section 4.3.5(D)(a) and Section 4.4.2(F) of this chapter.
357 SRM Regulation, art 2.
358 SSM Regulation, art 2 and art 6.
359 SRM Regulation, recital (38).
360 Financial Stability Board, *Recovery and resolution planning for systemically important financial institutions: guidance on developing effective resolution strategies*, pp. 14–16.

As referred to earlier, Article 114 TFEU is the legal basis for the enactment of the SRM. Therefore, it is also supposed to be the basis for the legitimacy of its key part, the SRF. The SRF is essential for the construction of the SRM, without which the SRM could not function properly. However, according to the rules about financial arrangement in the BRRD, the funding of a resolution is still to remain at the national level. In that case, the link between sovereignty and resolution and the weakness in cross-border issues would still persist. Within that context, the SRF could help to ensure a uniform practice in financing resolution and orderly liquidation, and it could help to avoid the obstacles for the exercise of powers and the distortion of competition in the EU due to different national practices.[361]

The building of the SRF seems to be a great leap forward in the advancement of Union power against the sovereignty of Member States in resolving the large banks. Thus, it attracted very intense criticism. In the end, although Article 114 is the basis of the SRM, transferring funds collected in accordance with the BRRD to the SRF is based on an Intergovernmental Agreement (IGA).[362]

According to the IGA signed by the relevant Member States of the EU, the fund will be built up over a time span of eight years. It will reach a target level of at least 1% of the amount of covered deposits of all credit institutions authorised in all the participating Member States according to the BRRD.[363] It is estimated that the size will amount to about EUR55bn.

The IGA applies to the contracting parties whose institutions are subject to the supervision of the SSM and the SRM. It requires the contracting parties to transfer the contributions raised at the national level according to the BRRD to the SRF established in accordance with the SRM.[364] During the transitional phase, the SRF will initially consist of compartments corresponding to each contracting party. But it will be gradually merged over the eight-year transitional phase. This mutualisation of funds starts with 40% in the first year and a further 20% in the second year. It will keep increasing by equal amounts during the subsequent six years until the SRF is fully mutualised.[365]

In the transition period, the order to bear losses is: (i) the compartments corresponding to the contracting parties where the institution or group is established or authorised; (ii) available means in the compartments of the fund corresponding to all the contracting parties; (iii) any remaining means in the compartments corresponding to the contracting parties referred to in (i); and (iv) ex-post contributions transferred to the fund from the contracting party referred to in (i).[366]

---

361 SRM Regulation, Recital (19)–(20). See also BRRD, art 102.
362 Council of the European Union, *Member states sign agreement on bank resolution fund,10088/14,PRESSE 302* (21 May 2014).
363 BRRD, art 102.
364 Council of the European Union, *Agreement on the transfer and mutualisation of contributions to a Single Resolution Fund* (May 14, 2014), art 1.
365 Ibid, art 5.
366 Ibid, art 5.

Based on the provisions of the IGA, although the EU takes on the function of controlling the SRF, it does not seem to impinge on Member States' budgetary sovereignty or impose on them excessive fiscal responsibility. It can be seen as providing ex-ante contributions to a mutual fund, which is used to facilitate dealing with banking operational risks in the future in Member States. Although it sounds pretty sensible, it has still attracted many critics.

Having said that, at least the IGA and the transferring of contributions to the SRF are consistent with the current EU framework, such as in the relevant case law in *Pringle*.[367] In the case, Mr Pringle, a member of the Irish Parliament, against the Government of Ireland sought a declaration that the amendment of Article 136 TFEU by Article 1 of Decision 2011/199 constituted an unlawful amendment of the TFEU Treaty and that by accepting the Treaty establishing the European Stability Mechanism (ESM), Ireland would undertake obligations incompatible with the Treaties on which the EU was founded.[368] The court's major argument in regard to the EU exclusive competence vs. international agreement is that:[369]

> Member States are prohibited from concluding an agreement between themselves, which might affect common rules or alter their scope. However, the arguments put forward in this context have not demonstrated that an agreement such as the ESM Treaty would have such effects.

In other words, where the EU have exclusive competence, international agreement between Member States is not allowed if it would alter the EU framework. With regard to the SRF and the IGA, it falls into the competence of the EU according to TFEU provisions. However, it will facilitate the functioning of the internal market and 'common rules' on the resolution of banks in the EU. Thus, it does not violate the case law in *Pringle*.

That said, compared with using Article 114 TFEU as the basis, the IGA has two weaknesses in providing legitimacy to the SRF. First, the IGA might undermine the autonomy of EU law. According to the autonomy principle of EU law, the powers and functions of the EU could not be affected by any international agreement.[370] As indicated in recital 19 of the SRM regulation, the SRF is the essential part of the resolution regime, without which the SRM cannot function.[371] According to the IGA provisions, it can only enter into force if approvals or acceptances have been deposited by signatories participating in the SSM and the SRM that represent no less than 90% of the aggregate of the weighted votes of

---

367 *Case C-370/12 Thomas Pringle v. Government of Ireland, Ireland, The Attorney General [2012]* *ECLI:EU:C:2012:756.*

368 Ibid.

369 Ibid, para. 101.

370 Jan Willem van Rossem, 'The autonomy of EU law: more is less?' in *Between autonomy and dependence* (Berlin: Springer 2013), pp. 13–14.

371 SRM regulation, recital (19).

all Member States participating in the SSM and the SRM.[372] Thus, although it is not the truth in reality, if the ratification had failed, then the SRM would not function effectively, which is in direct contradiction to the autonomy of EU law.

Second, relying on the IGA bypasses the existing EU mechanism and the involvement of European Parliament de facto. This also compromises the legitimacy of the SRF. What is more, because the international agreement always increases the availability for judicial review, this includes the possibility of striking down the agreement.[373] In addition, although the IGA also provides provision for inclusion of Member States whose currency is not the euro through a decision by the Council of the European Union or participation action by Member States, the IGA would still inevitably exclude some States.[374]

Therefore, the IGA undoubtedly provides the SRF with legitimacy. Be that as it may, the weaknesses of the IGA in providing legitimacy to the SRF obviously exist: bypassing the EU framework, subjecting it to more scrutiny by Member States, not including all Member States, etc. Those would also constitute impediments to an efficient SPE resolution framework according to the FSB's requirements.[375]

D THE WEAKNESSES IN THE MECHANISM IN TERMS OF THE SPE STRATEGY

In the context of the Member State-based resolution framework under the BRRD, the SRM was established along consistent lines with the BRRD, but aims at introducing a centralised decision-making process at the Union level for covered institutions. This section analyses its weaknesses in achieving this purpose in terms of the SPE conditions referred to earlier.[376]

(a) The Single Resolution Board and the fragmented decision-making process. Under the SRM, a centralised decision-making body with regard to bank resolution in the EU, the SRB, would be established consisting of a chairman, a vice chair, four permanent members, and the relevant national authority representatives where the failing bank has its headquarters or branches or subsidiaries.[377] The representatives from the ECB and the EC would act as permanent observers. In the Regulation, the assessment of whether an institution is failing or likely to fail

---

372 Council of the European Union, *Member states sign agreement on bank resolution fund, 10088/14, Presse 302.*

373 Zavvos, ' The Single Resolution Mechanism in the European Banking Union: legal foundation, governance structure and financing', p. 45.

374 Council of the European Union, *Agreement on the transfer and mutualisation of contributions to a Single Resolution Fund*, art 8.

375 Financial Stability Board, *Recovery and resolution planning for systemically important financial institutions: guidance on developing effective resolution strategies*, pp. 14–16.

376 The key conditions and features of SPE are discussed in Section 4.3.3 of this chapter. Ferran, 'European Banking Union: imperfect, but it can work', without denying the weaknesses of the SRM and SSM, Eilis Ferran holds a comparatively optimistic view that the EBU will still work well despite the political compromises.

377 SRM Regulation, art 42 and art 43.

is within the mandate of the ECB. However, the SRB also has the power to make the assessment if, at the request of the Board, the ECB does not make it.[378]

The SRM is a complex mechanism involving many players.[379] Therefore, its decision-making process seems also to be a complicated one.[380] For a start, the SRB can trigger the resolution process on its own initiatives or by communication from the ECB when the following conditions are met: (i) the entity is failing or is likely to fail; (ii) there is no reasonable prospect that any alternative private sector measures would possibly prevent its failure within a reasonable timeframe; or (iii) a resolution action is necessary in the public interest.[381] On the other hand, the SRB can also trigger the resolution process and do the assessment by itself on its own initiative. To do so, two conditions must be met: (i) it must inform the ECB of its intention; and (ii) the ECB fails to do the assessment after three calendar days starting from the receipt of information.[382]

Then, when these conditions have been met, the Board shall adopt a resolution scheme which includes: (i) placing the entity under resolution; (ii) deciding the application of the resolution tools; and (iii) deciding the use of the SRF to support the resolution action.[383]

Subsequently, after the adoption of the resolution scheme, the SRB needs to transmit it to the EC, which will transmit it to the Council within 12 hours of receipt from the SRB. The EC will need to decide within 24 hours from the transmission of the resolution scheme from the SRB whether: (i) to endorse the resolution scheme, or (ii) to object to it on the discretionary aspects of the resolution scheme not covered by the Council's mandate.[384]

The Council's mandate includes making decisions by simple majority within 24 hours from the transmission of the resolution scheme, on suggestions from the EC to either: (i) object to the resolution scheme for not fulfilling the criterion of public interest; or (ii) approve or object to a material modification of the amount of the fund to be used in the resolution scheme.[385]

Finally, the resolution scheme can only enter into force when no objection has been made either by the EC or the Council within a period of 24 hours since the transmission from the SRB.[386]

From the design of the decision-making mechanism, compared with the single powerful resolution authority referred to by the FSB, such as the US OLA, it is a

378 SRM Regulation, art 18. See also European Commission, *European Commission Memo, A Single Resolution Mechanism for the Banking Union – frequently asked questions.* (Brussels, 15 April 2014).
379 Rosalind Z. Wiggins, Michael Wedow, and Andrew Metrick, 'European Banking Union B: The Single Resolution Mechanism', *Yale Program on Financial Stability Case Study*, pp. 5–6.
380 Eilis Ferran, 'European Banking Union and the EU single financial market: more differentiated integration, or disintegration?' University of Cambridge Faculty of Law Research Paper pp. 16–20.
381 SRM Regulation, art 18(1).
382 SRM Regulation, art 18(1).
383 SRM Regulation, art 18(5).
384 SRM Regulation, art 18(7).
385 SRM Regulation, art 18(7).
386 SRM Regulation, art 18(7).

centralised system with fragmented powers. But even at the EU level, due to the sophisticated power distribution among different agencies within the ECB, the SRB, the EC, and the Council, its efficiency can be hugely compromised. The ECB as the supervisor of the EU's significant credit institutions essentially has only the power to assess the resolvability of institutions and maintain the status of observer in the SRB.[387]

As a matter of fact, it is fair to say that the resolution decision-making power distribution is another good example of political compromise at the EU level. In the original proposal, the EC was entrusted with important decision-making powers, and the SRB was only designated with an executive role. However, after contentious debate, the final adopted text provides many limits to the power of the EC, while empowering the Council in many ways.[388] The key decision-making body, which includes independent experts and members appointed by the NRAs, is the SRB. The EC is empowered to either support or object discretionary elements of the resolution scheme, which might controversially not be consistent with the Meroni jurisprudence.[389] The Council, however, is empowered to decide under the suggestion of the EC on whether public interest criteria have been met and on the matter of the use of the SRF. This sophisticated process of decision-making reflected a compromise between two stances: some Member States, such as Germany, advocated for a Council-dominated mechanism, while other Members States and the European Parliament suggested a greater role should be played by the EC. One of the huge challenges of such a sophisticated process is the efficiency of decision-making, especially within such a limited timeframe (24 hours).

By empowering the Council in this case, it reflected the lack of democratic legitimacy of the EC representing the EU in dealing with resolution policies and matters. This would be even more true if the Council were to act on behalf of the dominated Members rather than the Union as a whole. In the end, the interests of the Union as a whole might possibly be compromised by this sophisticated mechanism design.[390]

Thus, even though the SRM seems like a big step towards a Union-level resolution mechanism, its power of decision-making is severely compromised by this complicated and non-unitary process, unlike in a singular decision-making process such as in the FDIC and the OLA in the US.

(b) Decentralised execution. To a certain extent, the resolution decision-making process in the SRM is a mixture of a centralised yet fragmented resolution decision-making process at the EU level and a decentralised execution at the Member State level.

---

387 SRM Regulation, art 43.
388 European Commission, *COM (2013) 520: Proposal for a Regulation of the European Parliament and of the Council establishing uniform rules and a uniform procedure for the resolution of credit institutions and certain investment firms in the framework of a Single Resolution Mechanism and a Single Bank Resolution Fund and amending Regulation (EU) No 1093/2010 of the European Parliament and of the Council* (10 July 2013), art 16.
389 *Case- 9/56 Meroni v. High Authority [1958] ECR 133*, p. 153.
390 Zavvos, 'The Single Resolution Mechanism in the European Banking Union: legal foundation, governance structure and financing', p. 31.

The SRB would adopt a resolution scheme, determine the resolution tools to be carried out, and decide the funding to be used in a real case of resolution. On the other hand, the NRAs would take any necessary actions to implement resolution decisions in relation to SRM covered entities.[391] However, the SRB could also delegate tasks to the NRAs and coordinate their actions.[392]

(c) The SRF and its weaknesses. The above section indicates the weakness in the legitimacy of the SRF and the limits of the IGA. The SRF has more than that to be worried about. In the SRM Regulation, the target size of the resolution fund will be at least 1% of the covered deposits of all banks in all participating Member States,[393] which, in absolute terms and based on 2011 data on banks' balance sheets, made the size of the fund around EUR55 billion in 2014.[394] The target size of the fund will increase automatically if the banking industry grows.

The size of the SRF has been sharply criticised. Furthermore, the European Parliament pushed for the original date for the full size of the fund being made available to be brought forward to eight years from ten years, starting from the SRM's entry into force.[395] The GFC highlighted that it will always be difficult to forecast how much liquidity would be needed in a systemic crisis. Thus, there is still sufficient reason to be sceptical about the size of the fund in terms of whether it will be credible to support the resolution of many banks, especially in a systemic failure.

In addition, the SRF lacks sufficient backstop should the above insufficiency concern materialise.[396] According to the SRM Regulation, the SRF will receive banks' contributions raised by Member States' resolution authorities according to the provisions in the BRRD and transfer these to the fund in accordance with the IGA. Although the SRM regulation also has provisions on voluntary borrowing between resolution financial arrangements and alternative funding means, it does not provide any further backstop that is comparable to the Treasury's 'last resort role' in the Dodd-Frank liquidation procedure.

In the EU case, the source of liquidity could be guaranteed at three levels: (i) the high level of bail-inable debts at the top parent level; (ii) the sufficiently large SRF (which can be integrated with private recapitalisation channels) and; (iii) the ECB as the effective backstop.[397] Some scholars have argued that the European Stability Mechanism (ESM) could act as the backstop for the SRF in the case of a systemic crisis.[398] However, it could also be argued that in a systemic

---

391   SRM Regulation, art 29.
392   SRM Regulation, art 7 and art 29(2).
393   SRM Regulation, art 69.
394   European Commission, *European Commission Memo, A Single Resolution Mechanism for the Banking Union – frequently asked questions,* p. 9.
395   SRM Regulation, article 69–70.
396   Christos Hadjiemmanuil, 'Bank resolution financing in the banking union', pp. 19–22.
397   Jeffrey N. Gordon and Wolf-Georg Ringe, 'Bank resolution in the European Banking Union: a transatlantic perspective on what it would take', p. 41.
398   Dirk Schoenmaker and Daniel Gros, 'A European Deposit Insurance and Resolution Fund: an update', *CEPS Policy Brief,* pp. 2–4

crisis perhaps only the ECB could play the role of backstop due to the fact that it can provide unlimited amounts of liquidity when necessary to the markets.[399] The fact is that the ESM can be an alternative in providing extra funding support, but it cannot replace the function that the ECB could play.

(d) The role of Member States and the NRAs. In the SRM regulation, the NRAs play an important role in the resolution process. Specifically, the NRAs will be responsible for implementing the resolution decisions for the SRM-covered entities in accordance with national law, which has transposed the BRRD frame-work, and carrying out the resolution of entities not covered by the SRM.[400] It should be noted that to ensure a balance between the EU and Member States' powers, the Board has the authority to monitor the execution by the NRAs of its decisions at the national level. If, however, an NRA is not acting in accordance with its decisions, it can make executive orders directly to the troubled banks.[401]

The NRAs reserve the power of resolution of institutions not covered by the SRM. They would carry out the following tasks: (i) adopting resolution plans and assessing resolvability; (ii) adopting measures during early intervention; (iii) applying simplified obligations or waiving the obligation to draft a resolution plan; (iv) setting the level of MREL; (v) adopting resolution decisions and applying resolution tools; and (vi) writing down or converting relevant capital instruments.[402]

Thus, although the decision-making power of resolution has shifted partly to the Union level, the role of Member States is still significant. It is possible to act as a counterweight to a unitary resolution mechanism in the EU in terms of the SPE experience in the US.

(e) The structural issue. According to the FSB guidance on an effective SPE strategy, a firm should be 'legally and operationally structured in a way that supports effective resolution, so that the continuity of its critical functions can be maintained in resolution whilst allowing for an orderly wind down of business lines when necessary'.[403]

Although the SRF is provided, a bail-inable approach should be prioritised before resorting to the SRF. The reason is obvious: allowing losses to be internalised is better than relying on external funding. Under the SRM, although the MREL requirements are provided, there are still concerns about their size. There is no definitively effective way to predict how much liquidity might be needed in a failure. Thus, there is always the risk that recapitalisation might not be successfully achieved and the continuity of the financial services will be terminated and hence trigger an adverse spill over effect.

---

399 Hadjiemmanuil, 'Bank resolution financing in the banking union', pp. 19–22.
400 SRM Regulation, art 7.
401 SRM regulation, art 29(2).
402 SRM Regulation, art 7.
403 Financial Stability Board, *Recovery and resolution planning for systemically important financial institutions: guidance on developing effective resolution strategies*, p. 8.

Aside from the requirement for sufficient bail-inable capital, another step is to deal with bank failures by relying on structural reform as indicated in the previous chapters.[404] Legislative prodding could be used to change the institutional and financial structure of the banks. The US experience has taught us that the BHC model could best relieve the concerns about the continuity problem. With regard to the structure of banks, it is still up to the future legislation based on the BSR.[405]

From the discussion in these sections with regard to the resolution strategy under the SRM Regulation, it still seems to share many features with the MPE approach and is different from the features of an SPE resolution mechanism. According to the evaluation and assessment, what we need to do next is discuss how the MPE approach as applied in the EU resolution can be more aligned with the SPE approach applied in the US.

4.3.6 What next for the EU: the FSB benchmark and the SPE

From the discussion on the resolution framework under the BRRD and the relevant SRM, the resolution system in the EU lacks the required preconditions for an efficient SPE-based resolution regime. The framework under the BRRD is basically a bank resolution harmonisation mechanism instead of various resolution procedures in all Member States. It still lacks efficiency in addressing the remaining problems after the Lehman case, especially the run on short-term creditors and the cross-border issue. Its resolution design is less efficient than a standard SPE approach: a resolution decision-making process and execution through a single entry point carried out by a unitary authority.[406] With regard to the framework under the SRM Regulation, it was envisaged that an EU-level centralised resolution mechanism would be built rather than one at the Member State level. But its effectiveness is compromised by many factors, such as the very complicated decision-making process, the limitations of the SRF, the limits of current legal and organisational structures of banks, and the dynamic tension between the EU and its Member States.[407] These weaknesses are especially obvious when comparing with the US mechanism.

After the comparison between the EU resolution mechanism and the SPE based-resolution system in the US, the US experience could shed some light on the EU framework. The following are some suggestions for reform of the EU resolution in terms of the SPE strategy: (i) to improve the resolution authority's decision-making efficiency; (ii) to ensure an efficiently operated funding system;

---

404 The structural reform is discussed in detail from Chapter 3 to Chapter 5. See also Chapter 5, Section 3.3.3.
405 European Commission, *Proposal for a Regulation of the European Parliament and of the Council on structural measures improving the resilience of EU credit institutions, COM/2014/043 final*, art 6–8.
406 Armour, 'Making bank resolution credible', p. 31.
407 Ibid.

(iii) to strengthen the resolution power; and (iv) to facilitate the bank structure and capital restructuring.[408]

(a) To improve the resolution authorities' decision-making efficiency. As indicated earlier, the weakness of the resolution decision-making process in the SRM mechanism is brought about by a fragmented distribution of power. The ECB conducts an assessment on whether a bank is 'failing or likely to fail', the SRB adopts a resolution scheme and transmits it to the EC, and the EC transmits it to the Council.[409]

The fragmented decision-making process adds many uncertainties to the resolution process, and leads to adverse effects for the failing banks. To criticise the inefficiency and weakness of the decision-making mechanism, Stefano Micossi said:[410]

> This cumbersome apparatus clearly reflects the attempt to establish a balance between the main interests involved: the ECB, the NRAs, the SRB and the EC. However, it does not only seem overly complex but also incompatible with the requirements of speed, decisiveness and confidentiality needed to move from the early intervention phase to resolution. The intervention of multiple actors entitled to participate in the decisions, the passage of information and documentary material between them, and the complex procedural steps are bound to take time and generate leaks and rumours, notably when there are different views on whether and how to proceed.

This complicated decision-making process is both time consuming and lacks decisiveness, and is also lacking in the merits of confidentiality.[411]

Therefore, according to the features of the SPE, what needs to be done is to change the fragmented decision-making process into a centralised and unitary one, drawing on the experience of the building of the FDIC in the US banking resolution. As a matter of fact, the creation of the FDIC was among the responses to the weak state-based insurance systems that failed to prevent the interstate bank failures in the Great Depression.[412] Therefore, lawmakers chose to federalise deposit insurance to safeguard the security of the banks. The same concern also exists in the EU banking sector. After the Lehman failure, the bank run issue, and the spill over and cross-border issues have become major problems in bank failures in the major economies, including the EU.[413]

---

408 Ferran, 'European Banking Union: imperfect, but it can work', pp. 13–14. The resolution framework is a 'near dictatorial' mechanism. It needs more powers to carry it out.
409 SRM regulation, art 18.
410 Stefano Micossi, Ginevra Bruzzone and Jacopo Carmassi, 'The new European framework for managing bank crises', 304 *Policy Brief*, p. 7.
411 Armour, 'Making bank resolution credible', p. 11.
412 Carnell, Macey, and Miller, *The law of banking and financial institutions*, p. 62.
413 See Rosalind Z. Wiggins, Natalia Tente, and Andrew Metrick, 'European Banking Union C: cross-border resolution – Fortis Group', *Yale Program on Financial Stability Case Study*. See also Skeel, 'Single point of entry and the bankruptcy alternative', pp. 5–7.

The imperativeness of avoiding both overlap and conflict of power in resolution requires that a centralised and unitary authority in both early intervention and in the assessment of 'failing or likely to fail' would be the best option for the ailing banks. It maximises the speed of decision-making and prevents the possibility of information leaking and avoids to the largest extent possible a run on creditors. The unitary role could be played by the ECB, which would correspond with the US FDIC controlled resolution mechanism. Opponents argue that the change would be not in the interests of many Member States. They are very reluctant to give up their power in the field of bank resolution and believe that this change requires modifying the TFEU.[414] But this arrangement does de-link the connection between tackling bank failures and sovereignty. It could address the bank run and cross border issue to a large extent.[415]

(b) To ensure an efficiently operated funding system with a backstop. In an SPE resolution mechanism, the losses would be absorbed entirely by shareholders and creditors. However, given the threat of possible systemic crisis and disruption and the unpredictability of the sufficiency of MREL in a systemic crisis, an eligible financial arrangement should have adequate financial resources as the backstop to support resolution actions.

In the FDIC resolution mechanism, the Treasury would provide a credit extension to the FDIC as the main resource of funding and the funding would not be on an ex-ante basis. In return, the credit extension would enjoy priority repayment over the assets of the resolved institutions. Moreover, the Treasury can provide guarantees for the obligations of the bridge bank, backed by the credit of the US government.[416]

In the EU, the SRM Regulation and the BRRD provide the resolution fund requirement to back their activities; the financial arrangement in the BRRD is transferred to the SRF in accordance with the IGA. However, there is probably still a need for a last resort fiscal backstop to cover possible residual losses, especially in the case of a systemic crisis.[417]

Drawing on the experience of the US, the liquidity for the resolution mechanism is supposed to be guaranteed at three levels: (i) the bail-inable debts at the top parent level; (ii) a sufficiently large SRF (which can be integrated with private recapitalisation channels) and; (iii) the ECB as the backstop. The SRB would need access to immediate liquidity funding by the ECB just like the FDIC has the support of the US Treasury.[418]

---

414 Micossi, Bruzzone, and Carmassi, 'The new European framework for managing bank crises', p. 8.

415 Jeffrey N. Gordon and Wolf-Georg Ringe, 'Bank Resolution in the European Banking Union: a transatlantic perspective on what it would take', p. 33.

416 See Dodd-Frank Act (U.S), section 210(n)(5).

417 Micossi, Bruzzone, and Carmassi, 'The new European framework for managing bank crises', pp. 13–15.

418 Jeffrey N. Gordon and Wolf-Georg Ringe, 'Bank resolution in the European Banking Union: a transatlantic perspective on what it would take', p. 41. See also Hadjiemmanuil, 'Bank resolution financing in the banking union', pp. 19–22.

But during the phasing in of the mutualisation of the SRF, the capital shortfall might still need to rely on other sources: (i) private channels; (ii) a recapitalisation of the bank using public funds; or (iii) recourse to the ESM after exhausting national backstops.[419]

(c) To strengthen the resolution power. Looking at the operation of the FDIC, it is empowered to use a series of strong and credible tools to resolve the failing banks without causing major economic disruption and without giving rise to unnecessary losses for taxpayers. Comparatively, the SRB will also have the power to decide whether the best solution is to restructure the bank as a going concern (through bail-in), to restructure it, or to wind it down.

The SRB is empowered with four measures: separation, transferring, sale, and bail-in; and three steps: preparation, early intervention, and resolution. This provides the SRB with enough powers and tools to carry out resolution in theory. Compared with the US, the tools and powers at the SRB's disposal also seem to be sufficient. But what needs to be improved is the implementation at national level within the context of the power struggle between the Member States and the Union. There needs to be more clarification on implementation at the Member State level to ensure consistency and coordination. For instance, there is insufficient clarity on whether and under what circumstances the conversion tool would apply rather than proceeding with a write down, which leaves a discretionary element to the resolution framework.[420]

(d) Change the bank structure and restructure the capital ready for bail-in. For the US-style SPE to work, there are two preconditions with regard to the bank structure. First, the legal and organisational structure of the bank should ensure that each entity within the group has comparative independence, so that it permits the bankruptcy of one unit without disrupting the going concern of any other constituents. On the other hand, the capital structure should include up-streaming debts and down-streaming capital. The group has in its liabilities sufficient convertible assets at the top level or the parent level.[421] With the two preconditions met, in the event of a bank failure, the SPE style could be carried out to resolve an entity at the top or parent level without disrupting other constituents of the group.

The US banks meet the two requirements, whether intentionally or incidentally, as a result of the regulation mechanism in the US arming the US banks with a bank holding company structure, which meets both the organisational and capital structural requirements referred to earlier. In the past, the 'business

---

419 Micossi, Bruzzone, and Carmassi, 'The new European framework for managing bank crises', pp. 13–15. See also *Council statement on EU banks' asset quality reviews and stress tests, including on backstop arrangements. Economic and Financial Affairs Council meeting* (November 15, 2013), para 9.

420 Micossi, Bruzzone, and Carmassi, 'The new European framework for managing bank crises', p. 10.

421 Financial Stability Board, *Recovery and resolution planning for systemically important financial institutions: guidance on developing effective resolution strategies*, p. 16.

of banking' provision in the Glass-Steagall Act bars banks from providing many other financial services.[422] Even after Glass-Steagall was abandoned in 1999, banks remained prohibited from securities' underwriting and related investment banking activities, but banks could engage in investment banking and other financial services through the holding company structure and affiliation.[423]

That, however, is not the case in Europe. The US BHC group model is not that popular in European countries. But, the point to be made here is that current regulation and supervision can be changed to provide banks with incentives to alter their organisational and capital structures to meet the two requirements. Stimulated by regulatory incentives, Switzerland is the first European country to use the legal approach to provide a stimulus for banks to change their organisational structure. According to the FINMA position report, both G-SIB banks in Switzerland had subordinated and senior unsecured debt at the parent level equating to between 30 and 40% of their risk-weighted assets.[424]

4.4 Resolution and the weaknesses of the SSM

The establishment of the SSM was the first step in establishing the EBU. Among all three pillars of the EBU – the SSM, the SRM, and the DGS – the BRRD and the SRM have been analysed, so this section focuses on the SSM, the effectiveness of which is directly related to the resolution framework.[425] The effectiveness of the SSM is of significant importance for the overall map of the EBU. The SSM and the resolution framework under the BRRD and the SRM are interdependent.[426] To a certain extent, an efficient SSM would be the safety keeper of banks and key players in preparing for recovery and resolution. It should be noted that an efficient SSM would contribute to the safety and soundness of banks,[427] facilitate the decision-making process of resolution,[428] and make resolution proceed more efficiently.[429]

With regard to the DGS, if a self-insured SPE resolution mechanism is set up effectively, then the reliance on it would be very limited.[430] Thus, here we only discuss the effectiveness of the SSM and its relevance to the effectiveness of the EU resolution mechanism.

---

422 12 U.S.C § 23(7). See also Banking Act of 1933, sections 16, 20, 21, 32.
423 The Graham-Leach-Billey Act of 1999, 12 U.S.C §§ 843(k)(4)(H).
424 FINMA, *Resolution of global systemically important banks: FINMA position paper on Resolution of G-SIBs*, pp. 7–8.
425 Stijn Verhelst, 'Assessing the single supervisory mechanism: passing the point of no return for Europe's banking union', 58 *Egmont Paper*.
426 European Commission, *Communication from the Commission to the European Parliament and the Council: A Roadmap towards a Banking Union*, COM(2012) 510 final, pp. 1–5.
427 See generally, CRD IV and CRR.
428 See SRM regulation, art 18.
429 For instance, it can ensure that the bail-inable assets condition is met in banks to facilitate bank self-insurance without affecting other banks. See BRRD, art 44.
430 A resolution mechanism and appropriate structural requirements, together with sufficient bail-inable tools would make the banks self-insurable. It is believed by many scholars that these measures would eliminate the need for the DGS because loss would be absorbed within the banks. See Armour, 'Making bank resolution credible', pp. 19–24.

Ideally speaking, a seamless cooperation between the resolution mechanism and the SSM would facilitate the effectiveness of bank resolution in the EU. According to current legislation, however, the truth might not live up to expectations. As usual, politics at the EU level always stand in the way of good public policy; the decisiveness of reform would always be compromised by Member States' non-concerted incentives and resolutions.[431] One of the most contentious issues that arose on the establishment of the SSM included: to whom should the power be delegated? Should the power be conferred on an established institution, which requires no EU framework change, or is a newly established and specially tailored institution more preferable? Finally, it transpired that the latter would be practically difficult but seemed to be more effective. In contrast, the former turned out to be a pragmatic alternative with fewer obstacles in its path.[432]

Anyway, the political compromise on establishing the SSM may somehow blunt the sharpness and effectiveness of the mechanism, and it might fail to live up to the expectation of the resolution mechanism.

4.4.1 Tension in the recovery mechanism: consolidating supervisor vs. NCAs

In a previous section on the recovery framework, it is indicated that the intragroup support measures, the recovery planning, and the early intervention mechanism are useful measures for resolution notwithstanding their weaknesses.[433] Despite the fact that some elements of these measures have all been provided by the CRR and CRD IV, the provisions in the BRRD have made these measures more detailed to facilitate the resolution process and its implementation. But a major weakness of the recovery framework is related to the decision-making process for adopting relevant measures, such as RRP, intragroup support, and early intervention. This section analyses in general how efficiently the recovery framework could be carried out under the SSM. Apparently, there are conflicts between the supervisor of the group (usually the ECB) and the NCAs in the decision-making process of the recovery framework.[434]

A THE SIGNIFICANT ROLE FOR THE NCAS IN THE JOINT DECISION MECHANISM

It is indicated earlier, group recovery planning requires the joint decision of the consolidating supervisor and the relevant NCAs, in the absence of which respective choices are allowed, subject to the EBA's decision upon request.[435] The intragroup support measure also requires approval by the consolidating

---

431 Schillig, 'Bank resolution regimes in Europe: recovery and resolution planning, early intervention, resolution tools and powers', pp. 20–21.
432 P. Craig, 'Two-speed, multi-speed and European future: a review of Jean-Claude Piris on the future of Europe (2012)', 37 *European Law Review* 800. Paul Craig explains how the generic recognition of reform plans would inevitably surrender to reality.
433 The decision-making process is discussed in detail in Section 4.2 of this chapter.
434 BRRD, art 8.
435 BRRD, art 8(1)–(4).

supervisor and a joint decision between national competent supervisors.[436] Besides, in the implementation phase, the competent authorities have the power of objection at their disposal.[437] As regards early intervention, a decision could be made at the parent level or the institution level individually by respective supervisors; but to be implemented in more than two institutions, then the requirement is also a joint decision, in the absence of which respective choices are allowed, subject to the EBA's decision upon request.[438] The NCAs even play a consulting role in the development of group resolution plans.[439]

Therefore, it is not inappropriate to say that although the recovery measures are determined in a coordinated way, the NCAs still play a considerable role in it.[440] If not managed appropriately, the tension between the NCAs and the consolidating supervisor (usually the ECB) would impede the effectiveness of the recovery framework.

B THE ROLE OF NCAS IN PRUDENTIAL REQUIREMENTS

Empowering both the consolidating supervisor and the NCAs would probably create a tension between the two. As indicated earlier in regard to the challenges to the recovery framework, the political resolve does not seem to be very strong across all Member States.[441] Just as Jed S. Rakoff said when analysing the Department of Justice's lack of incentive and resolution in indicting bankers:[442]

> On the one hand, the government writ large, had a part in creating the conditions that encouraged the approval of dubious mortgages. Even before the start of the housing boom, it was the government, in the form of Congress that repealed the Glass-Steagall Act, thus allowing certain banks that had previously viewed mortgages as a source of interest income to become instead deeply involved in securitizing pools of mortgages in order to obtain the much greater profits available from trading. It was the government, in the form of both the executive and the legislature, that encouraged deregulation, thus weakening the power and oversight not only of the SEC but also of such diverse banking overseers as the Office of Thrift Supervision and the Office of the Comptroller of the Currency, both in the Treasury Department.[443]

---

436 BRRD, art 20.
437 BRRD, art 24.
438 BRRD, art 30.
439 BRRD, art 10.
440 Valia Babis, 'European bank recovery and resolution directive, recovery proceedings for cross-border banking groups', p. 16.
441 The role that the competent supervisor could play in the recovery framework is also discussed in for instance Section 4.2.2 of this chapter.
442 Jed S. Rakoff, 'The financial crisis: why have no high-level executives been prosecuted?' *New York Times*, www.nybooks.com/articles/archives/2014/jan/09/financial-crisis-why-no-executive-prosecutions/, accessed March 5, 2015.
443 See also Schillig, 'Bank resolution regimes in Europe: recovery and resolution planning, early intervention, resolution tools and powers', p. 36.

Therefore, it is only right to argue that NCAs might be a counterweight to implementing the RRP if being empowered excessively. If we have a closer look at the recovery framework in the BRRD, it is not difficult to see that the trigger or implementation of these measures would be related to some basic requirements including prudential requirements. With regard to recovery planning, one of the criteria to assess a plan is that the plan is reasonably likely to restore the viability and financial position of the failing institution, and the viability of the firm would certainly include meeting the basic prudential requirements.[444] As regards the intragroup support, it is clearly stipulated that the condition is that it would not jeopardise the liquidity or insolvency of the group entity, and that it would not cause the group entity to violate the capital requirements.[445] Similarly, the trigger for early intervention is that an institution is breaching or about to breach the prudential requirement.[446]

It is undeniable that the NCAs' role with regard to enforcing these prudential requirements, which are closely related to the implementation of the recovery framework, is very significant.[447] Apparently, in the process of enforcing the requirements, the discretion of the NCAs is considerable according to the current regulatory mechanism.[448]

To give an example related to this discretion, in the Liikanen Report the proprietary trading and investment banking activities are required to be separated. Under additional separation, the NCAs could require the institutions within their jurisdictions to comply with higher capital and prudential requirements. Higher prudential requirements sound very reasonable and beneficial to the safety of the banks; however, it can also act as a pretext to block some potential recovery measures or plan.[449] Therefore, it is theoretically possible that Member States might intentionally use the structural separation, which is envisaged to ensure the safety and soundness of the banking sector, in an opportunistic way to avoid some collectively necessary yet individually burdensome recovery measures, such as intragroup support.

According to the CRD IV, the NCAs also have discretion in many aspects.[450] In enforcing the capital requirement, the supervisors still have flexibility to apply the capital buffer, such as the capital conservation buffer, the institution-specific countercyclical capital buffer, the G-SII capital buffer, the O-SII buffer, and the systemic risk capital buffer.[451]

---

444 BRRD, art 6.
445 BRRD, art 23.
446 CRR, art 102.
447 See generally the Basel III and the CRR.
448 Karel Lannoo, 'Bank bonus compromise bodes ill for the Single Supervisory Mechanism', 8 *CEPS Commentary.*
449 Liikanen Erkki, *High-level Expert Group on reforming the structure of the EU banking sector,* pp. viii–x.
450 Lannoo, 'Bank bonus compromise bodes ill for the Single Supervisory Mechanism', p. 2.
451 See generally Basel Committee on Banking Supervision, *Basel III: International framework for liquidity risk measurement, standards and monitoring* (December 2010). See CRD IV, art 28–131.

In the large exposure requirement, institutions shall not incur an exposure to a client or group of connected clients, the value of which exceeds 25% of its eligible capital. The CRR provides many exceptions on the large exposure limit, such as asset items constituting claims on central governments, regional governments, and international organisations.[452] Anyway, the NCAs also have much discretion to exempt their banks from complying with certain exposure restrictions, including of course intragroup exposures.

With regard to the relevant liquidity requirements, this is still a matter for requirement harmonisation at the international level. The Basel III introduce the liquidity ratios concept, which means the introduction of minimal liquidity standards to make banks more resilient in a crisis, including the liquidity coverage ratio (LTR) and the net stable funding ratio (NSFR). The BCBS tried to harmonise such standards with predetermined parameters, but only in the case of a few of these parameters do NCAs still have any discretion.[453] In addition, it should be noted that the phase-in period seems to also add to the flexibility of the NCAs with regard to these prudential requirements.[454]

Therefore, the tension between NCAs and the consolidating supervisor could always persist in the recovery framework. This might undermine the capacity of the framework in enhancing cooperation and coordination in restoring failing banks.[455]

4.4.2 The weaknesses of the SSM that might impede resolution

Following the previous section pointing out the conflict problem between the ECB and the NCAs, this section analyses specifically the weaknesses of the SSM that could bring about problems and obstacles to resolution.[456] In particular, the SSM suffers from weaknesses in structure, scope, task, governance, and member structure, which might reduce its credibility as an effective supervision mechanism contributing to effective bank resolution under the BRRD and the SRM.[457]

The EU legislative basis of conferring power on the ECB is essentially based on the Article 127(6) TFEU:[458]

---

452 CRR, art 395–400.

453 Avgouleas, *Governance of global financial markets: the law, the economics, the politics*, p. 333.

454 See generally Basel Committee on Banking Supervision, *Basel III: International framework for liquidity risk measurement, standards and monitoring*.

455 Avgouleas, Goodhart, and Schoenmaker, 'Bank resolution plans as a catalyst for global financial reform', pp. 210–218.

456 Anne Sibert, 'Banking union and a single bank supervisory mechanism'.

457 Eddy Wymeersch, 'Banking union: aspects of the Single Supervisory Mechanism and the Single Resolution Mechanism compared', ECGI – Law Working Paper, pp. 5–9.

458 Consolidated versions of the Treaty on European Union and the Treaty on the Functioning of the European Union 2012/C 326/01 (TFEU), art 127(6). The ESCB shall according to the provision 'contribute to the smooth conduct of policies pursued by the competent authorities relating to the prudential supervision of credit institutions and the stability of the financial system'.

[t]he Council might after consultation with the European Parliament and the ECB and by a unanimous vote, decide to confer on the ECB the specific task concerning the policies related to the prudential supervision of credit institutions and other financial institutions except insurance institutions.

Unlike the legitimacy weakness that arguably exists in the SRM, the possibility of the ECB acting as the supervisor is explicitly provided by the Treaty.[459] Thus, the delegation restriction in the *Meroni* case is not applicable here. Besides, were it not for Article 127(6) TFEU, Article 114 might also provide sufficient legitimacy to the delegation of power to the ECB according to the jurisprudence in the UK short-selling case.[460]

A THE STRUCTURE OF SUPERVISION: A SYSTEM

To discuss the weaknesses of the SSM in detail and how this adds to the ineffectiveness of the resolution mechanism, the analysis should start with a conceptual introduction of the supervision mechanism in the EU. Under the SSM Regulation 2013, the supervision in the EU is constructed at three levels and the entity level is divided into two frameworks.[461]

First, the entity level supervision consists of the ECB supervision and the NCAs' supervision framework. According to the scope of the SSM, those deemed to be significant entities would be supervised by the ECB; those not falling within the scope would still be supervised by the NCAs designated by Member States.[462] In either framework, the other would play the assistance role with regard to supervision.[463]

Second, supervision on a consolidated basis is on a different level. For groups falling within the SSM scope, it depends on whether there is any entity presence outside the SSM. If the answer were no, then the group consolidated supervision and group-level decision would be carried out by the ECB. If the answer were yes, the consolidated supervision would be carried out by the ECB, or the NCA where the parent is located in a non-participating Member State, while the supervisory college would undertake any group-level decisions.[464] But, the ECB would of course be included in the supervisory college.

Third, there is a need for coordination among the supervisors. Due to the fragmentation of supervision, the EU has also designed specific powers for the integration and coordination of supervision. The EBA is the agency

---

459 Wymeersch Eddy, 'The Single Supervisory Mechanism or "SSM", Part One of the Banking Union (2014)', pp. 20–22.
460 *Case C-270/12.United Kingdom of Great Britain and Northern Ireland v European Parliament and Council of the European Union [2014].* See also *Case - 9/56 Meroni v. High Authority [1958] ECR 133.*
461 Valia Babis, 'European Bank Recovery and Resolution Directive, recovery proceedings for cross-border banking groups', p. 20.
462 SSM Regulation, art 4.
463 The cooperation between NCAs and the ECB will be further discussed in detail, see infra Section 4.4.2(B).
464 SSM Regulation, art 4(1)(g). See also CRD IV, art 111 and art 116.

responsible for the coordination task, facilitating the exchange of information between the competent authorities, carrying out non-binding mediation upon the request of the competent authorities or on its own initiatives, notifying the European Systemic Risk Board (ESRB) of any potential emergency situation without delay, taking all necessary measures in case of the emergence of a negative situation to facilitate NCAs' cooperation, and centralising information received from NCAs, among others.[465]

In addition, the ECB also performs the function of settling disagreements between the competent authorities in a cross-border situation.[466] Thus, apart from the EBA, the ECB also has the function of coordination. For instance, it should cooperate closely with the EBA, the ESMA, the EIOPA, and the ESRB and other authorities within the European System of Financial Supervision (ESFS) to ensure adequate supervision in the EU. When necessary, the ECB should enter into a memorandum of understanding with both the Member State NCAs and the non-participating NCAs with regard to how they would cooperate with one another in performing the supervision responsibility.[467]

Therefore, the building of the SSM, as indicated in the regulation, is a system of financial supervision including the SSM, the NCAs, and a cooperation mechanism. It is not a single unitary supervisor for the EU institutions.[468] This basic conceptual design makes conflict between supervisors unavoidable.

B THE SCOPE OF THE SSM AND ITS DRAWBACKS

(a) **Exclusion of 'less significant institutions'.** In the beginning, according to the EC proposal, the scope of the ECB supervision would cover all Euro area credit institutions, which means that the SSM would be responsible for the supervision of more than 6,000 credit institutions. The follow-up feedback by the European Parliament also seconded the position in terms of the scope.[469]

However, the Council took a different approach with regard to the scope of the credit institutions, and the final adopted text was also not the same as the EC's original text. It empathises the duty of cooperation between the ECB and the NCAs in supervision. Specifically, the NCAs shall have the responsibility to sort out 'less significant institutions', which would be assessed based on size, importance for the economy of the EU as a whole or certain participating Member States, and significance of its cross-border activities.[470]

465 Regulation (EU) No 1093/2010 of the European Parliament and of the Council of 24 November 2010 establishing a European Supervisory Authority (European Banking Authority), amending Decision No 716/2009/EC and repealing Commission Decision 2009/78/EC [2010] OJ L 331/12(EBA Regulation), art 31.
466 EBA regulation, art 19–20.
467 Regulation (EU) No 1024/2013 of 15 October 2013 conferring specific tasks on the European Central Bank concerning policies relating to the prudential supervision of credit institutions [2013] OJ L 287/63 (SSM Regulation), art 3 and art 4.
468 SSM Regulation, art 2(9).
469 SSM Regulation (Commission text, September 2012), art 4.
470 SSM Regulation, art 6(4)(1).

The SSM mechanism further defines the criteria for significant institutions. The following institutions are not to be considered as less significant unless special circumstances indicate otherwise: (i) the total value of its assets is more than EUR30 billion; (ii) the ratio of its total assets to GDP of its Member State exceeds 20% unless the total value is below EUR5 billion; and (iii) not meeting the foregoing criteria, but upon the notice of the NCAs, the ECB could still conduct an overall assessment of relevant factors to establish its significance.[471] Likewise, the ECB is allowed to conclude an institution is significant under another three circumstances: (i) the institution has established subsidiaries in more than one participating Member State and its cross-border assets represent a significant part of its total assets;[472] (ii) those for which public funds have been requested or received should not be seen as less significant; and (iii) as a backstop provision, even when not meeting the above standards, the ECB can still carry out its task within the framework of the SSM in regard to the three most important credit institutions in each of the participating Member States.[473]

It should be noted that the problem discussed in this book is about tackling the cyclicality and resolvability issue in the TBTF bank structural problem. Thus, it might be argued that the exclusion of less significant institutions would not be a problem because according to the criteria of less significant institutions,[474] they are not going to have any significant disruptive influence on the economy if failure were to happen, and they are definitely not on the list of SIFIs defined by the FSB.[475]

But this argument ignores the fact that one of the most critical factors of the GFC is interconnectedness and homogeneity, which could cause a spill over effect, either from SIFIs or from less significant institutions.[476] Thus, this argument is not entirely valid. Instead, what should be noted is that the ECB's supervision framework would not be the optimal one to facilitate effective resolution if it fails to supervise those institutions whose failure could potentially have as equally an adverse impact on other institutions as the failure of SIFIs or significant institutions.

(b) The exclusion of other non-credit financial institutions in the SSM.
The scope of institutions also excludes other non-credit financial institutions,

---

471   SSM Regulation, art 6(4) (2).
472   SSM Regulation, art 6(4).
473   SSM Regulation, art 6(4).
474   SSM Regulation, art 6(4)(2).
475   Financial Stability Board, *2013 update of group of global systemically important banks (G-SIBs)*, p. 2. The November FSB 2011 report noted that the group of G-SIFIs would be updated annually according to new data and published by the FSB in each November, starting with the November 2012 update.
476   Steven L Schwarcz, 'Protecting financial markets: lessons from the subprime mortgage meltdown', 93 Minn L Rev 373. On the size scope of the structural reform, more analysis in detail can be found in Section 4.2 of Chapter 3.

including insurers, investment banking, central counterparties, and other infrastructure providers. But it should be noted that other institutions, especially in the shadow-banking sector, tend to act as a more aggravating factor affecting overall financial stability compared with credit institutions.[477]

The restriction is not originally from the ECB Regulation, rather, it is clearly defined in Article 127(6) TFEU that the task conferred on the ECB relating to financial supervision excludes insurance companies.[478] This restriction might possibly make the mechanism suboptimal from the start.[479] For instance, investment firms would not be covered by the SSM on the basis of direct supervision. Although they are supposed to be supervised under the MiFID II and partially subject to CRD IV, such regulation still, to a certain extent, lacks sufficient coordination and consistency in different Member States. Besides, there are many other categories of institutions that are not qualified as banks, which are not under the supervision of the SSM. This could be a problem now that these categories of institutions are of equally significant importance to the overall economy. For instance, Central Clearing Counterparties (CCPs) are of fundamental importance for the clearing of securities and derivatives. However, due to the fact that they are not banks, they would not be included under the SSM supervision, although their significance is unquestionable. As a matter of fact, with a few other entities, for example Central Securities Depositories (CSDs), stock exchanges, or Multilateral Trading Facilities (MTFs), they are deemed to be part of the market infrastructure.

The fact is, the exclusion of entities from supervision might be an impediment to a successful mechanism of bank resolution within the context of the TBTF bank structural problem. It would be inappropriate to simply exclude some entities definitively and claim that these entities are not significantly important to affect the stability of the financial markets. Actually, it is worth mentioning that the universal banking model and financial conglomeration have been prevalent in the financial sectors in the EU for decades.[480] Within such a context, a newly established supervision mechanism should be constructed to respond to the universal banking model, rather than to artificially separate the supervision of

---

477 SSM Regulation, art 4.
478 TFEU, art 127(6).
479 Ferran and Babis, 'The European single supervisory mechanism', p. 6. That argument is not without controversy, but the author argues that this exclusion evades the decision of bringing non-banks within the purview of the SSM which are deemed to be systemically important, such as in the UK and the US. 'For example, taken place in the UK with respect to the boundary line between those firms (not just banks) that are to be prudentially supervised by the Prudential Regulation Authority (PRA) and those (less systemically important firms) that are to be prudentially supervised by the Financial Conduct Authority (FCA). Furthermore, the constraint means that the SSM will not have the flexibility found in both the United States and the UK systems for non-banks to be brought within the purview of the ECB if they are deemed to be systemically significant'.
480 Robert J. Shiller, *The subprime solution: how today's global financial crisis happened, and what to do about it* (Princeton, NJ: Princeton University Press 2008), pp. 10–40. It should be noted that universal banks are financial institutions that are able to offer all kinds of financial services and that this model has been prevalent in the EU since the late 2000s.

different entities according to different business lines.[481] Such a division of supervision would undoubtedly compromise the effectiveness of supervision in the financial sectors and hence compromise the effectiveness of resolution.

C THE SUPERVISORY TASK AND ITS CHALLENGE

The powers conferred on the ECB are a very exclusive set of competencies, which also partly correspond to the CRD IV package.[482] It includes the authorisation and withdrawal of authorisation of credit institutions; assessing notifications of acquisition and disposal of qualifying holdings in credit institutions; ensuring compliance with prudential requirements; ensuring compliance with robust governance; carrying out supervisory reviews including stress testing; carrying out supervision on a consolidated basis over credit institutions' parents established in Member States; supplementary supervision of conglomerates in relation to credit institutions; carrying out supervisory tasks with regard to recovery and early intervention in credit institutions.[483] The ECB also has the power to receive information about covered institutions either directly from the institutions or from the relevant NCAs.[484]

As regards the macro prudential tasks, the NCAs of the participating Member States shall apply requirements for capital buffers to be held by credit institutions at the relevant level according to the relevant EU law. But the ECB may decide to apply higher requirements for capital buffers than those applied by the NCAs of participating Member States to be held by credit institutions.[485]

Among the above tasks, one that is deeply related to the resolution framework is the supervisory task on recovery and early intervention plans. It is directly relevant to the resolution regime under the BRRD and the SRM. According to the current reform in the major economies, such as in the US, the FDIC carries out the recovery and resolution, and it emphasises the importance of the implementation of a 'living will'.[486] No matter what kind of resolution strategy is to be undertaken, a seamless cooperation between the 'living will' planning and resolution cannot be over emphasised.

A related question to be answered is what authority should be conferred on the power of supervision and preparation for resolution. There are different approaches in other major economies. In the UK, after the Financial Services Act, responsibility for prudential supervision and for resolution both falls within the mandate of the BOE.[487] The US adopted a different approach, the FDIC, as the

---

481 Eddy Wymeersch, 'The structure of financial supervision in Europe: about single financial supervisors – Twin Peaks and multiple financial supervisors', 8 *European Business Organization Law Review* 237.
482 See CRD IV art 4–27.
483 SSM Regulation, art 4.
484 SSM Regulation, art 6(2).
485 SSM Regulation, art 5.
486 Dodd Frank Act, 12 U.S. Code § 5381.
487 Financial Services Act 2013(UK), ss1–2.

resolution authority, and does not perform the supervisory function according to US banking regulatory structure, including the Fed, the FDIC, the Office of the Comptroller of the Currency (OCC) and the states.[488] It is hard to tell theoretically which approach is better. However, any resolution design would require a clear and efficient allocation of responsibilities to the extent that the transition from supervision to resolution should be swift and convenient.

Taking that into consideration, the major concern for the task of implementation in the SSM would be the cooperation between the ECB and the SRM in the Bank Union framework. The conferring of supervisory power on the ECB and the function of the SRM are dependent on one another. The major challenge ahead is how to reach seamless and effective cooperation between the two.[489]

D THE ECB VS. NCAS CONFLICT

As indicated in the SSM regulation, the SSM means 'the system of financial supervision composed by the ECB and the national competent authorities of participating Member States'.[490] The mechanism for single supervision is not through a single supervision authority. The difference is quite subtle; allowing the ECB and the NCAs to work together, instead of just using the ECB, would avoid the risk of conferring too much burden on a new single authority. But in the meantime, it also allows for the possibility of encroachment of power by the NCAs towards the ECB.[491] Thus, a clear division of power is of critical importance.[492]

For institutions that fall into the direct supervision of the ECB, the NCAs are still responsible for assisting the ECB in performing its tasks according to the Regulation.[493] Assistance can be in several forms and includes: (i) submitting draft decisions to the ECB in regard to significant supervised entities established in its participating Member State; (ii) assisting the ECB in preparing and implementing acts relating to the tasks conferred on the ECB, such as the day-to-day assessment of the situation of covered entities; and (iii) assisting the ECB in enforcing its decisions.[494] In addition, the joint supervisory team (JST), as the supervisory organ, is comprised of staff members from both the ECB and the NCAs.[495]

---

488 Edward V. Murphy, 'Who regulates whom and how? An overview of US financial regulatory policy for banking and securities markets'.

489 Ferran and Babis, 'The European single supervisory mechanism', p. 8.

490 SSM Regulation, art 2.

491 Jeffrey N. Gordon and Wolf-Georg Ringe, 'Bank resolution in the European Banking Union: a transatlantic perspective on what it would take', p. 24. Apparently, many Member States did not appreciate a federalised mechanism, for instance, in the designing of a single resolution authority. German and France argued that may be a 'college' style design would be better.

492 Ferran, 'European banking union: imperfect, but it can work', pp. 6–8.

493 SSM Regulation, art 6(3).

494 Regulation (EU) No 468/2014 of the European Central Bank of 16 April 2014 establishing the framework for cooperation within the Single Supervisory Mechanism between the European Central Bank and national competent authorities and with national designated authorities (ECB/2014/17) OJ L 141/1 (SSM Framework Regulation) art 90–92.

495 SSM Framework Regulation, art 3.

According to the Regulation, the NCAs will continue to exercise supervision with respect to the less significant credit institutions. In addition, the NCAs will continue to perform supervisory activities in accordance with their national legislations, following the guidelines and instructions issued by the ECB as a part of its oversight function.[496]

The Regulation provides for a cooperation framework between the NCAs and the ECB. The ECB has the power to oversee the system:[497] (i) it issues regulations, guidelines, and general instructions for NCAs; (ii) it may request reports from the NCAs about how they have performed their tasks; (iii) it could pre-empt NCAs regarding one or more banks on its own initiatives by either addressing instructions to the NCAs, or directly to the banks; (iv) it can call for information from the NCAs and from less significant banks; and (v) it can undertake investigations, including on-site inspections.

Therefore, the efficiency of the SSM would largely be dependent on the coordination mechanism due to the division of power between the ECB and the NCAs.[498] In addition, according to the provisions, there are many occasions where the boundaries between the ECB and the NCAs might ambiguously overlap in practice and need to be more clearly defined.

For instance, the ECB Regulation has excluded the direct supervision of 'less significant institutions', which fall under the remit of the NCAs, except that it can also exert direct supervisory power over them when 'it is necessary to ensure the consistent application of high supervisory standards'. [499] In addition, with regard to macro prudential tasks and tools, the NCAs of Member States can apply the requirements of capital buffers including countercyclical buffer ratios; the ECB, however, is able to apply higher standards of capital buffer requirements on its own initiative.[500]

What is more, the decision-making mechanism in the ECB on supervision also raises some concerns on the conflicts between the ECB and the NCAs.[501] The main decision-making body of the ECB would be the Governing Council, which comprises the members of the Executive Board of the ECB and the governors of the national central banks of the Member States whose currency is the euro. Its responsibility is to adopt guidelines and take decisions necessary to ensure the performance of the tasks entrusted to it.[502] But, the supervisory decision body is the Supervisory Board, which is composed of a chair, vice chair, four representatives from the ECB, and one representative from each participating Member State. Decisions should be made in the interests of the EU as a whole.[503]

---

496 SSM Regulation, art 6.
497 SSM Regulation, art 6(5). See also SSM Framework Regulation, art 20.
498 Rosalind Z. Wiggins, Michael Wedow, and Andrew Metrick, 'European banking union A: The Single Supervisory Mechanism', *Yale Program on Financial Stability Case Study*.
499 ECB Regulation, art 6(5)(b).
500 ECB Regulation, art 5(1)–(2).
501 The two decision-making bodies and possible conflict will be further discussed in detail in Section 4.4.2(H) of this chapter.
502 Protocol (No 4) on the statute of the European system of central banks and of the European central bank, art 10 and art 12.
503 SSM Regulation, art 26.

However, this decision-making mechanism engenders the concern about the conflict between the EU's interests and the Member State's interests. The NCAs might be overrepresented so that they might trump the overall interests of the Union, especially with respect to recovery planning and early intervention. On the other hand, there are still many powers reserved to the NCAs. According to the statute, the exercising of the ECB's powers would not be prejudicial to the powers of the NCAs.[504]

The division of power between the NCAs and the ECB seems to be inevitable from a pragmatic perspective and it makes sense because it is quite irrational to entrust all supervisory powers to one single authority which has no previous background or experience in financial supervision. It might lack sufficient institutional structure and resources to implement direct supervision. However, it is also unfair to deprive them of the opportunity of even trying in the first place now that the Treaty has provided sufficient legitimacy for the ECB to carry out bank supervision. The ECB is supposed to contribute or even partly replace the policies pursued by NCAs with regard to the prudential supervision of credit institutions and the stability of the banking sector.[505]

Therefore, although the remits of the NCAs and the ECB are defined, there still lacks an exact clarity as to the allocation of responsibility and there are some overlapping areas which might also compromise the efficiency of the mechanism. Lack of clarity and the existence of conflict between powers in supervisory roles would be an impediment to carrying out orderly supervision and orderly resolution in the future.

E EFFICIENCY OF THE COLLEGE OF SUPERVISORS

According to the Capital Requirement Directive IV, the college of supervisors is a vehicle set up to facilitate the exercise of the tasks of supervision on a consolidating basis, ensuring appropriate coordination and also coordination with relevant third-country supervisory authorities.[506] The colleges are set up to make supervisory authorities join forces, share knowledge, and use skills and resources more effectively and efficiently.[507] It should provide a framework for the consolidating supervisor, the EBA, and other competent authorities to carry out the task of information exchange, determining supervisory examination programs, increasing the efficiency of supervision, and ensuring the consistent application of prudential requirements.[508]

According to the SSM Regulation, the home and host issue could be very complicated, especially in the context of non-participating Member States.[509] For supervision on a consolidated basis according to the SSM, coordination

---

504 SSM Regulation, art 1.
505 TFEU, art 127(5).
506 CRD IV, art 116.
507 EBA Regulation, art 21.
508 CRD IV, art 116.
509 Wymeersch Eddy, 'The Single Supervisory Mechanism or "SSM", Part one of the banking union (2014)', pp. 30–35.

between competent supervisors – the ECB and the supervisor of the foreign parent or subsidiary – follows the existing procedures on coordination through the college of supervisors.[510] If the head office of the banking group is located in the Euro area, the ECB will chair the supervisory college including also the supervisors from the non-participating countries where the subsidiaries are located.[511] On the other hand, where an entity in the Euro area is part of a banking group located in a non-participating state, the college will be headed by the non-participating EU state, with the ECB and the supervisors where these subsidiaries are located being invited as members of the college.[512]

The college is created to promote cooperation and coordination; however, as far as the recovery and resolution proceedings are concerned, it is still not be very clear whether it could promote seamless cooperation between the competent authorities or not. Specifically, there are at least two obstacles. The first obstacle is the conflicting interests. This mainly comes from the composition of the supervisory college. It basically is comprised of the ECB and the NCAs. It is very likely that the decision-making process of the college might be obstructed by the conflicting interests, or a decision might be influenced by some majority participants, or even dominated by some interest groups.[513]

In addition, even in the absence of intentional obstruction of decision-making, there are still many other differences which might stand in the way of seamless cooperation in decision-making in the college. For instance, there is a difference in prudential requirements and a difference in institutional organisation. These differences would all compromise the efficiency of supervisory decision-making in terms of the recovery framework. Therefore, a lack of efficiency in the college would also possibly make the host-home inconsistency problem become more serious in the SSM.

F MONETARY POLICY VS. SUPERVISORY POLICY

As indicated in Article 127 TFEU, the main objective of the ECB is to maintain price stability, and without prejudice to the main price stability objective, it can support the general economic policies in the Union.[514] However, under the framework of the SSM Regulation, the new objective would be the safety and soundness of the credit institutions, the stability of the financial system, and performing the financial supervision function.[515] Thus, there might be obvious conflict on the objectives of the ECB between the two different functions: monetary function and supervisory function.

---

510 SSM Framework Regulation, art 8.
511 SSM Framework Regulation, art 9.
512 SSM Framework Regulation, art 10.
513 Duncan Alford, 'Supervisory colleges: the global financial crisis and improving international supervisory coordination', 24 Emory Int'l L Rev 57.
514 TFEU, art 127(1).
515 SSM Regulation, recital (2) and art 1.

Having said that, the Regulation also explicitly requires that the ECB's supervisory task shall neither be interfered with or be determined by its tasks related to monetary policy.[516] The rationale of the provision is to protect the separation from monetary policy. To some extent, the TFEU also gives a solution to the conflict in the functions: Article 127(6) allows for the existence and carrying out of the new supervision function in the SSM Regulation, despite the main objective being price stability in the monetary policy.[517] The logic is that, since the new function is conferred on the ECB, new objectives can be set as a condition of the new function. The 'new functions, new condition to exercise' seem to be sensible. In the SSM regulation, there is a requirement for function separation: when carrying out the tasks conferred by the Regulation, the ECB shall pursue only the objective clearly provided.[518] However, in reality, it is doubtful that the 'new functions, new condition to exercise' logic can be practical.[519]

A main reason for the doubt might be the lack of institutional structure for the new supervisory function in the ECB. With regard to the monetary function, the main decision-making body is the Governing Council and the Executive Board in the ECB. The division of responsibility is quite clear: the former is responsible for the making of monetary policy, while the latter is responsible for the execution.[520] The Governing Council should adopt the guidelines and take the decisions necessary to ensure the tasks are entrusted to the ECB under the Treaty.[521] The division of power over the monetary function is very clear.[522]

The institutional and decision-making designs for the supervisory function are not as clear as those of the monetary function. Specifically, the Supervisory Board is empowered to carry out supervision tasks entrusted to it by the SSM Regulation.[523] Although guarded by the independence provision, it is very difficult to exercise real untrammelled power like that operated by the Governing Council. The drawback of the supervisory organ within the ECB is evident in at least three aspects. First, the legal framework does not cater for the possibility of clear and discretionary autonomous power for the Supervisory Board, due to the fact that its draft decisions are subject to adoption by the Governing Council (non-objection principle). According to the principle, the Governing Council has the power to reject the draft. It might change the content or require further deliberation by the Supervisory Board within 10 days, or 48 hours in emergency situations.[524]

---

516 SSM Regulation, art 25.
517 TFEU, art 127(6).
518 Eddy Wymeersch, 'The European banking union, a first analysis', pp. 9–10.
519 See SSM Regulation, art 25.
520 Protocol (No 4) on the statute of the European system of central banks and of the European central bank, art 12.
521 Protocol (No 4) on the statute of the European system of central banks and of the European central bank, art 12.
522 Zsolt Darvas and Guntram B. Wolff, 'Should non-euro area countries join the Single Supervisory Mechanism?' 4 *Danube* 141, pp. 149–151.
523 SSM Regulation, art 26.
524 SSM Regulation, art 26(8). See also Wiggins, Wedow, and Metrick, 'European banking union A: The Single Supervisory Mechanism', pp. 12–13.

Second, the lack of sufficient autonomous power by the supervisory board might automatically cause the non-euro participating country to be treated as a second-class citizen due to the fact that their NCA can only be represented in the Supervisory Board and not in the Governing Council.[525] The membership of the Governing Council is limited to the Euro area central banks. This serious concern might make non-euro Member States be hesitant about participating in the mechanism.[526]

Last, the specific procedures of the Supervisory Board's operation still needs to be improved in detail to achieve the objectives of the SSM.[527] For instance, its decision-making mechanism adopts a simple majority rule; all four ECB representatives also have a voting right.[528] The Regulation only requires that all members of the Supervisory Board should act in the interests of the Union as a whole, but this aim is not reflected in the voting mechanism. It does not, for example, include any rules relating to vote casting in cases that directly affect the banks of a specific Member State where the Union's interest is obviously in conflict with that of the Member State.[529]

Thus, the lack of clarification on the two separate functions in the same institution would possibly make conflicts become very common and compromise the effectiveness of supervision and preparation for resolution under the SSM and the BRRD.

G INDEPENDENCE VS. ACCOUNTABILITY

It is widely accepted that the principle of independence is of critical importance for an effective bank supervision mechanism, especially to ensure that the operation is not influenced by other EU agencies. Article 30 TFEU indicates that when exercising the power conferred on it by treaties with regard to the operation of the ECB and the ESCB, neither the ECB nor a national central bank shall seek or take instructions from other Union-level institutions or Member States or any other institutions.[530] The principle is to protect the banking supervision function from any political influence either at the Union level or at the Member State level. According to the Regulation, the members of the Supervisory Board and the Steering Committee shall act independently and objectively in the interests of the Union. Any public or private body (either from the Union or Member States) shall not exert influence over it.[531]

---

525 Ferran and Babis, 'The European single supervisory mechanism', pp. 14–15.
526 Many other non-euro Member States have shown their hesitation to join the SSM; this will be discussed further in detail in Section 4.4.2(H) of this chapter.
527 SSM Regulation, art 26(8).
528 SSM Regulation, art 26(6).
529 Wymeersch Eddy, 'The Single Supervisory Mechanism or "SSM", Part one of the banking union (2014)', pp. 52–53.
530 TFEU, art 130, see also the ECB regulation, art 19.
531 SSM Regulation, art 19.

If independence is at one end of the scale, the concept of accountability is at the other end.[532] To maintain a functional equilibrium, the principle of accountability should not be ignored. It should be noted that the accountability mechanism for the monetary function is very weak.[533] A similarly weak accountability mechanism for the supervisory function is inappropriate because the supervisory power would have such a significant influence over covered banks. As a matter of law, with growing powers there should also come more accountability.[534]

In the SSM Regulation, at the EU level, the ECB is accountable to the European Parliament and the Council: (i) it is obligated to supply reports to the European Parliament, the Council, the EC, and the Euro Group;[535] (ii) at the request of the European Parliament, the chair of the Supervisory Board shall participate in a hearing on the execution of tasks by the committee of the European Parliament; (iii) questions in writing can be addressed to the ECB by both the European Parliament and the Euro Group, and be answered orally or in writing;[536] and (iv) the European Court of Auditors can examine the efficiency of the management of the ECB and the ECB is obligated to cooperate with any investigation by the European Parliament.[537]

At the national level, the ECB is required to forward reports to Member States, and national parliaments can address their reasoned observations to the ECB or even request a reply in writing by the ECB to any observations or questions submitted by them.[538] Furthermore, the ECB can require the chair or a member of the Supervisory Board to participate in an 'exchange of views' meeting.[539] The Regulation also provides for the due process and administrative board of review process to strengthen accountability.[540]

Having said that, the major concern is that the Regulation does not provide concrete provisions on how a judicial review is to be applied, and how Article 266 TFEU on judicial assessment can be exercised in this context.[541] As discussed earlier on the weaknesses and obstacles to RRP, the political resolve of Member States to carry out the recovery framework may not necessarily be very strong. Within that context, a lack of strong, effective supervision under the SSM can add to the impediments to the recovery framework.

In other words, if there is not a sufficient accountability mechanism for the powerful SSM supervisor, the ECB may not have a strong incentive to carry out supervision diligently. In this case, the reparation step for resolution would be

---

532 Darvas and Wolff, 'Should non-euro area countries join the Single Supervisory Mechanism?' p. 145.
533 Ferran and Babis, 'The European single supervisory mechanism', p. 17.
534 Ibid.
535 SSM Regulation, art 20(1).
536 SSM Regulation, art 20(6).
537 SSM Regulation, art 20(2)–(9).
538 SSM Regulation, art 21(1).
539 SSM Regulation, art 21(2)–(4).
540 SSM Regulation, art 22 and art 24.
541 TFEU, art 266.

compromised, especially for these procedures that are extremely dependent on effective supervision, such as recovery planning and early intervention.[542]

The SSM is only applicable to euro Member States, a decision which attracted much criticism for excluding other EU Members. But based on the Regulation, the SSM can also effect supervision in non-euro Member States through a 'close cooperation' by means of a memorandum of understanding (MoU) with Members voluntarily joining the SSM.[543]

(a) **Opting in and concerns.** The Regulation provides for the possibility for non-euro Members to enter into the SSM. There are also incentives for non-euro Member States to participate in the SSM. Members whose banking groups have large operations in the SSM might have a strong willingness to join the SSM. By so doing, banks can enjoy the advantages of operational simplification, cost savings, and reputational advantage.[544] It is only reasonable to think that the markets would prefer a unitary supervision mechanism for the ECB that is not subject to any national bias.[545] This could bring about more favourable interest rates, credit ratings, and equity prices, for example. In addition, even if close cooperation does not work out well in the end, the Regulation provides a regime whereby non-euro Member States can join the SSM, but can also leave it if disagreements emerge.[546]

Giving other non-euro Members the option to join,[547] different countries have various stances on this. For instance, the UK and the Czech Republic have shown considerable opposition to it, while other countries, such as Poland and Sweden, have also expressed their concerns.[548] However, since joining is optional and welcome, it is necessary to assess how the participating mechanism function works.

To start with, it is necessary to examine the conditions to be met for other Member States to join: (i) the joining State notifies other Member States, the EC, the ECB, and the EBA of their request to enter into close cooperation; (ii) the Member State has to ensure that its national authority is willing to abide by the ECB; (iii) it also has to ensure that requests for information from the ECB are effectively implemented, which also applies to implementation of individual measures ordered by the ECB; and (iv) the Member State must adopt relevant legislation to ensure its national authority's compliance with the ECB.[549]

---

542 BRRD, art 27.
543 SSM Regulation, recital (14).
544 Wymeersch Eddy, 'The Single Supervisory Mechanism or "SSM", Part one of the banking union (2014)', pp. 60–61.
545 Darvas and Wolff, 'Should non-euro area countries join the single supervisory mechanism?', pp. 148–149.
546 SSM Regulation, art 7(6).
547 SSM Regulation, art 2(1) and art 7.
548 Ferran and Babis, 'The European single supervisory mechanism', pp. 21–22.
549 ECB Regulation, art 8(2).

Through the establishment of close cooperation, the ECB will carry out its supervisory function as it does in the Euro area. With regard to termination, after an initial three-year period, termination is allowed to take place at the request of that Member State at any moment, and the ECB can decide to terminate the agreement.[550] A second kind of termination or suspension may happen if the Member States does not take corrective action in accordance with ECB guidance, or no longer meets the conditions for admission to the SSM.[551] A third possible situation for termination is when the participating non-euro Member State objects to a draft decision proposed by the Supervisory Board to the Governing Council or objects to the Governing Council to the Supervisory Board's draft decision.[552]

Therefore, by accepting the supervision of the SSM, the joining State also gains extra powers and privileges. First, it is represented on the Supervisory Board, which makes it part of the decision-making process, and benefits from the unitary supervision. Second, it has the right to notify the ECB of its reasoned disagreement with regard to an objection of the Governing Council to a draft decision of the Supervisory Board; if the Governing Council insists on the objection, the participating state can choose not to accept the decision.[553] If it disagrees with the draft decision by the Supervisory Board, it can also inform the Governing Council of its reasoned disagreement.[554] Finally, it has the right to terminate cooperation with the ECB.[555]

It seems that by participating in the SSM, a Member State and its regulatory authority would both be entitled to rights and be obligated to perform certain duties at the same time. The further question is to what extent it would really be treated equally in the SSM? The fact is that although it can be represented on the Supervisory Board, it cannot be represented on the Governing Council, which is the major decision-making body to ensure the carrying out the functions entrusted to the ECB according to the Treaty.[556] A lack of representation on the final decision-making body would make it suspicious as to whether the participating States would be equally treated in the mechanism.[557] On this matter, Article 127(6) TFEU could be blamed because it provides insufficient possibilities to take action to modify the internal structure of the ECB to accommodate the needs of the participating States. This is also why Eddy Wymeersch proposed

---

550 ECB Regulation, art 7(6).
551 ECB Regulation, art 7(5).
552 ECB Regulation, art 7(8).
553 ECB Regulation, art 7(7).
554 ECB Regulation, art 7(8).
555 ECB Regulation, art 7(8).
556 Protocol (No 4) on the statute of the European system of central banks and of the European central bank, art 12.
557 Ferran, 'European banking union and the EU single financial market: more differentiated integration, or disintegration?' Eilis Ferran believes there are enough legal safeguards for participating states according to the unity protection principle in Article 1 of the SSM, many other functional provisions, and the new adjustments to the EBA.

that the reform could have recourse to Article 352 TFEU for an ECB internal change when Article 127(6) has not provided sufficient possibilities for change.[558]

Apart from this problem, there are other concerns to consider for States that might join. For instance, would the mechanism set up for the 17 Euro States be sufficient to accommodate 28 Member States?[559] Would the participating States be bound by other relevant rules, such as the DGS? Would the ECB be able to perform the two conflicting functions well enough: the monetary function and the supervisory function?[560] All these uncertainties might stand in the way of equal treatment for participating States. The absence of any clarification in the rules would make the participating mechanism impractical in reality.[561]

(b) The Member States staying out and their concerns. According to the Regulation, the non-euro States can also choose to stay out of the SSM mechanism. As indicated earlier, joining the SSM would enable the participating Member States to gain some extra powers and advantages and reputational benefits.[562] Thus, choosing not to join raises several concerns, in particular to what extent the new supervisor, the ECB (representing mainly Euro members), would possibly challenge the powers of the EBA and the ESRB, which represent all EU Members.[563]

First, there is the possible existing conflict between the EBA and the ECB. As the regulatory agency in the banking sector, the EBA is responsible for a large set of tasks including the establishment of high quality regulatory and supervisory standards, contributing to consistent application of legally binding acts, developing draft regulatory technical standards, developing draft implementing technical standards, conducting peer reviews, assessing market development, and fostering depositor and investor protection.[564] In addition, it is also responsible for the settlement of disputes between competent authorities in cross-border situations.[565]

In 2013 there was a new Amending EBA Regulation essentially modifying the balance between the EBA and the ECB.[566] This Amending Regulation takes the

---

558 Wymeersch, 'The European banking union: a first analysis', p. 24.
559 Wiggins, Wedow, and Metrick, 'European banking union A: the Single Supervisory Mechanism', pp. 3–4.
560 Ferran and Babis, 'The European single supervisory mechanism', pp. 13–14.
561 Darvas and Wolff, 'Should non-euro area countries join the single supervisory mechanism?', pp. 155–156.
562 Ibid, pp. 148–149.
563 Ferran, 'European banking union and the EU single financial market: more differentiated integration, or disintegration?' Eilis Ferran suggests that the banking union is not likely to be a gamechanger and lead to an upturn in mass-level public opinion towards the EU in non-euro States. But she also refutes the disintegration concerns of the EU within the context of the EBU.
564 EBA regulation Regulation (EU) No 1093/2010 of the European Parliament and of the Council of 24 November 2010 establishing a European Supervisory Authority (European Banking Authority), amending Decision No 716/2009/EC and repealing Commission Decision 2009/78/EC [2010] OJ L 331/12 (EBA Regulation) art 8.
565 EBA Regulation, art 19–20.
566 Regulation (EU) No 1022/2013 of 22 October 2013 amending Regulation (EU) No 1093/2010 establishing a European Supervisory Authority (European Banking Authority) as regards the conferral of specific tasks on the European Central Bank pursuant to Council Regulation (EU) No 1024/2013 [2013] OJ L 287/5 (Amended EBA regulation).

form of increased powers for the EBA (Article 10 and Articles 17 to 19). An essential change to the previous EBA Regulation is that the EBA is placed in a position where it exercises its competence equally with other supervisory bodies.[567]

There is an obvious concern that the ECB would be in conflict with the other supervisor. There are at least two areas where an overlap of power might happen: (i) the EBA is responsible for the development of a 'European Supervisory Handbook', which might be in conflict with the ECB power to develop its supervisory techniques;[568] and (ii) according to the Regulation, the ECB can undertake stress testing on an individual basis as part of its regular supervision; however, the EBA will also engage in Union-wide 'assessments of resilience' in cooperation with the ESRB.[569]

So due to the existence of possible overlaps, the major challenge in practice is how to avoid conflicts, especially avoiding a scenario where the ECB (representing the Euro States) encroaches on the powers legitimately entrusted on the EBA, which represents the interests of the Union as a whole. While there could be overlaps in power, compared with the ECB, the EBA has two weaknesses. The first is the EBA lacks sufficient resources, both in financial and human terms. The Board of Supervisors is the decision-making body of the EBA, including the chairman, the head of national public authorities, representatives of the EC, the ECB, the ESRB, the ESMA, and the EIOPA.[570] But, according to the Amended EBA Regulation, it should be noted that although it includes Members from the Supervisory Board of the ECB, they do not have any voting rights.[571]

Another weakness is the harmonisation nature of the EBA. The objectives as provided in the EBA Regulation is that the EBA should enhance the functioning of the internal market; ensure the integrity, transparency, efficiency, and orderly function of the financial markets; strengthen international regulatory coordination; and prevent regulatory arbitrage and promote competition fairness and equality.[572] Thus, it could be argued that the nature of the EBA and its competence is regulation harmonisation in the EU. Defining the concept of harmonisation has its own limitations and tends to counter any challenge to its legitimacy. Just as was described in *United Kingdom v. European Council and European Parliament* (opinion of AG Jääskinen),[573] 'the conferral of decision making powers under that article on ESMA, in substitution for the assessments of the competent national authorities, cannot be considered to be a measure for approximation'.[574]

---

567 Amended EBA Regulation, art 1(5).
568 Amended EBA Regulation, art 8(1)(aa).
569 Amended EBA Regulation, art 22(1)(a).
570 EBA regulation, art 40.
571 Amended EBA Regulation, art 40(1)(b).
572 EBA Regulation, art 1.
573 *Case C-270/12 United Kingdom V Council of European Union and European Parliament, opinion of AG Jääskinen*, para 37.
574 The AG insisted that the powers vested in the ESMA in this case under Article 28 of Regulation No 236/2012 go beyond internal market harmonisation for a series of reasons. See *Case C-270/12 United Kingdom V Council of European Union and European Parliament*.

Compared with the EBA, the EU basis of the ECB is Article 127 TFEU, although it has not gone as far as the unification of supervision completely. However, it still has a stronger basis for legitimacy than the Article 114 harmonisation clause.

After the establishment of the SSM, it is unavoidable that the convergence of supervision for Member States would lead to more and more rule-making and arrangements which might in conflict with the remit of the EBA. For non-participating Member States, a likely concern is that the EBA might be marginalised by the expansion of the ECB due to the lack of any defence against the encroachment of its powers. This means the EU as a whole might be reduced to a secondary priority compared with the SSM members.[575] In this case, those Member States that are out of the SSM but in the EU are likely to be harmed.

Second, there are also possible conflicts between the ESRB and the ECB. The ESRB was set up to carry out the macro prudential policy in the Union and the monitoring of systemic risk.[576] It is responsible for the following tasks, among others: identifying and prioritising systemic risk, issuing warnings about systemic risk, and issuing recommendations for remedy action. If not content with a response, it can decide to make any warning public.[577] With regard to macro-prudential tasks, the ESRB's power is to issue recommendations and warnings, while the ECB has access to the full prudential toolkits. The ECB can impose macro-prudential tools, such as the imposition of additional own funds, a countercyclical buffer, or any other measure.[578] In addition, the ECB also acts as a prudential micro supervisor because individual risk and systemic risk are often strongly interrelated.

In its governance design, it is fair to say that the ECB has considerable control over the ESRB due to the composition of the ESRB decision-making body. The chair of the ESRB is also the chair of the ECB; the first vice chair will be elected by and from the Governing Council of the ECB.[579] In addition, the General Board, as the main decision-making body is comprised of the president and vice president of the ECB, the governor of the national competent authorities and representatives from other authorities.[580]

From the relationship between the ECB and the ESRB and their mandates in reality, it is not unreasonable to say that there might be potential conflict between the two in the exercising of macro-prudential tools and tasks. When these conflicts arise, it is also possible that the ESRB might be marginalised by the ECB due to the control and influence it has over the ESRB.[581]

---

575 Goyal et al., *A banking union for the Euro area*.
576 ESRB regulation Regulation (EU) No 1092/2010 of the European Parliament and of the Council of 24 November 2010 on European Union macro-prudential oversight of the financial system and establishing a European Systemic Risk Board [2010] OJ L 331/1 (ESRB Regulation), recital(1)–(2).
577 ESRB Regulation, art 3.
578 SSM Regulation, recital (15) and art 5.
579 ESRB Regulation, art 5(1).
580 ESRB Regulation, art 6.
581 Ferran and Babis, 'The European single supervisory mechanism'.

(c) **A dilemma ahead.** Therefore, for the non-euro Member States, there seems to be a dilemma facing them. Were they to join the SSM, the governing structure might be not in their favour despite some visible advantages they could gain. However, if they were to stay out of the SSM, they might face the risk that the increasingly powerful ECB (representing the Euro Members) might be able to encroach on the mandates of other Union agencies, such as the EBA and the ESRB.

4.4.3 SSM might impede resolution: more SSM and SRM cooperation

To sum up, according to the latest BRRD and the SRM, the SSM-ECB relationship will be of critical importance for the resolution mechanism in at least three aspects: (i) with regard to the recovery framework, the ECB and all other NCAs will be responsible for recovery planning of the banking groups under their supervision; in addition, the supervisors will have the power to carry out supervisory tasks in relation to recovery planning and early intervention;[582] (ii) it would be the ECB and other NCAs who decide whether a bank is 'failing or likely to fail', after which the resolution authority would decide to start the resolution action;[583] and (iii) the ECB and all other NCAs would also give advice on resolution planning, to be drawn up by the resolution authority; the competent supervisors would closely cooperate with the resolution authorities in charge of the resolution and contribute to the preparation of resolution plans but without being entitled to take the decisions.[584]

But, from all these discussions about the establishing of the SSM, it might be fair to say that there are still many weaknesses in it which might compromise the effectiveness of the SSM, and therefore the effectiveness of the resolution regime under the SRM and the BRRD to resolve the banks.

In summary, it is flawed in many aspects: its multi-layered supervision mechanism compromises efficiency; it naturally excludes non-banking institutions and non-systemically significant banks; there is a conflict between the monetary policy and supervision policy; it cannot effectively deal with the conflict between accountability and independence; and it cannot effectively deal with the relationship between non-participating States and SSM States. These flaws could act against a successful resolution regime.

Putting aside the weaknesses of the SSM and its influence on carrying out the recovery and resolution framework under the BRRD and the SRM, there needs to be closer cooperation between the SSM and the SRM to ensure the orderly liquidation of banks.[585]

In sum, it should be noted that bank supervision is a continuum starting from the authorisation of a bank to its resolution. Thus, a seamless cooperation

---

582 BRRD, art 5, art 8, art 10, and art 27.
583 BRRD, art 32.
584 BRRD, art 10 and art 15.
585 Wymeersch, 'Banking union: aspects of the Single Supervisory Mechanism and the Single Resolution Mechanism compared', pp. 5–6.

between the supervision and the resolution framework is extremely important to maintain consistency and avoid conflicts. For instance, under the SSM and the SRM, the ECB supervision and its supervisory decisions are directly applicable to its covered banks according to SSM Regulation; however, the SRB resolution decisions need to be implemented by NRAs. Therefore, there is obviously the possibility for conflict here that needs more cooperation to address it in order to really tackle the TBTF bank structural problem.[586]

5 Conclusion: resolution effectiveness and the BSR

The recovery framework under the BRRD corresponds with the living will approach to maintaining the failing bank as a going concern; but it also faces many challenges, such as the lack of a centralised decision-making mechanism and weak political incentives. The resolution framework provides many tools and powers to deal with bank failure and thus provides certainty in resolution. But, as an MPE-based framework, it cannot perform well in dealing with major problems, such as a run on short-term creditors and the spill over effect, together with cross-border difficulties.[587]

The pro-integration framework under the SRM Regulation might still not be able to change this situation and address the remaining problems effectively due to the political compromises in its design.[588] To make the SRM aligned with the US-style SPE strategy, it needs to be armed with a more centralised decision-making and execution mechanism, sufficient funds and backstops, powerful resolution powers, a more robust bail-inable capital structure, and a more centralised and effective supervisory mechanism under the SSM.

In the long term, there is also the suggestion of pressing on with the EBU towards a fiscal union, and the establishment of a political union including a 'Big Bank' (the central bank as the last resort to support resolution) and 'Big Government' (the US-style Treasury support to liquidation) to deal with a systemic bank failure.[589]

Putting asides its weaknesses, the resolution framework under the BRRD and the SRM is possibly capable of addressing the remaining cyclicality attribute of the TBTF structural problem, i.e. the resolvability difficulty following the BSR's intention to address the structural attribute. The operation of resolution framework could provide a last-resort-guarantee to the BSR in addressing the TBTF bank structural problem.

---

586 Ibid, p. 9 and p. 11.
587 Financial Stability Board, *Recovery and resolution planning for systemically important financial institutions: guidance on developing effective resolution strategies*.
588 Ferran, 'European banking union: imperfect, but it can work'. Eilis Ferran agrees on the deficiencies of the SSM, but holds a comparatively optimistic stance towards the SSM, stressing its progress compared with previous regulation.
589 Zavvos, 'The Single Resolution Mechanism in the European banking union: legal foundation, governance structure and financing', pp. 51–53.

What is more, the key to the success of bank resolution in dealing with the cyclicality attribute is also dependent on the structural reform under the BSR. In other words, the resolution framework under the BRRD and the SRM would be more effective if the BSR were to reduce complexity and interconnectedness successfully.

In the BSR as it stands, it does not provide many provisions for connecting the separation reform and the resolution reform. In this regard, the UK structural reform and the Liikanen additional separation reform are doing a better job by trying to take loss absorbency and resolvability into consideration.[590]

To sum up, to make sure the TBTF bank structural problem could be effectively resolved, the connection and cooperation between the structural reform and the resolution reform should be strengthened.[591] The two reforms compensate each other in dealing with both the structural attribute and the cyclicality attribute of the TBTF bank structural problem.[592] The BSR needs to be strengthened by having regard to necessary resolution elements. The SPE resolution framework can only be made possible based on robust structural reform.

---

590 Independent Commission on Banking, 'Final Report, recommendations' p. 151. See also Prudential Regulation Authority, *The implementation of ring-fencing: consultation on legal structure, governance and the continuity of services and facilities – CP19/14* (October 2014).

591 European Commission, *Commission staff working document impact assessment accompanying the document Proposal for a Regulation of the European Parliament and of the Council on structural measures improving the resilience of EU Credit Institutions and the Proposal for a Regulation of the European Parliament and of the Council on reporting and transparency of securities financing transactions, SWD/2014/030 final* (January 29, 2014)

592 The structural reform and the resolution reform need each other; this is also partly discussed in Section 6.3 of Chapter 6.

7 Conclusion

The main issue covered in this book is the TBTF bank structural problem (Chapter 1). It concerns the co-existence of an all-encompassing set of activities made up of mainly client-oriented activities and transaction-oriented activities. The TBTF bank structural problem includes two distinct but inextricably inter-related attributes: the structural attribute and the cyclical attribute. The structural attribute is reflected in the four features of universal banks that engage mainly in trading activities: behemoth size; complexity and interconnectedness; ignoring low probability events; and the domino failure effect. On the other hand, the risks and instability in universal banks come not only from their trading activities, but also from the cyclicality of banking, which constitutes the cyclicality attribute of the TBTF bank structural problem.

Innumerable anomalies can be seen in the development of the TBTF bank structural problem (Chapter 2). These behavioural factors and anomalies are categorised according to two variables: the subjects whom people distrust (inves-tors, government, and industry), and the source of that distrust (ignorance and greed).[1] Behavioural analysis is of critical importance in the analysis of the TBTF bank structural problem because, besides confirming the structural attribute ana-lysed in Chapter 1, it further substantiates the way behavioural factors interact with the universal banking model and increase risks, and therefore proves the cyclical attribute of the TBTF bank structural problem.

Building on the two attributes of the TBTF bank structural problem, two reforms could provide possible solutions: (i) the structural attribute makes a case for a structural separation reform as an ex-ante solution; and (ii) the fact that behavioural factors interact closely with trading-oriented activities and strengthen the cyclicality attribute indicates there could be some unavoidable failures even with structural separation rules being at the regulators' disposal, and makes a case for a resolution reform as an ex-post solution.

On Solution 1 (Chapters 3–5): exploring the solution to the structural attribute of the bank structural problem, there is considerable regulatory progress in the EU with the BSR proposal made by the EC (Chapter 3). Newly adopted legisla-tion in other jurisdictions, such as the US and the UK, have also been advancing.

---

1 DellaVigna, *Psychology and economics: evidence from the field.*

From a comparative perspective, the EC proposal (the BSR) is an approximate mixture between the Volcker style prohibition rule and the Vickers style ring-fence rule. Therefore, it can incorporate the merits of both US and UK rules.

The essential approaches used to analyse the BSR are a behavioural finance approach and a comparative approach. To assess the effectiveness and efficiency of the BSR according to its envisioned objectives, the embodiment of the behavioural finance approach in this book includes a market failure analysis (MFA) and a cost benefit analysis (CBA), both inspired by the FCA, which has been making progress in applying behavioural finance in strengthening financial regulation.[2]

The first test of the BSR is the MFA (Chapter 4). The normative implication of the discovery of behavioural influence on the development of the TBTF bank structural problem is to adjust legal intervention to minimise this influence and curb the risks caused by such influence.[3] It transpires that legal regulation having regard to behavioural finance not only shows imperativeness but also requires distinctive and unconventional measures despite behavioural finance's normative paradox. In this regard, distinct from the price-based approach, the BSR includes the interaction between the behavioural factors and the structural problem and risks thereof: (i) it significantly reduces the mutual interaction between behavioural factors and the trading entity; and (ii) it de-links the behavioural factors and the CCI.

We found that the BSR is effective in bringing about safety and stability to the banking sector, especially to the CCI. Given the prohibitive rule actually prohibits the universal banking model, it could evidently make banks safer, especially CCIs.[4] The reason is that the risks that triggered the bank failure emanated mainly from the trading entity, and behavioural factors only loomed largest in the universal banks. Although not as effective as the prohibition rule because of the difference in its strength, the ring-fence rule would also ensure the CCI was insulated from the risks hidden in the trading activities and therefore make it safer despite the concerns about its non-mandatory nature.

Having said that, the BSR would also have many challenges ahead. There is the possibility of trading activities migrating to other less regulated areas or less regulated regions. In addition, fragmented international structural reform also puts the effectiveness of structural reform to the test.

The second test of the BSR is the CBA (Chapter 5). It can be seen that the BSR represents a mixture of both the Volker Rule and the Vickers Rule. By undertaking the CBA, it seems that the BSR is able to accommodate most of the benefits

---

2 Financial Conduct Authority, *Financial Conduct Authority(2013), Applying behavioral economics in Financial Conduct Authority, Occasional Paper No. 1.*

3 Akerlof and Shiller, *Animal spirits: how human psychology drives the economy, and why it matters for global capitalism*, pp. 167–177.

4 European Commission, *Commission staff working document impact assessment accompanying the document Proposal for a Regulation of the European Parliament and of the Council on structural measures improving the resilience of EU Credit Institutions and the Proposal for a Regulation of the European Parliament and of the Council on reporting and transparency of securities financing transactions, SWD/2014/030 final*, pp. 33–34.

of the two reforms in terms of reducing complexity, interconnectedness, and enhancing resolvability. On the other hand, it seems to minimise many of the significant costs of both reforms in terms of implementation costs, hedging costs, market-making costs, diversification costs, and liquidity costs. Therefore, the BSR is able to retain substantial advantages from the universal banking model.

To a certain extent, an absolute decision of either Choice C (Vickers style) or Choice D (Volcker style) (see Table 3.1) is a rather difficult one in terms of their respective balances between benefits and costs.[5] Therefore, the choice in practice is really more a political matter than a technical one. Therefore, the two-tiered suggestion in the BSR would possibly bring about a balanced interest for the EU banking industry.

The BSR arguably pays due attention to the balance between financial stability and banking competitiveness. But one of its pitfalls is also evident: it lacks a direct link with relevant resolution reform in the EU. Therefore, unlike the Vickers proposal, which provides many provisions on loss absorbency, and the Liikanen Report, which includes the resolution-oriented additional ring-fence rule, the BSR also needs to take possible resolution requirements into consideration.

On solution 2 (Chapter 6): building on the analyses of the BSR, the book continues by looking at whether the current resolution mechanism in the BRRD and the SRM is sufficient to address the remaining cyclicality attribute in the TBTF bank structural problem, i.e. the lack of resolvability issue. The new resolution regime's effectiveness in dealing with the lack of resolvability is largely contingent on whether the design of the resolution powers is such that it can both swiftly direct resolution to avoid a creditors' run and also promote international coordination to avoid the spill over effect, as happened with Lehman Brothers.[6]

The practical effects of the recovery framework, including recovery and resolution planning, intragroup support, and early intervention, are yet to be tested, and will depend on the way they are to be implemented. But the framework faces obvious challenges: Member States still reserve the main controlling power in decision-making and implementation, which creates difficulties in coordination. Also, both firms and Member State regulators probably lack any strong incentives, and are uncertain about the new supervisory mechanism under the SSM.

Despite its progress in promoting coordinated resolution, the EU resolution framework under the BRRD still mostly corresponds with the MPE resolution strategy: multiple point of entry at both the parent level and the group entity level, multiple resolution authorities, and financial arrangements at the Member State level. Its ineffectiveness still persists for two reasons: (i) not enough protection for short-term funding; and (ii) the lack of concentrated capacity to absorb losses.

In contrast, the SPE resolution strategy, represented by the US, addresses these remaining concerns through the following means: (i) resolution tools are conducted on a top-down basis from the top of a group by a single resolution

---

5   Ibid, p. 65. See also supra Chapter 3, Section 4, Table 3.1.
6   Skeel, 'Single point of entry and the bankruptcy alternative', pp. 4–6.

authority to avoid the necessity for coordination of several agencies; (ii) losses in a firm are addressed by writing down a part of the equities and converting unsecured creditors' assets into equities at the group level; and (iii) using a bailinable capital structure, amending the firm's structure, and providing backup funds.

The pro-integration resolution framework under the SRM is a big step in promoting resolution at the EU level. But compared with the SPE and the US model, it is still a resolution mechanism with fragmented decision-making powers and decentralised execution. To make the SRM more aligned with the US-style SPE strategy, it needs to be armed with a more centralised decision-making and execution mechanism, sufficient funds and backstops, and a more robust bailinable capital structure and firm structure.

In addition, to be aligned with the US-style SPE resolution, a more robust supervisory mechanism is also important. It might be fair to say that there are still many weaknesses in the current SSM which might compromise the effectiveness of supervision and therefore the ability of the resolution regime under the SRM and the BRRD to resolve the TBTF bank structural problem. The flaws mainly include: its scope, the conflict between two policies, the conflict between accountability and independence, and the complicated relations between non-participating EU Member States and SSM Member States.

It should be noted that for the above recommended resolution to work, it also requires cooperation with the structural reform in general. This is especially true in terms of the element of bailinable capital structure and firm structure which are directly dependent on bank structural reform.

To sum up, to successfully address the TBTF bank structural problem, its two attributes, i.e. the structural attribute and the cyclicality attribute, need to be dealt with simultaneously. On the one hand, the structural reform tackles the structural attributes, but it needs the resolution reform to resolve the remaining cyclicality issue to provide a last resort guarantee for its supervision; on the other hand, the resolution reform also needs the structural reform to facilitate it by reducing complexity and interconnectedness. Therefore, setting aside the respective disadvantages of the BSR and the resolution framework under the BRRD and the SRM that need to be addressed, the connection between the two needs to be strengthened to resolve the TBTF bank structural problem.[7]

---

7 European Commission, *Commission staff working document impact assessment accompanying the document Proposal for a Regulation of the European Parliament and of the Council on structural measures improving the resilience of EU Credit Institutions and the Proposal for a Regulation of the European Parliament and of the Council on reporting and transparency of securities financing transactions*, SWD/2014/030 final.

Index

For Product Safety Concerns and Information please contact our EU
representative GPSR@taylorandfrancis.com Taylor & Francis Verlag GmbH,
Kaufingerstraße 24, 80331 München, Germany

Printed and bound by CPI Group (UK) Ltd, Croydon, CR0 4YY

08/05/2025

01864327-0006